"This is a very useful and competent account of the development of human religious consciousness and behavior encompassing the entire human race from prehistoric beginnings to the present age. It is not a book of spirituality or of theology or philosophy, though all of these play a role and can be helped by this book. Neither is it a history of religions. It is, as the subtitle indicates, the story of human religiousness. The book is free of jargon and reads easily. It is a very useful introduction to the phenomenon of religion."

Robert F. Harvanek, S.J.
Loyola University of Chicago

"...an excellent introductory textbook. Barnes begins historically by describing the development of religious structures and functions from primitive religion to the breakthroughs of universal religions focused on an absolute. He ends with a very fine discussion of the issues of religion and modernity. The chapter on belief is excellent...Highly recommended."

Charley D. Hardwick, American University
Religious Studies Review

"This book is a stunning achievement and is must reading! Barnes knows his stuff—analysis of religion by sociology, psychology, anthropology, philosophy, and the history of religions. A clear and helpful introduction to the nontechnical reader."

Donald G. Luck
Trinity Seminary Review

"I find this to be an attractive book for several reasons. It reads easily. The writing is both fresh and crisp. There's no fat here. No jargon either. It is a well thought out book. It touches all the bases in a fresh way. I feel quite comfortable recommending without reservation this book as a textbook in such courses as Introduction to Religion/Religious Studies on the undergraduate level. The book is really well done."

Richard Penaskovic, Auburn University
Religious Education

"An exemplary text (... ;y of religion for older teens, college people,

D. Campbell Wyckoff
...ton Theological Seminary

"This book is a tour de force, a synthesis of technical and professional scholarship, yet easily understood by any intelligent reader. Barnes organizes his material tightly and writes clearly throughout, with lucid introductions to and summaries of each section."

Eugene C. Best
Marist College

"This is a graceful and engaging work, written with warmth and wit. It comprehensively treats human religiousness as one phenomenon, common to our race, yet all the while deftly describing and analyzing that phenomenon.... The comparison of religions, philosophical reasoning, and psychological perceptivity are neatly intertwined. An intensely human book."

Robert T. Fortna
Vassar College

"The college student will find in this book a well-defined context for religious reflection. The college teacher might well find it a good text for an introduction to religious studies."

Daniel Liderbach
Canisius College

"...the inclusion of illustrative anecdotes adds space to the underlying themes."

Spiritual Life

"Teenagers as well as adults can use this book with profit."

The Living Church

MICHAEL HORACE BARNES

IN THE PRESENCE OF MYSTERY

An Introduction to the Story of Human Religiousness

TWENTY-THIRD PUBLICATIONS

185 WILLOW STREET • PO BOX 180 • MYSTIC, CT 06355
TEL: 1-800-321-0411 • FAX: 1-800-572-0788
E-MAIL: ttpubs@aol.com • www.twentythirdpublications.com

Dedication

To my parents
Horace and Corlin
with love and gratitude.

Seventh Printing 2003
Third Revision 2003

Twenty-Third Publications
A Division of Bayard
185 Willow Street
P.O. Box 180
Mystic, CT 06355
(860) 536-2611
(800) 321-0411
www.twentythirdpublications.com

ISBN:1-58595-259-1
Library of Congress Catalog Card Number: 2002111929
Printed in the U.S.A.

Contents

Preface

Six years after the first edition, *In the Presence of Mystery* had evoked enough suggestions to call for a second edition. Now, more than ten years after the second edition, other suggestions have come for additional changes, especially to take into account new aspects of the study of religions and theology. The most evident change since the second edition is the addition of a fifteenth chapter and an Epilogue. Chapter Fifteen asks again about the future of religion but now at a time when the secularization thesis seems rather weaker than it did twenty years ago, and in a time of postmodern thought, environmentalism, the increase of Islamic "fundamentalism," and New Religious Movements. The Epilogue takes up more fully the question of how to approach the study of religion, mentioned only briefly in this Preface. The Epilogue asks whether we can or should evaluate religion(s). It surveys options—sympathetic vs. critical, seeking to understand vs. seeking to explain—and explores reasons for and against trying to evaluate religion from the outside. Other changes are listed below in a special section, to guide those who use this as a textbook.

The Nature of the Book

Over the years I have heard complaints, albeit mild ones, from those who say that this book is either a) too religious or b) not religious enough. On the one hand it is sympathetic to religion and seeks to present religion as religious people experience it and to present their own arguments in defense of it. On the other hand it includes a fairly thorough survey of critical questions that have been directed at religion over the centuries. I have found in my own classes that those students who enter it religious tend to leave it still religious. A few say they have learned to appreciate religion more; some are more critical of religion. I have also found that those who enter it as skeptics usually leave still skeptical, but usually saying also that their earlier form of skepticism was simplistic and not sufficiently appreciative of the many human dimensions of religion. The Epilogue provides the student with a chance to look back over the whole book and think about her or his own options and reasons critically.

As I reflected on the content of the new Epilogue, I became more explicitly aware of differences between this text and other introductory texts in religious studies. Many such texts are simply a sympathetic and detailed description of major religions of the world. Some texts also offer an introduction to critical approaches in the study of religion. This text does both, but also has a third layer of explicit philosophical or theological analysis, of the sort associated with philosophy of religion. Some of these analyses are supportive of religion; some of them are not. Early in the book, to alert the reader to provocative issues in the material to follow, the second chapter takes a first look at some critical analyses of religion, by noting the approach of certain skeptics like Sigmund Freud or Stewart Guthrie. But this chapter also presents Mircea Eliade's defense of religiousness in his claims about the *sui generis* character of the sacred. A few chapters contain theological material in defense of religious belief. In every chapter there are likely to be a few lines, or sometimes paragraphs, reflecting on the plausibility of a certain religious belief or on the value of a certain approach to the study of religion. These reflections are sometimes drawn from religious people and sometimes from nonreligious. The voices of the religious believer, the sympathetic scholar of religion, and the critic of religion are all made present. At the end the Epilogue offers a survey of ideas about analyzing and evaluating religion.

Every book on religion has its own philosophical or theological perspective, sometimes not identified, however, as only one possible perspective among others. Many who teach and write about religion, for example, simply claim that religions in general are different modes of response to the sacred, and that the sacred is a *sui generis* reality. That is not the underlying assumption of this book. The not-so-hidden philosophy or theology behind this text is the conviction that we humans share an openness to the infinite, that there is always a mystery beyond the horizon, and that religion is a response to mystery. As the introduction will note, the focus of this book is not so much on the mystery itself as on us humans, as those who live in the presence of mystery, and on what this tells us about what it means to be human.

Specific Changes

There are numerous changes besides the addition of a new chapter and a new Epilogue. Several chapters have additional information on Islam, including Sufis and Wahhabis, and on Islamist movements. Further distinctions concerning agnosticism and atheism appear in the Introduction, distinguishing between weak and strong forms of each. Biology-based theories about aspects of religion, including ideas from evolutionary psychology, have been added and analyzed where they are relevant, as in Chapter Two on theories of the origin and function of religion. The section on Eliade's defense of religious experience has been expanded in this same chapter, to introduce ideas about the *sui generis* nature of religion and the phenomenological approach, topics which are taken up again in the Epilogue. This chapter also has a new section on syncretism, a topic that appears in Chapter Fifteen also. Some adjustments have been made to fit better with more recent scholarship, as in Chapter Three about estimates of the century in which Zarathustra lived, or about sacrificial practices among the Aztecs. Greater mention of the Upanishads appears in this chapter also (though for simplicity not of the Brahmanas).

Comments by students have led me to add the word "limits" and "limit-experiences" in the fourth chapter to Tillich's word "estrangement." Though estrangement is still part of the lives of many young people, others claim that they do not feel a significant estrangement. The issue of religious tolerance and religious pluralism has come to the fore in various ways in recent years, so there is more on this in Chapter Six and a new section of Chapter Twelve is devoted to it. Some corrections have been made about the caste system in India in Chapter Six. In deference to renewed disputes concerning nature and nurture Chapter Seven has replaced "Born without Identity" with the more flexible idea of "Born Unfinished." In Chapter Eight I have followed recent work by Rodney Stark which confirms other sources that in primitive cultures the spirits generally do not care about moral issues. In the same chapter the name "acceptance morality" has been changed to "allegiance morality," a phrase that just works better. Chapter Eight also now has a brief section on "virtue ethics." The introduction to Part IV has expanded the list of characteristics of modern religion, to make explicit reference to religious tolerance, individualism, and humanism. It also questions whether an emphasis on rationality is peculiarly modern (and peculiarly Western, for that matter). Current arguments about naturalism in science are now parts of Chapters Eleven and Thirteen. Chapter Thirteen now contains a section on whether science is based on a kind of faith. Chapter Fourteen has descriptions of the anthropic principle and intelligent design.

The list of readings at the end of each chapter has been brought up to date. This especially includes more materials relevant to feminist interests. I was tempted to add some URLs for websites on various topics, but there are far too many such sites, and they are all easily available to students through any of the regular search engines.

Religion and Culture Have Evolved

A number of comments I received after the first edition were directed against the thesis on which the book is built, the claim by Robert Bellah and others that there is an evolution of culture and religion.

There was in fact much that was wrong with earlier evolutionary interpretations of religion and culture. The famous early nineteenth-century theory of August Comte, for example, identified religion with primitive and archaic belief styles, philosophy with classical (or "historical") cultures, and science with modern culture. *In the Presence of Mystery*, following Bellah, claims instead that religion (as well as science and philosophy) has primitive, archaic, classical, and modern forms, as the first chapter here explains. Religion does not belong only to primitive and archaic styles of thought, as Comte claimed.

The nineteenth-century theories of cultural evolution were also misused as a justification for colonialist imperialism, on the grounds that the superior culture of Europe ought to dominate lesser culture. There were other problems with many of the nineteenth-century formulations, enough for the anthropologist Franz Boas to lead the movement away from such interpretations of the cultures of the world, and towards a greater degree of cultural relativism. Each culture deserves to be appreciated as its own functional unity, its own coherent pattern of life, said Boas and his followers; do not claim that European culture is the norm against which all other cultures can be judged.

There is a great deal of wisdom in Boas's approach. Nonetheless, many anthropological studies in the last thirty years or so have tested the degree to which changes in economic and social complexity, as from primitive foraging cultures to populous agricultural-trading cultures, produce parallel changes in notions about the spirits and gods and in the form of the stories about them. Various studies have explored how Jean Piaget's theory of cognitive development and the formulations of Lawrence Kohlberg about the development of moral reasoning correlate with degrees of social complexity and differentiation in various cultures. The result of these studies has been to substantiate a general idea of cultural evolution as well as Bellah's specific outline of religious evolution. There is much that is still unclear and much that is in dispute about cultural and religious evolution. There are still dangers of misusing any theory of cultural development to oppress others. So it is best to speak cautiously. But the general fact of cultural development is well supported by numerous anthropological studies.

To illustrate the range of studies let me mention a few significant sources on the topic. David Levinson and Martin J. Malone, *Toward Explaining Human Culture* (HRAF Press, 1980), analyze and compare studies on a large number of different cultures. Pierre R. Dasen and Alastair Heron, "Cross-Cultural Tests of Piaget's Theory," *The Handbook of Cross-Cultural Psychology*, Vol. 4 "Developmental Psychology" (Boston: Allyn and Bacon, 1981), Ch.7, 295-341. John R. Snarey, "Cross-Cultural Universality of Social-Moral Development: A Critical Review of Kohlbergian Research," *Psychological*

Bulletin 97/2, 1985, 202-232. Dean Sheils, "An Evolutionary Explanation of Supportive Monotheism," *International Journal of Comparative Sociology* XV/1-2, 1974, 47-56. For somewhat more popularized descriptions of cultural evolution, see Ernest Gellner, *Plough, Sword, and Book: The Structure of Human History* (London: Collins Harvill, 1988), an expert interpretation of cultural development. Or see the second half of Merlin Donald, *The Origins of the Modern Mind: Three Stages in the Evolution of Culture and Cognition* (Cambridge, MA: Harvard University Press, 1991). Jared Diamond, *Guns, Germs, and Steel: the Fates of Human Societies* (New York: W. W. Norton & Co., 1997) argues it is climate and physical context, not any difference in innate abilities, that have allowed the people of some cultures to dominate others recently. And my own work, *Stages of Thought: The Co-Evolution of Religious Thought and Science* (New York: Oxford University Press, 2000) provides detailed evidence about the long-term cultural evolution of religious thought.

Debts to Various Sources

Comments on the book have attributed the underlying theme of mystery either to Paul Tillich or to Karl Rahner. Both estimates are correct, though my own original appreciation of mystery came through a study of Aquinas' notion of God. Tillich's twentieth-century existential theology contributed notions about ultimacy, estrangement (treated also as "limit"in this third edition), and symbols. This book originated from brief notes to introduce first-year college students to Rahner's notion of infinite mystery as the ultimate context of human life. This notion is valuable both for understanding a major element in many contemporary theologies, and also for recognizing the peculiar character of us humans as the beings with the capacity for open-ended reflection and choice. For first-year students the notion of mystery as it appears today in theologies and philosophies is rather sophisticated, hard to grasp. My own teaching experience convinced me that it was a notion that I had to sneak up on very slowly with a lot of specific information, a lot of concrete instances and images, of the sort you will find here.

William C. Tremmel's book *Religion: What Is It?* showed me how a textbook might be both informative and interesting. His use of Tillich's categories reverberated with my own Rahnerian background, and part of his outline suggested to me how I might take it a step further using Bellah's theory. Finally, as I have reworked the book it has proved very useful to keep checking James Fowler's *Stages of Faith*, a seemingly simple but powerful synthesis of theories of individual development, a synthesis partly formed as the result of extensive, carefully evaluated interviews.

The Use of Repetition

The structure of the book reflects my own teaching experience in another way. Even a long and clear exposition of any one aspect of religion gets lost among the many aspects and is readily forgotten. So the reader will find each major idea described once in the context of one chapter's topic, and then find it again in the context of one or more later chapters and their topics. The repetition of the same idea in different contexts helps both to make it clearer by showing it from different angles and to fix it more firmly in the reader's memory through repetition.

Acknowledgments

Let me take the time here to extend words of thanks: once again to former graduate assistants John Lay and Joy Karl for research; to Mark Moorman and Mary Lou Baker Jones for careful readings of the manuscript; to Matthew Kohmescher, James Heft, Tom Martin, and Terry Tilley for their support as chairpersons; to Rita Vasquez, who taught me better how to use this book as a classroom text; to Pat and Neil Kluepfel, wonderful publishers and people; to Mary Carol Kendzia, editor on this revision; to both Jim Dunaway and Steve Ostovich for their many specific and very helpful suggestions for revisions based on their own classroom experience with the text; to Carolyn Ludwig, administrative assistant; Jeff Rahl, a budding geologist with a critical eye; Andrew Knight, student aide; to the University of Dayton honors students class of 2005 for comments on Chapter Fifteen and the Epilogue; to Matt Eggemeier and Scott Wagner for their challenging questions; to student proofreader Jeremy Somerson; and, finally, to the several thousand students who have made teaching an ongoing joy.

If anyone has questions about the content, perspective, and sources of this book, I will be happy to respond to inquiries. I can be reached at barnes@udayton.edu

Introduction

There is a tale told by Australian aborigines about the beginning. Once there was no death in the world. But one day Purukupali the hunter returned home to find his son Jinini dead from the heat of the sun. Grieving, he picked up the body of his child and walked into the sea to drown himself. As he stepped into the swirling waters, he shouted that because his son had died, so must everyone else from that day on. And so it has been ever since.

Purukupali was one of the original people of the world. Just before him had been Mudungkala, the original mother who rose out of the ground with her children, crawled about making hills and rivers, and decreed that the bare ground should grow green things for food and for creatures to hide in. And so it has been ever since.

Stories such as these may represent the earliest human attempts to express and come to terms with the great mysteries of life such as where the grass and the rivers come from and why we must all die. For the last forty thousand years or so, we humans have been engaged in an adventure of self-discovery. Over and over again we have discerned a dimension of mystery in our existence, in the fact of life and death, in the patterns of love and indifference and anger, in the reality of pain and the surprise of joy. In all this there is mystery—why it is so, what promise or threat it holds, how we can deal with it.

Few things reveal as much about us humans as the story of how we have responded to the dimension of mystery. That story, for the most part, is the story of religion.

Facing Mystery

There are many ways to define the word "religion." It is difficult to settle on a single clear definition. You can find this out for yourself by trying to create a definition that applies to all the patterns of thought and practices that you would call religious but which does not include any patterns that you would not call religious. A British armchair anthropologist named Edward Tylor (1832-1917) declared rather simply that religion is a belief in spiritual beings. But another armchair anthropologist, Lucien Levy-Bruhl (1857-1939), later proposed that primitive belief in spirits was probably not true religion, because primitive people do not worship the spirits, they only seek to manipulate them at times. Buddhism is usually listed among the great religions of the world, yet others say it is a philosophy rather than a religion, because Buddhism does not believe in God or other single Ultimate Being. Some define religion so broadly that they include patriotism or Marxism as religion, on the grounds that patriotism or Marxism may be the major object of devotion for some people. The anthropologist Clifford Geertz (1926-) offers a rather complex but well-known definition of religion as a symbol system. "A religion is 1) a system of symbols which acts to 2) establish powerful, pervasive and long-lasting moods and motivations in men by 3) formulating conceptions of a general order of existence and 4) clothing these conceptions with such an aura of factuality that 5) the moods and motivations seem uniquely realistic." Whether this definition is really better than Tylor's is something you can decide when you have finished this book.

For reasons that will become more apparent by the end of the Part I of this book, the definition of religion used here will begin with the claim that religion is a human response to mystery. A primitive tribesperson is uneasy about the mysterious forces that cause rain, bring good luck, and make strange emotions enter the heart. The primitive tribesperson names these forces, gives them faces and tells brief stories about them, in order to deal with them. Later cultures develop greater and more complex myths, describing the mysterious forces of nature as gods and families of gods. Through symbol, ritual, and elaborate story, humankind gives mystery concrete forms in order to tame it and make it less threatening.

Eventually, we humans discover that mystery is endless. About twenty-five hundred years ago, the major cultures of the earth stumbled upon the realization that beyond all the specific forms and faces we give to the mysterious forces that exist, there is an ultimate and infinite context of our lives that is an all-embracing mystery. There are various religious ways to label the mystery. In the West it is usually thought of as an Ultimate Reality called "God." Buddhists speak of nirvana, an incomprehensible state or condition. Other cultures have other ways for speaking of ultimate mystery.

Even when we are not consciously aware of it, ideas about the ultimate mystery of life may be influencing us. When you have lunch, for example, you may decide what to eat on the basis of the social consequences, such as sharing a meal with a friend. Your friendship in turn will be based on various things, such as who it is easiest to laugh with, who seems to like you more, who shares your values, or even who can help you socially. All of these criteria in turn are related to your basic feelings about what values are most important in your life, whether it be your own social success or having a friend to rely on in life's troubles or being able to take some satisfaction in your helpfulness towards others. And each of these in its turn may rest on an even more fundamental sense of what life is finally all about. Are we but solitary strangers in a dog-eat-dog world? Or are we children of God awaiting another life? Or are we brothers and sisters on an adventure of life?

Without knowing it at times, we carry in us ideas about such things, ideas that are our implicit answers to life's mysteries. At a certain point in our thoughts we shrug our shoulders and say to ourselves that we will not try to ask some of these questions because we cannot see how to answer them. That is the point at which we have discovered mystery. We may then choose to ignore it, but it is still there. And the way we deal with it affects our lives one way or another.

We can deal with it in nonreligious ways. Some people have formally declared the dimension of mystery to be simply the unknowable and therefore to be ignored. This is the position taken by agnostics. This label covers two positions, nearly the same but not quite. We can call them tentative agnosticism and strong agnosticism. Tentative agnostics are those who say they do not happen to know whether God exists or not, because the whole topic is not clear enough to them, or because the reasons they have been given for belief in God are not convincing enough to settle the case either way. This leaves them open eventually to be convinced one way or another. Strong agnostics, however, are convinced that the existence or non-existence of God is strictly unknowable. No amount of future information or argument, they believe, is going to change that. (Chapters Twelve and Thirteen will explain more about how some people have arrived at strong agnosticism.)

Others have said that the mystery that surrounds us is just endless possibility, empty in itself with no direction or meaning. This is the position taken by atheists. There are also tentative and strong forms of atheism. Tentative atheists are those who find the available evidence and arguments about God's existence sufficient to make it more reasonable not to believe in God. Supposedly, however, new evidence or better arguments might change their mind. Strong atheists, on the other hand, are convinced that the available evidence is so strongly against the existence of God that it is clearly irrational to believe that God exists. There are even a few people we could call absolute atheists, who think they can prove that no God exists. But most of those who reject belief in God are more modest in their claims than this.

Agnostics and atheists alike find no ultimate meaningfulness in the basic mysteries of life. They turn instead to the projects at hand, of making a living, learning to love, preparing the way for future generations, finding some joy in great art and pleasant picnics and the laughter of a child. This is meaning enough, most claim.

All of these are treasures of life, but they have not satisfied everyone in history. Beyond living and loving and laughing, the "more," the mystery, the endless possible questions about who we really are, what we ultimately come from, whether there is any lasting purpose to our lives, can still nag us. Is it possible that we come from randomness, are accidents of nature, have no purpose in the end? These questions have haunted the great civilizations of humankind. Each of them has found religious ways to deal with mystery, treating it not as a deadly emptiness but somehow as a fullness in which lies the meaning of human existence, naming that fullness "God," or in India "Brahman," or in China calling it the Tao. In such religions the ultimate mystery is treated as sacred, as Mystery with a capital "M."

We will see more about the ways in which great classical religions of history such as Judaism, Christianity, Islam, Hinduism, Buddhism, and Taoism give a name to the ultimate Mystery. Some religions do not worry explicitly about whatever it is that is truly "ultimate" in reality. That is a fairly sophisticated idea, as we will see in Chapters Three and Four. But they do worry about the aspects of life that would be mysteries outside the realm of their understanding were it not for the ways in which their religious ideas give some name to these mysteries and explain them. They worry about the mysteries of why newborn children often die, why the floods come each year, why it is important to marry outside of one's village. Every society perceives mysteries in life at some level. Finding the answers to one set of mysteries can lead on and on, until a culture may come to awareness of the ultimacy of mystery.

A Basic Human Faith

Most people in history have been religious in some way or another in the face of mystery. This reveals aspects of our human character that are sometimes hidden from us. First of all, we are stubbornly courageous beings. The religions of humankind are all manifestations of a kind of courageous faith in the meaningfulness of life in the face of the mystery that surrounds us. Facing mystery, we could wander in confusion, feel great fear, or even despair. Instead we find the faith to see it as somehow valuable or intelligible. By naming it, embracing it, building a life in relation to it, we show a trust that ultimately it does not destroy but upholds the worthwhileness of our life. This is what Jews, Christians, and Muslims do when they say the Ultimate is God. This also, as we will see, is what Buddhists do by calling the mystery "nirvana," and Hindus by calling it "Brahman" or "Atman."

Beneath this stubborn and bold faith in the ultimate meaningfulness of life is something else especially human, which is that we are the strange being, the peculiar animal, that can be aware of mystery at all. We have the kind of consciousness that can ask questions, can wonder why things are as they are, and can become insecure as a result. We can think about ourselves, our identities, our place in the scheme of things. Because of that, we can worry whether it all really does make sense.

Most questions can be turned into problems-to-be-solved so that they are no longer threatening, but there is always some genuine mystery left over that remains a question without an answer. The horizon of mystery always remains there in front of us no matter how far we travel. We find ourselves always able to ask one more question about what is worth living (or dying) for, about what sort of person we should be, about what our destiny is. Even when we ignore such questions, we remain the animal with the endless capacity for them.

Another way of saying this is that we are the beings open to the infinite. We are the beings related to whatever is the ultimate foundation or goal of all things (if there is such a foundation or goal as religions claim), because our kind of consciousness is an openness to what is always beyond: the endless mystery. Our thoughts can "transcend" whatever limits we have so far experienced.

As the religions of the world have been our usual way of dealing with mystery, it is a study of these religions that can show us most about our own nature as the beings who are open to infinite mystery. Most of the time our religions provide very specific beliefs, values, and behavioral norms rather than general talk about mystery and the infinite. Religions provide symbols, rituals, moral codes, community life, and personal identity patterns. Each of these many and varied aspects of religion will be explored in some detail in the following chapters. But it is good not to forget that each of these specific forms of religion is significant for us humans precisely because each is one of the ways we bring our lives into a coherent and worthwhile focus in relation to the mystery around us.

The Development of Religion in Cultures and in Individuals

There are so many specific aspects of religion that it is very difficult to make a coherent story out of it. The outline for the approach in this book is taken from the sociologist Robert Bellah, who claims in a fairly famous article, "Religious Evolution," that religion has passed through certain stages of development. Not all scholars who study religion agree with this developmental theory. It is wise to be wary of theories; they are not always fully accurate. But Bellah's theory does a great deal to illumine and make sense out of the story of religion and the human capacity for the infinite that religion expresses.

Bellah's theory claims that religions generally pass through a progression of forms, from primitive and archaic to historic and modern. It also appears that each of us repeats this developmental pattern in our own lives. We are born primitive, and then we grow into archaic and eventually perhaps historic and even modern modes of thought. Descriptions of primitive tribespeople around a fire working their magic and invoking the spirits are also descriptions of something buried in your life's story and mine, in ways we do not always recognize. What the whole human race has experienced is still within us.

Human culture and individual lives expand gradually into broader visions of life. Primitive culture lives in a relatively small world populated by various spirits and magical powers. Archaic cultures perceive a larger and more complicated world with powerful gods at work. Historic cultures conceive of a universal power or Being that exerts its influence everywhere. Finally, the mystics of history and now a modern religiousness emphasize the infiniteness of the Mystery, called by such a name as "God."

Likewise each of us today may go through stages of understanding. Those raised to believe in God, for example, will begin by thinking of God as an invisible person, like grandpa perhaps except bigger. At some point in life they may picture God as a cosmic power, clearly and obviously intervening in history and nature. Later yet they may reflect more on God as infinite and mysterious, always present in a subtle and not obvious way. To abandon one way of thinking of God is not to cease to be religious; it may be only a change in the way of being religious.

The cultural developmental process is still just struggling into the most recent stage in Bellah's outline, the modern stage. It has been emerging only in the last couple of centuries, a brief time in the panorama of history. (Even so there are now also so-called "post-modern" theories of religion. This term has too many meanings to be entirely clear. Chapter Fifteen will discuss the nature of post-modern religious thought and seek what clarity is possible.) Modern religiousness has often been taken to be antireligious, especially by those who are most conservative in their religious feelings, because modern religion lets go of or reinterprets some older beliefs and practices. But modern religiousness is also a way of facing the mystery of our existence. To understand this modern mode of religion and culture we will have to start at the beginning, with primitive and archaic religion.

The Academic Study of Religion

A later chapter will introduce you to the study of theology. Theology is usually defined as rational reflection about the meaning and coherence of a religious tradition. Theology is most often done by those who accept and support the religious tradition they are reflecting on. Theologians are "insiders" for the most part. This book in general is not theology but is the study of religion. Such study is done, as it were, from the outside. That does not mean that it is necessarily done from a position of disbelief or skepticism, though it can be. You will find most of what is written here to be sympathetic to religion. But the perspective taken is that of looking in on our own human religious life, as though from the outside.

Another way of saying this is to note that some people study a religion to find out more about God and the supernatural and so forth. That is theology. Others study religion in order to find out about us human beings through our religiousness, to find in the religious beliefs and practices and symbols clear insights or at least good clues to our own inner selfhood. We human beings are hard to figure out. The study of religion is a great help for learning more about us. That is the purpose and the approach of this book. Only in the Epilogue will we finally look at the awkward question of making critical evaluations of religions, possibly to challenge various religious beliefs, values, and practices.

In the course of the next fifteen chapters you will find a great deal of information about specific aspects of religion, about spirits, magic, gods, God, Brahman, paradise and hell, heaven, belonging, identity, moral values, leaders and sacred texts, rituals and symbols, faith and reason, skepticism and modern beliefs. But throughout these chapters you will also keep meeting a strange side of ourselves, that capacity for the infinite that our mode of consciousness possesses that keeps us always on the edge of mystery. It is the capacity for reflection and freedom, for hope and despair, for responsibility and commitment. It is our humanness.

For Further Reflection

1. Which seems more accurate, to think of religion as a set of answers or to think of it as an awareness of unanswered mysteries? Explain.
2. What would you say is life's ultimate meaning? Express as best you can why this is a difficult question to deal with.
3. Can most people get along quite well without any active concern for what is mysterious and uncertain about life? Explain.
4. Explain what you currently believe about the evolution of cultures. Do you find it plausible to say that humankind has gone through stages of cultural development for the last forty thousand years?
5. What purpose do you have in mind for studying human religiousness? Is there anything about studying religion from an "outsider's" viewpoint that bothers you? If so, what?

Suggested Readings

Denise and John Carmody, *The Range of Religion: An Introductory Reader*, 1992. A good collection of readings from various religious traditions and about religions.

Robert S. Ellwood and Gregory D. Alles, eds., *The Encyclopedia of World Religions*, 1998. Informative and up-to-date articles.

James L. Peacock and A. Thomas Kirsch, *The Human Direction*, 1980 (third edition). A general presentation of cultural evolution.

Robert Bellah, "Religious Evolution," *American Sociological Review*, 39:3 (June 1964), pp. 348-374. This can be found also in Bellah's *Beyond Belief*, 1970.

James W. Fowler, *Stages of Faith: The Psychology of Human Development And The Quest For Meaning*, 1981. An excellent synthesis of several theories of individual development in relation to basic faith or trust in life, with many illustrations from life.

James Thrower, *Religion: The Classical Theories*, 1999. Describes religion from the viewpoint of both believers and skeptics.

Theodore Roszak, *Unfinished Animal*, 1975. On the religious impulse and a sense of mystery.

Part I

The Numinous

One of the most difficult aspects of describing religion is that there is no single good word for what religions are concerned with. The best ordinary word is "sacred," but it has its limitations. It has to be stretched, for example, to cover the demonic forces many religions believe in. The sacred is also usually thought of as "holy," whereas most of the gods of ancient religions are not very holy at all, in the usual sense of the word. Other words are limited also. "Divine" will not quite cover magic and spirits. To many people, "supernatural" suggests only ghosts and not also an infinite God.

Rudolph Otto (1869-1937), a German theologian, used a more obscure word in his book, *The Idea of the Holy* (1917). He borrowed the word "numinous" to refer to the "fascinating and awesome mystery" known as God. The word can serve a wider use here, to stand for the many ways that the mysterious dimension of existence has been encountered and given some religious name by the generations of humankind. Stage by stage, from primitive to modern, the numinous has taken on new faces, names and roles. Descriptions of each of those stages in the next chapters will clarify the meaning of "numinous." The descriptions will also enable us to look again at ourselves as the unusual beings who live with an orientation to mystery.

Chapter One

An Enchanted World

The Numinous in Primitive and Archaic Religion

Primitive Religion

If you were to awake some misty morning in the central highlands of New Guinea, in the thatched and stilted home of a native tribal family, you would find yourself in a world alive with invisible powers and beings. Before dawn it would not be entirely safe to intrude upon the spirits who roam at night, so you would lie within the hut talking quietly, or begin to eat breakfast inside until sunlight made the outdoors more safe. When you went out you would have to respect the rights of certain snakes. To stare at them openly could provoke them to return as spirits when you slept again and make you ill. Perhaps, though, you were born with a special aura of power about you. If so, the snake might not be able to see you, so you would be safe. At any rate, you would know some ritual techniques of your own to counteract the snake's power. In fact, you would know many kinds of magic to cause illness to your enemies and health to your pigs, and to deal with threatening spirits.

The daily life of mountain tribespeople of New Guinea provides a good example of what is meant by primitive religion. There are only a few places in the world where this is true, but in the mountains of New Guinea and Southeast Asia, in the Kalahari desert and the rain forests of the Congo, in the upper reaches of the Amazon and in the deserts of Australia, there are tribes almost following the old ways still. Contact with other societies over centuries, and recently with modern societies, has had an impact. The old ways are fading now and being replaced by new modes of thought, for better or worse. But during the last one hundred years or so, anthropologists have learned to live among the tribes, to study their languages, to observe their customs carefully and sympathetically. These outsiders may never have fully seen life and reality as it appears to the tribespeople, but they have provided such precise and thorough descriptions of tribal life that we can form a picture of it that is probably close to the truth.

What the anthropologists tell us about the primitive tribal groups gives us our best available basis to estimate what religion may have been like before there was any civilization on this planet. This is important information because it is not just information about the past; the study of primitive beliefs is also a study of ourselves, of what we might be like without our extra layers of cultural accumulations. Primitive thought is woven into the greater complexities of later cultural forms including our own. Primitive religion still lives in the niches of contemporary culture and in the corners of our personalities. We can begin to understand this by looking at the universe as primitive people see it, one full of numinous powers of limited size and power.

The Nonliving Numinous Forces: Luck, Magic, Mana, and Omens

Primitive people are conscious of many mysterious forces at work around them. Sometimes berries grow; sometimes they do not. Disease comes at unexpected times. A brother who is usually quiet and calm runs away screaming. For these and other events there must be causes, but often these are not evident. Sensibly enough, primitive people believe there must be invisible causes at work in the world, affecting people's lives. One category of invisible and mysterious causes is the category of nonliving numinous powers. There are many forms of it, and many names.

Luck is one form. This is not mere accidental luck, not chance or happenstance, but luck as a real force to make good things (or bad) take place. Some inanimate things have it, such as medallions that can ward off evil. Some once-living objects have it, such as rabbit's feet which bring good luck (though not to the rabbit, apparently). Some people have it. In every tribe or group someone is born luckier than others, possessed of an inner power to succeed, be healthy, eat well, please people. Other people are jinxed, afflicted by a power that attracts harm to them and those around them.

Magic is another name for this numinous power. Rituals have magical power to affect the weather, put snakes to sleep, insure pregnancy. Medicines in general are all full of strange power. (The English word "pharmacist" comes from an ancient Greek word meaning "magician" or "poisoner.") Water from sacred streams has magical power to cure or to kill. Special signs made with the fingers can inflict harm or ward off demons.

For many primitive people names have a kind of magical power. To label something is to control it. Children experience this when they discover they can influence the large warm creature who holds them by saying, "Mama." In some tribes, people hide their true names so that no malicious spirit can control them by calling their name. The mere name of a spirit sometimes has power over other forces, a power to bless or a power to exorcise evil influences.

There is a power in similarities. Pouring water on the ground from a gourd may stimulate further water on the ground from the sky in the form of rain. Painting a bison on the wall of the cave and hurling spears at it may help in tomorrow's hunt. There is power in contact also. To touch a dead person without later purification can make a person ill. What belongs to you, your hair and saliva and food that has been in your stomach, has some relation to your whole self and can be used in magical ways to affect you. The connections of similarity and contact can be used together in sorcery. If you construct a doll similar to a person you wish to harm and also use bits of hair or clothing from the person, that will make doubly certain that any harm done to the doll will affect the person it represents.

Those who believe in magical powers often do not claim to know what such forces really are or why they really work. So often all a person can do is to memorize what does work. Notching the ears of cattle protects them from evil disease. Hex signs keep demons away. It is not necessary to understand why this works, so long as it does.

To make it easier to talk about this invisible nonliving power, a name will help. The one used most commonly now by anthropologists is "mana." In 1891 a missionary, Bishop Codrington, wrote to a colleague in London about the Southwest Pacific culture of the Melanesians. These tribes, Codrington reported, share a belief in an invisible power which is "the cause of all success in life that surpasses the ordinary." They called this power "mana." The name has stuck, as has its companion name "taboo" (or "tapu" or "tabu"). Mana-power can be good or bad, but because it is power it is often dangerous. Places, people, or objects with too much mana are therefore taboo—dangerous—and are to be avoided or handled with great care.

Mana-power may also make its presence known by peculiar effects on the environment. Spirits do the same, as the next section will mention. Such signs of numinous power are called "omens." The derivative word "ominous" suggests that omens are warnings about bad things to come. Vultures flocking over your house may be an ominous event. But there are also good omens and neutral ones. An itchy palm is an omen you will receive some money, it is said. A fire that flares up signifies that visitors are on their way, perhaps friendly, perhaps not. Primitive people live in a world where there may be numerous signs every day. Any odd occurrence is likely to foretell something. It is important to be alert to the signs.

Divination is a name for the practice of reading omens. For the most part anyone can read the signs that appear in nature and daily life. It is especially handy to have available some reliable method of divining. In some cultures bones or marked pebbles can be cast down on the ground to be read. In another the shape of the clouds can be trusted to foretell the immediate future.

Numinous omen-power is useful in many ways. The English used to throw a murder suspect into a pond that had been blessed. If the suspect floated, the holy water was rejecting him. He was therefore guilty. (If he drowned, his innocence assured him of a good afterlife.) A New Guinea tribe discovers who is guilty by cutting off the head of a chicken and letting it loose to run around until it drops. Where it stops indicates who is guilty.

The numinous power in luck, magic, or omens can be good or bad, strong or weak, easily controlled or completely independent of human choice. It is a force residing in spirits, people, animals, inanimate objects, or daily events. It is a nonliving power, though some omens are signs given by spirits. It is unexplained in the sense that, by and large, it is just there in reality, affecting people even when no one can say why or explain what it is. Primitive people perceive it as relatively limited and local. As we will see, archaic people believe in much more powerful forms of it.

Living Numinous Beings: The Spirits

The world of the primitive is at least as crowded with spirits as it is with mana. However big the tribespeople conceive their universe to be, it is alive with invisible living beings, forces that are not only numinous powers but also conscious, with thoughts and feelings like those of a person. The more similar the spirits are to humans, the more they can be called "anthropomorphic" (human-form).

A vast array of small nature spirits live in different places and things. Each tree, river, field, rock, cove, cave, and mountain top is likely to have its spirit. Often the spirit has a personality like the place where it lives: the spirit of a brook is talkative and lively; the spirit of the thunder is loud and angry. Every animal has its own spirit. Or we could as easily say that many spirits have animal-form (are "theriomorphic."). Nature has a hundred thousand souls.

Many pests and demons, small invisible beings, care only to cause trouble. They make you forget your stew on the fire until it burns. They trip you, so you break a leg. They turn your milk sour and make your apples rot. Some of these are strong enough to cause major troubles such as disease, miscarriage, deformed children, and even death.

Many people have attendant spirits. When you are born, perhaps you have an invisible twin who will accompany you through life, or even two of them, one helpful and one harmful. Perhaps you have a spirit partner you must entertain and keep happy lest it get angry with you. Or it may be more like a guardian angel, a protector, or source of luck.

The spirits of the dead are rarely very far away. Sometimes they live at the edges of the campsite or village. At other times they stay in the land of the dead, but might return to visit out of loneliness, or to cause trouble out of envy for the living, or to demand more remembrance and attention than has been given them, or to give advice in dreams, visions, or omens.

The original ancestors of the tribe may still be present. They established the tribe's customs. In a very few cases they watch to punish anyone who violates those customs. Or they act as guardians and give warnings through omens. The ancestors of the animals sometimes show up also, as talking animals in a dream, or metamorphic—shape-shifting—beings, sometimes human in form, sometimes not.

You yourself are a spirit-being; your life is your spirit. It is even possible that within you are various spirits that together make up who you are. One tribe, for example, says each person has three spirits. Upon death one spirit dissolves, another remains to roam around on earth, the third goes to the sky to live. Another tribe believes that it is possible to capture one of the spirits of each person you kill in battle. A strong warrior grows in strength because each victory over another person allows the warrior to inhale the other person's spirit with its additional energy, to add its strength to that of the other spirits which the warrior already possesses. A person who has killed too often, though, may lose control of the many spirits within him and go mad.

Among all these numinous spirit-beings are other strange and numinous ones that are not spirits, yet not human either. There are elves, gnomes, trolls, leprechauns, and such. They are a little too solid to be spirits, yet they are in touch with the numinous in special ways. They can bless or curse a person or give warning signs, so it is advisable to remain on good terms with them.

No single tribe is likely to see around them all of the forms of spirit-beings described here. Among the many spirits that a given tribe does believe in, only a few will have much importance. The spirits of the dead, a local nature spirit or two, an animal whose spirit is of special significance to this tribe, a few spirits who frequently produce omens to guide people—these and one or two others might be the only spirits a child learns much about. Yet no tribe is surprised to discover that the world is full of spirits, some of whom the tribe had not known about before.

Dealing with Numinous Powers

Because primitive existence is crowded with mana and spirits, it is of obvious importance to know how to deal with them. A child growing up in a primitive culture learns about the various mana powers the way a modern child learns about household appliances. Each has its use. Some open cans; others toast bread. A child learns to use them, even without understanding how or why they work. It is the same with magical rituals, or "oracle" bones that foretell the future, or musical instruments that are taboo because they possess intense mana. A child in a primitive culture learns not to tread on taboo ground and not to dribble saliva where a sorcerer can get it and use it to do harm to the child. Magical potions can make someone fall in love with you or can make an enemy fall over dead. The proper song can attract the opossum close enough to hunt. The power-filled symbols on your chest can prevent spears from striking you. Mana-power is everywhere, to be used when possible, to be avoided when necessary.

Dealing with spirits requires some care also. Spirits are like people, with similar needs and feelings. Persuasive techniques can help. The spirits may be lonely and seek company. That is why they want to take your children's spirits, even though that means your children will die. Keep the spirits away from the village if you can. If you cannot, pour a bit of beer on the ground now and then as a little gift, and they may leave you in peace.

Some bothersome spirits can be threatened or driven away. Firecrackers at festivals, and loud gongs and clattering sticks at funerals will keep little demons or the spirits of the dead at a distance where they will do no harm. Some spirits are not too bright and can be tricked. When disease is spreading, leave a dummy image of yourself in front of your hut. The sickness spirit may mistake the dummy for you and curse it with the disease, leaving you safe.

Magic is important for dealing with spirits. Certain signs or symbols can keep spirits away. There are formulas or substances for summoning spirits and for casting them out. Psychotropic drugs or alcohol can aid in making contact with spirits or using their power. Garlic has a noticeable mana, strong enough to drive away evil spirits.

The best magic is coercive magic, guaranteed to work provided only that the whole magical ritual is performed exactly right. Unfortunately, some demons also know magic and can cast contrary spells. Others will make you stumble in your speech and actions and thereby weaken the power of the magic. Some spirits are too strong to be coerced by magic. It is best just to avoid them as much as possible.

In all these ways of dealing with spirits there is no worship. Some ancestors or spirits may be addressed with respect. A hunter may respectfully thank the spirit of the deer he has just killed. The Ainu of northern Japan, for example, have a bear ritual in which they honor the spirit of the bear which they have just killed for their feast. But they do not worship the bear spirit, as a superior spirit being. For this reason some anthropologists in the past decided that primitive beliefs and practices of this sort are not true religion. Once again, it depends on how "religion" is defined. For convenience, we can treat these primitive practices and beliefs as the simplest form of religion.

Primitive Religion Is Called Animism

Near the end of the nineteenth century, an Englishman named Edward Tylor

(1832-1917) decided that the beliefs of primitive tribes in a multitude of spirits needed a name. He used the word "animism," from the Latin word *anima*, meaning soul or spirit. People who believe that there are many and varied spirits invisibly roaming the world and affecting our lives are called animists; they also usually believe in some form of mana-powers.

Primitive tribes are all animistic to some extent. So Tylor guessed that animism is the origin of all religion. Many people were offended by this conclusion, because it seemed to imply that religious belief is fundamentally primitive.

In defense of religion others pointed out that no one really knows what went on among people ten thousand or twenty thousand years ago. Perhaps the earliest human religion was belief in a single supreme God, and animism was only a later corruption of this noble belief. This theory happened to fit better with what the Judaeo-Christian scriptures seemed to say, that the first human beings knew that there was one supreme God, so this theory was more popular among people who adhered to traditional religious beliefs. The Catholic anthropologist Father Wilhelm Schmidt (1868-1954) promoted this idea in the early decades of the twentieth century.

The dust has settled somewhat since the days of the most turbulent arguments. Though there is always room for revision, we can treat primitive animism as the earliest form of religion and the roots of later religious beliefs and practices. This need not imply, however, that religion is necessarily animist at its heart, as we will see.

Animism is still part of life today. There are numerous forms of contemporary belief in mana. People still believe in good luck and bad luck. Baseball players will not play without their lucky cap or socks. Actors refrain from wishing one another well because that is unlucky. They say "break a leg" instead. Hostesses will not seat thirteen people at a table and hotels have no thirteenth floor. Some people wear blessed medals or use holy water for protection.

Belief in mana is sometimes disguised in pseudo-scientific forms. Some people claim that the pyramid shape can focus cosmic rays to clear your mind, preserve raw hamburger, and sharpen razor blades. The magician who used to move objects by "magic" now advertises his exceptional ESP talent of telekinesis, which empowers him to bend forks with his mind and stop clocks at a distance.

Belief in spirits is less common today than it once was, yet we still buy books of stories of haunted houses. People fear ghosts. Others claim to be reincarnations of ancient heroes. Some television personalities claim to bring messages from the deceased to people in a studio audience. Films about dead people communicating with the living are popular. We hear stories at night of demonic possession and tremble a little, even in our skepticism.

Animism today also sometimes appears in the guise of science. Researchers have discovered that people whose hearts have stopped beating for a time report similar "out-of-the-body" experiences. We are tempted to take this as scientific evidence that we are all embodied spirits. When strange lights are seen in the sky, it somehow seems possible to believe there are living beings within the unidentified flying objects. Unseen beings from outer space are replacing some of the invisible spirits that hovered around our ancestors.

The overall life, culture, and religion of the primitive tribes that exist today are like surviving remnants of the common beginnings of all human culture. But the modern "tribes" that are the great industrialized and computerized nations retain the past also in all the little ways we find mana-like powers and spirits all around us still.

The Culture of the Primitives

The numinous is ordinary. The numinous elements, living and nonliving, that are part of the primitive person's reality blend into the everyday and ordinary aspects of that reality. A child grows up memorizing the names and habits of invisible spirits and living cousins without thinking of one of them as being more "religious" than the others. They are different but all part of the same world. The child learns which snakes to avoid, which rocks have spirits, and which tree is full of mana, all as part of everyday practical knowledge. The spirits are part of the everyday world; the numinous powers are all part of the family's homeland.

The world is a loose collection of various powers and beings. There is no overall unified order to the spirits and mana-powers. Each spirit has its own story; each bit of magical power has its location or use. The world as it now exists is the result of a thousand different and more or less unconnected events. The porcupine has quills because once it was a person who burned someone's hut. The owners of the hut threw spears at the arsonist, sticking him all over. The person crawled into a log and came out days later looking as he does now, with tiny spears all over his body. Clouds are wet and the snake is shiny and people die and no one should marry a brother or sister, each for a different reason. The world cannot be understood any more than that. Once upon a time, certain different things happened for different reasons, and that is why the world is the way it is today. Primitive people are as intelligent as people of any culture. They show great ingenuity in the ways they categorize and cross-categorize things, or apply everyday logic skillfully in making tools. But their culture does not train them to use their intelligence in the same ways as other cultures, as we will see.

The collection of customs rules life. The customs give form to daily life and prevent it from breaking into chaos. Many times fights erupt out of jealousies, anger, or pettiness. A small argument leads to great insults and on to physical injury or even death. Suddenly whole families are caught up in tensions, fearful about who will attack whom. Customs may restore peace by dictating a certain specific reparation or banishing an offender. Custom and chaos sway back and forth in uneasy balance. Words of wisdom from one person or astute reading of omens by another may provide guidance. Those tribes with the stronger and more effective customs, we can presume, are the ones that endure in the face of the human impatience, pride, passion, and pettiness that is part of life everywhere.

Primitive life is usually called egalitarian, because there are no hereditary or official rulers in primitive societies. Any person with good social skills or great strength or other special qualities may in fact exert greater influence in the tribe than others. But primitive people usually resent anyone among them who tries to claim extra power or privilege.

Tribespeople live day by day and generation by generation, juggling a thousand forces both numinous and ordinary, balancing between customs and impulses. There are rarely plans for long-term projects. There is no well-structured social hierarchy, no kings, no full time priests. There are just the people in families, bands, and tribes, digging up edible roots, planning a feast, preparing an initiation ritual, driving out a harmful spirit, cooking a meal, making signs to ward off sorcery, nursing a child, stealing from an enemy, falling in love, growing old, and telling the stories about how things are in the world.

From Primitive to Archaic Culture

As far back as ten thousand years ago, some part of the human family transformed its existence by inventing agriculture. Primitive people live by hunting and gathering, sometimes also with small gardens or with a domesticated animal or two. Some cultures became more complex when they extended their gardens or began to herd large numbers of animals. But large scale agriculture brought much greater changes. In the fertile crescent in the ancient Near East (from present day Palestine up through Syria and into Iraq) a few people began to plant various grains that could be tended and harvested in bulk. Ever larger numbers of people could live off the produce of one area of land.

Villages turned into large towns where there were inherited distinctions between an upper and lower class of people, the rulers and the ruled. Eventually cities appeared. Social and economic classes multiplied: landowners, the military, merchants, peasants. The role of chief or king took on greater power. Even religion was put into the hands of full time specialists. Priests were consecrated to offer sacrifices to gods in official acts of worship. In the temples, prophets had full time jobs reading omens in the entrails of animals. As culture changes, religious beliefs and practices change. Primitive beliefs in mana and spirits were retained (as they still are in weaker form even today), but were absorbed into a somewhat different pattern of belief known now as archaic religion.

ARCHAIC RELIGION

The Birth of the Gods

The archaic stage of religious development is a stage in which people begin to think of some of the spirits as numinous beings of very great power, more awesome than ordinary spirits. We usually call these great spirits "gods." Like all spirits they are personal in that they have thoughts and feelings. The word "personal" here does not necessarily mean friendly or warm. Although the gods can be helpful and kind, they can also be petty, vengeful, and destructive.

The gods are not as neighborly as are most of the lesser spirits. Even if the gods live nearby in a shrine or sacred place, they are nonetheless like great chiefs or kings, endowed with majesty and deserving of respect and fear. Many of the gods live far away in the skies, on a high mountain, or deep in the earth.

Human society is no longer egalitarian as it is in primitive culture. Archaic cultures have a hierarchy of power among people, from peasant to landlords and military leaders to king. Among the gods and spirits it is often the same. Many local spirits might live their lives on their own for the most part, but still be under the power of a god. The spirits that live in underwater caves and in various harbors might all have to bow to the greater power of a great god of the sea. Occasionally, there is an explicit line of authority as in the case of Zeus who ruled all the sky gods because he is their father, or of Marduk, god of ancient Babylon, who ruled the other gods of that area as his reward for having defeated monstrous enemies of the gods.

The anthropologists have sometimes used the name "high god" to label a god who is not merely greater than an ordinary spirit but who dominates even other gods in some sense. The category of high god is a fuzzy one. Sometimes it applies to any god like Zeus or Marduk who is the dominant one, albeit not all-powerful. At other times the title "high god" belongs to the god who created the universe as it now exists, perhaps forming it out of some primordial ooze or out of the bodies of defeated monsters. Or perhaps one god is just so appreciated by people that the other gods are overshadowed. (Wilhelm Schmidt, mentioned earlier, claimed that all cultures have or had some form of high god, but this does not seem to be true of genuinely primitive cultures.)

Awesome as they are, the gods are not always of particularly noble or gracious character. The very size of their power tends to spoil them. Little spirits can be as willful, vain, and petty as children. Unfortunately the gods are too, but they have such power that their whims must be respected. Even kings can act childishly, so it is no surprise if gods do likewise. When the gods go on a rampage, bringing floods or epidemics, people can only cower in fear, offer the greatest gifts they can find, and hope that their offerings and praise will eventually soothe the divine anger. Archaic people simply do not expect much of what we would call emotional or moral maturity in their gods.

Religion and culture develop together. When chiefs and kings appear among the people, gods appear among the spirits. When a hierarchy of classes arises in society, a hierarchy of powers arises among the spirits. When cultures perceive a larger world of manifold and changing complexities, the gods inhabit larger spaces and give rise to complex stories of various plans, struggles, victories, and defeats. This would seem inevitable. On the one hand, people can really conceive of only what their own language, tradition, and experiences prepare them to be able to find words for. On the other hand, since they do have new experiences, they will eventually find the language to begin to describe them in new ways. Whether religion comes from the active presence of the numinous among people or from human imagination or from both, it will still be conceived of and portrayed in ways that the life experiences of the people incline them. Religiousness, like all aspects of life, finds its expression in the cultural forms available to people.

Great Mana

Just as the archaic cultures think some spirit-beings are great enough to be gods, they think of some mana-power as very great. Most great power was usually personified; even time (Chronos) was a god in ancient Greek thought, as were heaven and earth (Uranus and Gaia), rather than nonpersonal or nonliving forces. Yet occasionally there have been forms of belief in some massive numinous forces.

The ancient Chinese, for example, perceived two complementary forces, the yang and the yin, at work in all aspects of the universe. The ancient Hindu priests believed that in their rituals they generated a kind of cosmic power. (A later chapter will say more on all of these.) Astrological belief in the influence of the stars and planets on our lives is very old. There is no way of knowing how long human societies have taken notice of the effect of the moon on the tides, or even a correlation of the twenty-eight-day lunar month with menstruation (a word based on *mensis*, the Latin word for "month"). Nor do we know which societies of the Northern Hemisphere first noticed that when the constellation we call "Cancer" arose at night, the days were longest and the sun brightest. But out of these and similar observations, ancient peoples like the Babylonians and the Chinese devised elaborate descriptions of various kinds of numinous forces that emanate from the heavens and influence human affairs. Still today millions of people check with their astrologer before they make any significant decisions or take important actions.

Perhaps equally ancient is the belief that numbers represent great mana. Sums and propositions have a wondrous regularity. With measurements, angles, and designs, for example, the end of the sun's retreat into winter and its return for spring can be identified. (The structures of Stonehenge in England are just one example of this.) Among the Babylonians, numerology shared popularity with astrology. There were "lucky" numbers, numbers with positive power. The numbers of a person's name established how a person's life would intertwine with the number-value of other places and peoples and powers.

Dealing with Gods and Great Mana

The primitive person lives as a near-equal to the spirits and the local forms of mana; but the archaic person faces numinous powers that loom large over the landscapes of life. The gods are too strong to be controlled by magic or any other means. At best, it is persuasion, not control, that a person must bring to bear on the gods. Worship appears for the first time in history.

No one need worship spirits; they are human-sized and can often be controlled by magic. But the great gods are beyond easy control. People must try to influence them by bribes and flattery, albeit with great respect. Bribery takes the form of respectful offerings; flattery appears as dutiful worship. These acts of persuasion cannot be too brief, or occasional, or casual. Long rituals and celebrations are expected. Formal shrines and temples become common. A whole priesthood with its temple rituals develops eventually. Worship becomes the major business of religion. (Some scholars have argued that religion begins with worship of gods, and that primitive practices are really pre-religious. It all depends on definitions.)

Even with all this, it can still be difficult to please the gods and keep them helpful or at least benign. Subject to their own passions, pride, and pettiness, they might still send a plague, destroy crops, or flood a city. But anger against them in such cases will not help. The gods can be like abusive parents; the children can only submit helplessly. To blame the parent may only evoke more punishment.

To some extent, people can adapt to great mana. Parents can choose a name for their child that has lucky numbers the sum of which is also lucky. They can try to arrange when pregnancy occurs so as to give birth to a child whose sun-sign, for example, is that of Leo, a force producing strong and generous leaders. Yet in the end, the forms of great mana hover over a person's life with such unavoidable and unchangeable force that the only course open to people is submission. The stars and sun will not change in their course; the yang and yin of nature flow unaffected by human decision. Much of life, therefore, can only be an acceptance of what is and will be, with perhaps some modest improvements in things through the occasional help of spirits and gods, the use of magic, and a wise coordination of activities with the patterns of the great numinous forces.

Polytheism: A Name for Archaic Religion

The name alone says most of what archaic religion is, a belief in many (*poly*) gods (*theoi*). There is not a clear line between animism and polytheism, because there is no way to fix a standard as to just how powerful or important a spirit-being must be to deserve the title "god." The ordinary sky spirits of the Australian aborigines have been called gods by some outsiders. On the other hand, the high god of the Delaware Indians, for example, was referred to by many colonial residents of America as a Great Spirit. In general, though, it is useful to reserve the name "god" for a spirit of great power, superior to other spirits and people.

Polytheism developed after animism. Most primitive societies today do not exhibit beliefs in extremely powerful spirits. Some societies we loosely call "primitive" believe in a high god, but these usually are not really primitive societies. As a rule, for example, these have a chief or king, which denotes a hierarchical ordering of power that is part of an archaic culture. The most primitive societies, such as those of the highland tribes in New Guinea, Australian aborigines, or tribes of the Amazon basin, have neither chief nor powerful gods. The best estimate is that primitive animism preceded archaic polytheism by thousands of years, and that the belief in local mana, which is part of animistic religion, also long preceded the belief in great mana found in archaic cultures.

Archaic Style Religion Today

Archaic beliefs are still fairly common. There are first of all explicit forms of polytheism alive today; many cultures of Africa have been polytheistic to this day. The popular religion of India is strongly polytheistic, with gods almost beyond numbering filling up the spaces of the universe.

There are also less obvious ways in which the old gods have been replaced by their equivalents. In some major branches of Christianity the saints in heaven are accorded great influence. Strictly speaking, they are not to be worshiped as gods, because they are totally subordinate to the one God. Yet people appeal to them and have formal and elaborate ceremonies in their honor in order to benefit from their influence. In his own sinister way, the Satan of popular Christian belief is also a spirit of godlike (though not God-like) power.

The old beliefs in great mana exist today also. Astrology is still strong enough to generate a multi-million dollar industry of book publishing, chart reading, and newspaper columns. Those who believe in pyramid-power sometimes speak of this power as an awesome cosmic force. Those who use TM, transcendental meditation, often interpret it as a way to tap a numinous energy that flows through the whole universe. (To speak of cosmic forces or of the whole universe is normally a sign of "historic" classical or universalist religions. But not all who learn from these religions understand them in the same way. Chapter Four will discuss this further.)

As is the case with belief in small mana, belief in great mana today has also taken on quasi-scientific forms, disguising its sense of the numinous in technical jargon. Pyramid-power can be couched in the language physics uses to speak of cosmic rays. The Transcendental Meditation movement brought to England and the U.S. by Maharishi Mahesh Yogi, once guru to the Beatles, still connects its belief in a universal energy to certain medical practices. The mystery of the numinous is only half-tamed and half-hidden beneath all the technical language. Archaic beliefs live with primitive ones in our midst and within us.

Archaic Culture

Archaic culture is one of greater complexity than the primitive. In archaic cultures the numinous powers range from the ordinary everyday spirits and magic, inherited from primitive times, to the awesome and more distant gods and great mana. This wider range of the numinous is a clue to the greater world in which archaic people live. Life in the large village or in the city is a life with a more complex kind of knowledge about the world than is usual in primitive societies. There are more social roles and thus more complex relationships to be learned. There is often opportunity for more forms of trade with outside cultures. Local villages, each with its own customs, fall under the influence of a powerful city. Eventually, small empires arise, as in ancient China, India, Mesopotamia, and Egypt.

One result of this is that the universe appears to archaic cultures as no longer merely a collection of events and patterns to be learned and assimilated as the one single reality. Instead, the universe looks complex enough to require more elaborate explanations. There are more options about how to live, and so each culture needs some reasons why its ways are better than other ways. The great myths of literate archaic cultures portray and explain the complexities of life to archaic people. There will be more on this when we speak of myths in the next chapter.

The many facts of reality are not just scattered facts, as they most often are to primitive people. The facts are organized into more complex categories and put into a hierarchy of power or importance. In Egypt the sun that gives light and life was above all life so the sun was the most important god, called Amen or Ra. Lesser gods had to take subordinate positions. Osiris and Horus had special presence, though, in the Pharaoh and the Pharaoh's power over the Egyptians, so these gods outranked most others. In the ancient religion of the Indo-European people, whose language and thought is the parent of much of Western language, the sky is the dominant numinous realm. The power of sun and storm, of light and darkness, overwhelmed all else. So the sky god was high god. In ancient Greece his name was Zeus. Under the high god was often a hierarchy of other specific gods. Under Zeus, for example, were his children such as Aphrodite, Helios, Hermes, Athena. Below the gods were the extraordinary beings such as the giants and the monsters. Below the extraordinary beings were the ordinary ones, the spirits and the humans.

In archaic cultures, however, this hierarchical ranking was usually rough and unsettled. Alliances of power were made and broken. Competing major gods might divide reality among them, as Zeus took the sky and open air, Poseidon the sea, and Hades the underground. Archaic cultures perceive a greater amount of unifying order in reality than do primitive cultures, but it is still an incomplete order. There is no overall unity as is found in monotheism and other great classical religions, as we will see.

Summary

This chapter has presented some interpretations of the ways primitive and archaic societies perceive numinous mysteries, as magic and spirits and great mana and gods. Primitive religion is a way of living with a multitude of smaller numinous powers in a relatively small universe. Mana and spirits are plentiful, each to be dealt with to make life run smoothly. Archaic religion, an aspect of a more complexly structured society, still acknowledges magic and spirits but also worships the more distant powerful spirit-beings known as gods, whose influences can extend over many parts of the world, and may seek to conform life to grand powers like the stars and numbers.

Behind the fact of such beliefs is the question of why these beliefs exist. The various answers people offer are valuable because they give us clues about our own human character, needs, and hopes. That is the topic of the next chapter.

For Further Reflection

1. List all the kinds of mana-like powers, spirits, and numinous realities in general that people today believe in. (Look at the magazines sold at your supermarket checkout counter to get some ideas.)

2. To what extent do you find it reasonable to believe in numinous powers like spirits, magic, or gods? Explain why or why not.
3. Explain how coherent or integrated the many forces of the universe seem to you. What sort of single underlying unifying order is there to all things, if any?
4. Are you comfortable with the claim that religious ideas and practices change as the culture changes? Is this true of the religious traditions you are most familiar with, including your own? Explain.

Suggested Readings

Tim Ingold, David Riches, and James Woodburn, eds., *Hunters and Gatherers I: History, Evolution, and Social Change*, 1988. Contains anthropological articles about the nature of primitive beliefs and practices.

Napoleon Chagnon, *Yanomamö: The Fierce People*, fifth edition, 1997. Examines this primitive people closely and vividly.

Alice B. and Irvin L. Child, *Religion and Magic in the Life of Traditional Peoples*, 1993. Includes information about both primitive and current "archaic" style cultures.

Robin Horton, *Patterns of Thought in Africa and the West*, 1993. A collection of Horton's many influential articles about non-literate tribal cultures in the twentieth century.

Peter J. Wilson, *The Domestication of the Human Species*, 1988. Describes the shift from semi-nomadic primitive life to the settled life of early agriculture.

Elizabeth Hallam, general ed., *Gods and Goddesses: A Treasury of Deities and Tales from World Mythology*, 1996.

Lotte Motz, *The Faces of the Goddess*, 1997.

Desmond Morris, *Body Guards: Protective Amulets and Charms*, 1999. Describes dozens of magical objects still in use in modern societies.

CHAPTER TWO

The Human Quest

The Origin and Function of Belief in the Numinous

THE FACT OF BELIEF

Every culture in the history of humankind has included belief in the numinous as a major part of its understanding of reality. In fact, most people in history have considered it self-evident that the gods are real, or that ancestors guide them, or that demons cause sickness. Does the sun rise and water run downhill and the eagle soar in the sky? Of course. Do spirits roam, and does magic exist? Of course. The numinous and the non-numinous are equally obvious, especially to people of primitive and archaic cultures.

Later developments in human history, though, included some degree of disbelief. In the classical or historic cultures, as we will see, people began to doubt some primitive and archaic beliefs. In contemporary times, there are those who doubt all beliefs in the numinous. In theory such doubts would have been possible all along; the numinous beings are usually invisible, after all. Why believe in something you cannot see? In our view, there is little evidence that magic is really efficacious. How is it that most people preceding us have believed in it or some equivalent mana-power?

The possibility of doubt makes it all the more striking that so few doubts have existed. If disbelief could have existed at any time, the fact that it has been quite rare indicates something about human beings in general.

Individual religious traditions have proposed that the reason for belief lies in the actions of the divine power. Western religions, for example, have claimed that they believe in God because this God revealed himself to them. But these same believers do not think that Zeus really appeared to the Greeks or nature spirits to primitives. Have all the gods and spirits and mana-powers that people have believed in really given reliable and obvious evidence of their existence? If even most of these do not really exist, why is it that almost every culture in history has believed in so many of them nonetheless? Closely allied with this is the question of why people have not only believed, but have found those beliefs to be very important to them.

The answers to these questions can tell us much about ourselves, about our character and needs. They are descriptions of basic aspects of our existence. An investigation into the fact of nearly universal human belief in the numinous is an investigation into ourselves.

There are two basic types of explanations for religious beliefs and practices: religious explanations and nonreligious explanations. Religious answers are scattered through this book, in the chapter on religious leaders, in the chapters about scriptures and revelations, and in the chapter on religious responses to modern skepticism. So most of this chapter will describe nonreligious explanations of religion, though there will be some initial religious explanations offered at the end. It is relevant here, by the way, to recall that so far we are dealing mainly with religious *beliefs* and not with the many other major aspects of religion. Later chapters will take up such aspects.

Non-religious Explanations of Religion

There are four kinds of answers offered here, each of which says a great deal about us humans. They concern 1) the human search for intelligibility, 2) psychological needs, 3) the problem of social stability, and 4) genetic inclinations. All four are attempts to explain why humans perceive a numinous dimension in the endless mysteries of life.

The Search for Intelligibility

Ancient and modern beliefs in magic, spirits, and gods often appear to us to be a sign of ignorance. At the least we presume that we now have a better understanding of various natural things that were once thought to be numinous powers. But there is another side to animism and polytheism worth noting. Belief in spirits and gods, as well as in magic and great mana, indicates cognitive powers such as no other animal on this planet possesses. Even in our ignorance and superstition we are engaged in rather important mental processes: conscious attention, categorizing and naming, intellectual reflection. We can see this human power of consciousness and understanding at work in the various forms of belief in the numinous.

Belief in Mana

Every animal lives in an environment of wonders and never knows it. A woodchuck meandering through the woods is following its genetic programming: when hungry, start moving. Its eyes register the sight of a large brown thing in motion. It freezes for a moment, then darts away to pause in the nearest shelter, then to ramble on again. As far as we can tell, the woodchuck does not have conscious thoughts about any of this. It simply has senses that feed impressions into the central nervous system where genetic programs and learned responses compute the next activity.

Many animals employ some sort of signals. Chimpanzees have even been taught some sign language. But not even the most well-trained chimpanzee has yet shown much talent for what a three-year-old human child can do rather easily—to stop and take deliberate note of events that seem interesting, to consciously categorize them, to wonder explicitly about the cause of those events, to invent or discover ways of accounting for those events, and then to use complex language to share ideas with others.

Humankind has spent centuries taking note of events, labeling them, and devising and sharing explanations for them. People expect events to have causes. Whenever we can name or describe the cause of an event, we feel we have explained it. Many causes are clear and ordinary. A neighbor has a black eye because she ran into a tree. The bread is burnt because the fire was too hot. But there are other causes that are not so clear. Why does a sore on your leg fail to heal? Why is the rain so abundant this year? If there is no visible cause, then it is obvious there is an invisible cause. Evidently, the world is full of invisible powers because so many things happen without any visible cause.

The human race has been strangely insistent on finding or devising explicit and specific explanations for the events of life. We humans have been very reluctant ever to say merely that some things just happen for no particular reason or because of no particular cause. Primitive people (and others) ignore the possibility that events might be just random and accidental. There are always causes for things, visible and invisible.

The more significant or troublesome events in life are the most important to explain. Health and sickness, food and hunger, peace and war are issues that stir up people. Whatever causes them is more deserving of concern. The invisible causes of any of these things evoke an extra sense of awe, because being invisible, they are a little more mysterious. These are the causes more likely to be treated as numinous. They are the ones that go by such names as mana, magic, omens, spirits, and gods.

Thus, a major reason why people believe in mana-like powers is just the human tendency to insist that things be explained. However foolish or superstitious some beliefs might appear to us now, every belief represents human confidence that we can make sense out of things by discovering their causes. This confidence represents an implicit faith in the intelligibility of reality and in our power as thinking beings to understand it.

This tendency often leads to superstitious (i.e., false) belief. The psychologist B. F. Skinner provided a good model for showing how this can happen.

Skinner had a large box with a lever and a food tray. Every time a pigeon in the box pushed the lever, a food pellet dropped into the tray. Pigeons put in the box soon learned to push the lever in order to get food (although this "learning" is probably not conscious learning). One of the pigeons was not merely fat from eating well; it was also a little dizzy. It would turn in a complete circle, then push the lever and go to the tray for its food pellet. Apparently, the pigeon had once turned in a circle and then pushed the lever, thereby learning a combination of turning and pushing to produce food. Skinner called this superstitious behavior.

Today a softball player who wears a new cap and then hits a home run feels that wearing that cap helps her batting. In primitive society the person who hears a crow make loud cries just before bad news arrives thinks of crows as bad omens. Pigeons, ballplayers, primitives, and all of us have an inclination to believe that when one thing precedes a second, it caused the second to happen. By definition, that is superstitious if it produces a mistaken belief in a cause that does not exist, or in a cause and effect relationship that does not exist.

It is worth noting, though, that not all belief in invisible causes is superstitious. Natives of Peru knew that the bark of the cinchona tree had the magical power to cure the fever that came from walking too near the swamp where demons of illness lived. Today we agree. The quinine in the bark does in fact have the power to cure malarial fever. We simply no longer call this a numinous power. To us it has become too ordinary and easy to understand. There is genuine power there; there is genuine cause and effect relationship. The primitive person may well be right to believe that there are always explanations for what happens, even if the particular explanation the person uses does not now appear to be a very good one.

Belief in Spirits

Belief in spirits is also a sign of the human impulse to make sense out of things. In fact, belief in spirits adds an implicit extra-explanatory note about the numinous powers beyond what mere belief in mana provides. Magic, mana, luck, and other inanimate powers are inexplicable. What these forces are like or why they should have an effect on things is unknown and mysterious. Spirits are somewhat mysterious also. No one can be sure of their habits, desires, activities, presence, or absence. They too are invisible. Yet to think of numinous powers as living beings says something more about them. It explains their activities as motivated by the same kinds of desires and impulses that affect us. The spirits may be whimsical and arbitrary and unpredictable. Nonetheless, they do have motivations that we can understand to help us make some sense out of their behavior: they hurt us because they are angry or mean; they help us because they are friendly or because they like our gifts.

One theory to account for belief in spirits sometimes goes by the name Freud used for it: "projection." This is a process of explaining various events by projecting our own very familiar inner thoughts and feelings out into the world around us, believing that other people act for the same reasons we act. It appears that we project our inner states not just onto other people but also onto objects and animals and even invisible beings. We do this from childhood. Why does the sun set? Because it feels tired after being up all day, our parents say, and that makes sense to us. In fact, as children we often create invisible friends to talk to and play with. We start our lives projecting personality into many things. Perhaps it is just easy to continue to think this way, at least a little bit, when we grow up. It provides a handy explanation why some strange things happen. "The spirit led me." "The god saved me from drowning." "The devil made me do it."

This predilection may arise because of the common human process of developing what psychologists call a "theory of mind." At age three a child is not aware that other people have their own thoughts that may differ from his or hers. By age four, however, almost all children know that other people have their own thoughts, plans, and motives. This new "theory of mind" (really just an awareness of others' minds, rather than a theory) is useful in social interactions. The child can now think about the possible motives and plans of others and figure out how to win favors from others or make deals with them. Some psychologists have speculated that religion might arise from an over-extension of this. Perhaps when the thunder booms or a disease strikes or a child dies, from very early in life people may respond to such events by applying a theory of mind to whatever invisible cause might be at work. So people may treat the thunder as though it were the act of a person who could be appeased, and treat a disease as the work of a spirit the person might persuade to go away. Perhaps this theory of mind is the origin of "projection."

There are some kinds of human experience that could seem like good evidence for the existence of spirits. Edward Tylor made two different guesses, in fact, about ways in which people could feel that they had concrete evidence of how real spirits are.

First of all, there are many states of consciousness in which people find themselves face to face with talking animals or dead ancestors or numinous beings with magical powers. Everyone dreams, and sooner or later in our dreams we find ourselves talking with great-uncle Louis who died seven years ago, or perhaps with a wise elephant who understands human language. Primitive and archaic people are likely to interpret these dreams as real experiences of real people, real animals, and real spirits. Since spirits are mysterious beings, it makes sense that they should show themselves only in those strange experiences we call dreams, when it seems that our own inner spirit has entered into a world where the usual rules do not apply.

Dreams are not the only altered state of consciousness. Native Americans of the northern plains had the practice of going alone to a hill or woods to fast, meditate, and wait. After days with no food the person would be prepared. A spirit, often that of an animal, would appear and be a sign of what character and style in life the person should possess. Native Americans of Mexico have long used the mana-filled mushrooms to open themselves to special visions, some of them visions of the spirit-world. Many cultures have known that alcohol contains spirit power that can change people's perception and personality, and allow them to be strange beings. (Or maybe this is mana-power.) Altered states of consciousness, Tylor noted, are common to people everywhere. No wonder so many people have seen spirits.

Add to this a clue that language gives us and we can discover another kind of evidence for the reality of spirits. Many languages use the same word for both "breath" and "spirit." "Spirit" in the Christian New Testament is pneuma in Greek. This is the same word used in the English word "pneumonia," "breath illness." This breath is the power of life. When it leaves a person's body, the person dies, though this breath may go on living invisibly. In Hindu tradition a person's inner self is called "atman." You can recognize the connection to the English word "atmosphere," a sphere of air. If you blow on your hand you get concrete evidence that the breath in you, though invisible, is physically real.

Primitive Closeness to the Spirits and Mana

So far, we have talked about belief in mana and spirits as a way primitive people explain their world. But the word "explain" is not quite enough. Belief in spirits and mana does not merely explain the world; it also portrays it in story form so that the primitive person can feel at home in it and identify intimately with its ways.

Primitives have many folktales about reality, sometimes called myths but simpler in form than most myths. An Australian aborigine story, for example, tells how their land was created before the beginning in "dreamtime" (which is an English word that may or may not accurately translate a difficult aboriginal word). This was before the first sunrise, when there was no light and the earth was flat and naked. Then the old blind woman, Mudungkala, rose out of the ground with three infants, a boy and two girls. She crawled around on her hands and knees, leaving hills and paths for water behind her. Then she decreed that vegetation should grow and animals appear so that her children and the generations to come would have food. That is why the world looks as it does now.

Stories such as this tend to remain popular as explanations for things, even in archaic and later cultures. But among primitives, a story like that about Mudungkala provides a chance for people to relive the events at the beginning of things. In rituals the tribe can re-enact the first events that made the world as it is. In this way, the people portray the world to themselves as it is. They name it and its aspects once again in a vivid way, as though to repeat to themselves who they are and what their world is like.

From Primitive Folktales to Archaic Myths

In general, the more primitive the culture, the less unity and order there are among its stories. Australian aborigines, Kalahari bushpeople, the Nuer of the Sudan, the New Guinea mountain people, to cite a few, are all people who have many separate stories to explain things. They take it for granted that there are always explanations for things. But the stories often bear little or no relation to each other, and may even contradict each other. On festive occasions when various groups of the tribe convene, they may all tell their tales, one after the other, sometimes in a kind of historical sequence, but with no single unifying theme, plot, or conclusions. In general, primitive stories have the flavor of simple folktales unconnected with each other except that they are about the same single world.

Most tribal groups in the world today have had some contact with outsiders, in particular with Christian missionaries or through the wide-spread influence of Islam in some places or Buddhism in others. So it is not always easy to know which stories represent long-standing tradition and which are an amalgam of traditional and imported ideas. In the Pacific Northwest, for example, one group of Native Americans tell a simple but well-rounded story of the beginning of human life. The Old One descended on a cloud from the sky to the surface of the only thing that existed, the formless waters. From five hairs of his head he created five young women. He gave to each of them the choice of what to be. One chose to be a bad woman and to bear children who, like her, would fight, steal, and commit adultery. Another chose to be good and to bear children who, like her, would be wise, just, honest, and peaceful. The third woman chose to become the earth; the fourth, fire; the fifth, sweet water. From these five came the world in which people live. From them come all people, both good and bad. The Old One promised that eventually the good people would outnumber the evil and then all things would be made good.

This is a very direct story explaining how the world and its inhabitants came to be. It treats fire and water not just as accidental aspects of life, but rather as important natural forces established at the beginning of things. It explains the source of human evil, making sense of why it should exist at all; and it even promises an ideal future, when conflict will end. The beginning of life, its present condition, and its future fulfillment are all brought together in one story.

This group of tales includes stories of other sky beings. The sun, moon, and stars are in the sky now, but they were not always there. Father Sun mated with Mother Earth, but Earth nagged him saying he was nasty, ugly, and too hot. So Sun abandoned her, taking moon and stars with him. The Old One had to step in to put things back in order, the same order that exists now. At the same time the Old One taught people how to think and speak, how to make fire and to fish, to dig roots and build lodges, to sing and dance, to do anything. All of life, therefore, is not just a set of random practices. The order of the universe and of human life alike come from the work and wisdom of the Old One. Behind the evident confusion and disorder of events in life, there is a set of reasons for things.

It is unusual for tribal people, even for those with a rather more complex economic and social order such as the tribes that told these stories, to have a belief in a single personal supreme agent such as the Old One. It is also unusual to have a promise of a kind of salvation in the future when everything will be made right. But both of these beliefs are part of Christianity. So we cannot be sure that the Native Americans who tell of the Old One now have not adapted their stories to include some new ideas.

Nonetheless, we do have good evidence that as human societies began to grow larger and more complex, so did the stories about the gods and the origins of things. The invention of literacy seems especially to have had an enormous impact on the length and complexity of the stories of the gods. Denise Schmandt-Besserat describes what may be the origin of all writing in the Old World. Over hundreds of years during the fourth millennium BCE in ancient Sumer, writing arose very slowly, step by step. The idea of writing then spread to Egypt rather quickly, then later apparently also to the Indus Valley and probably also to China still later. One result of literacy was that the many folktales of older times were now incorporated into much longer and complex stories about the gods and various heroes. Out of the materials provided by earlier and shorter folktales from pre-literate times, different literate societies created grand myths. As one city conquered others and united them into a kingdom, all the gods of the various cities had somehow to be placed in a hierarchy. The ancient Egyptian kingdom had an official state religion that emphasized the importance of some gods over others by 3000 BCE. By the second millennium BCE the same was occurring in China, India, and Mesopotamia.

A word is in order about the nature of myth. What you and I first think of when we hear the word "myth" is "false story," for we no longer believe in most of them. But one should not forget that these myths arise from the human belief that reality is intelligible. Myths are invented or accepted by people because people will not settle for experiencing things but want to discover the sense of things. Around the world people tell stories of how the world came to be as it is, where people come from, why there is evil and death, why there are laws and customs, why there is winter, even why turtles are slow and snakes have no legs. Some stories are the simpler folktales of pre-literate cultures. Others are the grand myths of literate cultures, which tie together many aspects of life. All of them are the result of human intelligence beginning to make sense of things in the face of mystery.

They have a great impact on people, though not the way textbooks or formal education do. The myths are like motion pictures we might see today, which speak directly to our own concerns and feelings by drawing us into the story to the point where we begin to interpret our own lives in terms of the story. We accept the values by which the heroine or hero lives; we imagine ourselves facing the same dangers or challenges and overcoming them with the same virtues or skills. The world of mythic narrative becomes part of the person's life, helping to establish the person's identity and values and place in the scheme of things.

Psychological Theories of the Origins of Religion

When the beliefs, tales, and myths about the numinous provide a way to name and explain mysterious aspects of life, it is not just intellectual satisfaction that is achieved; there is also great psychological comfort in these stories. Without such stories to make sense of it the world often appears chaotic, full of random forces that intrude upon the more reliable patterns of life. If the unexpected is truly random and accidental, then there is no sense to it all. Perhaps what orderliness there is in life can be destroyed by mindless and senseless powers. Perhaps, as the Aztecs came to fear, the universe can come crashing down.

Merely to assert that every event has an explanation, a story behind it, is to express an implicit trust that life makes sense, that the dimension of mysterious powers is not a dimension of raw chaos threatening life, but one of some coherence and intelligibility. However threatening various numinous spirits, gods, and powers may be, they are less threatening to human security than the alternative possibility that behind the strange events of life there is just random senselessness.

Primitive and archaic cultures do not say such things explicitly. They do not write philosophical or psychological analyses about how their stories function. But the outside observer can say it for them: people bring coherence to their lives when they tell their "creation" stories or their epics of the gods. These are their "master narratives." Over and over again in folktales and great myths the world is brought into its present order out of a chaotic condition. A kind of sense is imposed by the ancestors, the Old One, the gods, on the formless waters, on the dark and lifeless earth, or on the monsters of chaos and disorder that live in the depths. The ability to believe that the numinous conquers chaos provides psychological comfort.

An added feeling of security comes from the fact that if you can name and describe the numinous powers that affect your life, you can expect to be able to exert some influence on them at times. From knowledge comes power. Mana can be manipulated by magical procedures to cure your children and your goats. The spirits who have dried up all the berries can be bribed or flattered into making new sweet berries grow. A child can be sacrificed to appease the great god who has sent a killing sickness in punishment for committing incest. There are many terrifying events in life. It would be very discouraging to feel helpless to deal with them. Techniques of magic, persuasion, and worship all provide a feeling of competence in dealing with problems.

Sigmund Freud (1856-1939) offered an influential nonreligious interpretation of the psychological function of religion. As children, Freud claimed, we obviously experience a great deal of helplessness. Our parents provide us with guidance and protection, thereby taking some of the anxiety out of our helplessness. But we grow up and discover we still are somewhat helpless in the face of disease, injustice, natural disaster, betrayals, and death. We no longer have parents as strong as they once were. It is now evident they too are limited humans, helpless as we are.

Our childhood experiences have prepared us to seek a solution to our helplessness by relying on a superior being, a parent, to guide and protect us. Thus we readily devote ourselves to a god, especially a high god with great power, who can continue to care for us as our parents did. We can appeal to this divine protector for aid; we can rely on the god for guidance. In addition we can feel that a strong parental figure cares for us once again, one who might even love and cherish us (though gods are usually not all that loving; Freud was talking about belief in God also).

Freud was an atheist. He thought religion was a neurotic illusion that we cling to out of psychological need. He compared it to the obsessive behavior that arises from inner anxieties. Yet even one who believes in and values a given religious tradition can agree with Freud's claim that religion can be a source of psychological comfort. It is safe to expect that anything in human history so widespread and powerful as religion must be fulfilling some important human needs. Otherwise, even if it were completely true, people would not be interested in it. (We will see more about the psychological function of religion in later chapters.)

Sociological Functions of Religion

Other nonreligious accounts of the origins of religion focus on social relations. Even the simplest tribe has a set of techniques for caring for children, distributing food, preventing fights, assigning mates and marital responsibilities, and so forth. There have to be some specifically stated rules: it is all right to steal from an enemy but not from kinfolk. There are various roles to be defined: men hunt and plant yams; women tend the gardens and cook the food. There are institutional patterns: the mother and mother's brother carry the basic responsibility for raising the mother's children. Every group, tribe, or culture has rules, roles, and institutions that make their lives together coherent instead of chaotic and deadly.

Belief in numinous powers makes these social arrangements intelligible by attributing them to the original beings or gods. Why must the young girl about to be married avoid everyone's sight for three days of fasting? Why can we eat pigs but not foxes? The answer to such questions is often the same: this is how things were established at the beginning by ancestor-beings, or how they have been decreed by the gods. Once again, the human search for intelligibility may lie behind religious beliefs, in this case beliefs concerning the social order.

But this explanation does not just satisfy the mind's curiosity; it also helps to maintain the customs. Human beings live close to social chaos in many ways. Disputes over pigs, huts, insults, marriage, or a hundred other things bring people into conflicts that can seriously impair the group's ability to get on with the activities that sustain their lives. There could be endless disagreements on how they should live with one another. The demands of the moment could lead to confusing changes in rules and roles. To primitive people it appears that the tribe must adhere to its traditional patterns, however, because there is no real alternative. The patterns were set up at the beginning, so that is the way it is. Reality is a "one-possibility-thing," as someone once expressed it. No one can go back and redo the origins. As it was in the beginning, so it must always be. Individual people can rebel, if they choose, but that puts them outside the one correct order of the tribe. It is even possible that the spirits, perhaps those of the ancestors, may punish them for that. By such beliefs, primitive people not only explain but also uphold their social patterns.

Archaic people do the same. Archaic peoples are a little more sophisticated on the average, especially the great archaic civilizations. They trade with outsiders more extensively, or interact with them in war. Through this interaction they gain greater knowledge about different possible rules, roles, and institutions in the world. If these are only human inventions, then a person might feel more free to break them. But archaic people typically claim that their social order was dictated by the gods or at least is upheld by the gods.

A person can still choose to break the rules, but the gods can send punishment for this. The gods, in fact, expect society to actively defend the laws the gods have set up. If society does not punish the person caught in incest, for example, the gods may punish the whole society.

The pioneer sociologist Emile Durkheim (1858-1917) was so impressed by the connections he saw between religious beliefs and social order that he thought society itself was the sacred reality that tribespeople unconsciously address when they honor their tribal totems through ritual. Like a divine force, society molds the individuals, gives them their beliefs and values, rewards and punishes them. Tribespeople unconsciously recognize this, Durkheim thought. When they engage in their rituals, then, they are not engaged in empty behavior; they are reinforcing the social order that nurtures and protects them.

A remarkable aspect of how religious beliefs help to maintain the cultural patterns is that the people involved usually do not realize that their beliefs are functioning that way. Incest, for example, is forbidden in some form or another in every society. There may be good reasons for this. It may be that banning incest decreases family tensions and promotes useful marriage alliances with other groups. Usually, however, the only reason people explicitly give for avoiding incest is to repeat the rules about which clan members may marry into which other clan and which marriages are not allowed, or to remind everyone what the gods have decreed.

Another example comes from Marvin Harris, an anthropologist, on religious respect in India for the cow. Many non-Indians mock this respect, saying it is foolish and even harmful, that the cows get in people's way, that they consume good food but cannot be eaten for food. This criticism is partly mistaken. Cows give milk and provide cow chips for cooking. When the cows die naturally, the lowest members of society can eat them for badly needed protein. The cows' hides can then be used for leather goods.

More significantly, reverence for the cow has a special benefit that is ordinarily not recognized at all. In times of drought people go hungry, Harris notes, and can be tempted to slaughter the cattle for food. But those who do so condemn themselves to long-term starvation because the cows and oxen are needed for plowing the fields. Without oxen, people could not feed themselves when the drought ended and the rains returned. So it is important that people have a strong motive not to kill and eat the cattle, even when that would keep some of them alive in the short term. In the villages where the strongest religious respect for the cow is maintained, the continuing existence of that village and its custom of veneration is most assured. Harris points out, though, that the villagers do not give this survival benefit as the reason for respecting the cow. They say it is because the cow is holy as an earthly form of the great mother goddess, Kali.

The sociobiologist Richard Dawkins agrees with Harris to a large extent, but uses different language. He would say that cow worship is a meme (an idea that can be passed on). Memes that contribute to the survival and health of the people that hold them are memes that survive and have a chance to spread, especially if societies or villages which do not have that meme are more likely to perish because they lack the meme. Cow worship is thus a self-perpetuating belief.

Today it is difficult to realize how thoroughly most societies in history have based their cultural patterns on religious beliefs. There are a few remnants of this today in modern industrialized society. Many people, for example, still say that the rules of marriage are not human inventions but have been decreed by God: one man and one woman entering into a life-long partnership wherein sexual relations are legitimate and in which the husband is dominant. Like other traditional beliefs, this one is undergoing some revision today. Less and less of our culture is explicitly based on religious beliefs.

In most of history until today, just the opposite has been true. The rules, roles, and institutions of a culture have been consistently portrayed by people as having originated in the choices and actions of numinous beings, whether the ancestral beings of folklore or the gods (or God), and perhaps as still supported by those numinous beings. This belief has been a major force in archaic cultures throughout history to sustain their rules and patterns, and to help maintain stability and order.

Once again folktales and myths are important for passing on the social rules. These stories tell of the days when the social order was established and how it came to be that men of the fox clan cannot marry women of the frog clan, or that a chief of the villages had power to be the judge over land disputes, or that the king was given power by the high god of the city to make laws. As the story tells it, so it is and must be.

Theories of Genetic Influences

A more recent psychological theory about the origin of religious beliefs comes from the new field of study called evolutionary psychology. It is the division of sociobiology that applies to human behavior. (Neither sociobiology nor evolutionary psychology are really all that new; early versions of them can be found in Charles Darwin's writings.) Evolutionary psychology is the study of specific behavioral tendencies that are supposedly produced by the influence of the genes. Evolutionary psychologists try to identify behavior that is common to almost all people everywhere. If, they say, people behave the same in similar situations, in spite of many differences among human cultures, then it is plausible that there is some common genetic influence at work that is shared by human beings in general. Belief in invisible spirit beings is indeed common to people everywhere. Perhaps Tylor has the best reason for this. But evolutionary psychology offers a different possibility.

Stewart Guthrie (1941-) has argued in his book, *Faces in the Clouds*, that religions are all manifestations of a general innate human tendency to anthropomorphize. We treat ships and cars as people, giving them personal names. We treat the nation as our mother or fatherland. We accept dancing stuffed animals in TV advertising, and so on. We may do this because our genes lead us to do this.

According to evolutionary theory, any gene package that inclines its carrier, the organism in which it resides, to engage in behavior that assists the carrier to survive and reproduce is a gene package that is more likely to survive and get reproduced. So it will spread.

Anthropomorphizing probably aids in survival. When there is a rustling in the brush or an odd sound from outside the camp, it may be better to jump to the conclusion that it is an enemy or a dangerous animal than to ignore the sound. Any genetic tendency to make a person even slightly more likely to suspect there is some living being behind events in life will increase at least slightly the chances that the person may be more likely to escape being killed or maimed by some enemy. So they will survive to reproduce, and soon there will be more people around with that genetic tendency. If there are more people with those genes, more of them will end up having sex with each other and producing children with an even stronger tendency to anthropomorphize. Eventually the tendency becomes strong enough to account for the evident human tendency to anthropomorphize extensively.

Guthrie's theory is compatible with the "theory of mind" approach. The tendency to anthropomorphize would account for why children, and adults also, over-extend the theory of mind and apply it to things that otherwise seem quite lifeless and mindless. These inclinations could work together to make people ready to perceive the influence of person-like beings with conscious intentions behind whatever takes place.

Religious Explanations of the Origins of Religion

The nonreligious reasons for belief described here so far can all be used in such a way as to cast doubt on the truth of religious beliefs. By describing the motivations people might have to believe, they show that people might believe in numinous realities even if none such existed. Mystery exists: unanswered questions, unexplained events, uncertainty about the future, confusion about how to live. Perhaps to deal with mystery human beings would feel compelled to invent numinous powers out of their dream experiences, their imaginations, their tendency to "projection," their wishful thinking, their needs for psychological comfort and social stability, their genetic tendency to anthropomorphize. None of this disproves the existence of the numinous, but it raises suspicions.

This sort of suspicion has gone by the name of reductionism. This name is used to suggest the idea that all religious beliefs can be reduced to the status of sociological fictions or psychological illusions or by-products of genetic influences. Reductionism began as a by-product of rational inquiry as in philosophy or science. Science explains events by showing their natural causes. Anthropologists, psychologists, and sociologists have all tried to be scientific by showing the natural causes of religious behavior. Having found all sorts of possible natural causes for religious belief, the science-minded have sometimes declared that these are the only causes, that people have no genuine experiences of true numinous powers or beings, not even of God, as causes of their religious beliefs. So belief in the numinous is entirely a mistake, the reductionists claim.

Everyone tends to be reductionist about other people's beliefs. We usually assume that we are being rational when we explain belief in magic and gods as false beliefs. The thoroughgoing reductionist just extends this attitude toward all religion. Be objective, this person says, and admit that all religion is false. This is not quite as objective or scientific as it might sound, though. It would be difficult to show that all religious belief is false, to establish that there is no numinous reality of any sort. Someone could argue that our intellectual, psychological, sociological, and genetic inclinations only heighten our sensitivity to the numinous dimension rather than lead us to invent it. Through history there have been a number of more specific ways to respond to doubts that can be raised about religious belief. Here are a few, though others will appear in later chapters. (And the Epilogue will return to this issue again.)

Syncretism as a Theory

One of the earliest religious responses to skepticism about belief in various gods can be found in ancient pagan "syncretism" (from a Greek word meaning to join together). This is a name for a way of reconciling diverse polytheisms. In India, Persia, Mesopotamia, Egypt, Greece, Rome, and among the Celts and the Germans, people worshiped different gods. Perhaps all of these gods really existed, side by side, spread across the earth. Yet if Zeus were the god of the sky, as the Greeks believed, how could there be another god of the sky in India and yet another one in Egypt? The same stars, sun, and moon were in the same sky in all these places. The syncretists—largely citizens of the Hellenistic world around the Eastern Mediterranean in antiquity—solved this problem by proposing that there is only one main sky god, but that different nations know this god under different names and worship it with different rites. Syncretists then gave similar accounts about various other gods and goddesses. But syncretism took for granted that gods existed. It was not really an explanation as to why people everywhere believed in gods at all.

Early Christians did doubt that there were gods. The Christians were sure that there was only one God. Augustine (354-430), bishop of Hippo in North Africa, claimed that the gods were really demons, whose superior wiles allowed them to deceive people into worshiping them. Augustine also offered a moving answer as to why people might be inclined to believe in any divinity. In his autobiographical *Confessions,* Augustine recognized in himself a restlessness with most of what earthly life had to offer. He attributed this restlessness to his capacity for God. "You have made us for Yourself and our hearts are restless until they rest in You." Centuries later, John Calvin (1509-1564) adapted Augustine's idea to his own explanation of wide-spread belief in gods and spirits. God made humans with an instinctive awareness of the reality of God. But sinful humans wanted to reject God's rule, said Calvin. Yet even in their pride, the heathens could not escape entirely this inner inclination to believe in God; instead they managed only to diminish and pervert it by changing it into belief in gods.

Experience of the Sacred

Historians of religion today who reject the explicitly nonreligious approaches described earlier tend to explain nearly universal belief in numinous beings and forces through a few closely related ideas. One is that underlying the many forms of religion in the world is a common human experience of the sacred (another word for the numinous). A second is that the sacred is *sui generis*—a unique reality that cannot be analyzed adequately by psychologists, sociologists, or anthropologists. The third is that experiences of the sacred therefore ought to be bracketed off from skeptical analysis and simply studied with an eye to understanding and appreciating how things look from the viewpoint of those who enjoy such experiences.

This third idea is usually labeled a "phenomenological" approach. The word is odd. In current English usage the word "phenomenon" stands for something strikingly unusual. But it is a Greek word that just means "that which appears." The phenomenological approach tries to understand and appreciate religion just as it appears, without asking all the skeptical questions raised by nonreligious speculations on the origin of religion. The skeptics think that sacredness is only in the eye of the believer. The phenomenologists say that they have no right to make that judgment. Whether objects or beings or places are truly sacred in themselves is only for believers to judge, not outsiders.

In practice the phenomenological approach is very supportive of religion. Those who follow it tend to write as though the sacred were in fact a real objective quality and not just a characteristic that believers attribute to certain places or things or beings. Mircea Eliade, a historian of religion, is a well-known phenomenologist. The experience of the sacred (the numinous) has been so overwhelmingly prevalent in human history, Eliade argues, that it is not very objective or scientific to casually dismiss it as though none of it could be legitimate. In his many books Eliade indicates how thoroughly a sense of the sacred permeates the atmosphere of human existence. Awareness of the sacred dimension resolves many of the tensions of life and also keeps people open to further values and realities that transcend our present limits. The sacred is, therefore, too important to be dismissed, Eliade insists.

What Eliade suggests is that while many specific beliefs about magic and gods and such may well be false or inadequate, these may just be just the limited attempts various people have so far made to express the mysterious dimension that surrounds us. However inadequate some specific expressions of belief have been, there may nonetheless truly exist a sacred or numinous reality, one perceived imperfectly, but still too important to ignore.

As the next chapter will explain, classic historic religions—Judaism, Christianity, Islam, Hinduism, Buddhism, Taoism—have all given some indirect support to the idea that we can be correct in believing in the reality of the numinous or sacred even while we are incorrect in our way of describing it. These religious traditions all say that there is an Ultimate Reality that is the final answer to life, but one which human language and concepts can never adequately capture. Phenomenologists of religion usually suppose that belief in spirits and magic and gods is also just an inadequate way to express the reality of the numinous, the sacred.

It is certainly true that the dimension of mystery is always present in life; it is also true that this mystery eventually must be addressed by the human spirit seeking to discover the truth and value of being human. No one can adequately explore the human condition without taking the story of religion seriously, because that has been at the heart of the human effort to address mystery.

Summary

This has been a brief look at four kinds of theories about why we humans have so readily and so often believed in mana powers, in spirits, and in gods. Theories claim that we have intellectual, psychological, sociological, and genetic motivations that might lead us to appreciate or even invent belief in numinous powers and beings. But the phenomenological approach suggests that belief in the numinous or sacred arises because there really is such a dimension to reality, one which people have experienced and expressed in limited ways but which is there nonetheless.

The beliefs found in primitive and archaic cultures are not restricted to those cultures. People today still find such beliefs comfortable in many ways. But there is yet another set of beliefs that has embraced archaic and primitive thoughts in a much larger and well-integrated framework. That is the style of classical or historic culture and religion, the topic of the next chapter.

For Further Reflection

1. Are there really any compelling reasons not to believe in magic, spirits, and gods? Describe the ones that make most sense to you.
2. Do you think that nonreligious answers can explain why all events happen as they do, and why all of reality is the way it is?
3. To appreciate the power of myth, describe some story, motion picture, television drama, or play that seemed so real and vivid to you that you imaged yourself as part of the story.
4. Do you think it is true that people think of gods or God as a superparent? If so, explain whether you think this is good, bad, or just a fact.
5. Cite any current claims you have heard that there is one correct set of social norms that is commanded or supported by God?
6. If almost everyone in history has believed in the existence of the numinous, does that make it more reasonable for you also to believe in it? Explain.
7. Can we human beings get along all right without belief in the numinous? Intellectually? Psychologically? Socially? Explain.

Suggested Readings

Brant Wenegrat, "Belief in Unseen Beings: Its Evolutionary Basis and Its Effects on Morality," in Robert Wesson and Patricia Williams, eds. *Evolution and Human Values*, 1995. Brief descriptions of theories of religion based on evolutionary psychology.

Stewart Guthrie, *Faces in the Clouds*, 1993. Provides extensive evidence about the tendency to anthropomorphize.

Joseph Campbell, *Myths to Live By*, 1972 (Ch. 2 especially). An influential work on the emergence of human culture through myths.

Sigmund Freud, *The Future of an Illusion*, 1928. Offers his biting critique of religious belief.

Peter Berger, *The Sacred Canopy*, 1969 (Ch. 1 in particular). A now-classic statement of the function of religion to maintain social order and identity.

Mircea Eliade, *The Sacred and the Profane*, 1961 (Ch. 4 in particular). A phenomenological approach to the history of religions.

CHAPTER THREE

A Supreme and Awesome Unity

God and Other Ultimates in Historic Religions

HISTORIC RELIGION

The Axial Age and Universalist Religion

Around the sixth century BCE, a double shift in thought took place in many major cultures, particularly in China, India, and certain Western areas including especially Greece. In these areas an intellectual elite began to use a broadly systematic logical mode of thought and argumentation. They also used this new style of thought to seek out an ultimate unity to the entire universe. For all we know, many individuals may have thought in this systematically logical way on their own in previous times, but it was not until sometime around 600 BCE or later that this thought style became publicly influential and valued. The philosopher Karl Jaspers thought this was a breakthrough so important that he labeled this era the axial age, as though all history revolved around it as on an axis.

In each of these major centers of civilization at least a few influential people looked beyond the individual things and events and patterns of the universe to find some final and all-embracing explanation for everything. These people created universalist philosophies and theologies. This chapter will describe some of the major religious universalist views.

There are degrees in the amount of order a person might perceive in the world. If a person looks superficially at the world, reality can appear to be just a collection of things and happenings with no particular order. Even primitive cultures, however, are able to look at reality and see some order. They see cause and effect relationships. They sometimes perceive general categories like the numinous and the ordinary, the personal and the nonpersonal, the important and the irrelevant, the rewarding and the threatening. They usually have detailed categories for foods, plants, terrain, weather, and spirits. But their concerns are "local," as is their religion.

Archaic polytheistic cultures recognize greater and partially systematic order, represented by their great myths that connect many events into a single narrative and by their belief in gods whose power unites many parts of reality. The world does in fact look a lot like the polytheist pictures it. Reality is a mixture of little things and various large patterns. Trees, rocks, lakes, and clouds are all individually influenced by or are a part of large valleys or major weather patterns. The many activities of the city, the shops and the gate-guards, the streets and the temples, the neighborhoods, the festivals, are all influenced by the king. Thus there is some large-scale order to reality, order that archaic cultures attribute to gods of the land or the weather or the city and so on. The large cities and even empires of archaic culture have what might be called a more "national" or "imperial" viewpoint, embracing much more in its vision than a primitive tribe would. (The word "national," as used of archaic religions, can be misleading; it indicates simply a large area of civilization, not a modern nation-state with well-defined borders.)

An archaic perspective, however, does not see any overall order and unity. The land needs water but the skies withhold it this season. The god of the underworld erupts through the mountain, pouring down ash and fire. The great god of the city is defeated by the god of a neighboring city in a battle where the king is killed, as nation fights against nation. Life goes on, both ordered and disordered, always a little dangerous and confusing.

Once there were only archaic and primitive cultures, with their "local" and "national" perspectives, in which people accepted reality as it appeared, partially stable and ordered, partially disordered and unreliable. This was reality. What else is there to do with reality except to acknowledge it and accept it? Neighborly spirits lived close at hand; the gods were more distant and awesome, requiring worship. Society dealt with them individually, or grouped a few of them together, hoping to keep the numinous beings happy and helpful as much as possible. Life was as it appeared. All that people could do was to scratch out as much safety and happiness from it as they could.

Then came the axial age, when human consciousness dared to go beyond how things appeared in order to discover a universal order that rose above, "transcended," all the separate parts of reality, an order that included all those parts in its all-encompassing unity. Philosophy appeared. This included attempts to describe the ultimate principles and patterns and stuff of the entire universe at once and to show how it all logically fits together in one coherent system. Science appeared also, as part of philosophy, trying to do what philosophy in general did, to provide an all-embracing set of explanations of how all things work and why. This new consciousness therefore also included a vision of how human life fit within the logically coherent system of the universe, and how life therefore might be made whole and ideal rather than torn between the conflicting forces of earthly life. This new consciousness produced a new way of being religious, one built upon the achievements of primitive and archaic forms, but one that absorbed them into a more unitary and idealizing religiousness. This is now called historic or classical religion.

Historic religion took many forms in the East and West, each form arising out of its own cultural context. But beneath all the varieties of forms and ideas are four characteristics common to historic stages of religiousness. These are a belief 1) that there is an ultimate unity to all things, 2) that the source of the unity lies beyond or beneath the complexities, changes, and limits of this world, 3) that this source of ultimate unity is a reality of total perfection, and 4) that such perfection must be an Absolute (a word that will be explained later). In briefer terms, historic religion focuses on a numinous reality that is a universally unifying and perfect Absolute. The rest of this chapter will explain what that means.

There are two additional effects that characterize at least some of the universalizing religions. The first is what Robert Bellah has called "world-rejection." Apparently a vision of a realm of perfection that lies beyond ordinary life makes this ordinary worldly life seem very deficient by contrast. In India both Buddhism and Hindu thought say that escape from life as we experience it is the only true salvation. In Christian tradition this world is just a "valley of tears." A later chapter will explore such ideas. The second effect is some degree of "demythologization." The old myths are either reinterpreted to fit with the new universalist perspectives, as Augustine and Calvin did with pagan belief in the gods. Or the old myths are rejected in favor of more abstract theologies and philosophies. We will see instances of both of these effects in this chapter.

Historic Religion in the West

A Personal Supreme Being

According to the major Western religions, there is a universal and unifying order to reality because there is a supreme and transcendent personal Being that created, sustains, and rules the entire universe from end to end. Belief in such a Being is called monotheism. Most people in the West today would probably call themselves monotheists because they believe in an all-powerful Creator called God or Yahweh or Allah. The era of polytheism is over, it would seem. Yet monotheism is a more austere and difficult kind of belief than we are usually aware of. It is hard to think the way a thorough-going monotheist does. A look at some history will make this more clear, and will help to refine the meaning of the word "God."

Near-Monotheism: Two Cases from History

One of the oddities of history is that a kind of monotheism appeared in Egypt for a brief period of about twenty years, long before such an idea existed in other cultures. Whether it was a true monotheism or not is still disputed.

As far back as 3000 BCE, Egypt was a united kingdom with a vigorous archaic culture. In these early times the pharaoh was an earthly presence of the highest of the gods, the sun god Ra. Through the rise and fall of many dynasties, the sun god remained supreme, though he came to be called Amen or Amen-Ra. By the beginning of the fourteenth century BCE, Egypt was attaining its greatest power, extending its rule to Mesopotamia. It was as though the sun god Amen-Ra, whose divine power was present in the pharaoh, was extending his control over the whole known earth.

But this was not yet a monotheism. Other important gods existed such as Osiris, descendant of Ra in some accounts, the god of life, especially of life after death, as well as Osiris' son Horus, also identified with the pharaoh in those times. (Yes, it is very complicated. Archaic cultures do not make all their stories neatly logical and coherent.) All these polytheistic complexities suddenly gave way to an apparent monotheism, in the reign of Amenhotep IV (or Amenophis IV in some spellings) in the fourteenth century BCE.

This new pharaoh changed his name to Ikhnaton (or Akhenaton) in honor of a new sun god, Aton. Ikhnaton's name means "the Spirit of Aton." The pharaoh declared the old gods banished, and outlawed public worship of them. Some scholars have claimed that Ikhnaton was promoting a true monotheism, with Aton as the sole god over all the universe. As long as Ikhnaton lived, Aton had to be worshiped in the public temples as the sole and supreme god. But when Ikhnaton died, so did Aton's power. The next pharaoh to ascend the throne was Ikhnaton's son-in-law, Tutankhamen, the famous "King Tut," whose name signals the return to worship of Amen as sun god, and that of all the other traditional gods as well.

If the worship of Aton was true monotheism, it was not accepted enthusiastically by the people of Egypt. The old priestly caste that worshiped Amen may have resented their loss of power under the new god Aton. The people of Egypt, like all people, probably thought that the traditional gods were better for them. They were used to the stability and security represented by the old ways. On a local level, people also may have felt that Aton was too distant to be of use to them. The gods of the river, of life after death, of fertility—each had a special function. Each of these gods was closer to hand, although still somewhat awesome, in comparison with a god so big he ruled the universe. While Aton was running the whole world, who would answer their prayers concerning their individual needs? Egypt, like the rest of the world, was not yet prepared for monotheism.

Perhaps also as early as the thirteenth century BCE, another near-monotheism appeared in Persia (modern Iran) in the form of Zoroastrianism. The people of this part of the world had long lived by animistic and polytheistic beliefs. They saw the world as full of the spirits of their ancestors as well as other spirits and gods. An unusual aspect of their belief was that the spirits were either good or evil but not both. Most of the spirits and gods people have believed in throughout history have been an ordinary humanlike mixture of good and evil. These ancient Persians, however, perceived the human world as a battleground between the forces of good and the forces of evil. The evil in the world exists not because people and spirits alike all have their unpleasant side, their moments of anger or spite. Evil is a stronger and more unremitting force. It is the power of the evil spirits, called *daevas*. Good people are fortunate, though, because they can expect help against the *daevas* from good spirits known as *ahuras*.

One scholar claims that it was as early as 1300 BCE when a man named Zarathustra interpreted these older Persian beliefs in a new way, founding a religion that is known to us after the ancient Greek form of his name, Zoroaster. There are very few Zoroastrians in the world today. The last sizable group are the Parsees (Persians) of Bombay, India. But Zoroastrianism left its mark on the other major western religions.

We do not have any of the original writings of Zoroaster, though there may be some verses from his era that still offer clues about his message. According to a seventh century BCE version of Zarathustra's teaching (perhaps a serious revision of his original thought), there is one supreme god named Ahura Mazda ("wise Lord") or Ormuzd. This wisest of good spirits was perfectly good, hating evil. He was the creator of the entire universe, originally a beautiful place of joy and happiness. But Ahura Mazda had an opposite, the evil one named Ahriman. The goodness of the world was offensive to Ahriman so he began to curse it, bringing war, disease, suffering, and death. It was Ahriman who created the daevas, and together with them tried to seduce the minds and hearts of humans to follow evil ways.

Ahura Mazda immediately set about fighting to bring goodness out of all this evil. For three thousand years there would be a battle between all the forces of good and of evil. People would have to take sides, choosing to follow Ahura Mazda or Ahriman. In the end, the entire world would be destroyed in the conflict, and all people would meet in judgment. Those who had pursued goodness would cross a wide bridge into Paradise, a lovely garden. Those who had followed the ways of Ahriman, father of lies, would find the same bridge thin as a knife's edge and would fall from it into the burning pit they deserved.

In one version of these beliefs, after three thousand more years of burning, the former sinners would be purged of their evil and rejoin the good people in a perfect world prepared by Ahura Mazda. Then all evil and all its effects would have been totally destroyed. Ahura Mazda's power and goodness would have unquestioned supremacy over everything.

Though extant historical documents are not fully clear about early Zoroastrianism, it looks as though it was struggling towards monotheism. Ahura Mazda was creator of the entire universe and in the end would exercise complete power over everything. Yet he had to engage in actual battle with Ahriman, just as the gods of polytheism sometimes fought one another. If monotheism is a belief in a God whose power is total, then a being like Ahura Mazda is not really God-like because his power is limited by another such as Ahriman, even if for just a time.

The problem that Zarathustra and later Zoroastrians faced was how to reconcile belief in a supreme and perfectly good Creator with the all too evident fact of evil in the world. If the Creator is all good, then it seemed he could not be willing to tolerate evil. He would not merely eliminate it all at the end of time, but would not allow it to exist in the first place. But evil does exist. Rather than accept the idea that Ahura Mazda was uncaring or imperfectly good or incompetent, Zoroastrian thought chose an alternative: Ahura Mazda is not all-powerful. He is the most powerful, finally able to conquer even Ahriman and all the forces of evil Ahriman created to help him. But Ahura Mazda does not have all power. He is not unqualifiedly supreme.

Many people who are supposedly pure monotheists may actually be closer to the Zoroastrian type of belief. As long as the god worshiped is most powerful in the universe, one who will win out in the long run, that is enough. It is sufficient, perhaps, to picture the god as not too distant from the troubles of human life, not so absolutely supreme as to seem as distant from people as Aton once seemed to the ordinary Egyptian. A god that has to battle against forces of evil, as people themselves must do, is one that may be easier to identify with. But this is a limited god.

The Evolution of Jewish Monotheism

The formal beliefs of Judaism, Christianity, and Islam have usually defined Yahweh/God/Allah not merely as the most powerful being in the universe but as the absolutely, totally supreme Reality from all eternity, Creator and ruler of everything, limited in no way at all. By custom the name for this Creator is spelled with a capital letter: God. There is a history behind this belief in God, a history that can make more clear what an unqualified monotheism is.

The major formative influence in Western monotheism is the early history of Jewish monotheism, which developed out of the religious beliefs of the ancient Hebrews. These people were Semitic nomads who settled in the land of Canaan (present day Palestine/Israel) sometime in the second millennium BCE. Some of them somehow ended up in Egypt. A pivotal event in the history of Western civilization was the escape of some Hebrews from Egypt under the leadership of Moses about 1250 BCE, an event known as the Exodus. Moses returned to his kinfolk from the Sinai peninsula where he had been living for a while, and brought them a new god called Yahweh, who would be able to protect them from the Egyptian gods in their attempt to escape.

Moses might have been a monotheist of some sort, believing that no God existed except Yahweh, though many scholars now doubt this. It is clear that Moses' Hebrew followers were not monotheists. Like all people of their time, they showed great willingness to worship any god they thought might help them. When these Hebrews eventually settled in Canaan (Palestine) they happily worshiped the local high gods, the Elohim (a word meaning simply "gods"), including especially Baal and his consort Astarte, gods of fertility and the skies. For that matter, as their scriptures attest by complaining about it, these Hebrews also believed in spirits, sorcerers, and omens. They and their descendants were polytheists and animists at heart. It probably would not have occurred to them to take seriously the idea that no god existed except one absolutely supreme God.

Yahweh was nonetheless a very important god to them. He was clearly a good war god because he had led the Hebrews to victory in many battles. In general, Yahweh was a good god for historical events like wars, escape from Egypt, the invasion and settlement of Canaan. But their Canaanite neighbors taught them that Baal was the god to worship for fertility in the family, flocks, and fields. And Hebrews and Canaanites alike would presume that when visiting in foreign countries like Egypt or Babylon, it would be prudent to pay some thought to Amen-Ra or Marduk.

A step closer toward monotheism was a belief that grew among the Hebrews, that Yahweh was a jealous god, not one to share worship with other gods. The Hebrews believed that many gods existed, but sometime between the tenth and eighth centuries BCE their leaders came to insist that they should ignore all gods except for the one that was distinctively theirs, who specially guarded and guided them and gave them their identity through their laws and customs. Scholars sometimes call this "henotheism," a word invented in 1880 by German religion scholar F. Max Müller to identify primary devotion to a certain major god among other gods in India. "Monolatry" may be a better word, meaning worship restricted to only one of the various gods. (Akhenaton may have practiced monolatry rather than true monotheism.)

There is a famous story in the history of Israel illustrating the tendency to monolatry. In the ninth century BCE, Ahab, king of the northern tribes of Israel, had a wife named Jezebel. She came from Phoenicia where her father, also a king, had followed the royal ways approved by Baal, the main god of many Phoenicians. The ways of Baal allowed the king great powers over his subjects. The ways of Yahweh, however, coming from a time before there were kings over Israel, demanded what today could be called civil and social rights. With Jezebel's encouragement Ahab was acting like a tyrant, contrary to Yahweh's will.

From out of the desert appeared a wild-looking man, Elijah. He challenged the ways of Baal by proclaiming that if Ahab did not follow Yahweh's customs, Yahweh would cause a drought. This was a striking challenge in most people's minds because rain was supposedly under Baal's power, as god of fertility. Eventually, as the story goes, the contest between Yahweh and Baal was focused on Mount Carmel near the Mediterranean where altars were set up, one to each god. The priests and prophets of Baal danced, sweated, sang, and cut themselves to get Baal to show a sign of his power. Nothing happened. Elijah suggested that Baal was hard of hearing or off resting. Then, at Elijah's prayer, Yahweh sent a mighty bolt from heaven to burn up the offering and show his power. Before long, there appeared on the horizon a small cloud, "no bigger than a man's fist." The cloud grew quickly until it let loose a downpour. Yahweh had shown that he was God of nature's fertile rain. For generations after this, the priests and prophets of Yahweh would often urge that other gods be ignored, that people abandon Baal and worship only Yahweh. Yahweh might not be the only god that existed, the leaders said, but he was the only one his people should acknowledge as their god. He could take care of all their needs—war, fertility, and anything else.

This attempt at monolatry was only partially successful. For the next two hundred years and more, people were still inclined to hedge their bets, catering to all gods who might have some power. Then came a catastrophe that established belief in Yahweh as a genuine monotheism. In 587 BCE Babylon conquered Jerusalem, capital of Judea. All the leading Judeans (hence "Judaism," from whence the word "Jew" derives) were taken into captivity so they could not instigate a new rebellion against Babylon. The city walls of Jerusalem were destroyed as was the glorious temple of Yahweh built by Solomon. The Judeans were in exile, living in a foreign land ruled by the great god Marduk. Many of the Judeans undoubtedly came to the most logical conclusion, that Marduk had defeated Yahweh. Other Judeans, however, a "faithful remnant," reaffirmed their loyalty to Yahweh. Babylon was Yahweh's tool, they said, used by him to test them and purify them, to teach them that Yahweh alone is God, that all other gods are but lifeless clay and sticks. Yahweh is so great a God as to be God over all the nations of the earth. There is no God but Yahweh.

This Jewish monotheism has proclaimed itself in the famous prayer, "Hear, O Israel, the Lord our God, the Lord is one." Christianity inherited this belief, as did Islam: "There is no God but God (Allah)." Jews, Christians, and Muslims are sometimes highly conscious of the differences among them, but all three faiths are monotheistic.

The God of Western Theologies

The Jewish-Christian-Islamic God is a God we probably all think we can define rather easily. It is the Creator, Lord of the Universe. But it is not really easy to pin down what is meant by "God." Here is a list of five major characteristics that the three main Western monotheisms have tended to agree upon. You may want to test your conception of God against these.

First of all, God is all-powerful ("omnipotent"). This does not mean merely that God has more power than anything or anyone else, such as Ahura Mazda had. It means literally that nothing exists except what God has created and sustains in being. Philo of Alexandria (ca. 20 BCE-50 CE), a great Jewish philosopher, spelled this out by saying that God creates out of nothing (*ex nihilo*, in Latin). Only Hindu tradition has a similar belief about the origin of the universe. Primitive folktales, archaic myths, and many philosophers all supposed that there is a primordial stuff, perhaps in chaotic form, that must be put in some coherent order by divine power. But Judaism and Christianity interpreted the first lines of Genesis, "In the beginning God created the heavens and the earth," as a statement that before creation there was nothing at all. The Qur'an, the sacred text of Islam, echoes this Genesis statement. It also says that "God holds the heavens and the earth, lest they remove," to use one translation from the Arabic (XXXV, 39). Without the divine power upholding the existence of the heavens and earth they would be removed from existence.

God's omnipotence also implies that nothing can happen unless God makes it happen, or allows it to happen, or empowers forces and beings in creation to make things happen. God's control over the course of all events is known as Providence. Every lily that grows, sparrow that flies, volcano that erupts, does so under God's providential guidance. Human beings are said to have free will. But to exist at all depends on God's power; to continue to have freedom depends on God's decision to make people free; and God may influence free will very much (though different groups disagree on how much). Within Islam the reality of human freedom is an unsettled question, so strong is the Muslim insistence on God's power as the cause of all events. There are lines in the Qur'an that have led some traditionalists to say that God determines even our choices.

Secondly, the Western God is all-knowing ("omniscient"). There is absolutely nothing that happens that God does not know. God sees all, down to the most minute detail. A traditional belief, in fact, has claimed that God knows everything that will ever happen, that God has known perfectly from before the beginning of time every event that would ever take place. Whatever it is that any person freely decides to do, God already knew about that free choice and took it into account, along with every other free choice ever to be made, as part of the divine plan. Therefore, it would seem, everything is bound to turn out exactly as God has planned all along. The control that God exercises over the eventual destiny or outcome of each person's life is often called predestination, or sometimes predeterminism.

Western monotheism has not been consistently predeterministic. Islam has favored this view most strongly. All things happen "as Allah wills." In Christianity a line of thought runs from St. Augustine in the fifth century to John Calvin in the sixteenth, which says that some individuals are predestined by God even before their birth to end up in heaven—or in hell, Calvin added. Jewish thought has been the least predeterministic or predestinarian of all.

A third traditional concept about God in the West is that God is perfectly good. In the earlier parts of the Judaic scriptures, written in archaic times, God is pictured as sometimes angry and vengeful. But around the axial age the Jews began to conceive of God as utterly perfect and, therefore, utterly good. Human weaknesses such as emotional outbursts of jealousy or impatience seemed increasingly inappropriate for God. Some religious believers then and now, however, have not considered jealousy, anger, impatience, or vengeance to be imperfections. They manage to assert simultaneously that God does have something like these emotions but is also perfectly good. The idea of "good" can vary, evidently. (Chapter Eight will discuss different meanings of "good.")

A more serious problem with the concept of God as perfectly good is that there seems to be a great deal of evil in the world. One cause of evil is human free choice. People have freely decided to murder and torture one another, or to allow pain and hunger when it could be prevented. Why are people like this? The events of nature also cause evil. In the course of human existence, a billion people have been killed or crippled by disease, drought, earthquake, and flood. For the most part these have all been things that human beings were powerless to prevent. Why is nature like this? An all-good God cannot be callous or indifferent to such things. An all-powerful and all-knowing God presumably could have arranged things to operate less destructively (unless omnipotence and omniscience are somehow compatible with incompetence).

Western religions have faced the problems posed by the existence of evil and have produced various answers. Such answers are now called "theodicies," a word coined by the philosopher Gottfried Leibniz in the early eighteenth century. (Theodicy literally means "God-justification.") One theodicy is the story of the original sin of humankind committed in the garden of Eden, as told in the third chapter of the book of Genesis. It wasn't God but human sin that caused evil by throwing life and nature itself into disorder. Augustine expanded on this, arguing that everything that God creates is necessarily good. Evil is a kind of non-existence, however; it is the absence of a good that should have existed but does not. It is a *privatio boni*, a deprivation of good. And every case of *privatio boni* is the result of human sin, especially original sin. In answer to why God would allow this deprivation of the good at all, Augustine answered that God allowed it to bring even greater good than would otherwise have been the case. The free will that allows people to sin also allows them to love God and eventually enjoy heaven.

Leibniz himself had a suggestion along these lines. He proposed that this was "the best of all possible worlds." It is better to exist than not to exist. But only God is perfect. If there is to be a world at all, it will have to be imperfect. When God created, God must have considered all the alternative worlds that might be able to exist, and then selected the best possible out of all of these. That is this real world. So even this flawed world with its evils is better than no world at all; it is a greater good than not existing.

A different theodicy is reflected in the First Epistle of Alexander Pope's famous poetic Essay on Man. "Whatever is, is right." Even though things appear seriously flawed to us, if we had divine knowledge we would be able to see that all events work together for God's holy purposes, that all events are part of a plan we cannot understand. Those things that seem to us to be terrible will eventually prove to have been exactly right.

Some recent theology, like Zoroastrian thought long ago, has suggested that God has limited power and so should not be blamed for everything that goes wrong. The "process theologies" based on the ideas of Alfred North Whitehead argue that God operates only persuasively, not coercively. For centuries people have struggled with this problem of evil, producing various answers. The notion of a perfectly good God is not as simple a notion as it first seems.

The fourth major characteristic of God in Western theology is personness. This can be a tricky concept because it can have a variety of meanings. The

Yahweh of early Hebrew thought was very much a person, as were Baal and Marduk and other gods. They were divine persons rather than human ones. They means they were immortal, very powerful, and normally invisible. But they thought and acted like humans and had emotional needs and feelings like humans. These gods were anthropomorphic ("human-form"), not necessarily in appearance but in their personalities.

Early monotheism retained much of the anthropomorphic language about God from earlier polytheistic (or monolatrous) times, but it reinterpreted this language. The all-powerful God was beyond all humanlike limitations and weaknesses. The personhood of God was what a person would be like if a person were not confined to bodily forms and were totally perfect in every way possible. Judaism came to conceive of God, for example, as utterly perfect wisdom. Christian texts spoke of God as perfect love. Islam describes God as perfectly merciful and compassionate. These are all characteristics of a person, yet a perfect Person in this case and not a merely humanlike god such as Zeus.

As monotheism continued to develop in the West, much of the formal theologies moved even further away from any suggestion of anthropomorphic thought. While the average religious person spoke of God as attentive and caring, as wise and merciful, the theologies warned people not to take such language too literally. Theologians proposed that "God" is the name for the infinite, changeless, eternal Being that is the Cause of all else, a Being beyond the capacity of a finite mind to understand or a language to describe.

When people say that God is personal, therefore, what they should mean, according to the theologians, is that God is in some incomprehensible way what the total perfection of life, consciousness, and free choice are like when these are aspects of an infinite and eternal Reality that is perfectly good (also in a way not comprehensible to us).

This theological way of speaking avoids anthropomorphic talk about God, or at least asserts that anthropomorphic talk is useful poetic imagery but not literal truth. But there is a price to pay. A God that cannot be described literally as a caring and attentive person is a God far from many people's needs. Most people might well prefer a very good, powerful, personally attentive god, someone like Zeus turned into a benevolent helper, rather than an infinite, eternal, but incomprehensible perfection of personness.

The fifth major characteristic of God in much of Western theology nevertheless calls for such nonanthropomorphic language. God is described as Absolute, which means that God is unqualifiedly beyond every limitation of any kind whatsoever. God is not only totally perfect, God is beyond even perfections as we humans could conceive of them. God is the infinite, the incomprehensible fullness that is eternal Mystery. God is the Absolute.

This rather extreme and abstract way of thinking arose in a way that was perhaps inevitable. Once people begin to search behind the confusions and imperfections of the world for a supreme and unifying perfection, they found it hard to stop at any finite reality. "God" is the name given to the absolutely ultimate cause of everything, the final answer, the origin and goal of all else. God can be this only if God is truly ultimate, beyond which there is nothing else. If there is anything beyond God or independent of God in any way at all, then God is not the ultimate unifying cause of all that is, for there is at least some other and competing reality, such as Ahriman was to Ahura Mazda's supremacy.

A way to conceive of God as unqualifiedly ultimate is to do what a Christian theologian, Anselm, did in the eleventh century CE. He defined God as "that than which nothing greater can be conceived." God, therefore, is not merely a being that happens to be greater than anything else. "God" is the name for that being which by its nature is necessarily greater than anything and everything else that even might exist. "God" is the name for a reality which cannot be "second" in any way to anything. The only way to be that great, it seems, is to exceed every possible limitation. And that is to be infinite. So at least the traditional argument went. (Chapter Eleven will further explore reasons for this conclusion.)

That conclusion eliminates all anthropomorphism. In fact, it makes it hard to say anything. A finite reality can be defined; its limits are what describe it. It is like this and not like that. But if God is totally unlimited, then God is actually beyond all categories and labels. God is called a Mystery, then, not merely because God's ways are sometimes puzzling but because the absoluteness of God is always beyond what any finite mind can conceive.

In spite of this, Jews, Christians, and Muslims do describe God. They do it by a balancing of ideas. On the one hand, God is the supreme personal Creator from whom all else receives its existence, in some sense totally good, all-powerful, and all-knowing. On the other hand, God is Absolute, the infinite Mystery. God somehow is goodness, somehow personness, somehow power, but all in ways beyond human understanding.

If you find it difficult to deal with the notion of God as Absolute, you are not alone. Nonetheless, it is an idea that the human mind seems to arrive at eventually in its search to make sense of reality in the face of mystery. Most people do not feel any individual need to affirm the utter absoluteness of God. Yet in the major religious traditions some such idea occurs anyway. This is evident not just in Western monotheism but in Eastern thought also.

Historic Religion in the East

Nonpersonal Ultimates

There are two major centers of ancient civilization in the East: India and China (and it would be legitimate to include Persia as yet another). Each of these two has a complex religious history, and they both produced religious movements that portrayed an ultimate numinous reality as nonpersonal rather than personal. The infinite and universal power in some Eastern religious traditions is not so much a Being as a Force, not a personal reality but simply a Cause. It may be easier to understand this way of thinking by beginning with a description of some less than infinite nonpersonal forces that have appeared in cultures other than Eastern ones.

Non-Eastern Great Numinous Forces

The Mexica rulers of the Aztecs of Central Mexico believed that the earth and heavens had been brought out of chaos four different times, each time ending in horrible destruction. Now, they believed, we live in the fifth and last age. The universe must be held together for there will be no other chance beyond this. If the universe collapses again, the gods themselves would fall into destruction. And so day after day, year after year, the Aztecs offered up human sacrifices on the altars. These sacrifices were offerings to the gods, but they generated a cosmic energy necessary to keep the universe in balance, gods and all. These ritual forces were capable of maintaining the coherence of the universe. (Whether this belief represents archaic or an incipient historic consciousness is difficult to say.)

In ancient Greek mythology before the axial age three numinous beings, the Fates, controlled the destinies of all people. By the axial age or during it, some Greeks came to think of the Fates as a single, nonpersonal Force that assigned situation and status in life to humans and gods alike. Therefore, one of the most foolish and dangerous things a person could do was to aspire to rise above the station in life Fate had assigned. Such desire was called hubris, pride. It was the arrogance of daring to believe that you could be or accomplish more than Fate had decreed.

Out of this belief in Fate, perhaps, came a similar notion, from a group of philosophers known as Stoics (because their founder Zeno had lectured on a porch (*stoa* in Greek). The Stoic movement arose after the axial age had begun and believed that there was a universal and divine power that ruled even the gods. Every event in history is predetermined by a cosmic Logos or principle of rational order, they said. It is a divine Intelligence, of which human intelligences are dim reflections. Out of respect for tradition the Stoics called this principle Zeus, thereby transforming the god Zeus from a person-like being into a cosmic and divine rational Force.

Around the same time, another Greek philosopher developed a theory about a supreme force that is hard to classify as personal or nonpersonal. That is the Unmoved Mover, described by the great Aristotle around 330 BCE. He decided that there must be some continuing and primal force or being unceasingly producing motion or change in the universe; otherwise everything in the world would naturally grind to a halt. Oddly enough, Aristotle reasoned, the prime force that made everything else must itself be unmoving. If it moved, it would be necessary to look for what caused it to move. This would result in an infinite regression, i.e., an infinite series of movers moved by another mover, which in turn was moved by another, and so on. Aristotle claimed that there had to be a First Mover, itself unmoved and unmoving, for us to make sense of the continuing fact of motion in the world. (He never doubted that we could make sense of reality.)

The only kind of reality Aristotle knew about that could remain motionless yet move other beings was something desirable. An ice cold drink on a hot day can move us into action without its having to do anything except be there in front of us. So the unmoved mover must be the supremely desirable reality. This in turn meant to Aristotle that it must be perfect in every way. An imperfect reality would not be supremely desirable. The most perfect kind of thing Aristotle knew of was thought, for it is thinking that reveals to us what is perfect and eternal. So the unmoved mover must be pure thought. But there is nothing higher than the unmoved mover. If it is thought, it must be self-thinking thought, not a thought dependent on someone else's mind. Aristotle concluded then that the ongoing cause of all activity in the whole universe is a self-thinking thought, perfectly desirable, the Unmoved Mover.

A self-thinking thought, a Logos that controls our lives and keeps each of us in our place, a ritual-power, generated from human sacrifices to keep the universe moving—this is a strange miscellany. Yet each notion represents an attempt by people to make sense of reality. Each culture or thinker had become aware of some puzzle or mystery: why does the universe act as it does? What makes it go? How does it influence our lives? Is there anything an individual can do in response? The desire to make sense out of life in the face of mystery is one that no culture seems able to resist. Each tries to respond to mystery as well as it can, given its history, culture, and experiences. China and India gave their own responses also.

The Taoism of China

Long before the beginning of recorded history, the peoples of China were animists and polytheists. By historical times many Chinese worshiped a high god. In the Shang dynasty of the eighteenth to eleventh centuries BCE, the great Ti, ruler of heavens, watched over the Shang kings. A neighboring kingdom ruled by the Chou dynasty also had a high god, one called T'ien, "heaven." In the eleventh century BCE the Chou conquered the Shang and combined the two gods into one. Shang-Ti and T'ien became just two different names for one high god of the skies (another instance of syncretism).

T'ien or Shang-Ti was a personlike god. Ancient Chinese literature speaks of T'ien as one who sees all and hears all, who blesses and protects people and punishes the wicked, who in fact created the Chinese people with their particular character. The Chou dynasty encouraged people to think of T'ien as the one who upheld the power of the king as long as he ruled wisely and benevolently, and who would overthrow a corrupt dynasty like the Shang in order to provide a new and good government for the people.

But from ancient times in China there was another belief, in a regular natural order of things. The day and the night follow one another and the seasons progress year after year. All things follow a pattern of growth and decline, everything is balanced by its opposite. The Chinese summed all of this up into one fundamental pattern—yang/yin.

There is a yang aspect to nature that is warm, dry, male, heavenly; and a yin aspect to balance it, which is cool, moist, female, earthy. The list of opposites can be extended indefinitely: active and passive, loud and quiet, hard and soft, and so on. In discovering the yang/yin, the Chinese had found a way to organize all the categories of nature into one grand scheme. Human intelligence was at work again, refusing to accept the world as a variety of disconnected happenings, forms, or things. The Chinese mind sought a higher unifying order running throughout all reality.

The yang/yin are opposites, but not antagonists. They blend into one another. They are the alternating aspects of nature. There are moments when one or the other dominates. The hot and dry days of summer and the cold and wet days of winter are such times. But these extreme days are also the moment of a return back to the mingled moderation of spring or fall when yang/yin are more evenly balanced. The moon that wanes also waxes; the seed that flowers then withers and drops new seed to the ground. Yang/yin are not good/evil; both are valuable and necessary aspects of the unity of nature. They are not gods or spirits, but the fundamental forces of nature.

From about the eighth century BCE the Chou dynasty itself fell into corruption. The rule of law broke down and no one could be sure of receiving justice in the courts, protection from bandits or from greedy landowners. It was the time known as "the warring states." Most of the Chinese continued to pray to T'ien (Shang-Ti) or the ancestors. Some Chinese, however, became skeptical about T'ien. As the centuries went by, conflict continued. It seemed that T'ien was either powerless or callous. Hope for help from the high god diminished.

Out of all this came a particular school of thought known as Taoism. Sometime between 600 and 300 BCE two writings appeared, one ascribed by legend to a figure named Lao-Tzu, another written by the wise man Chuang-Tzu. These two works are in agreement that there is one supreme force, a truly ultimate one. It includes everything that exists within the scope of its influence. It has universal power and presence. This ultimate reality is called Tao (pronounced "Dow").

The word "tao" is a rather ordinary one. It means way, or pattern, or order. The Chinese had long sought the right way (tao) to live and to organize society. For most Chinese the ancestors and the high god T'ien/Shang-Ti had been of major importance in establishing the correct way. The writings ascribed to Lao-Tzu and Chuang-Tzu proposed something different. We all know that there is a way to nature, they said. This is the yang/yin pattern, the eternal process of the world. These are the two forces at work in the three parts of the universe: heaven, earth, and living beings. These three parts move through the four seasons, which in turn are a blending of the five elements: earth, water, fire, wood, and metal. But ultimately, behind the five, four, three, and two, is One. That is the Tao that is the way of all the universe. "Tao bore one, one bore two, two bore three; three bore ten thousand things," says *The Book of the Tao*, in its usual obscure way.

This ultimate Tao is beyond all categories of five or four or three or two. It cannot fit within any definition at all. Therefore it is ineffable, unable to be spoken. Whatever can be expressed, thought, felt, or imagined, is not Tao. "That which imparts form to forms is itself formless," says Chuang-Tzu. Tao is self-existent; there is nothing that accounts for its existence. It just is. Eternal and unchangeable, it is not outside the universe but is in and through all. It is the nameless principle behind everything that happens.

Western scholars have sometimes translated the word Tao as "God." It is easy to see why. The ultimate Tao, like God in the West, is the universal power at work in all that happens. This view is close to pantheism, a notion that all of nature is divine and worthy of worship. It may be more accurate to call Taoist belief a near-pantheism in that it considers all of the events of nature to be manifestations of the supreme power called Tao, which lies within nature, but is not identical with it.

On the other hand, the ultimate Tao is not what Westerners usually expect when they think of God. The Tao is not a supreme Person who knows what is going on in the world and who guides the path of history. The Tao does not and cannot hear or respond to prayer. The Tao is not caring toward people, but neither is it uncaring. It is beyond such categories. It simply is, eternally and unchangeably incomprehensible. It is the nonpersonal way from which there somehow emanates the yang/yin way of nature. So says "philosophical" Taoism, at least.

In actual practice most of those who call themselves Taoists today acknowledge the reality of the ultimate Tao but do not devote much time or attention to it. This is partly because the Tao is nonpersonal and cannot care for people or listen to them. Most Taoists are involved on a daily basis with the spirits and the ancestral beings that are personal. They are also attentive to the many spirits and concerned with the lesser nonpersonal power in omens, mana-filled rituals, and various quotidian forms of yang/yin. This is often called "popular" Taoism. If ordinary people pay scant attention to the supreme Tao, it is probably because this ultimate Tao, like all ultimate realities, is a little too hard to grasp, too general or abstract or philosophical to evoke ongoing interest. Yet belief in it shows again how far the human mind can reach.

The Ultimate Reality in the Religions of India

It is impossible to easily represent the range of religious thought that has developed in India. Hindu, Buddhist, Sikh, and Jain religious traditions had their origins there. Hindu thought alone can count many different theological schools as well as hundreds of local traditions. But we can describe a few particularly significant Indian themes about the ultimate.

There is, for example, the extremely austere theme of earliest Buddhism. The Buddha, prince Siddhartha Gautama, was a very practical person in his own way. He proposed that human salvation consisted in achieving nirvana, a sort of self-extinguishing (more about this in Chapter Five). The condition of nirvana was the ultimate reality, according to the Buddha. What was nirvana like? Do not ask, the Buddha replied. No one can know. There is no use wasting time on empty speculations. This answer did not satisfy all Buddhists, however. Eventually, many Buddhists began to describe Buddha-nature as a kind of supreme divinity, once manifested in the prince Siddhartha as well as in other earthly and godly beings. Yet beyond even Buddha-nature lies the state of nirvana, the true goal ultimately of even Buddha.

Buddhism came out of an older and still enduring Hindu tradition, one that in India reabsorbed Buddhism into itself. In this there are two lines of thought about the ultimate that have converged at least partially and have had major influence. One originally concerned the power of ritual; the other was about a search into a person's innermost self.

The best starting point for discussing these ideas or any Hindu traditions is the Vedas and the Upanishads. By around 500 BCE, perhaps earlier, two sets of sacred writings were assembled. The first of these is the Vedas, four major collections of the ritual prayers of very ancient Hindu practices, but containing all sorts of information, instruction, and even magic. The second is a set of somewhat philosophical interpretations. In the sixth century BCE, the axial age, a late segment of Vedic literature appeared, known as the Upanishads, a set of commentaries on certain passages in the Vedas, especially the collection known as the Rig Veda. Until this time Hindu belief and ritual had been polytheistic, but the Upanishads (and a very few lines in the tenth book of the Rig Veda) added something important. They struggled with questions about the ultimate cause of all things, and how the entire universe fit together. The two lines of thought, about ritual and about the self, appear in the Upanishads. (There will be more on Vedic literature in Chapter Nine.)

From very ancient times the priestly caste, those whose right and duty it was to perform the ritual, had emphasized the importance of ritual power. A word for ritual-power (sometimes translated as "prayer") begins with the letters brhm. The priests therefore were called brahmins and the mana-like power generated by the ritual was called something like "brahman." The Upanishads re-interpreted the notion of brahman. They proclaimed that Brahman was not just a power, but was the single Ultimate Power in the universe. A number of Hindu thinkers asserted that there is one supreme and ultimate reality, infinite and incomprehensible, that lies behind the entire universe, a reality to be called Brahman. It is the ocean of Being, the fullness of Power, the Really Real.

This idea eventually intersected with another ancient tradition, belief in the Atman or "Self" (a word to be used cautiously). As early as the time of the Upanishads, some Hindu thought had begun to turn inward away from the outer world. The world we live in is one of confusion and pain, of unreliable things that come and go. To find some peace a person must try to close off the world and retreat into the inner self. One of the Upanishads compared it metaphorically to falling asleep to the outer world in order to find something else inside the person.

In dreams or special states of consciousness a person perceives a reality that is not subject to the usual limitations imposed by time and space. Dreams are partial freedom from the world. In deep dreamless sleep a person goes a step further, beyond even the dream-reality into a kind of no-self, a state of non-consciousness as though the self had disappeared for a time. But this is a temporary no-self. The inner self of a person actually lasts through this dreamless sleep, as is evident when the person wakes up. The dreamless state was just a temporary freedom from involvement in the passing jumble of events in life. To attain a fuller freedom a person must go even deeper, beyond even dreamlessness, to get totally beyond individual self. It is not easy to take this metaphorical journey beyond waking and dreams and dreamless sleep into full no-self. The path to it is not through actual sleep (Chapter Five will describe the path). Few ever achieve it. But the path leads to the ultimate Self. It is called Atman, a word that originally meant just inner self or spirit (recall "atmosphere"). It is the infinite and universal Self, the truly ultimate reality. At times it is called pure consciousness as befits a Self, or pure bliss as a kind of state of consciousness. Yet because it is truly the Ultimate, it is also eternal, unchanging, and unbounded. It is a consciousness and bliss utterly beyond what we can comprehend. Each person's inner self/atman is not truly an individual self; it is really a drop in the infinite ocean of Self/Atman.

Different Hindu thinkers responded to ideas about Brahman and Atman in different ways. Many decided that since each was said to be ultimate reality and there could be only one truly ultimate reality, it must therefore be that Brahman was Atman and vice versa. To some this meant that Brahman-Atman was and is pure Consciousness, as though Brahman-Atman were the ultimate Self or Personness. Another school of thought pushed the ideal of ultimateness all the way. The truly ultimate is that beyond which there can be nothing else. As ultimate, it must therefore be the infinite. As infinite, it must therefore be beyond all categories, even the categories of consciousness and bliss. Brahman-Atman then must be Nirguna Brahman: Brahman without attributes. This is all certainly confusing. But it is difficult to think clearly about a reality that lies beyond the ability of thought to grasp it.

A fairly extreme but widely held philosophical position is that of the Hindu thinker Shankara. He lived and wrote in the early ninth century CE, relatively recently, and he claimed to be bringing to completion what was already in the Vedic writings, especially the Upanishads. He argued that Brahman is indeed the incomprehensible, infinite, ultimate Reality. It has the fullness of realness and infinitely so. That means that in some sense nothing is really real except Brahman's eternal and changeless "realness." At this point, other thinkers concluded that because the world is real it is therefore part of Brahman. Not Shankara. He concluded that the world we live in and perceive and take to be real is just the opposite. It is a shadowy, insubstantial thing. It is "maya," a word sometimes translated as "illusion." Like those concerned with the inner self and Atman but in his own way, Shankara turned away from the world. Brahman-Atman alone is real, he declared, in its infinite incomprehensibility.

This is the extreme expression of a belief in a nonpersonal Ultimate. The Tao is nonpersonal and ultimate, but the Taoist values this world and its yang/yin order as manifesting the universal influence of the Tao. The Brahmanist who accepts Shankara's ideas claims that nothing is truly real except the infinite and incomprehensible Nirguna Brahman. The world has no true existence. Nor do you and I have any true existence, except that we have within us beneath our individual selfhood the Self (Atman), which is actually even beyond Self, for it is ultimately identical with Nirguna Brahman.

TALKING ABOUT THE INCOMPREHENSIBLE

It is difficult to try to make sense out of a position that says that we are not real the way we think we are, and that the best way to think about the Ultimate is to recognize that it is unthinkable. But within the complexly woven threads of Hindu tradition there is a basic thought common to East and West. It is that beyond or beneath the various events and realities of life as we experience and comprehend it, there is a single and infinite incomprehensible reality: God as Absolute, the formless Tao, Nirguna Brahman. In the West, in China, and in India, three major historical centers of world civilization, religious thought passed beyond animism and polytheism, beyond even everyday monotheism, in search of the ultimate unity to everything. The search has led to a great mystery, the incomprehensible and absolute Ultimate.

These different civilizations followed different clues towards the Ultimate. Western religion pursued the idea of a personal Creator-God. By asking who created everything, it arrived at the notion of the Absolute from whom somehow reality comes. Chinese Taoism looked to the yang/yin order of nature as its best clue to the ultimate, and discovered a nonpersonal Cause of the patterns of nature. Hindu Brahmanist thought speculated both on the Atman-Self within a person and on the nonpersonal sacred power in rituals in order eventually to find the ultimate Brahman-without-attributes. The differences among these three approaches deserve books of their own, but what is the same is this: all three discovered an Ultimate, a reality that transcends or exceeds all boundaries and all comprehension. All three concluded that to understand that which we cannot really understand is the most valid understanding. All three concluded that the Ultimate is Mystery.

If the religious traditions had stopped at that and insisted firmly on nothing but that, these traditions might quickly have lost strength among most people. Ordinary religiousness includes more than an awed acknowledgment that the Ultimate is Mystery. Mystics may relish contemplating the infinite Mystery. Most people, however, seek something else in their religion.

These traditions remained alive for two reasons. The first is that most religious believers have not worried much about these rather abstract conclusions. In India, for example, most people worship one or more gods rather than focus on the absolute Being of Brahman-Atman. Each of the gods is said to be a lesser symbol of the supreme divine Self (Atman), which in turn is somehow a mode of presence of Brahman. But most believers do not worry too much about that. It is enough to worship the gods. Similarly, in China Taoism takes a less abstract and popular form, attending to the ancestors, manipulating magic powers, and dealing with spirits. Most Taoists do not break their heads over the formless Tao. In the West people are usually happy to speak in somewhat anthropomorphic ways about God. Jews, Christians, and Muslims will say that God is a Mystery and certainly not an anthropomorphic being like Zeus. Yet they will also speak of God's love or mercy or God's plans and activities the way we all speak of human persons, without worrying much about how precisely correct this is. Religious traditions do not usually insist that all believers hold to the most austerely proper and rigorously logical forms of speaking about the supreme numinous reality, be it God, Tao, or Brahman.

The second reason why religious traditions have been able both to claim that the supreme reality is an incomprehensible Ultimate and to have it still remain important to them is that they have found workable ways of talking about the incomprehensible. They do this by focusing on the clues to the Ultimate. The existence of persons, the order of the world, reflections on ritual-power and on the inner layers of one's self—these point in the direction of the Ultimate. In the Western historic religions, for example, God is said to be personal. This is taken to mean that when we understand what a person is—life and consciousness, freedom and love—we are then orienting ourselves in the direction of what God is rather than away from God. It is legitimate, therefore, to call God personal, although it must always be added that the ultimate nature of divinity is personhood in a way utterly beyond all limitations and therefore in a way that cannot be comprehended. (If you find such a philosophical qualification too technical and intellectualist to want to include it as part of your daily religious thoughts, the religious traditions will not insist upon it.)

Summary

This chapter has provided a survey of the various ways different religious traditions have agreed that behind the diversity and conflicts of life there is a single unifying Ultimate Reality. Because it is ultimate, it is also beyond our human ability to describe it adequately. Each culture has its own perspectives about the Ultimate. Each perspective provides a different view of the value and reality of human personness, of nature, of the universe.

It is striking that we humans should find it possible to believe in and care about an ultimate unity to all things. It is doubly striking that we should maintain this belief even if it leads us into ultimate incomprehensibility—into Mystery. The next chapter will explore the human condition to see what it is about us that perpetuates such belief as the core of historic religion.

FOR FURTHER REFLECTION

1. How disorderly does this world appear to you? Do you find it plausible that there is an ultimate unity to all things? Does the religion you know best claim that there is such a unity? Explain.
2. If you had to describe the main characteristics of God, would you agree with the image presented here of the Judaeo-Christian-Islamic God? Why? Why not?
3. Would you call the nonliving Tao by the name "God"? What about Atman-Brahman? Explain.
4. Where do you look for the best clue as to what is truly ultimate? What clue or clues are most meaningful to you?
5. What value can you see, if any, in saying that God is an ultimate Mystery?

SUGGESTED READINGS

Huston Smith, *The World's Religions*, 1991. An updated version of one of the most eloquent description of world religions.

William A. Young, *The World's Religions: Worldviews and Contemporary Issues*, 1995. For another interpretation of the same topics.

Karl Jaspers, *The Origin And Goal of History*, 1953. Chapter 1, on the axial age.

Guy E. Swanson, *The Birth of The Gods*, 1960. A description of the original times of the historic religions.

Michael Horace Barnes, *Stages of Thought: The Co-Evolution of Religious Thought and Science*, Ch. 5 "The Axial Age and the Classical Style of Thought," 2000.

S. A. Nigosian, *The Zoroastrian Faith: Tradition and Modern Research*, 1993. A rather scholarly analysis of the probable dates and teachings of Zarathustra and later Zoroastrianism.

Swami Prabhavananda and Frederick Manchester, *The Upanishads: Breath of the Eternal*, 1957 [or any edition of the Upanishads]. Axial age Hindu thoughts on the Ultimate.

Chapter Four

The Endless Quest

The Human Basis of Belief in an Ultimate

Chapter Two described reasons why people believe in magic, spirits, and gods. Animism and polytheism offer ways of making sense out of the events of life. These beliefs provide psychological comfort and social stability. Some beliefs may have roots in our genes. Most of us usually assume that belief in a single, universal Ultimate such as God also offers equivalent mental, emotional, and social benefits. But it should be clear now from Chapter Three that monotheism and its equivalents can take a rather extreme form as belief in an incomprehensible Absolute and Ultimate Reality. Belief in a single Ultimate sounds quite simple: it is belief in one God instead of many. But this belief is actually rather complex; it claims that contrary to appearances there is a universal unity to everything. It passes beyond familiar anthropomorphisms into austere statements about infinity and incomprehensibility. In spite of this, it is a belief that has been maintained firmly and widely for many centuries. That is what needs to be explained.

God as a Merely Perfect Person

It is odd to speak of God as a "merely" perfect Person. It should be no "mere" thing to have a God who is a truly perfect Person. A perfect Person exceeds by far the gods of polytheism. Such a Person is often pictured as something less than truly infinite and ultimate. But we might be excused for not objecting to this. God as a "merely" perfect Person would seem to be preferable to an Incomprehensible Ultimate for several reasons. Hindus likewise may prefer to think of Vishnu or Shiva, and some Buddhists of Amidha Buddha, as a "merely" perfect Person, instead of attending to Nirguna Brahman or meditating on nirvana.

First of all, God as a perfect Person is totally good. No person need fear that God will be fickle, unreliable, unfair, petty, greedy, or vain. The gods suffer from all these imperfections that we ordinary humans also experience, because the gods are not perfectly good as God is. At the same time, as less than the Absolute, God can be more readily portrayed in a personal way. Sometimes supposedly monotheistic religious leaders or writings go too far in that direction and describe God as though God were only a god. They do this, for example, when they say that God is impatient or angry or needs attention. Monotheism intends to establish at least this minimum about God, that God's goodness is totally unflawed. This should mean, for example, that when God is poetically portrayed as a parent, the image should represent a perfect parent who recognizes that the way to respond to a child's faults and failings is by loving and supporting the child, by showing compassion and understanding, and by using corrective measures when necessary but never out of anger or impatience or to fulfill selfish needs.

A perfect Person is also all-knowing and thus will never harm anyone through mistake, inattention, or ignorance, as mere gods might do. There is no real need ever to call God's attention to problems, as must be done with the gods. Nothing that God does is aimless or useless, even if people fail to understand the purpose behind it. Of equal importance is that an all-knowing merely perfect God is one who truly understands us. Other people fail to see us as we are or appreciate what we have to offer. Others ignore us at those times we most need to be accepted. Others pressure us into play-acting our lives to earn their approval. But God sees within, knows a person fully and accurately. As all-good God does not merely know us in our inner selves, feelings, and needs, but cherishes us deeply.

Furthermore, a merely perfect Person is all-powerful. God's knowledge and goodness lead God to know and choose exactly what is best for every person. "All-powerful" means that God can also accomplish what is best; no power in the universe can stand against God's choice. If anything seems evil or chaotic, we can nonetheless be assured that it happens only as the all-powerful, all-knowing, and all-good God has chosen to make it happen, or at least has allowed it to happen. If human beings have any special needs for miraculous help, divine care, special guidance, or even life after death, there is no doubt that God can provide such things.

The gods of polytheism can also provide some divine guidance and care. They can even give life after death if that is needed. Miracles, divine commandments, special attention, and eternal life are not things that only a perfect God can do. But belief in God as perfect Person adds the confidence that because God is perfect as the gods are not, people can place unqualified and unhesitating trust in God. God will never fail us because of limitations such as inattentiveness, carelessness, ignorance, weakness, confusion, or emotional immaturity.

This portrayal of God (or Vishnu, etc.) as Perfect Person makes it obvious why many people have adhered to at least some limited form of monotheism throughout centuries. Belief in a perfect God can offer much more psychological comfort than belief in lesser numinous powers and beings. Whatever can be done with mana or magic or luck, God can do better, and can be counted on to do what is best. Whatever it is the spirits or even the gods can provide, God can do more and will do it with unfailing love. This same God is also a more certain reference point for social stability than the gods can be. When God delivers laws to be obeyed or provides wisdom for guidance or establishes patterns of human life, every person can be sure that these are the best possible laws, wisdom, and patterns. Conformity to them will never be wasted effort, for God knows all and has a plan for everything. Thus God can be pictured in somewhat anthropomorphic terms as a parent or friend. God is a friendly and helpful Being rather than just an incomprehensible Absolute. God is Lord, Leader, or Lawgiver, not just an Ultimate.

In spite of this, theologies in historical or classical religions have maintained that we all should push beyond our anthropomorphisms, beyond the comfort and security of an image of God as a merely perfect Person, on to belief that the ultimate truth is that God is infinite and incomprehensible, that there is a Nirguna Brahman beyond perfect Self, that the Tao is formless. There are philosophical reasons why the traditions have described the Ultimate this way. We will see these reasons in Chapter Eleven on the proof for the existence of God (or equivalent). Some religious thinkers say that we have semi-mystical experiences of infinite mystery upon which the universe and our lives depend. That too will be discussed in another chapter. This chapter has a more ordinary but important question to answer.

The search in the next few pages is for the way our own lives present to us a dimension of ultimateness that we cannot easily avoid. We will understand a great deal about ourselves as human beings when we understand why the rather austere and difficult notion of the Ultimate as incomprehensible Mystery has been maintained at the core of major religious traditions. What we will be looking for are the kinds of feelings and ideas that everyone might have sooner or later in life that would make a person aware of questions so big and disturbing that only belief in some truly Ultimate or Absolute reality can answer. Thousands of years ago, our ancestors set out to find answers to the many mysteries of life. They did not know it, but they were setting out on an endless quest. The human mind has such an unlimited capacity to wonder and question that it is in the very nature of humanness to live in the presence of infinite mystery. The next section will try to explain that.

The Ultimate Questions

There are certain questions that we are capable of asking because we have human minds, but that are odd because they can only be answered (if at all) in the way historic religion does, by talking about an ultimate reality that is relevant to the entire universe at once. These questions are not raised by everyone everywhere. It may be that most people would just as soon avoid being bothered by them. And people in primitive and pre-literate archaic cultures do not seem to ask them, at least not explicitly. Yet they are universal questions in the sense that they ask about the whole of all things at once. These questions seek the final or ultimate explanation for everything at once. In a pure monotheism or its equivalent, the ultimate explanation for everything is a single reality rather than multiple realities (as in polytheism), a single reality that is the Cause or Power or Being behind the whole of things.

Part of the reason why we ask ultimate and universal questions is that we have available to us a style of thought that makes it easier to formulate such questions. People in historic (and modern) cultures are no more intelligent than people in primitive and archaic cultures. Humankind seems to share in the same basic human intelligence everywhere. But folktales and myths are stories of specific beings and events. As narratives, these stories must provide concrete images of activities and their consequences. The axial age, however, brought with it not just certain ideas about universal order or unity but also a mode of thought better able to express such ideas. In the axial age, the old stories continued to be told, though sometimes were reinterpreted. But a new and more abstract mode of thought gained currency among the intellectual elite of various great cultures. Explicit logic, formal rules of argumentation, and highly abstract language were the tools of the new philosophy, science, and theology. They made it possible to ask the ultimate questions. Perhaps they even made it inevitable that people would ask them, though we cannot know this for sure.

There is really just one ultimate question, though it has many aspects: "Why is everything?" It will be easier here to approach the one single ultimate question by looking at three different forms the question might take:

1) What is the origin of everything (if any)?

2) What is the order or nature of everything (if any)?

3) What is the purpose of everything (if any)?

These three questions ask about the entire universe at once, where it all comes from, what it is like, and where it is going. Because we are part of this universe, these questions also appear as follows: Where did we come from? Who are we? Where are we going?

It took many thousands of years of human development before whole civilizations became aware of these universal questions. It is as though human cultural development preceding the axial age had not yet reached the stage in which such questions made sense. This is also true of each individual. Not until adolescence do human beings begin to achieve the capacity to recognize the significance and range of the ultimate questions. Even then we do not find it easy to exercise that capacity. It takes practice before we get used to thinking in such broad, all-inclusive, and abstract ways. Not until the axial age do we find cultures that encourage the use of this ability.

Asking the Questions in a Contemporary Context

From primitive times people have been asking about the origin, nature, and purpose of things. As we have already seen, primitive peoples use folktales to explain each bit and piece of reality. Literate archaic people develop elaborate myths about how the god or gods brought order out of chaos and how the present division of authority among gods came to be. Historic religion looks further, for a single unifying all-inclusive explanation of all things.

It is difficult for us to try to understand how new ideas about reality have startled people in a different culture into asking ultimate questions. We may never be able to share the sensibilities of former generations and other societies. Rather than try to reproduce the complex analyses of the Chinese, Indian, or Jewish thinkers of ancient times, we can get a better idea of how ultimate questions can arise by considering information that is part of our own era, information from astronomy about the physical universe. It is seemingly harmless information, but if any of it begins to evoke some uneasiness and stir up some uncomfortable questions in your mind, then you will know a little better how previous generations as long ago as 500 or 600 BCE felt when they stumbled across ultimate questions in their own cultural contexts.

Current astronomical theory says that the universe is about fourteen billion years old. The estimates vary and new information could change the estimates, but generally speaking this picture of the universe is a well-supported theory. About fourteen billion years ago, it says, all the matter and energy that is the universe today was condensed so compactly that less than a teaspoonful would have a mass equivalent to the entire universe. The density was so great that its energy made it explode, scattering itself outward, spinning and crashing and expanding on and on until today. The universe we live in is that explosion still scattering outward. All the stars and galaxies of stars and the matter and energy in between are clusters of stuff blowing outward since the "big bang" that began fourteen billion years ago.

Perhaps this exploding universe will expand endlessly, with everything becoming more and more scattered and spreading itself ever thinner until the universe that we know becomes dead, every bit of it lost from every other bit in the unending cold. Another possibility, one that currently looks less likely, is that the mutual gravitational attraction of every bit for every other bit will slow down and stop the expansion of the universe and then drag it back together, faster and faster, all of it falling in toward everything else until it is so condensed again that there will be another big bang and the universe will start all over again, and then again, and so on. Such a cycle would recur perhaps about every eighty billion years or so, the theory has it. It seems there could be an endless series of cycles, explosion and collapse, explosion and collapse, explosion and collapse, one after the other.

Meanwhile, we live in this continuously expanding universe. It is a very large one. To get an idea of the amount of matter and space involved, begin with a pea about one-third of an inch in diameter. Let that stand for the earth (a little less than eight thousand miles in diameter). Put the pea next to a very large beach ball, one full yard in diameter, to represent the sun (eight hundred sixty-four thousand miles in diameter). Now put the pea at one end of a football field and the ball at the far other end, about one hundred ten yards apart. That approximates the average distance between earth and sun (ninety-three million miles). The earth is quite close to the sun compared to the outermost planets. Pluto's average distance from the sun is forty times as far as earth's. If the whole solar system out to Pluto were shrunk to one inch, on that scale the nearest star would be ninety yards away. Our solar system is three-fourths of the way out from the center of a cluster of stars known to us as the Milky Way, a galaxy with as many as perhaps three hundred billion stars. There are an estimated hundred billion such galaxies in the known universe, each of them averaging another hundred billion stars or so. This speck of rock called earth can seem insignificant in a universe where even our entire Milky Way galaxy is lost among a hundred billion others. In a few million years our sun will follow the normal course in the life of a small to medium sized star, first bloating out into a "red giant" burning the earth raw and then collapsing and dying.

The astronomical theories have disturbing implications. They may imply that the whole universe is a rather chaotic collection of random events, that we tiny humans are the merest specks of life on a rocky mote whirling in vast emptiness as a momentary phase in the unending aimlessness of time and space. Is that the whole story of the ultimate origin, order, and purpose of the entire universe?

How should we respond to a question like that? We can ignore it and get on with the practical things of life. That is a successful tactic most of the time. We can also fall back on traditional religious beliefs and just say that no matter what the universe looks like to astronomers we are sure it is all under

God's purposeful guidance. That response works well for many people. But to understand better the human significance of ultimate questions we will have to look into them more deeply. We might even get in over our heads here and there, looking at problems we cannot answer. It will all help, though, in understanding why ultimateness, universality, infinity, and other such incomprehensibles keep intruding into human history in historic religions.

What Is the Origin of Everything?

This is the first form of the ultimate questions, the most intellectually abstract of the three. There is a dilemma inherent in any attempt to ask about the origin of everything. Neither of the two horns of the dilemma is a comfortable place to sit. One is the possibility that there is no origin, that the stuff of the universe always existed, everlastingly before every person's life and, seemingly, everlastingly after. Things keep on happening, one after another, every event passing away endlessly, all events and lives swallowed up eventually in an infinite series of changes.

There are puzzling aspects to this. Can the universe really go on endlessly? If it could cease to exist or if the energy that composes it could ever be extinguished, then an infinity of time already passed should have been time enough for this to happen. Inasmuch as the universe is still active, then perhaps it goes on endlessly. That would be the same, it seems, as going nowhere in particular, because wherever or however the universe ends up at some given point in time it will never stop there but go on and on and on. Our minds can circle restlessly around possibilities like these.

The other horn of the dilemma, that the universe did originate some infinite amount of time ago, is embodied in the scientific theory of the big bang. The next question, then, is why there existed any matter/energy to go "bang" in the first place. Where did it come from? The monotheist answers this easily: God created it. But the answer is not as simple as it looks. Why is there a God? Did someone or thing create God?

The traditional answer is that no one created God because God always existed. This is a troublesome response, though, as the philosopher David Hume (1711-1776) pointed out over two centuries ago. If we think the universe had to have a start, what is it about God that says God did not have a start but can start everything else? Or if God could have existed endlessly, why not the universe also? But then if the universe could have existed forever, what need is there for a Creator? If the universe has existed forever, in fact, then all the problems from the first horn of the dilemma are back with us.

Indian and Western historic religions found it necessary in the face of such puzzles to make a major shift in their idea of the ultimate reality. God or Brahman is not everlasting, they said. To last endlessly is to endure through time. The Ultimate is not everlasting, they proclaimed; rather it is eternal. The eternal stands outside of time; it is timeless. It causes time, or affects the events of time, or is the reality hidden behind the appearances of time. But in the eternal Ultimate there is only utter changelessness. There is no before or during or after. The world experiences time, so it cannot be the ultimate. That is why there must be an eternal (timeless) ultimate to account for the world's existence.

We have seen another line of thought that led to this same conclusion. In the East and West the supreme Reality is thought to be totally perfect. Anything imperfect is a limited or flawed reality like a god or great mana. The reality behind all the universe must be unlimited or unflawed. Whatever changes is good or perfect in its own way perhaps (if it really exists at all), but it is not totally perfect. Whatever changes is always passing away in some respect. The totally perfect, therefore, is beyond change. What is beyond change is timeless, for time is nothing but change. So the logic went, at least. It is perhaps not water-tight logic, but it is the kind of thought that the West and East engaged in beginning in the axial age.

We may be a little intrigued by thoughts like this, or just tired and confused trying to sort it out, wondering whether it is really worth the effort. There is very little in our daily lives that makes such thoughts useful. But in the axial age about twenty-five hundred years ago this kind of thinking became an explicit part of human history. Human minds then opened wide enough to wonder about everlasting duration and timeless eternity. Ever since then, we have been asking questions that are so broad that they point toward infinite, absolute, and changeless perfection. This beginning leads to other ultimate questions, some more directly related to our ordinary life.

What Order and Purpose Is There to the Universe?

However you or your culture answers the question about the origin of everything, a further question remains unanswered: what order is there in reality as a whole?

Is there any real order at all? The astronomers' portrait of the universe as the fragments of an explosion is a hint that perhaps any kind of orderliness or pattern is just a momentary accident. In general our basic faith in the intelligibility of reality usually overcomes our doubts; we feel sure that somehow things do make sense. This basic faith, though, is always being challenged by reality. Order does exist to some degree; that much seems obvious. We can make a certain amount of sense of things. The success of science seems to be evidence that reality is intelligible and predictable.

But the order seems incomplete. Science says that nature on the whole is a cosmic explosion still chaotically fragmenting. Likewise in every person's life there is some chaos, confusion, conflict, and destruction. The simple faith that reality makes sense may then be too sweeping a judgment. Perhaps the evidence should lead us to say that reality makes only partial and temporary and local sense, that there are everywhere conflicting forces at work, that there is no universal order as historic religions claim but only partial areas of order as polytheistic interpretations see it.

Even if we find some way to assert that there is a basic order to all things, this order may not be to our liking. Perhaps this order is just a mindless fate to which we can only submit. Perhaps it is a dead, mechanical, automatic process. The laws and patterns of nature are all rather orderly in that they follow certain basic physical laws. But the laws may just operate without purpose or meaning. Order without purpose can be as humanly empty as chaos. Everything then runs smoothly but uselessly.

A person may well reject the idea that our existence is an accident subject to uncontrolled forms of chaos, or is order but of a mindless and purposeless sort. But is it bothersome or unsettling to you to take these kinds of ideas seriously? If so, then the questions of ultimate order and purpose are important to you. We do not always notice their importance because we tend to live by the unconscious faith that reality is intelligible, that there is purposeful order to it. It is not until that faith is somehow challenged that we become aware of its place in our lives.

Primitive, archaic, and historic peoples have all felt the threat of chaos, but it is the historic religious traditions that have worried and reflected most deeply about it. They have found ways to express their faith that in the end chaos is not victorious. The Taoist is confident that all moments of disorder will be balanced out in the long run by the Tao. The Western monotheist claims that even seeming disorder is part of a divine plan. God somehow maintains a meaningful order to everything even if that is not apparent to us. In India the Shankara school neatly eliminates disorder by declaring that all the events of the universe are not truly real, but only "maya." In each case the supreme reality must be of such power to assure that every event in the universe is assimilated in some way into an ultimate order or perfection.

It is an awesomely massive and complex universe to bring under a single order. There is an enormous extent of time and of real events and possible events, of countless billions of happenings even under a single jungle rock much less in a whole forest, continent, planet, solar system, or galaxy. Is there a God or cosmic force that can and does bring the events of one hundred billion galaxies into a coherent and meaningful order on each of a billion days? Questions like these have helped sustain the historic religions in their belief that the one God or Ultimate must be not merely a Perfect Person or Self but the infinite Absolute, able to encompass the immensity of the universe within its eternal power.

What Order and Purpose Is There to Our Lives?

All the thoughts about the universe, about its origin, order, and purpose, would be mere academic speculation were it not that the order and purpose to our lives are bound up in such questions. We do not often experience the connection. Our implicit faith in the intelligibility and value of life usually remains strong. We believe that to live and act and choose, to work and to plan and to love, are all somehow deeply meaningful.

Once in a while, though, reality falls apart in front of us and lays bare a frightening emptiness. Most of us only catch glimpses of this emptiness and comfort ourselves with the thought that it is not really there. Very few become convinced that emptiness is the final truth; some may be fortunate enough never to perceive it at all. Yet most people eventually get a brief look behind the seeming order and purpose of life into mysteries that can upset their natural faith in life.

The Unfairness of Life

One major way that reality challenges human faith that life is meaningful is by its "unfairness." By definition life would be fair if every person could expect to get out of life exactly what he or she deserves. If life were fully fair, the innocent would never starve to death or suffer a long and painful disease. If life were fair, those who conscientiously work and sacrifice to help those they love would never lose everything to flood or earthquake. The fact of reading this book probably means that by accident of birth you have received food, shelter, and education during your life; enjoyed the luxury of not having to worry about intestinal parasites, or about being killed in a revolution; and expect to live a reasonably long life. These are luxuries in the sense that most people in history would consider them true privileges. Have we done something wonderfully meritorious to have deserved these privileges? Probably not. Life is not fair.

It is one of the peculiarities of our contemporary situation that life appears basically fair to us, because we are protected against its many deadly uncertainties. And yet we are aware that the security of these comfortable conditions is tenuous. We too can be crippled by disease or made blind. Our children, our parents, our loved ones can suddenly die in a senseless accident.

The Fact of Death

There is a second major aspect of life that can stir up a deep uneasiness about the ultimate meaning of life. That is the fact of death. During our lives we build up a pattern of goals and accomplishments. We live towards the future, to enjoy, to do, to create. And then one day we discover that most of our future is behind us. There is a time limit. We all die. We will never enjoy all that we hope to enjoy. We will never find all the love, success, happiness, fulfillment we once hoped for from life. For a brief moment, the moving forces of the universe have produced the particular spark of life that is our identity, a brief candle glowing brightly and then sputtering out.

The fact of death easily becomes a symbol of our finiteness. Every person's life is a quick flash of hope, burning among a billion others, passing away like a billion others to be replaced by another countless billion. People leave behind families, monuments, great books and works of art, philosophies, nations, even religions. But everything is limited, partial, passing. In ten thousand years all but the very greatest or very worst will have been forgotten. A million years from now, a brief time on the cosmic scale, little will be left. "Eat, drink, and be merry, for tomorrow we die," said the Christian apostle Paul, mocking what he thought to be the Epicurean philosophy of life. If death brings an end to everything, then there is no lasting purpose to anything. In the infinite immensity of time, all things turn to dust.

Religious Answers to Death and Life's Unfairness

There are various ways to avoid the challenge to life's meaning. Some people manage to ignore the challenges. Others manage to maintain their basic faith in the worthwhileness of life out of some inner optimism. For most people, however, it is their religious beliefs that meet the challenges.

Historic or classical religion has a special power to overcome the threats of death and unfairness. The belief that there is one ultimate Being or Power is already a belief in a final order, in spite of apparent conflicts and contradictions in life. Belief in a God, for example, is a belief that the disorder of unfairness is conquered finally in some way by the ordering power of divine Providence. Belief in Brahman is a belief that the disorder of unfairness and death is only part of "maya" (illusion). Belief in the Tao is a belief in a transcendent order that reconciles all temporary disorder in some way. Likewise, belief that death is not just a passing away but a meaningful incorporation into an eternal reality beyond this life is a belief common to most historic religions.

When people face death and unfairness, belief in a God who is a merely perfect Person turns out to be helpful but not always enough. As long as each person thinks mainly of his or her own experiences of life's unfairness and of the approach of death, the person may be satisfied with a God who is guaranteed to be perfectly fair and loving and able to give everlasting life to that person. But larger questions can intrude. The death of millions through civil wars and the unfairness of children dying hungry can cause doubt about ultimate meaningfulness. The questing consciousness of human thought can begin to nose around the edges of infinity by asking where it all comes from, whether it all hangs together in some way, whether there really is some ultimate purpose to all things that can never be swallowed up by billions of years of time or by an endless sequence of happenings.

It is in answer to such thoughts that the historic religions have proposed there is an Ultimate that is more than even a merely perfect Person (though in Western monotheism the Ultimate is also somehow the infinite perfection of personness). As a result, there are whole theological libraries devoted to comprehending and speaking about the incomprehensible Ultimate.

In all these libraries of thought about the Ultimate is another topic, half-hidden, one a little closer to our lives than abstract discussions of the Ultimate. This is our own human orientation to the Ultimate or the infinite. From the first pages we have talked about our orientation to mystery and even about our capacity for the infinite. Our simple ability to think about the kinds of universalist questions we have been pondering is of very special importance and needs to be addressed more explicitly.

An Openness to the Infinite

Our Peculiar Kind of Consciousness

The ultimate questions represent something odd about human life: that we are unsure about where we fit in reality. Where do we come from? What are we part of? Where are we going? We do not always know for sure; at least, the human race has had a hard time trying to answer those questions. The most significant thing is that we are aware that these questions exist and can be asked, and that we do not always have satisfying answers. We are the consciously uncertain animal.

Once again compare a human being to any animal. Those animals are simply a part of nature. Each is aware of its environment, the air and smells and moisture in it, the earth and mud and rocks, trees and shrubs and stumps, rivers and rain, birds and insects and mammals. None of the animals, however, consciously names these things and wonders where they came from or what their purpose is. Animals are born, develop, live and die, in accordance with the patterns evolution has produced so far, and they do this without thinking about it. They do not ponder the meaning of their lives or ever worry about their future success. They simply live, from moment to moment, meal to meal.

We humans have some things in common with those animals. We also are born, live for a while, and die. We also have moments of pleasure and pain. But we can also reflect on these things. On any given day it may be that we are consciously aware of feelings of excitement about someone we are going to meet or frustration over failing to achieve something we hoped for. To be aware of having these feelings is a special consciousness, an ability to say about oneself "I am excited" or "I am feeling frustrated." We simultaneously remember times when we were less excited or frustrated. We can make conscious comparisons in our minds and feel better or worse through these comparisons. We can also consciously picture to ourselves others we know or have read about and use this mental picture as a basis of comparison. We can even consciously imagine possible future conditions for ourselves in which our excitement is spoiled or our frustration is overcome. We can make ourselves happy or sad by our memories, imaginings, and comparisons. We can create worlds of possibilities by which we measure what we actually have or lack.

This is an extraordinary ability; it is self-awareness. We can consciously possess our own selfhood by being able to say, "I am." It is also called self-transcendence. When we look at ourselves, at our lives, actions, and options, we are rising above (transcending) our ongoing existence, as it were, in order to look it over and reflect on it. In this lies our power of self-determination. Because we can rise above our ongoing life and look it over, we are in a position to direct that life, to choose in various ways what it will be like. This capacity for self-transcendence is therefore our freedom. It distinguishes us from all other beings. It is what makes us so distinctively human.

The Experience of Limit and Estrangement

Because we can consciously remember, imagine, reflect, compare, and see ourselves in a thousand ways, we can also stand in front of a mirror and say, "I wish that I could be…." We all have the kind of consciousness that allows us to dream of being as strong, good looking, intelligent, free, courageous, wealthy, famous, healthy, loved, and loving as someone else, real or imagined.

We all know that wishful thinking is not very profitable except about things that we can accomplish by hard work and training. We know that much of life must simply be accepted and endured. We know that the right attitude about what is can bring us happiness, instead of misery about what is not. We learn to deal with our consciousness of what might be, with our imagination and dreams. The significant thing about humans is that we must learn to deal with life's possibilities. Life is not automatic; we are not born into a programmed pattern of behavior to fit into a special niche in nature. We are adrift in reality, struggling perhaps to find a place, a home, a center of security and identity; or working to establish a direction, a set of goals that we can trust to guide us in our decisions.

Nothing is a greater blessing or advantage than our power to imagine what does not yet exist, to work with our minds, comparing options and reflecting on possibilities. Out of this has come our language, civilization, art, and humor. The uncertainty and desires that arise because of our kind of consciousness gives us our openness to change and the motivation to grow. But there is a price we pay. While our consciousness makes us the animal that is most fully alive, that same consciousness also makes us the only animal that foresees its own death. The consciousness that makes us desire wholeness and happiness also gives us a sense of limitation and makes us estranged.

Estrangement is an unusual word with a simple meaning: to be separate. In romantic contexts the word "estrangement" is used to describe a change from a feeling of affection to one of indifference or separation. Philosophers and theologians employ the word at times to reflect something of the romantic meaning in a new way. Human existence is like the tragic condition of two lovers who sought happiness with each other but somehow find themselves lonely and frustrated. The unity they once thought they had has turned out to be an illusion and mockery. Where they hoped to find meaning there is now nothing. It would be too painful to think about this often, so they do their best to forget or ignore the bright wholeness they once had. But there is now a feeling of restlessness within, a deeper, unnamed sense of wrongness to life, a state of separation or estrangement, a frustrating experience of limit.

The historic religions often declare that our whole lives are basically ones of estrangement from some ideal reality or some perfect Ultimate. The human ability to look at the conditions of existence and discover basic problems in life reached its greatest strength precisely when the human mind became able to dream of perfection. The same consciousness that allows us to dream of an ideal unity to things, of perfect goodness, knowledge, and love, also thereby allows us to recognize that in this ordinary life things fall far short of such perfection.

In the historic religions that arose in India and the West there is a sense of estrangement from the conditions of human life. These historic religions have described life as fallen, corrupt, sinful, or illusory. They see it as flawed beyond repair. (It will not be until the rise of the modern stage of religion that an appreciation of life in this world will regain strength.)

Forms of Estrangement

A modern theologian, Paul Tillich (1886-1965), distinguished three types of estrangement. A review of these kinds of estrangement can help a person today see the sort of thing historic religions have said about life all along.

First of all, we can feel estranged from the natural universe and the limits it imposes on us. We are cosmic orphans, as one person expressed it; we have no clear and settled place in nature. Physically we are natural beings, yet our minds allow us to step back from nature and look at it and decide whether to accept it or reject it, enjoy it or avoid it. We often like to see ourselves as part of a grand natural order. Yet that natural order includes our death. We like to admire the grandeur of nature, yet nature is so immensely grand that perhaps it is only a cosmic collection of accidents with no particular place for human consciousness. In the midst of nature's beauty there is also nature's destructiveness through disease and drought and earthquake. Perhaps nature is not a home for us but just a meaningless randomness.

Secondly, we can be estranged from one another. Every human being has a strong need to belong, to be accepted, to be loved. Each of us can look at the person next to us and recognize a common humanness in a common need to be close to someone. Yet there is probably no person who has ever lived that achieved so full and lasting a relationship that all loneliness disappeared for good. Communication between any two people is always imperfect. Misunderstandings arise. Lack of trust and openness is part of life. Jealousy, hatred, insecurity, boredom, irritation, possessiveness, bigotry—all leave little scars on the skin of life, making us tough enough to survive but also tough enough to be separate from one another in self-defense. Every one of us needs acceptance and support. Every one experiences some rejection and abandonment. We dull our minds and harden our feelings a bit so that we are not too painfully aware of it. We find the courage to live with it, but we are still estranged from one another.

Thirdly, we are even estranged from ourselves. Each of us as a child was taught what we must not be. We found ways of talking, dressing, laughing, and playing that earned approval from family, teachers, or friends. We did not always feel comfortable with some of these roles. We often faked it. We still do. When we were children, people occasionally told us that we were selfish or jealous and we felt like saying, "No, I'm not," because we had been taught that good little girls or boys were not like that. Without really being conscious of it, we have all learned to lie to ourselves about some of our true feelings in order to preserve our own self-esteem. A young boy walks to the seashore with his father and is frightened by the big waves. The father says, "You are not afraid, are you?" The child learns from this to pretend, even to himself, that he is not afraid. A teenage girl has feelings that are sexual but denies it to herself because someone has taught her that makes her dirty-minded. These kinds of examples are endless because they are so ordinary. There may be someone who lives comfortably without pretense of any kind; there may be someone who does not lie to himself or herself in hidden ways, but such a person would be very rare.

We do not have a ready-made identity. We must search for one as the years pass, creating it as we go. It is never ideal. We dream of who we might be. We look for unity with others and sometimes try to please them so they will like us. We hope always for an at-home-ness with the universe, others, and self, but it never works completely right. Most importantly, we are conscious of that. Because we can imagine what a more ideal life might be like, we are conscious of life's actual limits.

Overcoming a Sense of Estrangement

Sometimes we hope to overcome life's serious limits by human effort. Perhaps someday we will learn to understand ourselves, each other, and the universe, and from that understanding develop techniques for eliminating the sources of estrangement. Perhaps medicine can eventually prolong life so that no one need die until death finally looks appealing as a permanent rest or a transition to a new condition. Perhaps psychology, sociology, and other fields of study will enable us to grow up happy and satisfied, loving and open and supportive toward one another.

If we achieve such a marvelous state, however, perhaps we will become restless again by wondering what the point of it all might be, what the ultimate purpose or value is in living, however pleasant it might be. Now we can become restless because our minds enable us to look past present conditions to something better. Even in some supposedly ideal state our minds will still have the power to imagine, wonder, and dream. Even the smallest flaw, the humblest question about purpose, the slightest bit of unfairness, could make us wonder again and worry. The fact of limits may still haunt us. Human minds have been dreaming of perfection at least since the beginning of the axial age. Perhaps such dreams and the estrangement they can bring will never be eliminated unless we eliminate our ability to think.

Again, it is the historic religions that have often decided that earthly life is fundamentally flawed beyond correction. The new world or other realm cannot be one that only improves on current life. Some historic philosophies such as Stoic thought, proposed that we learn to accept the world as it is, adapting to its order. In recent centuries a modern style of religiousness has sought simply a deeper harmony with cosmic order. But at least some of the great historic religions pass a much more negative judgment on this world. They say that it must be transformed, destroyed, or abandoned completely in favor of a different kind of existence. Because historic religion is a religious consciousness of those who ask universalist questions, it is a consciousness that can dream of absolute unqualified perfection. Our human power of conscious awareness gives us an inner ability to seek that which transcends all limitations and overcomes all estrangement totally. In the following chapters we will see this more concretely.

Summary

This chapter has reviewed aspects of our existence that lead us beyond local spirits, magic, powerful gods, and great mana forces, behind the finite and comprehensible, to wonderment about what is ultimate and beyond all limitation. There are many specific issues that do this: the general ultimate questions, the problem of life's fairness and of death, the forms of estrangement. The power of these issues to take us beyond the finite is a sign of our own human capacity for the infinite. It is this capacity in the last analysis that leaves us always open to the infinite Mystery that goes by all the names described in Chapter Three.

END OF PART I

We are not at an end yet in talking about the stages in the development of religion. There is still the modern (and even a "postmodern," as we will see) stage. But that stage is so recent that it is as yet only a tiny part of the overall story of religion. The following chapters, therefore, will explore more of the ways in which primitive, archaic, and historic or classical religions have dealt with the mysteries of life. That will provide the background to understand better what is happening to religion today.

Very likely in the course of this study you will eventually discover that you are a modern person in some ways but, like most people, also partly historic and archaic and even primitive to a degree, with all of it mixed together in the flow of your life, thoughts, and feelings. The kinds of salvation from estrangement that appeal to you or make sense to you will provide some clues to this. That is the topic of Part II which follows.

FOR FURTHER REFLECTION

1. Express as clearly as you can the difference between a merely perfect Person and an Absolute Ultimate.
2. How do you feel about making the idea of a merely perfect Person only a way of imaging or symbolizing an Absolute Reality? Explain.
3. Is it possible that in five hundred years or more we humans will have learned to overcome the major forms of estrangement? Explain.
4. Describe the most significant limits, flaws, and failures in life you are aware of.
5. In what ways do you see yourself as a being with a capacity for the infinite? Explain.
6. Describe fully some example of a way in which our minds can ask questions so big that not even belief in God as a Perfect Person is adequate to answer them.

SUGGESTED READINGS

James W. Sire, *The Universe Next Door: a Basic World View Catalogue*, 1997 (third edition). Describes how several religious and nonreligious worldviews interpret the basic human situation.

Paul G. Johnson, *God and World Religions: Basic Beliefs and Themes*, 1997 and John Haught, *What Is God? How to Think about the Divine*, 1986. Describe which aspects of life and experience best symbolize God.

John Hick, *An Interpretation of Religion: Human Responses to the Transcendent*, 1989. An example of a crosscultural approach to transcendence.

John Shea, *Stories of God*, 1978. A mixture of reflections and stories about ultimate mystery.

Paul Tillich, *Systematic Theology*, Vol. II, 1957. See especially pp. 66-72 on his notion of estrangement.

D. Z. Phillips and Timothy Tessin, eds. *Religion without Transcendence*, 1997. Philosophical articles on the relation of religion to questions about the transcendent.

Part II

Salvations

Estrangement appears in many forms. The historic and modern religions are the most conscious of life's flaws, but primitive and archaic religions also can be restless with life. Human beings, whatever their culture, feel some need to overcome life's limitations and failings.

There are nonreligious means people can use to eliminate sources of estrangement. Some people place their hopes in science. Human techniques for handling nature and social relations and self-development include technology, sociology, and psychology. Medical progress, for example, has eliminated smallpox, one of nature's great killers. The virus still exists in a few laboratories, unfortunately, where it remains available for biological warfare. But perhaps in the next few centuries developments in the social sciences may make wars or terrorist attacks less likely. In general the sciences approach the threatening mysteries of life as problems to be solved. Compared to many of the religious techniques of the past, such as the use of magic or invocations of the gods, science is doing better in dealing with many former mysteries. Science is saving people from many limitations that primitive and archaic religions especially could not deal with so well.

But science cannot grasp all the complexities of human life, nor solve all of its problems, least of all those in the moral arena, as a later chapter will illustrate. The previous chapter on universal or ultimate questions should make clear that the mysteries of life, including the alienating presence of death, unfairness, and other basic evils, are not easily reduced to technical problems to be solved by good science or engineering. There always remains the human ability to wonder and compare and question and to become restless with the limitations of life.

Some mysteries are very threatening. When they cannot be solved like ordinary problems, their threat is unrelenting. Life in the presence of unrelenting threats would be hellish. Religions save people from a feeling of limit and estrangement by seeing the other side of mystery, not as threat but as promise. Religion saves people from feelings of estrangement by perceiving in the mysteries of life a numinous presence or power that offers hope. Earlier, religion was defined as a positive response to mystery. Here is a fuller definition: religion is a response to mystery as a numinous reality that has the power to provide some form of salvation from estrangement. Be aware, however, that the word "salvation" is being used very broadly here. Not all forms of salvation offer life after death, as we will see.

The following three chapters are about forms of religious salvation. There will be many examples of various religious beliefs in salvation, because there have been a great many notions about how best to be saved from the estranging threats that life poses. To bring some order out of the wealth of traditions, the chapters have been divided according to the kinds of threatening estrangements. Chapter Five will focus on ideas of an ideal life or universe, as answers to estrangement from the natural world, Chapter Six on forms of social existence as answers to estrangement from others, and Chapter Seven on ways of achieving an ideal selfhood in answer to estrangement from self. Each of these chapters will in turn describe primitive, archaic, and historic forms of beliefs and practices.

Beneath all these divisions and examples there is still a common human story. All the many beliefs and behaviors described here are signs of the human condition of beings with the conscious ability to ask endless questions and thereby discover mystery, and to have faith that behind or within the mystery is a numinous power that upholds rather than destroys the ultimate meaningfulness of life.

CHAPTER FIVE

Peace, Paradise, and Perfection

The World as It Should Be

This universe is not always kind to us. We face lives of troubles and uncertainties, and dream of an ideal situation where nothing threatens our safety and meaningfulness. Every religious tradition has some way of acknowledging that life is not what we would like it to be, and of portraying ideal conditions that can be achieved through proper relations to the numinous powers. The traditions usually describe simultaneously how to achieve the ideal world and to establish or maintain ideal relations with others as well as an ideal self; these three elements will appear somewhat intermingled here. But the emphasis in this chapter is on ideas about beliefs in an ideal world, a place or condition or universe that does not produce frustrating limits or a sense of estrangement.

In general, primitive religions seek a good life, in the world more or less as it is; archaic religions dream of a better life, even an idealized life, but usually do not hope to be able to achieve it; and historic religions seek to escape life's limitations entirely in some sort of perfect life. The hopes of humankind have gone from good to better to best. Like many generalizations, this neat progression is too neat to be entirely correct. But it is a useful guide to some major differences.

PRIMITIVE SALVATION: AN UNBOTHERED LIFE

The primitive person accepts the world more or less as it is. The tribesperson knows that it is not perfect; there is disorder within it; there are powers that cause disease and hunger. Nonetheless, the tribesperson has an unthinking faith in the universe as it appears, accepting it as reality and trusting that it can provide for a comfortable and safe life. For the primitive person, salvation consists mainly of a defense of the stable order of the world against disruptive forces.

There are three ways the comforting pattern of life can be disrupted. The first source of disruption is by a breakdown in proper tribal order. This order was established at the beginning of time, the original time of the world just a few generations prior to what living memory can reach, by the original beings. This is the one true way to behave, the right way, the safe way. This order is composed of all the customs, laws, roles, and other behavioral patterns that make the tribespeople who they are. Violation of these patterns causes chaos and confusion, fights and family disputes, bad luck and sometimes even punishment from the numinous. Maintaining the one correct order produces peace and happiness.

To preserve the order established in the primal time is to stay in contact with those times. Thus the Australian aborigines use the ritual retelling of these stories of the beginning as "dreamtime," when they identify themselves with their origin and become one with it again. In the modern world we value the changes that time brings, but for the primitive person time is an enemy because it contains the risk of change; it brings confusion and danger. It is better to maintain a kind of timeless identity between the "now" and the "then" of the beginning, and to avoid any future not identical with then and now. That is one form of salvation for the primitive person.

Even if the proper tribal order were faithfully maintained, there is still a second source of disruption: the activities or influences of mana-like forces and spirits. It is not enough, then, just to try to maintain correct roles, customs, and so forth; it is also important to learn about and to use the many techniques that can control the numinous powers. The spirits must be kept happy or at a distance. Mana-like power must be controlled magically or avoided. All these things contribute to saving the tribesperson from powers that can upset daily living.

The breakdown of proper order and the intrusion of dangerous numinous powers into life are the two main threats in this life that a tribesperson seeks relief from. Salvation from them means that day by day there will be good food, physical health, familial and tribal peace, individual happiness. But almost every tribe acknowledges the presence of a third disruptive force, one of great importance: death.

Some primitive tribes believe that only the death of very old and weak people is natural. All other deaths are caused by sorcerers using magic or by angry spirits. A number of New Guinea tribes, for example, believe that death is caused by enemy tribes using sorcery, and that the death of a tribesperson by sickness requires vengeance. The oracles are checked to discover which enemy caused the disease; then the tribe goes to war against that enemy. Very old people sometimes believe that even their deaths can be put off indefinitely by the proper magic. After all, no one has to die just today or even tomorrow. At least one more day of life is possible, and then one more. So the old men and women who feel their strength failing may try to hold on to life with the help of various charms, potions, and spells.

No amount of magic or vengeance, however, prevents death from finally coming. Many tribes hold farewell rites to put the dead person's spirit to rest or send it away so that it will not return to cause trouble. Primitive people assume that it is better to be alive than dead, and that spirits of the dead are apt to cause trouble out of envy for the living.

A common alternative belief is that those who have died live in a different place, but one more or less like the one they have just left. The Apatani hill people of Burma and Tibet believe that those who die pass on to a land of the dead which is very much like the usual Apatani village. The guardian spirits there ask each male spirit, for example, how much land he owned, how many wives and chickens and pigs he had, and how many cattle he sacrificed to the spirits. These spirits then assign to the new spirit the same possessions he had before, including the cattle he sacrificed. The new spirit lives another normal life this way until he grows old and dies once more. Then he passes on to yet another Apatani village of the dead, and so on. The Yanomami of the Amazon and the Tobriand Islanders of the southwest Pacific have similar ideas. By such beliefs, the sting is taken from death, even though the new life hoped for is very ordinary. Primitives like their lives, accepting them as the way things are. It does not usually occur to them to imagine a new life after death that is radically different from the life they know, except that it is more often pictured as boring and dreary rather than as pleasant.

Archaic Salvation: An Idealized Life

Archaic people live in a bigger and more complicated universe than primitive people. They know more about the world, about other cultures, about complexities in their own society. They have a greater awareness that there are ways of life other than their own. One way they show this is by picturing the gods as somehow different from themselves, living immortal lives in their own abode apart from mortal people. Another way is by dreaming sometimes of an ideal life that they themselves would like to lead, one quite different from the normal human situation in the world, which would save them from many of life's limitations and miseries.

Primitives seek to stabilize and maintain life as they know it, but also to free it from disorder and sorcery. Archaic people more often look beyond the conditions of life as they experience it to a vision of a better life, one they can imagine even if they do not expect to attain it. Different archaic cultures have different beliefs, some quite simple and others more complex. They often contain elements retained from a more primitive past. That means it is often difficult to classify some of the beliefs as primitive or archaic, but we can apply this rule of thumb: archaic religion is more conscious that this ordinary life is flawed, and is more desirous of a different and utopian mode of existence. Primitive people seek a good life. Archaic people often dream of a better life.

The Golden Age and the Fall

One way archaic people show their awareness that life is seriously flawed is by their stories or myths about a time back in the beginning when life was not flawed. These stories also make some sense out of the disconcerting fact that life is now flawed, by describing an original mistake or evil deed that caused the present miseries. A good number of cultures have some story of an ideal primordial state without sickness or death, without anger or war, without drought or flood, without vermin or poisonous animals. This past and ideal state is often called a "golden age."

The story in the Old Testament about the garden of Eden is an example of belief in a golden age. In this early Hebrew story from archaic times, Yahweh is pictured a little like a god of polytheistic beliefs (he walks in the garden in the afternoon to be cooled by the breeze). This Yahweh created a man and a woman and a garden of plenty where they lived. In the garden was the tree of life from which they could eat and therefore live forever, it seems. But there was another tree also, of the knowledge of good and evil, from which they were forbidden to eat. A serpent persuaded the woman to eat from this tree (women are frequently blamed for humankind's troubles—by men, of course). She persuaded the man to eat from it also. As punishment the couple was expelled from the garden. They were cursed so that ever since then people have had to earn their bread with sweat and weariness, women bear children with pain, and all people die and return to dust. Once there was a golden age but because of the primordial act of disobedience rust, rot, and sadness afflict everything.

Similarly the Nuer tribe of north central Africa tells of a time when heaven and earth were joined. The heaven in this story is not some invisible realm but simply the sky above where a great god named Kwoth lives. People once lived in heaven too. They were happy and healthy; they did not die. Heaven and earth were joined by a rope. One day a mischievous hyena cut the rope. Those people who had been temporarily down on earth gathering some food were trapped here. Unable to return to heaven people now grow old and weak and eventually die. Today their descendants are born, live for some years, and then also die. In another African story, that of the Tutsi, the ancestor of humankind, Nyinakigwa, lived in heaven. She broke her word to Imana, the high god of the sky. As a consequence, she and her children had to leave the heavenly realm and fell to earth, where to this day there is hunger, suffering, and death.

People today in our supposedly forward-looking age still also look backwards to the beginnings, to the original ideal society. Atlantis, Mu, Lemuria are all names of mythical or legendary empires of great power and accomplishments. Various books speculate that earth was long ago visited by space people. There are many tales of the wisdom of the Ancients, of the secrets of lost civilizations. People dream of returning to an idealized and innocent state of nature. Each of these ideas represents a suspicion that once things were better than they are now, that our present limits and liabilities are not natural or inevitable but the result of some primal fall from truth, wisdom, and power. If all of us felt truly at home in our present world, such stories would be less popular than they have been.

Sometimes the story about the original error or fall offers no particular hope that the error can ever be rectified. There is a kind of numb acceptance of the sad conditions of life. The Nuer tribal story that tells of the hyena and the rope does not offer hope for a day when heaven and earth will be reconnected, although they do believe that the high god Kwoth will continue to care for them on earth. The Tutsi, however, who tell of Nyinakigwa's fall, believe that one day Imana will no longer be angry and will allow all of Nyinakigwa's children to return to the sky, to happiness and unlimited life. Such a hope for the future, when the present sadness will be eliminated, is a hope common to much of humankind.

The Millennium and Apocalypticism

"Millennium" has come to be the label for any future utopia or ideal society. The best known millenarian beliefs in Western culture are those based on Jewish apocalypticism, which in turn may be based on Zoroastrian ideas described in Chapter Three. The word "apocalypse" is an ancient Greek word meaning "revelation." During the period of approximately 200 BCE to 150 CE many supposed revelations were circulating in Jerusalem and other places. A few of these writings are now part of Judaic and Christian scriptures, in the books of Daniel and Revelation, for example. They were said to be revelations from God or an angel or some ancient hero about future events. Jewish apocalyptic literature promised that foreign domination over Jerusalem would be overthrown by God's power. He would send his anointed one ("messiah" in Hebrew) who would then rule over a perfect world. As the prophet Isaiah had once promised, Israel would be a light to all nations, bringing peace and prosperity. In the Christian version Jesus would return to rule as the Christ (*christos* = "anointed" in Greek) over all the earth.

Some of these writings predicted a catastrophic end to this world-order. Fire would fall from the skies, the earth would tremble, the armies of good would clash with the armies of evil. Finally, all evil forces would be defeated. Then a new earth and a new sky above would be built out of the rubble. All those who had remained on the side of good would live on in the new earth, the heavenly kingdom of God on earth. In some of these revelations it was even said that good people who had died would be raised up from the dead and live on also in the new kingdom. The word "apocalyptic" has come to be used to label all visions that predicted a violent and sudden destruction of this world-order in order to usher in a new and perfect world-order. Even today, anyone who predicts a catastrophic end of the world is said to be preaching apocalyptic ideas.

In the Christian New Testament the last book is the book of Revelation of John ("The Apocalypse of John"). It too predicts the end of the world. There will be worldwide upheavals and natural catastrophes. The forces of good and evil—people, angels, and demons—will face off. On the plains of Meggido (Armageddon) in Israel the climactic battle between the Christ (Greek for "anointed," i.e., "messiah") and the Anti-Christ will take place. There the power of God will overcome the power of Satan. Then God will send the Christ to rule over a perfect kingdom centered on Jerusalem for a thousand years. (Later Satan will briefly be released only to be defeated again permanently.) The word for one thousand years is "millennium." Those who wait for the thousand-year reign of Christ are said to be waiting for the millennium to arrive.

Various Christians have used the book of Revelation as a guide to interpret the signs of their times. Many early Christians awaited the end of this world-order in their own times. During the Middle Ages in Europe there were many predictions that the end of this world was at hand and that Jesus was about to return. At times people left their farms and their families, devoted themselves to prayers and fasting, or went on pilgrimages, to prepare themselves for the coming of the end. Still today major religious groups such as Seventh Day Adventists and Jehovah's Witnesses expect the end of the world before too long, and many individual Christian ministers and believers see all around them the signs predicted in the book of Revelation coming true now, omens of the end of this world-order. Wars, pestilence or plague, famine, earthquakes, increasing immorality, and even an increase in knowledge (because of a single line in the Hebrew scripture's book of Daniel on this last point) are taken to be signs that the end is near.

There are many beliefs outside of the Christian tradition that anthropologists have called millenarian beliefs. In spite of the name, many of these beliefs do not involve any one-thousand-year period. And not all of them call for a destructive apocalyptic end of the current world. Any expectation that this current world-order will soon be ended and a new utopian life created is now labeled "millenarian." In North America at the end of the nineteenth century, the Native Americans of the Western plains began to preach a set of ideas associated with a ghost dance (or spirit dance). Dispossessed of their lands and the buffalo, dislocated and discouraged, Native Americans in the West began to spread the belief that if they would return to the old tribal ways established by their ancestors, then the ancestors' spirits (ghosts) would set things right, eliminating the foreign intruders, bringing back the buffalo, and creating a happy society. This was to happen soon, not in a thousand years. Nor was the happiness to last for just a thousand-year period. Nonetheless, anthropologists have called this a millenarian movement.

Other movements today can also be called millenarian, even in forms that do not appear to be religious. The hope of many Marxists, for example, had been that in a few generations the principles of Marxism would triumph, bringing peace, prosperity, and happiness to the human race. New Age enthusiasts hope for a state of cosmic harmony to arrive soon, a millennium of sorts but without a catastrophe to usher it in. Each of us at some times in our lives may have become attached to a utopian vision of a society to come, when everyone on earth would finally have learned to live in love and peace. Whether this utopia is ushered in by an apocalyptic catastrophe or by a gradual evolution, it would in either case now be called a millennium.

As you may be able to tell from the examples given, millenarian thought is also sometimes part of historic religion. The line between archaic and historic thought is blurred, because historic modes of thought arise out of and borrow heavily from archaic culture, and continue to mingle with it. Like archaic thought such beliefs are expressed in myth-like stories rather than in the systematic analyses found in historic theologies. They are also archaic in that the ideal life they seek is usually in an idealized world here on earth. We will see that the historic style in religion seeks something more than this. Finally such stories are archaic to the extent that they disregard the question of the Ultimate in a full sense. They settle for a godlike being powerful enough to win out eventually over all enemies, as Ahura Mazda wins out eventually over Ahriman.

From Archaic to Historic Religion

Humankind long ago stumbled toward monotheism, trying out beliefs like those about Akhenaton and Zoroaster, approaching a clearer belief in a universal and unifying numinous Power. At the same time many began to despair of this world as a place for human happiness or fulfillment. The human mind became more and more accustomed to thinking about unqualified perfection, as it did when thinking of an ultimate unity behind the confusions and conflicts of life. Human imagination began also to look beyond this incorrigibly flawed earthly existence to a fully perfect reality beyond. A golden age or a millennium began to seem merely ideal, a great improvement but not absolutely perfect. Only an utterly other-worldly realm would suffice. World-rejection did not appear suddenly in fully finished form. It began in late archaic and early historic times with a belief in an otherworldly but earthlike paradise, and its counterpart, hell.

Paradise: A Perfect but Physical World Beyond the World

The archaic beliefs in a golden age or millennium portray an idealized life on earth, past or to come. Archaic societies have also believed in some existence after death, though they do not always expect much from it for most people. It is pictured at times as a shadowy life of boredom, as in the Hades of Greek thought, or as a lifeless place of unending sleep, as in the Sheol of ancient Hebrew beliefs. A few heroes or favorites of the gods might have a very pleasant time of it, but not most people. As the axial age arrived, however, belief in life after death took a new turn.

Discouraged thoroughly by the newly perceived finitude of earthly life, estranged from life as it exists in this world, religious thinkers around the time of the axial age began to envision a perfect existence beyond this world. An early version of this is belief in a paradise. The word, which comes to us through a Greek form based on an old Persian word, meant a beautiful park with deer and fruit trees and flowing water. This is the sort of afterlife promised by Zoroaster to followers of Ahura Mazda. Islamic belief offers paradise after death to those Allah has chosen. Many Christians picture eternal life in a heaven as a paradise, although the trees and streams are sometimes replaced with clouds and harp-playing angels.

In the East, Hindus and Buddhists look forward to at least a temporary stay in a paradise, though this is not full and final salvation. Pure Land Buddhism, for example, popular in Japan and formerly also in China, made hope for paradise a focal idea. According to this form of Buddhism, there was once a golden age on earth when people followed the ways of the Buddha and achieved enlightenment as Siddhartha Gautama did. But as time passed, people slowly became less and less enlightened and finally lost their ability to follow the teachings of the Buddha at all. But the Buddha-power that existed in Siddhartha Gautama exists also in many beings, including the divine Amida-Buddha, a kind of godlike Buddha. Fortunately for people in this present fallen age, Amida has the power to transport those who trust him straight to a Pure Land after their deaths, to a paradise. In this Pure Land everyone can finally learn enlightenment as the Buddha did and then achieve the salvation that lies beyond all paradises (which we will talk about soon).

Hell: The Opposite of Paradise

In its earliest stages, historic religion has tended to believe not only in a perfect paradise rather than in just another life after death; it has also believed in various hells. Primitive and archaic religions believe that a person who is not buried properly, or whose death is not avenged, or who is not offered enough food through sacrifices, may end up troubled and unhappy. They have also pictured life after death as a shadowy and dreary state, not exactly hellish, but simply boring. That was the lot of those who went to the shadowy underground land of Hades or Sheol, which was like a place of sleep. (The ancient Egyptian belief in a happy afterlife for morally good people was unusual for a polytheism.) Early historic religion, however, has a tendency to create full-scale hells, some temporary and some everlasting.

From Zoroaster to contemporary times people in the West have often believed that there is a hell, a place of everlasting fire and torment. Many have claimed that such beliefs should not be taken too literally, but the words traditionally used make hell a truly terrible existence, a place of utter and unrelenting torment.

Some forms of Buddhism also have traditions about a hell or many hells. An educated Buddhist will say these descriptions are only poetic metaphors and not literally true, but popular beliefs portray hell very graphically. One such description describes hell as a place of excrement, of bitter-tasting dung mixed with molten copper in which there are worms with diamond-sharp beaks. The sinner who dies awakens in hell being eaten by the worms. They start with his lips, tongue, and throat, until finally the sinner is eaten from inside out, only to find himself alive again and due for more punishment. This particular hell is for anyone who kills a bird or animal for supper without feeling regret.

Zoroastrian and Buddhist thought, each in its own way, offer some assurance that hell will not be everlasting. Terrible as it is, someday it will come to an end. All evil, even the evil of being in hell, can pass away. Christianity has traditionally been less sparing. Those who have deserved hell will have to suffer there forever and ever. Some Christians in modern times have had doubts about how literally this should be taken. Perhaps, they have suggested, belief in an unending hell is just a dramatic way to express thorough antagonism to evil. An all-good God might also be all-forgiving. An all-powerful God might be able to conquer evil totally by leaving no pain or agony anywhere in existence.

Though belief in paradise and hell occur in early historic religion, these beliefs have distinctly archaic aspects. The angels and demons are like gods. They are spirit-beings, invisible to humans, but with great power. The beliefs are also expressed in mythic narratives rather than in the more abstract language that historic religions came to favor. This archaic character stands out when the ideas of paradise and hell are compared to more fully historic belief in a fully spiritual heaven, or absorption into Atman, or dissolution into nirvana.

Historic Religion: Perfection Beyond

Salvation through Cosmic Order

Before talking about a perfect reality beyond this world we should give some space to the idea of a perfect worldly order. The forerunner of this idea is the unspoken assumption among primitive people that the order established at the beginning of things is the way things are and now must be. This idea continues into archaic thought, such as Egyptian belief in "ma'at," a word sometimes translated as "truth," which is the basic order of the universe. In historic cultures the idea becomes even more explicit, as in the belief in India in a cosmic pattern of justice known as karma, and in the basic natural set of duties (dharma) people should obey.

China has been a civilization thoroughly dominated by the belief that there is a proper order to all things and that adherence to this order provides salvation. The two main forms of this are found in the two traditions native to China, Taoism and Confucianism. In each the historic interest in perfection eventually appeared, although these religions were more world-accepting than historic religion usually is. In general the history of China is harder to fit into Bellah's categories of religious evolution than are other traditions.

Confucianism is as much a social philosophy as a religion. It arose about the same time as Taoist thought and shared Taoism's indifference towards the high god or gods. The movement stems from the wisdom writings ("Analects") of Kung Fu-Tzu, "Confucius" in Latinized form. Confucius preached social order based on a harmony among human beings. This in turn came from adherence to "li," proper behavior and observance of customs. Conformity to li would bring about salvation from family discord, from social injustice, from political unrest, and from war. By CE 1200, a neo-Confucian called Chu Hsi had elaborated on the concept of li and described it as the cosmic right order to which all people ought to adhere.

Taoism also offered certain kinds of salvation through an understanding and acceptance of the eternal Tao and its major manifestation, the yang/yin pattern to all things. Some Taoists have always been more archaic than historic in their attitudes. In facing the problem of death, for example, many Taoists have sought to use their knowledge of yang/yin in a kind of magical way. They have analyzed the kinds of food people can eat to determine which has more yang and less yin. The ordinary person may want to mix beans and rice rather equally for lunch, because this would provide a nice balance of yang and yin aspects. Older people, however, are apparently losing yang, the more active and energetic principle, and need more of it. For vigor in old age, then, go heavy on the beans. Some Taoists spent years devising strange mixtures of gold and other elements into various kinds of food, in order to create a potion that could extend life indefinitely.

The more philosophical Taoists, however, found their salvation from the threat of death through a correct attitude. Meditation on the patterns of nature would produce an inner sense of the fundamental rightness of the natural. Death is as natural as life. So the Taoist would learn to accept it without fear or concern. Chuang-Tzu, the ancient Taoist, was found humming and making pottery in his yard the day after his beloved wife of many years had died. His friends were shocked that he should act so cheerful rather than be in mourning. Chuang-Tzu replied by asking what wisdom there was in mourning over what was as natural as eating or sleeping. A good Stoic might agree. Unlike philosophical Taoists and Stoics, however, the historic religions of the West or of India, including the Buddhism that eventually became very strong in China and Japan, looked away from this world to another reality. Bellah characterizes them as world-rejecting religions.

Heaven beyond Paradise

Western religions to this day have balanced the late archaic and early historic belief in a physical other-worldly paradise with belief in a spiritual heavenly existence wherein even the limitations of paradise are surpassed. (As we will see, the religions of India did something comparable.) For most of us, the idea of a merely perfect God is more appealing than that of an Absolute. Likewise, a merely perfect paradise can be more attractive than a spiritual heaven, as you may judge for yourself. Yet the same restless human mind that can conceive of ultimate, infinite, and incomprehensible Reality can also question the adequacy even of a physical paradise.

The movement away from belief in a mere paradise began with a change in the idea of spirit. As we have seen, primitive and archaic people think of spirit as physical stuff like air or breath, thin and usually invisible but solid enough to feel. When primitive and archaic cultures speak of a life after death for human spirits, they imagine it as a kind of earthly life, a physical place suited for physical spirits. If life is to be really human life, even after death, it would have to include the whole human person, body and spirit as one.

When historic religion developed in the West, it at first retained belief in a salvation for the whole person, body and spirit as one. The apocalyptic tradition in Judaism, one among various alternative traditions, had looked for a kingdom of heaven on earth. The living would enjoy it and the religiously faithful who had already died would be resurrected into a new whole life in this millennial kingdom. Christianity inherited this belief and preached a bodily resurrection of the dead into the kingdom of God in the new earth following the apocalyptic end of the old one. The Qur'an, Islam's sacred book, describes paradise in ways that make it a heavenly garden full of physical comforts.

These Western religions, though, have had a tendency to minimize or ignore the physical aspect of life after death and to describe it in a purely spiritual way. They have accepted a more radically distinctive meaning to the word "spirit" as something utterly unphysical and unearthly. This was due to the influence of Greek philosophy, and perhaps indirectly due to Hindu ideas as well.

Dualism of Matter and Spirit

In 399 BCE the Greek philosopher Socrates (469-399 BCE) died by drinking a cup of hemlock. He had been accused and found guilty by the citizens of Athens of denying the reality of the gods and of corrupting the youth of Athens by leading them away from traditional beliefs. He accepted the punishment as a way of showing his dedication to the ideas he stood for. But when it was time for him to die his friends began to cry. To console them he gave them a few reasons to believe that it would only be his body that died, not his soul.

The story of Socrates' death is contained in a short work called the Phaedo written by Socrates' disciple, the great philosopher Plato (427?-347 BCE). This story became one of the main sources in all of European civilization for the belief in the immortality of the soul. Plato begins his version of the argument with the idea that there are two major elements in each person, body and soul; and that these two elements are entirely different from each other.

Matter is limitation, Plato argued, using the figure of Socrates to say these things; whatever is material is imperfect, flawed, changeable, and therefore subject to decay. Spirit on the other hand belongs to the realm of what is perfect and changeless. The basic evidence for this is our own knowledge. The inner spirit-power we call mind is able to conceive of things as perfect and unflawed. For example, it can conceptualize the abstract idea of perfect oneness, a simple unity without parts, complexity, or division, even though in the actual physical world no such perfect oneness exists. Similarly the mind can conceive of perfect justice, a state wherein all things exist in perfect order, even though in the actual physical world justice is always partial and imperfect.

Plato concluded that there are two levels of reality: one is the space-time realm of matter; the other is the invisible and timeless realm of pure essences (also called Ideas or Forms). These essences are the basic, unchanging, and perfect natures reflected in mixed and confused form in the material world. Behind the material reality we perceive lies the eternal realm of perfect and pure goodness, truth, beauty, oneness, justice, and so forth. If you cannot form any image of goodness as such, not this good thing and that good deed but just pure goodness, you are on the right track. Pure goodness, pure beauty, pure justice, apart from all concrete instances, belong to the perfect realm of essences, which no images can adequately express. Only abstract concepts can categorize them. The fact that our minds can conceive of them abstractly is evidence that our mind is not material. If it is "spirit," it is an immaterial spirit, belonging not to material reality but to the eternal and perfect realm of essences. We can call this notion of spirit by the traditional name, "soul."

It is very strange, in fact, Plato thought, that we live a bodily existence at all. Plato believed that the human soul is like a prisoner in the body. Some primordial flaw, some unknown ancient mistake has trapped us for a time in material existence, in time and space. But bodies die. The human soul cannot die, for it belongs to what is eternal and changeless. Our souls are naturally immortal.

We should use our time on earth to train our minds to be open to what is perfect and eternal in preparation for the death of the body. If we prepare ourselves well, at death our souls will pass back into the perfect realm of essences. Then we will spend a timeless forever in blissful contemplation of the perfection of the essences. This will be our salvation from all estrangement, for then we will have found our true home and perfect happiness without end. If we do not prepare ourselves well, however, we will be reborn in another material body. Then we will have another chance to learn to love the realm of perfection and become worthy of it.

To exist forever in mental contemplation of perfect essences is not the average person's idea of a joyous life after death. Nevertheless, from Plato's time until today the idea of the soul as a purely non-material being, intrinsically immortal, has had great influence. Plato's thought affected Christian ideas about life after death (as well as those of Islam and Judaism in different ways).

The first Christians, as was mentioned, looked forward to an apocalyptic end of this world-order and the establishment of a millennial kingdom of God on a new earth. Those who had already died would experience a resurrection of the whole person, transformed into new life in this kingdom. Christian tradition has maintained that resurrection from the dead includes bodily resurrection. But this tradition has often been overshadowed by an emphasis on the life of the soul in heavenly existence after death, as a "beatific vision." The happiness of the soul in heaven will thus consist in an eternal contemplation of God. The mental vision of God's absolute and infinite perfection will overwhelm the soul and produce in it unspeakable and unending bliss. There is little mention of any bodily existence in the usual language about this beatific vision. The notion of "heaven" has also shifted from its original meaning as a name for the skies above where the planets and stars move about. Many Christians tend to speak of heaven as an utterly nonmaterial reality.

Another aspect of Platonic thought that has had an effect in the West is the notion that materiality is a trap or prison and that only the soul has eternal life and value. About the same time that apocalyptic ideas were gaining popularity among many Jews, a form of thought known as gnosticism was spreading among educated Greek-speaking people who were scattered all around the countries of the eastern Mediterranean. Gnosis is the Greek word for "knowledge." Gnostics were people who agreed with Plato that our inner self was an immortal soul belonging to the realm of perfect ideas. Most people, the gnostics argued, had lost sight of their true nature as minds that belong to the nonmaterial realm of spirit. In order to achieve a lasting freedom from being born into a physical body, people must come to know who they really are, and they must know this clearly and fully. They must live in the spiritual realm and not be distracted by their bodies.

These gnostic attitudes were accepted by many people. They may have influenced Mani, a Persian who lived in the third century CE and borrowed ideas from Zoroastrian, Buddhist, and Christian thought. Mani's movement, named Manicheism, preached that caring for the body would perpetuate the power of the body to hold the inner spirit captive. The way to liberation was the way of asceticism, the practice of denying oneself any pleasures. In particular Mani declared that sex was the pleasure most to be avoided because it had great power to keep people interested in physical existence. Manicheism and many forms of gnosticism together influenced early Christianity. In spite of biblical statements that God intended there to be sex and that God made this physical world and called it good, a variety of Christian groups in history declared that sex is either always sinful or at least mildly degrading, something to be avoided by anyone who is interested in spiritual values.

Platonic ideas also live on today, occasionally mixed with beliefs from India, in a number of fairly significant religious movements. (The compatibility of Indian and Platonic thought may not be coincidental; there are signs that one of them may have borrowed from the other.) For example, Christian Science, the belief of the Church of Christ Scientist founded in Boston in the nineteenth century by Mary Baker Eddy, says that people are basically souls. A soul should have power over the lesser forces of matter. True spiritual understanding and faith should make medical help unnecessary; mind should be able to cure body. There are also a number of theosophical schools of belief that proclaim that we are souls who have been assigned to our particular bodies and earthly lives in order to test and train us for greater spiritual and mental advances in a spirit realm or astral plane, as it is sometimes called.

In the Western historic religions today there is a range of belief in an ideal life after death, from the somewhat archaic-style belief in a millennial kingdom on earth, to the early historic paradise-like heaven, to an utterly spiritual heaven. It is generally safe to characterize Western historic religions as religions that look for salvation in a life to be achieved when this current world has been utterly transformed or rejected. This otherworldly emphasis has lasted until today. (We will eventually see that modern religiousness includes a return to a fuller appreciation of this world.)

Salvation in India as Dissolution of the Self

To reject this world completely is a fairly drastic way to seek salvation from the alienating conditions of life. Major religious traditions in India have gone a step further. Hindus and Buddhists say that to escape fully from pain and frustration, to achieve final and lasting salvation, a person must escape not only from the world but even from individual selfhood. Only when there is no longer an individual "you" at all is there salvation.

While people of the West hope for life after death, the Hindu and Buddhist are afraid that we are all condemned to have to live again after death. Hindus say that each of us is a soul or self that is born into the world and dies, and then is reincarnated again tens of thousands of times. In each one of these thousands of lives there will be suffering. Never mind that a particular life might be joyous or healthy, for it will eventually end and be replaced by more suffering.

We earn happiness by our good deeds and by our acceptance of our duties. The cosmic law of justice called karma guarantees that we are eventually repaid exactly for all our good and our evil in one or more of our reincarnations. Every action has its consequences, and no one performs only perfect actions. We make mistakes, grow weak, and sin, and so we earn more suffering. Popular Hindu and Buddhist beliefs say also that we spend time between our incarnations on earth in a paradise or hell, as we have deserved. But even these pass away, and we are each threatened again by rebirth into this world. We are trapped in a sequence of action and consequences, lifetime after lifetime.

The Buddha, Prince Siddhartha Gautama, lived in Nepal in the sixth century BCE. Buddhist tradition says that as he was growing up, his father had protected him from the sight of human misery. One day he wandered from the palace and was shocked by the sight of a hungry and ragged old beggar. He abandoned his home and family to try to discover how such misery could exist and what could be done about it.

After years of searching and learning, he finally reduced all his insights to a few essential ideas: all life is suffering; we suffer because we have desires; the only salvation from suffering consists of letting go utterly of all desires, all attachments and cares. Those who let go completely will pass into the condition called nirvana when they die instead of having to be reborn again. Nirvana is an extinction of individual self, a kind of not-being. (In fact the Buddhist teaching of anatta—literally "no-self"—says there really is no true self; each of us is just a collection of attachments that produce a new "self" when the old one dies.) Nirvana is also beyond comprehension, the Buddha said, so there is not much use in speculating on what it is like.

Since the time of the Buddha, many reinterpretations of his ideas have grown up and spread throughout the world. Many of these reinterpretations speak of a kind of Buddha-land where a self may dwell in happiness. But eventually a person must let go completely of all attachment, life, and self to attain nirvana. This alone is salvation.

The Hindu tradition has similar ideas about final salvation. Being born again and again is the basic problem. The only way to escape it is to cease to be a self at all, to bring a complete end to one's individual identity. That leaves, then, only what alone was real in a person, which is the presence of the eternal Atman-Brahman. It is as though when the individual self lets go, it is dissolved back into the cosmic ocean of Brahman.

The Hindu tradition says it can take many thousands of lifetimes to reach this letting-go. When we are born for the first time (why this happens is not quite clear), we have many desires. We find value in pleasure. It is perfectly natural, says Hindu belief, for a person to take great joy in good food and comfortable sleep and intimately loving sex, in majestic scenery and the excitement of adventure, in the beauty of great art and in the smile of a child. But when a person has devoted a thousand or ten thousand lifetimes to pleasure, it will all become dull. Then a person may find life's values in success, in fame and power and wealth. But eventually through thousands of lives a person will have achieved so many things so often that all success will be empty. Then a person will find life meaningful through devotion to the needs of others. A lifetime or ten thousand lifetimes can be spent in unselfish service: clothing the naked, feeding the hungry, consoling the wretched, loving the orphan, the bereaved, the lonely. But this too will prove to be an endless task, raising eventually in a person's mind a doubt about all life. Life itself will continuously produce more people to serve and be served. Generation after generation, the trail of human joy and misery goes on and endlessly on. Eventually each person comes to face the ultimate question of the purpose of things: what is any of it truly worth?

Even an endless life in paradise is not enough to answer this question. To endure forever is not sufficient as a purpose. For what purpose does one endure? The Hindu sees that the human mind can ask the ultimate questions, and because it can a restlessness will inevitably set in, even in paradise, and finally a sense of estrangement about all existence.

Thoughts like these have led Hindus and Buddhists to proclaim that the only full and lasting salvation is to pass beyond all individual existence and to fade into the cosmic ultimate, Brahman to the Hindu and nirvana to the Buddhist. In both cases salvation consists of eternal and unchanging identity with the ultimate reality. This condition is beyond our imagination because it is a union with the incomprehensible Mystery. Western religions usually deny that the individual self ceases to exist after death, but they too often proclaim that salvation is an incomprehensible and blissful union with the Ultimate mystery called God.

All of these ideas about salvation as an incomprehensible union with the Ultimate may sound vague or abstract as well as unappealing. When we worry about life's limitations and experience a sense of estrangement, hope for a millennial utopia or a paradise is usually satisfying enough. If paradise turned out to be boring in an eon or two, that would be time enough to start worrying about a subsequent form of salvation that was even more fulfilling. Yet the fact that Hindus, Buddhists, Christians, and others have looked beyond paradise to an incomprehensible and eternal union with limitless mystery indicates a continuing potential built into our humanness, a potential for the infinite. To be human is to be able to reach out endlessly more.

Summary

This chapter has surveyed the various ways religious traditions have dreamed of an ideal context for human salvation; a good life in primitive thought, a wonderfully ideal-world existence in archaic thought, an otherworldly paradise in early historic thought, and an utterly perfect existence beyond this world entirely in later historic thought. (Later we will see that the modern style of religion has come to appreciate this world again.)

Any ideal context, though, is ideal only if it somehow provides also for our need for acceptance and our need for a sense of worthy selfhood. We need to be saved not merely from a flawed nature or world but also from our estrangement from others and from self. These are the topics of the next two chapters.

For Further Reflection

1. Do you take it for granted that some aspect of ourselves survives physical death, or is this an implausible idea to you? Explain.
2. When you have thought about a life after death, how have you imagined it? Is it like earth in any way at all? Explain.
3. If there were no life beyond death, would this earthly existence be meaningful and sufficient in itself? Explain.
4. Can the world be improved enough to provide adequate earthly happiness for all people? Explain. Do you think that will ever happen?
5. Does it make any sense to you to hope for some kind of beatific vision or even a dissolution of self in relation to an infinite Ultimate? Explain.

Suggested Readings

Hiroshi Obayashi, ed., *Death and Afterlife: Perspectives of World Religions*, 1992. Contains articles by various experts on many major religions of the world.

Christopher Jay Johnson and Marsha G. McGee, eds., *Encounters with Eternity: How Different Religions View Death and Afterlife*, 1991.

Lawrence E. Sullivan, ed., *Death, Afterlife, and the Soul*, 1989. A selection of articles from the *Encyclopedia of Religion*, Mircea Eliade, general editor.

Bernard McGinn, John Joseph Collins, John Joseph, and Stephen J. Stein, eds., *The Encyclopedia of Apocalypticism*, 1998. Three volumes about the history of apocalyptic thought in the West.

Carl B. Becker, *Breaking the Circle: Death and the Afterlife in Buddhism*, 1993.

Daigan and Alicia Matsunaga, *The Buddhist Concept of Hell*, 1972.

Tony Walter, *The Eclipse of Eternity: a Sociology of the Afterlife*, 1996. Looks at the current decline in belief in an afterlife (but a renewed interest in ghosts and such).

CHAPTER SIX

Neither Lost nor Alone

Belonging as a Form of Salvation

When we hear the word "salvation," we usually think of a life after death where we are saved both from the trials of this life and from death itself. Most, though not all, of the beliefs about salvation presented in Chapter Five involved some sort of life after death. The main hope was for an ideal reality or world. Although many cultures expect such a world to be an alternative to this one, achieved after death or in the future, others think of that ideal reality as a here-and-now affair. Primitives seek a here-and-now proper order. Confucian and Taoist ideas emphasize a this-worldly balance to be attained and maintained in our daily lives. Some hopes are focused on a person's daily sense of fulfillment or worth. This chapter and the next will both be concerned with that sort of salvation, a present and ongoing salvation from threats of estrangement, achieved through a sense of personal worth and at-home-ness in daily life by relation to some numinous reality. This chapter will describe various ways religiousness provides a comforting and supportive sense of belonging.

In the course of the descriptions, three complexities will appear. The first is that "belonging" is a fairly broad word, which can include a feeling of being accepted by another person, as well as a conviction that one belongs to a whole community of persons. A person can also have a sense of belonging to something more impersonal such as a historical movement, a belief system, or a cosmic order.

A second complexity is that the notion of belonging overlaps with the topics of both the previous and following chapters. There is no way to be fully clear when salvation is a matter of finding an ideal reality and when it is a matter of belonging. These two blend together, as the concrete illustrations here will show. A sense of belonging is also part of a person's identity—the topic of the next chapter. The categories of estrangement from the universe and others and self are a little artificial. Our life is one; our problems are one;

our salvations are also one. All is one because underneath all the categorized compartments of our lives is one basic reality—the human person conscious of self and therefore needing to have a sense that life is meaningful in the face of the mysteries that our consciousness enables us to perceive.

The third complexity is one created by the outsider's perspective on the study of religion which we are taking here. The outsider can see a believer being saved from estrangement in ways the believer might not even recognize. Religious traditions sometimes tell the believer that just belonging to the tradition instead of being lost and alone is already a kind of salvation. We will see examples of this. But the outsider can see many instances when the feeling of belonging is not explicitly recognized by a tradition as a kind of salvation, even though this belonging does in fact free the believer from what otherwise would be a painfully estranged state.

As usual, there is some advantage in dividing up the topic into smaller and more manageable categories. The categories are only approximations. How many ways can a person feel lost and alone? How many ways can a person find a sense of belonging? In each case too many to count. But here are two main categories, each with subdivisions. The first involves a special one-on-one relation to a numinous being, power, or order. The second involves being part of a larger social context.

Individual Devotion to a Numinous Reality

Throughout time people have devoted themselves to offering attention, praise, gifts, affection, and obedience to various numinous powers. Often these offerings are simply means of persuasion carefully calculated to bribe, flatter, or seduce a spirit or god into granting some favor. But as was mentioned briefly in Chapter Two, at times the attention paid to the gods is a way of achieving a kind of psychological salvation through a sense of belonging. This world can be a dreary and disappointing place to many individuals. Hope for an afterlife, paradise, or heaven can sustain a weary and lonely person for a long time. Years of nothing but aloneness, however, of being only marginally significant to others, of being powerless in a world where others accomplish great things, is a very heavy burden to bear. Hope for eventual joy after death might not be enough to sustain a person. During life's long years there is a need for additional consolation and support. Devotion to a numinous reality can provide this.

Devotion to a Personal Numinous Being

Spirits, ancestors, saints, angels, gods, and God are not only numinous but are also personal. They are beings you can address as friendly, thoughtful, helpful, and even loving persons. Followers of the Hindu gods Shiva or Vishnu or the goddess Sri carry their statues in processions, build beautiful temples to them, and surround their statues with lights and burning incense. A small food offering, a bunch of flowers, a carved bit of wood honor the god. The many local spirits in Japan each have their own shrine, ceremonies, and day of celebration. Orthodox and Catholic Christians celebrate feast days of various saints and angels with processions and other ceremonies. All these numinous personal beings are treated with respect, affection, and praise. This is partly to win their favor, but it is also simply to rejoice in having them as benefactors with whom a person can be a friend or intimate.

The full value of having a numinous personal being as friend is manifest in the private side of devotion. Whether during a great public ceremony or in the quiet of a nearly empty shrine, each person can cherish the thought of the spirit, saint, or god whose attentiveness makes up for all the thoughtless people in life. The saint in heaven knows the innermost feelings of a person who is misunderstood by everyone else. The love given by Vishnu is not the critical and selfish love of a human partner but a forgiving and generous love. To know that Jesus loves you with enormous and divine love washes away your insignificance or failure and makes you equal in worth to the greatest person who ever lived. In fact, the gods, spirits, and God are often said to have a special love and concern for the weak, the forgotten, those who suffer in life. The same burdens of powerlessness and pain that threaten to crush people actually make them more significant, more worthy of divine care and affection. This belief is a form of salvation from feelings of insignificance and aloneness.

Whether the devotion be public or private, it can vary in degrees of intensity. For most religious people, to have devotion to a god or saint is important but not all-important. In every religious tradition, however, there are those who give their entire lives in service to a divine or numinous person. There are monks and nuns in East and West, priests, hermits, gurus and prophets, who devote their entire lives to prayer, attention, and devotion to a form of the Buddha, to Shiva or his consort Kali or to Jesus. We will see more about such people later. These find the entire worth of their lives in devotion to a numinous being.

As we have noted, there is a tendency around the world to believe that suffering somehow merits special attention from the gods or God. As though the pains in life that come to a person by themselves were not enough, out of religious devotion people will inflict additional suffering upon themselves. People have beat themselves with whips, starved themselves, lived in cold and darkness, all to show their devotion to a god or God. Some pain in life is unavoidable; at other times pain is deliberately accepted as part of a training program; but religious movements have included people who believe that suffering is somehow pleasing to the numinous being whose attention, forgiveness, or love they seek. Religious people are sometimes masochistic in their devotion, though they would probably deny that the god or God is a sadist who enjoys seeing suffering.

There are various guesses about why this masochism appears in religion. It may be that religion is often a way of making sense of life's sufferings. First we suffer, some of us much more than others. This can make life seem unfair or senseless. Secondly, we find a way of making sense of this mystery of suffering by a religious explanation: the spirits are punishing us for violating the customs; the gods are angry at our meager offerings; the balance of Tao's nature has been upset by our excesses; God is putting us to the test. Thirdly, we then come to think of suffering as a good thing because it helps to maintain the customs, improve the offerings, balance nature, and prove our worth. Fourthly, we go overboard and conclude that because suffering is good we should seek it.

There are other possible explanations for religious masochism. Perhaps childhood memories are unconsciously at work. When a child is hurt, parents grow very attentive and loving. Parents are sometimes angry at children until the children are punished; then the anger is gone. Perhaps suffering is a proof of devotion. We are touched by someone who makes sacrifices for us; we are sure then that someone truly cares for us. So we make sacrifices for our gods so they will know we truly love them. In any case, the greater our fears that the spirits or gods might not care for us, the greater the motivation to suffer in order to evoke their concern and merit their love. The greater a person's sense of guilt, the more a person might believe that only suffering can restore the person to favor in the god's eyes. If nothing else, religious masochism is a sign of the immense human need to be accepted, forgiven, and cherished. To achieve this is a form of salvation.

Devotion to the Right Order of Things

A person can live a life of devotion not only to personal beings such as spirits, gods, or God, but also to impersonal numinous order. In the previous chapter we have seen that the primitive person devotes energy to maintaining the order established at the beginning times. We have talked also about the beliefs of Confucianists, Taoists, and Hindus who believe in a sacred cosmic order. It is possible to achieve a sense of belonging by harmonizing one's life with such order.

For some who believe in a cosmic right order, adherence to this order is only a means to a later state of salvation. By conforming to the cosmic law of karma, a Buddhist will get a better chance at eventually achieving the enlightenment that is the gateway to eternal not-being, nirvana. Yet in all cases where people believe in a cosmic order, there is also a here-and-now sense of belonging that is worth treating as a kind of salvation all by itself.

Each of us would like to be able to feel that our lives are lived well and wisely rather than poorly and stupidly. We have to make serious decisions about our life's patterns, and we worry at times that we have made the wrong decisions. Whatever we have accomplished, whatever our work or our social success or our accomplishments, we can all have some doubts about the worth and rightness of who we are. If we are sure that there is one correct way to exist, one natural pattern to things, then we can achieve a sense of rightness to our lives by conforming to that pattern. Thus the ancient Egyptians strove after ma'at, the Stoic deliberately accepted the workings of the universe, the Taoist still seeks to flow smoothly in life with the eternal currents of yang/yin, living in a simple hut, raising a few chickens and radishes, at one with nature.

In each instance some degree of salvation from problems is achieved just for the practical reason that the one order of nature is the fact of things. People who struggle against the currents of nature and time are liable to wear themselves out and still lose in the long run. It can be good practical wisdom to learn to cooperate with the laws of reality. In addition to this practical common sense, there is also a deeper satisfaction that comes from feeling that we belong to the truth, to what is naturally correct, to what is the everlastingly right order to things. It does not matter as much then if on the surface our lives look unimportant, because the deeper truth is that our lives are at one with what alone is finally important, the cosmic order.

Devotion to the right order of things is often connected to devotion to a personal numinous being. If the ancestors or gods established the rules of living, then adherence to the rules is a form of devotion to these sacred beings. A person belongs to the god by accepting the god's decrees. If it is a universal power such as God that has created the natural order, then the person who tries to do what is natural thereby belongs to God. The person who perceives a divine plan and follows it shows devotion to God. For many people, devotion to God is accompanied by a general belief that God has a hidden plan for all things. Whatever happens is God's will; so to accept all things, however confusing or threatening they may be, is a way of accepting and belonging to God and takes the terror out of the universe.

Mystical Devotion to an Absolute

The word "mystical" has various meanings. It is used at times to refer to primitive or archaic style belief in magical powers or spirits. In classical or historic religion the word may be used rather broadly as a label for any strong religious feeling. But historic religions have also used the word for a very specific experience, of an intimate relation to the Absolute Reality, the infinite, eternal, and incomprehensible Ultimate that embraces all things at once. It is the One beyond all limits. It is God the Absolute, Brahman the incomprehensible, Allah the infinite, or the formless and eternal Tao that the mystic encounters in mystical experience.

According to the mystics themselves, this mystical encounter is not really describable because it is not experience in any usual sense of the word. It is not thinking or knowing because this experience takes a person beyond such limited states of consciousness. It may produce certain feelings or emotional states, but it is beyond mere emotions. It is not a seeing or hearing or touching, although metaphors based on sensation or sensory images can provide some poetic ways of speaking about it. The mystics attempt to describe it by saying it is a being-at-one with the One that is All. It is a momentary eternity, a few minutes or hours of identity with the Everything in comparison with which the person is nothing. It is bliss; it is nothingness. It is ecstasy; it is emptiness. It is a rapture or utter peace. Then, when they have said all these things in an attempt to describe it, the mystics finally reaffirm that it is.... Words might help point a person towards mystical union with the Absolute, but only the experience of it can let a person "know" what it is.

Such experience sounds far removed from the life of a normal person; it is rare, indescribable, strange. But each of the great historic religions has had its mystics. In each major civilization there have been those who have sought and found union with the One as the highest and fullest mode of religious devotion. This devotion is a kind of salvation. Like all people, mystics are aware of the limitations of life. They too have suffered from a sense of estrangement. Yet the union with the absolute One overrides all limits and estrangement by giving the mystic a sense of total belonging. Ordinary feelings of loneliness or dislocation are wiped out by the experience of belonging to the One in perfect union.

After the mystical experience, the limitations of life no longer give rise to feelings of estrangement, because in a moment of total mystical union, peace, bliss, love, and belonging, all earthly limitations have by comparison been made trivial and unimportant. The mystics say that this rewarding feeling is not the real purpose of mystical union. Because the One they seek is alone truly and ultimately of lasting value, it is deserving of unqualified dedication and devotion for its own sake. That, they say, is the real reason they give themselves over to this One. But the sense of belonging to this One is still a form of fulfillment. It is a kind of salvation.

Belonging to a Sacred Community

In many nations today religion is a relatively private matter. People have the option of adhering or not to any religious tradition. But this is a highly unusual situation. Down through history religion has been a shared social matter in a degree only suggested by what was said earlier in Chapter Two on the sociological function of religion. In spite of the option today of religious privacy and even solitude, most people still are religious in at least a semi-public way, in a community of believers. From this communal aspect of religion comes a sense of belonging.

Primitive Religion: Local Community

Religion, community, and individual identity are inseparable in primitive society. Each person discovers his or her identity by learning what the tribe sees as proper behavior, thoughts, and feelings. A given individual will, of course, have a unique personality, a special name, perhaps a singular role such as elder or warrior or mother of many, but these will be within the bounds defined by tribal tradition. Moreover, the traditions are right because they were established at the beginning of things by the original beings. Tribal customs are expressed and reinforced in religious ceremonies. Political, social, and economic decisions may be made with the help of the spirits who communicate by signs and through dreams.

Primitive religious communities are straightforward and clear examples of what sociologists claim when they say that religion functions to support the social order. Shared belief in spirits, taboos, and magic for healing and hexing are sacred threads that tie the pieces of social custom together. Through such beliefs and practices the individual tribesperson gains a sense of belonging not only to the present pattern of tribal life but also to an unchanging and reliable order. So closely united are society and religious practices in primitive society that, as we have seen in Chapter Two, the great sociologist Emile Durkheim thought that religious rituals were actually ways in which primitive people celebrated the power of their social order to rule their lives and give them their identity (though without being consciously aware that is what they were doing).

One of the great problems for tribal societies in today's world of quick travel and easy communication is that they must contend not only with occasional new ideas but with the presence of constant newness. Primitive tribal societies are likely to have a defense against outside influences in a belief common to many tribes, that what happens to outsiders is of no significance for their lives. In tribal languages around the world, the name a tribe uses for itself is the closest word it has to say "human being." When a Yanomamö in

Brazil or a Cheyenne in the American western plains used to say "Yanomamö" or "Cheyenne," they meant "people." In tribal thought the group says, "We are people; the others are not people as we are. We know the spirits and where the mana-powers are. Others do not. We know how to follow the ways of the ancestors, make the moon rise, preserve the truth about the rivers. Others do not. We live as it is correct for people to live in this place. Others do not." The primitive person lives smugly in this unified reality and identity, happy to belong. Much of this is religious, we would say. But for the primitive person the religious element is not distinct from life as a whole. There is usually no word for "religion."

Archaic Religion: "National" Community

Like primitive societies, archaic cultures offer the individual a sense of belonging through identity with a social order given by the ancestors or gods. Devotion to the gods in an archaic society is the same thing generally as devotion to the city, territory, or ruling family in the land. The highest form of patriotism in ancient Rome, for example, was called *pietas*. The religious connotation of the word still exists today in "piety," referring to devotion to God. Roman pietas was indeed devotion to the gods, especially to Jupiter and to Janus, god of war and peace. But this devotion in practice consisted of fidelity to Roman customs. A person who upheld the traditional social and family order was the one who was called *pius*. Even today, people often equate patriotism with religion, saying that God wants people to support their nation and its law and morality.

Through extensive contacts with foreign peoples or "nations," archaic cultures are rather conscious of the differences between themselves and other peoples. Each archaic culture tends to emphasize its own worth and value and disdains other cultures. The "others" are seen as mere barbarians if they are less advanced culturally. Or the "others" are seen as weak and decadent if they are highly civilized. One's own gods and the customs they provide and protect are superior to all others. This attitude, of course, does not exist only among archaic cultures. From primitive to modern times, many people still think in parochial (local) or nationalistic terms about the status and value of other people's thought, culture, and religion. It is a normal human tendency to assert that our ways are better than their ways, whoever they are.

Many archaic societies grew very large, uniting what originally had been smaller and more primitive localities into large cultural groups. This occurred in China, India, and Mesopotamia in the second millennium BCE, and in Egypt before that. In all these places the problem was how to achieve social unity among the various localities. People of different villages could be more united politically if their customs, beliefs, and values could be united. Only a unification of the gods, some form of syncretism, could achieve this.

The conquest of the Shang by the Chou in ancient China (c. 1100 BCE) has been mentioned here already as an example. After the conquest, the Chou king had the problem of how to consolidate his rule over the kingdom of the Shang, how to win the approval and acceptance of the conquered people, who had a sense of belonging to their own land, family, ancestors, and gods. When the Chou arrived, bringing strange gods and customs, there could have been continuing conflict between the two groups. The Shang had the difficult choice of how to maintain a sense of belonging by allegiance to the old ways without setting themselves at odds with the new rulers. The politically astute Chou king proclaimed that the Shang people could maintain devotion both to their god, Shang-Ti, and also to the new king. It was Shang-Ti, the Chou king said, who had empowered him to overthrow the Shang dynasty because that dynasty was corrupt and no longer taking proper care of the people. The Chou king proclaimed that his high god, T'ien, was the same god as Shang-Ti, but under a different name. Therefore, all the peoples of Chou and Shang territories could join together in allegiance to one and the same high god. All who lived in the new unified kingdom could share a common sense of belonging.

The caste system of India provides one of the most monumental examples of complex social organization and unity based on religious belief. The caste system originated in archaic times when the conquering Aryans from the North imposed their rule on the people of the Indus valley and later on other parts of India. At first, perhaps, there was simply the division between the Aryan conquerors who began to arrive around 1500 BCE and their new, darker-skinned subjects. The caste system gradually grew more complex, and was eventually absorbed into the historic-style religion of later centuries and has lasted up until today.

In the usual simplified account there are four basic castes. At the top are the Brahmins, the priests in charge of the rituals. Because they deal with sacred things, they are not supposed to make contact with anything unsacred. Next are the nobles or warriors (the nobility around the world were originally military leaders strong enough to grab territory and rule it). Third are merchants and landowners. At the bottom of the four castes are the many who labor at various tasks. As centuries passed, each caste subdivided. The most exalted Brahmin family might be twenty stages above the lowest Brahmin family group. None would think of being on casual terms with any person more than ten subcastes below his or her own. None would allow marriage to anyone more than four or five subcastes lower. Every person by birth belonged to a very precisely defined level of society with its rules, dietary customs, social privileges, and obligations.

Among the lowest caste some of the work was and is considered so demeaning that it renders the person performing it "untouchable" to those of higher castes. They were once known as "pariahs." Pariahs are not "outcastes." They simply belong to a very low caste. Mahatma Gandhi called them "Harijans," meaning "Children of God," a name that has gained currency. (The British and then the Indian government classified them as "scheduled castes.") A person who is born into a family that washes other people's dirty laundry is of very low caste, but not so low as those who empty latrines. Launderers will not wash the clothes of latrine-workers.

For centuries the people of India cooperated in maintaining this social structure. In every generation there were many individuals who tried to elude the restrictions of the system by pretending to belong to a caste higher than the one they were born into. The sacred writings of India predict severe consequences for those who dare to rebel in this way against the rules that assign them to a specific place in the social order. Every person by birth has a basic *dharma* (duty, set of obligations) to accept his or her place in society and fulfill the role appropriate to it. This dharma is not just a social rule; it is part of the cosmic order, it is the fundamental truth of things. For one born a merchant to seek to become noble is a grave offense against dharma. The person who rebels against the place assigned by birth will thereby deserve to be born the next time to an even lower caste or as a dog or worm. The only way to rise to a higher caste is to perform one's social role so well in this lifetime that it merits rebirth in a higher caste in the next lifetime, in accordance with the cosmic justice called *karma*. Even in a person's lifetime, though, it is possible to become a true outcaste—to have done something so terrible that the person has no social status whatsoever, not even of the lowest caste.

Historic Religion: Universal Community

Primitive, archaic, and historic societies alike all provide the people with assurance that the social order they belong to is correct for them, because that order comes from the numinous power or powers that guide them. Historic religion, however, gives a special interpretation to this.

Historic religion tends to universalize. It proclaims that there is one underlying unity behind the various aspects of nature, and one supreme cause of that unity. There is but one Brahman, one Tao, one God. If there is a divinely approved way, or a way that fits the nature of the supreme numinous reality, there is only one such way. There is but one ideal social order, one correct way to be human, one valid and morally proper behavior pattern, one true human identity.

If there are people in the world who do not follow that one true path, there are two basic ways a historic religion may treat them. One way is to fall back into a primitive or archaic exclusivism and to believe that the others are less than fully human. This is easy for any culture to do, historic or not. The basic tendency to favor one's own clan or people over others is probably innate, always there in tension with whatever historic universalism the culture or religion promotes. We have seen that the Yanomamö and Cheyenne think of themselves as people and others as not quite people. The Chinese always knew foreigners were inferior barbarians. The Europeans who first invaded South and Central America were so startled by the strange ways of some of the more primitive tribes there that they debated whether those tribespeople had souls as full humans do. Once you have decided that the strange people are naturally inferior, you can then justify conquering and ruling them. After all, God or some power made them inferior and thus it is divinely established that they are fit to be ruled by their superiors; or else some enormous sin of theirs merited them this lowly and flawed condition, and such great sinners do not deserve much concern.

The other alternative that historic religions have before them is to judge that all people are in fact equally human. This belief is more consistent with the universalizing attitude of historic religion, and is the actual position most take. It means that all people should live by the one true way for human beings. They should, for example, all worship the one true God, follow the one universally valid set of moral rules, and adapt themselves to the customs of those wise and virtuous people who have already accepted the one true way.

It may sound arrogant for a religious group to claim to have the truth for everyone in the world, but there is also a kind of logic behind the claim. If in fact there is one Tao and one yang/yin order throughout the universe, or if the only real salvation for anyone is dissolution in Brahman, then it would be very wise and most practical for everyone to share these beliefs. If polytheism is true there is no single unifying order or truth to all reality. If atheism is true there is no ultimate meaningful order to human existence at all. But if monotheism or its equivalent is true, then there is one, true, all-encompassing plan or order to reality. Logic then implies that there is one basically correct vision of life that is valid for every human being. On these grounds the Roman Catholic Pope Boniface VIII declared in 1302 that because the Pope is head of the church and the church contains the sole truth for all humankind, therefore all people on earth were subject to the authority of the Pope whether they knew it or not. On these grounds a good Muslim knows that the Qur'an provides the final truth for all people everywhere and should be the universal religion of humankind.

There is usually not only logic but also compassion behind the universalizing claims of historic religion. If people believe they possess the truth that can set all humankind free from estrangement and give them salvation, it would be ungenerous to keep that truth to themselves. Buddhist missionaries went forth for centuries to gently preach the wisdom of the Buddha, out of compassion for all people, though in the third century BCE the emperor Ashoka imposed Buddhism on most of India by force. Islamic forces have waged *jihad,* holy war, to overthrow the kings and armies that oppose Islamic belief, in order to allow people to choose submission to Allah. It would be a great benefit to the whole human race, a Muslim believes, to have all people submit to the holy and divinely wise laws of the Qur'an in a worldwide house of Islam. Christian missionaries have traveled the world to teach people the only way to escape eternal damnation. The missionaries have usually brought with them helpful medicine and education; but they have also accompanied military conquerors. In all of these cases, the outsider can perceive a religious imperialism, but the believer can do no less than share what he or she takes to be a true blessing for all peoples.

A further consequence of the logic of historic religion is to maintain an alliance between church and state. We who live in contemporary industrialized societies are accustomed to think of religion as private and separate from the public structures of government and civil laws. This is a rather modern notion. Boniface VIII would have said it is a foolish and evil idea. One of his later successors, Pius IX, explicitly agreed, listing it among major basic errors of modern times, as he saw it. If the religious authorities have God's sole and universal truth, including divine laws governing all aspects of life, then of course the government should be guided or ruled by the church or by the religious authorities. Belief in a separation between government and church was not officially accepted in the Roman Catholic Church until the 1965 declarations of the Second Vatican Council.

In many Islamic countries it is still maintained that the government must follow the rules laid down in the Qur'an. In the 1970s the ayatollah Khomeini in Iran agreed emphatically with this. He established a ruling council of religious leaders who can reject or revise laws that go contrary to God's will as expressed in the Qur'an. Saudi Arabia is governed by strict religious laws. The governments of Afghanistan and Pakistan have tried to do the same. Such religious rule over the government is called a theocracy. Islamist movements promote theocracy wherever there is a Muslim majority.

This historic tendency to impose a single correct way of life appears in nonreligious forms also. Since the thirteenth century, Neo-Confucian philosophy was the basis for all governmental and family patterns in China. Marxism aspired to become the sole socio-political form of government for people everywhere. The historian Francis Fukuyama proclaimed in a 1992 book that democratic liberal society was the end point of all human history.

Some religious groups in modern industrialized nations still also insist that the governmental laws should uphold the basic moral laws established by God about sex or marriage or abortion and so on. The collection of movements known in the U.S. as the "Religious Right" is such a group. Their goal is not a full theocracy. But they do share a desire that at least some civil matters conform to their religious values.

A historic religion tends to promote its own dominance rather than accept peaceful co-existence with other religions. Religious pluralism has been unappealing to many historic religions. Antagonisms are common, not only between two rather different religious traditions, such as Christianity and Islam, but even within a general religious tradition.

In Europe in the seventeenth and eighteenth century, for example, the divisions among various Christian groups in the wake of the Reformation led to vicious religious wars. Europe learned religious tolerance as much out of exhaustion as out of any high moral ideal. Tolerance came very slowly. The first development was segregation, as each ruler made his or her territory officially Catholic, Lutheran, Calvinist, or Anglican. Tired of internal strife, France tried to achieve mutual tolerance between Huguenots (French Calvinists) and Catholics. The Edict of Nantes of 1598, allowing people religious choice, did not prevent continued hostilities. The dominant Catholics slowly squeezed the life out of the Edict with both military attacks on Huguenot cities and with legal restrictions in the early seventeenth century; later in the same century the Edict was abolished.

Similarly, differences within Islam created mutual antagonisms. In the period after Muhammad's death disputes erupted on who should follow as his successor, or "caliph." The leadership position first went to one of Muhammad's "generals," but Muhammad's nephew Ali thought he should be leader. Eventually Ali ruled but then was assassinated. When his younger son Hussein later tried to become caliph, he and his followers were massacred. Hussein's followers were dispersed but remained powerful in what is now Iran and Southern Iraq and a few other places. The word for "partisan" in Arabic gives rise to the name of this group: Shi'ites. They developed what is sometimes called a clergy, though it is more like a rabbinate, because like Jewish rabbis these are leaders by virtue of their education, not through ritual power (a distinction that will become clear in a later chapter). Those rejecting Ali's claim still constitute the majority of Muslims (perhaps eighty-five percent) and their practices are closer to original Islam. They are called Sunni (Sunna = tradition.).

From among the Shi'ites in Iran (Persia at that time), another movement gradually emerged, now called Sufism. The Sufi sought to experience mystical union with Allah, and elaborated their ideas in both poetry and philosophical form. Many of them formed monastic communities of different sorts. Sufism spread throughout the Muslim world. Most Muslims in the

Sudan, for example, adhere to one of several forms of Sufism there. Among all these groups some degree of mutual intolerance is common. In Saudi Arabia a rather strict form of Sunni Islam arose in antagonism to aspects of Sufism. Shi'ite Iran found it natural to go to war with the Sunni-dominated populace of central Iraq.

Mutual tolerance among groups whose religion is historic is not the norm. We human beings do not seem very ready to follow whatever instructions historic religions may pass on to love one another or respect all life or have compassion for even the stranger and foreigner. We will return to this topic in Chapter Twelve.

Holiness Communities

In various religious traditions, some people feel called to belong to a special holiness community within the larger religious context. If not everyone will strive to live perfectly, at least these few will try.

From early archaic times, the priests or prophets of the temples were sometimes set aside from ordinary people and lived as a holiness community within the larger community. The historic traditions have produced the greatest number and variety of holiness communities. Here the historic ideal of perfection finds an appropriate style of life. The core of traditional Buddhism, for example, is the life of the *sangha*, a community of monks. Buddhism teaches that the cessation of all desire and attachments is the way to salvation. But the ordinary lives of people distract them from salvation by involving them in countless concerns for family, job, friends, entertainment. So life in the sangha is the best way to achieve release from desire. The monk leaves all possessions behind except simple clothes and a bowl with which to beg for food each day. Avoiding all attachments and physical comforts and especially the great distraction of sex, the monk devotes time to meditation on what alone is eternal and worthwhile: release. In the Orthodox and Catholic communities of monks and nuns the details of dress and food-gathering have been different, but the rest is very similar. The goal in all of these is to step aside from the distractions of worldly concerns, to leave behind the world, the flesh, and the devil, and to devote oneself entirely to God.

The explicit goal of a traditional monastic life has been to prepare for an eternal salvation: nirvana or heaven. But this life also provides the person with an ongoing sense of belonging. The monastery is a community of people who share the same vision of life and confirm one another's lifestyle. They pledge themselves to live in harmony and mutual kindness. And as the community is thought to be close to the divine or numinous, it is especially uplifting to be able to belong to it. The lifestyle of holiness communities also prepares a person to enter into mystical contemplation of the Ultimate.

Separation of Society and Religion

The human desire to maintain a unified sense of belonging to family, culture, and religion all at once is very strong, but no person will find total belonging in all aspects of life. There is always some disjointedness, some estrangement. While religion usually helps to overcome such estrangement, occasionally it is a cause of estrangement from some aspects of family or society. Sometimes religion demands that a person make a choice between belonging to the family and society that have nourished that person, or to a religious movement that challenges the family values and societal order.

Possibilities of Separation of Society and Religion

Until modern times, all aspects of life—politics, economics, medicine, family, social class, and so forth—were so intricately tied up in the threads of religious beliefs and values, as we have seen, that any distinction between religion and society has been limited. The cultural context provided each person with religious beliefs that became so familiar as to appear to be the obvious and only truth. The religious beliefs in turn provided the justification for the various cultural patterns. That, at least, is how things most often have been.

Modern experience has made us more aware, though, that religions and culture can diverge or contradict each other. We live in a pluralistic society where many religious traditions exist side by side, and none of them is totally in harmony with all aspects of the culture. From this vantage point we can look back in history and around the world and recognize various modes of separation between religion and society.

Primitive and Archaic Religion

A primitive religion cannot be separated from its social context. The social rules on marriage, for example, could be called religious rules, in that they carry a burden of taboo for the person who violates them. Similarly, the tribe's diet may be dictated partly by the fact that some animals are tribal totems. Religion and society are one. To lose attachment to one is to lose attachment to both simultaneously. As was mentioned, the primitive person's world is a "one-possibility" thing. The person must belong to this social-religious pattern or belong nowhere at all.

Archaic societies also see their social order and their religion as one, but these societies are internally more complex than primitive societies, offering each person alternative roles to play. Archaic societies segregate the roles of priest, king, merchant, landowner, and peasant. The gods are somewhat segregated from daily life also, to the extent that they are more distant than local spirits and mana-powers. All of this creates the possibility that one aspect of society can be in explicit tension with another. The power of the king, for example, cannot simply exist; it must struggle against the individual powers of landowners who do not always want to support the king. Each side in a struggle may claim that the gods are on its side. Because the gods are sometimes fickle, they may even be bribed to change sides.

Historic Religion

Historic religion can be both an intimate part of a social order and a critic of that order at the same time.

Unity between religion and society is easy to find. Hindu thought supported the caste system. Islamic law forbids carved or painted images. Christian tradition declared chaste celibacy to be superior to married life. In each of these cases, religion formed the culture or vice versa, so that they blended into a unity a person could belong to without inner division. Yet the perfectionism of historic religion contains within itself the element of separation from society.

The era of monolatry in ancient Israel provides a very early example of the high moral ideals usually found only in historic (and later) religion. In the eighth century BCE, the prophet Amos felt called to speak in Yahweh's name against social injustices. Amos saw abuses all around him. He saw widows and orphans in poverty; he saw rich people and religious leaders condoning oppression of the poor; he saw people bought and sold into slavery. Amos shouted out that Yahweh rejected these customs and would punish all who "sold the innocent for silver." He declared that the standard religious offerings in the temples were useless; what Yahweh desired was compassion and justice.

Historic religions usually treat compassion and justice as universally valid ideals. Such religions tend to be perfectionist. We have seen that historic religion arose when the human mind became accustomed to thinking about the universal and the perfect. But this world is highly imperfect. There is often a conflict between historic ideals and social reality. Every time people take to the streets today protesting in God's name against injustice, they are demonstrating the kind of tension that inevitably exists between historic religious ideals and society. Archaic religions can do this too, but historic religions by their very nature, by their ability to dream of perfection, are meant to be social critics.

As we have seen, perfectionism can also lead to world-rejection. For some Hindus the world is maya—illusion. For traditional Christianity the world is a vale of tears, made good by God but so corrupted by sin as to be no longer a fit home for humankind. Such thoughts make a person feel he or she does not belong to earth or any part of it, not even to earthly society and culture. No lasting compassion or true justice can be achieved in this world. All earthly things pass away; in comparison with eternity they are neither lasting nor of value in themselves. A sense of detachment is the proper attitude. Belong to heaven, to the eternal, to the otherworldly. Do not put your trust in princes. Do not store up treasure where it can rust. Join a holiness community perhaps.

Ordinarily the religious believer will feel enough at home in the society not to reject or criticize it; it is still true that social and religious belonging usually merge together. After all, it is usual that the society a person grows up in provides and even reinforces the religious beliefs. But when a time of conflict comes, when a person becomes angry at human failure, or is uncomfortable with a social pattern, or cannot accept a cultural value, then religion provides one way of justifying a separation from earthly society. It is not one's true home; it is not where one really belongs.

Some sociologists employ three terms to illustrate how historic (and sometimes archaic) religiousness can function in relation to society: "church" (and sometimes also "denomination"), "sect," and "cult."

Church

A church is an organized body of religious believers that is very closely tied to its cultural context. Like any historic religion, it has some sense that its patterns of belief and practice belong to the divine order rather than the earthly. Yet every religious group is made up of people, and people make up society. So the normal state of affairs is that the same religious people who feel that their practices, morals, and beliefs link them to the eternal are the people whose practices, morals, and beliefs are actually closely linked with society. The word "church" is used by the sociologists to label this normal condition, that of conformity between religion and culture. The strongest form of this is the "established" church, one that is the official religion of the state, as the Lutheran Church is in Norway and the Anglican Church in England.

We see conformity between culture and religion every day. As long as a culture says that only men can be leaders, no women can function as priests. When the culture changes to admit women to leadership, religious groups conclude that it would have been right all along to eliminate any discrimination against women. For centuries Christianity and Islam both condemned usury—lending money at interest. Yet as commercialism increased in Europe, the Catholic Church decided that charging interest on loans was sinful only if the interest was excessive. People who have a sense of belonging to their own society and culture as well as to a historic religion, one that supposedly represents the one universal way of things, will ordinarily find ways to integrate these two forms of belonging. Religion and society blend together on the whole, with moments of tension passing into some workable accommodation. Most religious people today find it easy to blend social and religious belonging.

Sect

Sociologists define a sect as a religious movement that derives many of its ideas from the same dominant religious tradition as the churches, but whose members adhere more fervently and strictly to their beliefs than the average church member. In any society some individuals discover that they are not comfortable with the social reality they have learned from family and neighbors. Some find society to be too immoral, too chaotic, or too uncertain about its beliefs. Others find regular churches to be much too casual and lighthearted about basic matters of rules, roles, and purposes. Sects are a kind of nonmonastic holiness community. (The holiness communities in Orthodox and Catholic Christianity have functioned all along as sectarian elements, practicing the religion in its purer and stricter form apart from the general society.)

In the United States there are a number of vigorous sects. The Seventh Day Adventists believe firmly in the Bible, as the other Christian churches also say they do, but they are strict observers of a code of behavior that includes a ban on the use of tobacco, nicotine, and meat. Their rules separate the Adventist from the rest of society to some extent. They reinforce a sense that the real purpose of life is not to conform to society but to prepare oneself for the end of this world. Likewise, the Church of Latter Day Saints (Mormons) and Jehovah's Witnesses derive many of their beliefs from the larger Christian tradition, but add further interpretations and usually expect a more rigorous adherence on the part of the believer than the mainstream churches do of their members.

Cult

In popular usage the word "cult" is often used to indicate that a certain group has bizarre beliefs or is under the dominance of an unstable leader. But sociologists want to be cautious about classifying unusual behavior as bizarre or charismatic leaders as unstable. What seems strange or erratic to one person may appear quite meaningful and sound to another. For this reason some sociologists would prefer to avoid the word "cult" entirely. To those who do use this language a cult is usually any group that defines itself in terms that are significantly foreign to its cultural context.

In North America and Europe, for example, the Hare Krishna movement is a cult in sociological terms because its roots are in India, and it is quite different from Western religions. It invites people to live in a strict community of believers who give up ordinary earthly attachments in order to devote themselves to praise of the Lord Krishna, whom they believe to be the major form of the Ultimate divinity. In clothes, food, methods of prayer, and a dozen other ways, the Krishna follower abandons Western culture and absorbs the belief and lifestyle of a devotee imbued with a form of Hindu-inspired ideas. In the community house, the ashram, the believer finds a sense of belonging in a new identity and social pattern.

Other groups may be classified as cults even if they are only half-foreign. Scientology has been influenced by a European adaptation of Buddhist ideas, by Freudian thought, and by modern technology. This movement uses electronic E-meters to determine where mental blocks are inhibiting the release in the person of the basic spiritual or mental power we possess. (There will be more on Scientology in the next chapter.)

The Unification Church ("Moonies") is also difficult to classify. It teaches a system of thought that is somewhat Judaeo-Christian. Jesus tried to initiate the ideal human family, says the Reverend Sun Myung Moon, but failed. Now it is up to the Unification Church to create the perfect worldwide family and bring unification and total peace to all. It aspires to transform society eventually according to its beliefs and so become no longer a cult or sect but a mainstream church in a society made compatible with its beliefs. The differences between categories of church, sect, and cult are often blurred in reality, but they provide useful guides, nonetheless, for perceiving patterns of religion.

Those who join cults may do so because they find their own society, family, and culture unsatisfying. They may feel so little at home that only a radically different perspective appeals to them. But sociologists find that the main reason people join cults is for social involvement. It is most often friends and family of cult members that join, usually after a period of socializing with members of the cult. Eventually the beliefs and practices that seemed a bit strange at first become familiar. The cults also tend to have a rather high turn-over in membership, indicating that people who join still maintain their own perspective, enough to make a decision to leave the group eventually. Claims by outsiders that cults practice "brain-washing" are often exaggerated or unfounded.

Belonging as a Source of Intolerance

The great human need to find a home in a social community has a dangerous side. The need to belong can produce a fierce sense of loyalty to one's own group that goes beyond loyalty and passes over into the intolerance mentioned earlier in the chapter. There are various causes of intolerance. One is a psychological fear of anything that calls into question the rightness, the validity, the true worth of the community a person belongs to. If our ways are correct, why should anyone refuse to follow them? If other communities do not follow our ways, are they suggesting that our ways are wrong? The more a person feels insecure about the validity of the group he or she belongs to, the more that person may be tempted to attack anyone or anything that threatens it. Intolerance, hatred, bigotry, even physical attacks can result, as we see in the history of the Ku Klux Klan, Nazis, and other such groups. We will see more about this in relation to the problem of identity in the next chapter.

Evolutionary psychologists think that bigotry may just be the flip side of what they call "kin-favoritism." Evolutionary psychology claims that we have a genetic inclination to favor those with whom we are raised. The theory is that in doing this we are carrying out instructions from certain helper-genes we carry in us, instructions to aid copies of those helper-genes, copies that exist in people around us. The genes in us cannot really know where their copies are. (The genes in fact know nothing; they are just chemical recipes for producing proteins.) But if a person has a tendency to help whomever he or she was raised with, it is likely that there are kin among those people, and kin have some of the same helper-genes. So helping kin, to survive and to reproduce eventually, helps copies of the helper-gene to survive and get reproduced.

Even when they are not bigoted, community members easily fall into patterns of mutual reassurance in which they praise their own ways and make demeaning jokes or comments about outsiders. At times this takes the more charitable form of condescension. If the community has the truest and best pattern for human life, then a person can sympathetically speak of the depraved, ignorant, or misguided outsiders who must still suffer the lack of what believers have now been blessed, wise, or humble enough to accept. Of course, this is all perfectly logical. Jews see themselves as God's chosen people. Christian tradition has insisted that outside the church there is no salvation. Islamic faith declares that only members of the House of Islam can expect to reach paradise right after death. These ideas can tempt the believer to look down upon the outsider.

These religions, like all historic religions, assert that all people are of equal worth before God or the Eternal. All people share in one human community. We are all brothers and sisters. We are all equally deserving of compassion and love and support. Occasionally a great leader inspires people to see through differences and to cherish everyone. In this century Mohandas Gandhi and Martin Luther King, Jr., led crusades for freedom and justice. Yet both insisted firmly and repeatedly and at great personal risk that even the oppressor must be protected against harm. Both required nonviolence from their followers on the basis that all people, even the oppressor, are to be loved. Both tried to maintain a sense that Indian and British, black and white, all people, are part of one human family. This is the ideal that historic religions preach; but we humans have a very hard time learning to accept it and live by it.

Summary

This chapter has described the ways in which feeling of belonging is itself a kind of salvation. As an answer to a feeling of estrangement, of being adrift without a true home or acceptance, religions can offer a God to belong to, a natural order to conform to, and most especially a community of companion believers. Usually society as a whole has been the religious community people belong to. But in historic cultures sects, cults, and holiness communities may stand aside from the mainstream of life and provide special and separate opportunities for belonging. (We will speak later at greater length of the religious pluralism of modern culture.)

When we have found where we belong, though, we might still feel uneasy about ourselves. Are we truly all right, secure in our selfhood and truly worthy? That is the topic of the next chapter.

For Further Reflection

1. Do most people find it very important that there is a God who understands, loves, and forgives them? Why do you think this is so?
2. Would you find it comforting to feel that you are part of a cosmic unity? Why? Why not? Is it true that whatever is natural is good?
3. Identity the community of people you feel most thoroughly at home with. Do you belong to many communities? Which of them are religious communities in any sense?
4. Have you ever supposed that your community's way of life is the best one for all humankind? Why? Why not?
5. Are there standards for life that are or should be the standards that all people everywhere live up to? What are they?

Suggested Readings

Elizabeth M. Bounds, *Coming Together/Coming Apart: Religion, Community, and Modernity*, 1997. A somewhat dense but brief review of basic current issues.

Robert Carter and Sheldon Isenberg, eds., *The Ideal in the World's Religions: Essays on the Person, Family, Society, and Environment*, 1997. Some chapters in this are relevant to the other two chapters in Part II here.

Gibson Winter, *Community and Spiritual Transformation: Religion and Politics in a Communal Age*, 1989.

Donald L. Gelpi, ed., *Beyond Individualism: Toward a Retrieval of Moral Discourse in America*, 1989.

Robert Bellah et al., *Habits of the Heart: Individualism and Commitment in American Life*, 1996 (second edition). The content deals only indirectly with religion.

Harry C. Triandis, *Culture and Social Behavior*, 1994. Crosscultural anthropology by a social psychologist.

Rodney Stark and Roger Finke, *Acts of Faith: Explaining the Human Side of Religion*, 2000. See Part 3 on "The Religious Group."

CHAPTER SEVEN

A True and Worthy Selfhood

Identity as Salvation

Religious salvation is freedom from estrangement through a positive relation to a numinous reality. The salvation achieved by attaining some heavenly condition is the kind of religious salvation we most often think of. The salvation from aloneness that comes from belonging to a divine being or a sacred community is not quite so obvious, yet it is plain enough once it is described. The salvation that is least obviously religious is salvation from confusion about one's own identity. The topic of identity sounds more like a matter of psychology than of religion. Yet estrangement from self is a basic problem for every human person, and there are fundamental ways that religiousness has entered into this problem as it has into others. Our identity has an intrinsically mysterious dimension to it, and so the question of who we are is one that religions address in one way or another.

THE PROBLEM OF IDENTITY

We may have felt a need at some time to get to know ourselves as individuals better. It is common in popular psychology to speak about getting in touch with our feelings, or finding ourselves, learning who we really are. Perhaps we have had only an occasional restlessness about our inner character and feelings. Or perhaps we have stumbled upon some deeply upsetting desire, bias, or habit that sets us apart from others and makes us worry about our own normalcy, worth, or sanity. We all can experience unsettling moments about ourselves because we are born with an incomplete identity and must learn who we are to become as we grow. As we grow we change, so our identity is always changing in some way.

Born Unfinished

We are unfinished animals, said sociologist Peter Berger in his book *The Sacred Canopy*. He was not trying to be insulting; he was just pointing out a contrast between us and all other living beings. Every dog, kangaroo, and monkey is programmed so thoroughly by its genetic make-up that the offspring of each species does not need to be taught how to be an adult.

A puppy is born with an array of specific directions inside its cells telling it how to become a full-grown dog not only biologically but also behaviorally. A puppy raised apart from all other dogs has only a minimal need to learn at the appropriate age how to bark, how to mark off territory by urinating in the right places, how to catch food if necessary, how to recognize when it is time for mating. It will not have to be taught doggy thoughts or doggy values. The same is true, generally speaking, of all species on the planet, except for us human beings.

Human identity is a highly complex mixture of several elements. The first element is our inherited behavioral tendencies. Evolutionary psychologists, the people who claim that we are inclined by our genes to favor our kin (or actually whoever we grow up with) or to anthropomorphize inanimate objects, think that there are a lot of these tendencies. Men are naturally more promiscuous than women, they say. Our tendency to overindulge in sweets and fats is inherited. So is the tendency of parents to care for their offspring even at great personal sacrifice. So is the tendency of infants to explore sounds as part of the process of learning language. There is strong evidence that we do inherit a number of behavioral, emotional, and even intellectual tendencies, though the number and strength of these tendencies are disputed.

The second element in human behavior is human flexibility. There are great differences in how societies address our common inherited tendencies. We do not all share the exact same rules on how to treat our kin. We do not share the same anthropomorphic beliefs. We must invent or discover ways of thinking and acting, in ways that go even far beyond the specific influences of our genes. Long ago the human race, or our ancestral hominids, began to shift from dependence on instincts to dependence on learning. Over many thousands of years, with some prodding from residual instinctive tendencies, the cultures of humankind built up such vast reservoirs of ideas about family life, food gathering methods, mutual defense, land use, possessions, stages of life, mysterious powers, the use of tools, making music—all the categories and structures of human life—that even an encyclopedia could barely list and describe them. Because these are invented rather than inborn, they have to be learned. We have to spend many years learning and practicing how to be a human being in accordance with the norms our society has provided for us.

Because so many of these norms are invented rather than inborn, they are also somewhat arbitrary, varying greatly from culture to culture. In many cultures nudity is so customary no one thinks to notice it. In America's warm summers, on the other hand, few businessmen notice how strange it is to wear a suit and tie designed originally to keep people warm in England's cool climate years before central heating was invented. Some modern military groups exclude homosexuals. Yet in the fierce military units of ancient Thebes, love among men was thought to increase the soldiers' devotion to one another in battle. North Americans feel oddly uncomfortable talking to someone who stands too close. Latin Americans, Arabs, and others perceive North Americans to be a little cold and distant because they stand so far away when talking with them. Fat white worms that grow in rotten logs are nourishing and tasty to many people. Others enjoy the flavor of well-aged eggs but think that the rotten milk product known as cheese is disgusting. A cup of warm blood taken directly from the neck of a grazing cow is a main part of some diets.

A third element in human behavior is neither specifically inherited nor learned. It derives from the middle ground of common challenges, which arise simply because we humans are all generally intelligent, language-using, and social beings who have evolved on the same planet. We are beings who must all worry about food and water and shelter, who must all create rules for communication with different people, who must all decide how to care for the very young and the very old, who must all determine whether some people get more attention than others in community affairs, who must all respond to disease or drought, and so on endlessly. These problems do not arise from very specific genetic tendencies but from our common human situation and nature.

This third element is a meeting place between nature (inherited tendencies) and nurture (all the many invented ideas we need to learn from our culture). How that meeting is negotiated by a culture is itself changeable. When a society reaches a certain level of affluence, for example, the problems of food and water change rather dramatically. When some diseases turn out to be readily curable through medical technology, expectations concerning health and longevity may change. In fact, the long history of cultural development from primitive to modern is evidence of an openness to change, an incompleteness in human nature.

Validity of the Social Norms

Clothing, sexual values, conversational styles, and dietary customs are only samples of the kinds of things which we humans have invented and which we pass on through generations. In becoming an individual personality with a complex array of elements and characteristics, each of us draws upon all the inventions that constitute our culture. This happens gradually, so the "I" emerging into selfhood interacts with the culture to produce each next bit of selfhood. It is not a completely passive process. Yet eighty percent or more of the specific personal characteristics that have to be learned are the cumulative product of the inventiveness of our ancestors now encoded in our culture.

Our everyday impression of our customs and identity can mislead us. We might fail to note that our social manners, our notions of success, our sexual roles, our musical chords, our hours of sleep, our family structures, our methods of law are merely human inventions that could easily have been different. We are accustomed to them. They collectively make up our consciousness of what life is like and how we fit into it. We do not remember how for years we carefully watched, imitated, practiced, and became persons in the way our culture defines a person. We forget the troubling years of early adolescence when we watched each other, adopted the right habits, laughed at those who diverged from approved behavior, and reinforced one another's conformity to the restricted range of behavior that we learned to know as normal, natural, sane, and acceptable.

We humans want to develop in ourselves some conformity to others in order not to be isolated, but the motivation is deeper than that. Even if we found ways never to be alone, always to belong to others in some way, we would still have a further need: to feel we are worthwhile and valuable, to feel we have an identity that does not merely fit with that of others but is praiseworthy in its own right. We need to feel fully at home with our own identities.

Berger tells us, however, that our identities are doubly precarious. First of all, our identity is vulnerable to attacks from those who think we are individually inadequate, odd, abnormal, silly, insane, corrupt, or perverted. Each of us is under constant pressure not to deviate too far from accepted norms. Each has some fear of being embarrassed, looking foolish, not being accepted. Each fears association with people our culture considers deviant, inferior, or strange. These are all signs of how precarious our individual identity is. We are not quite secure enough simply to be who we are regardless of the social standards, or to accept others for who they are in spite of social pressure. We achieve our security by adhering to the standards.

Our identities are precarious in a second way to the extent the social standards themselves are largely human inventions. The social norms we use to measure ourselves and assure ourselves we are all right are largely invented rather than inborn. Anyone who manages to develop an identity fully in tune with the culture may then feel secure because the culture accepts and praises that identity. But the culture's standards can be doubted, challenged, and changed. When this happens, then the old secure identity may now be mocked by others and rejected. The "housewife" was once praised above all other women. Now her identity is less secure because society has opened up more options for women. There are people whose sense of importance is still based on a racism that assures them that their race is better than others. Fortunately, this norm is changing. On a more prosaic level, those who smoke cigarettes once were thought to look relaxed, or sophisticated, or tough. Now they may appear foolish and repugnant. Because social patterns are precarious, so are the identities built on these patterns.

Religion as Source and Support for Identity

In human cultures the major source of support both for the individual's sense of worthwhile identity, and for the security of the social pattern that much of that identity is based on, has been the religious traditions of the cultures. These traditions have told great stories about the origins of things, the place of humans in the world, and the goal of human life. These narratives hold up ideal humans whose lives and teachings are to be imitated and followed. A person can find a proud and significant identity by accepting a role within such a story of how things are and should be.

Both the section on the sociological function of religion in Chapter Two and the discussion in Chapter Six on the interpenetration of religion and culture indicate how important religion has usually been in supporting social patterns. Every culture has inertia of its own and would tend to maintain itself for some time, presumably, even if religion were weak. At times religious groups oppose aspects of their culture and try to change it into something they can support. By and large, however, most societies have been quite confident that their ways are precisely what God, gods, or the ancestors established, or are in conformity with the numinous forces.

The belief that numinous powers support the culture works in two ways. First, it provides assurance that the customs are correct because they come not from confused human opinion but from the power or wisdom of the numinous. If anyone rebels against them, that person is simply and obviously wrong. Second, the numinous powers often can be expected to enforce their rules. In Melanesia and Polynesia, for example, if the king errs, the god may punish the whole people. In medieval Europe it was a common opinion that God would punish those who rebelled against the king. In fact, because the rebels are certainly wrong, they must be either mentally crippled to stray so far, or else maliciously evil. This justifies any actions by the rest of society to restrain or punish the rebels.

Thus the individual's identity can be made more secure by the power of religion to maintain the customs and values of the grand narrative on which the identity is based. There are numerous specific ways in which religion supports the narratives, the social order, and individual identity. The rest of this chapter will describe a number of them.

Worthwhile Identity and Religion

Special Status of a Few People

Every culture has some people whose significance depends on their special connection with the numinous, whether official or unofficial. Each such person can feel his or her life is worthwhile, therefore, in a special way. Each is a somebody, because he or she is in touch with what is truly powerful and worthwhile.

There are many official roles. A later chapter will speak for example of those who are official religious leaders. It may include magicians and sorcerers who know how to manipulate mana-power, as well as the shaman who deals with the spirits of disease and death. The priest, official performer of ritual, has special status. So also are the official augurs and prophets of the temples.

Many people have unofficial ways of achieving worthwhileness or significance through religion. Numerous people today find themselves possessed by a divine spirit who gives them wonderful powers of healing or speaking in tongues. These Christian charismatics or Pentecostals believe they have received these powers as gifts (*charisma* in Greek) from the Holy Spirit, as happened to the apostles on Pentecost in Jerusalem or the Christians of Corinth a few years later.

Among religious believers with special roles or gifts there are inevitably a few who are consciously eager for high status in society or a feeling of importance. Most presumably are intent on genuinely religious devotion for its own sake. Nonetheless, whether intended or not, to achieve special religious status is also to achieve a sense of being right and being worthy. Even if no one else were to know that a person received special gifts from God or was able to deal successfully with spirits, that person would have some added sense of worth from this special relation to the numinous.

Special Status for Everyone

It is not only the special individuals such as priests and charismatics who get a sense of clear and worthwhile identity through relation to the numinous. In most cultures everyone receives an identity in some ways through religious beliefs or practices.

Most cultures give identity a clear form through religious rituals. This is especially true of the "rites of passage," those rituals by which a tribe, culture, or religious tradition marks off the main points of a person's life (Chapter Ten will deal more fully with ritual). Birth rites acknowledge that a person has been born and acquired a specific identity as a member of this family, with its tradition and its gods. Baptism, for example, is a naming ceremony in which the infant is officially made a member of the religious group. The person's identity comes from belonging to the group.

Puberty rites, when childhood is left behind, are important rites of passage in many cultures. The notion of adolescence as a period between childhood and adulthood is a recent invention. For most societies the young person who is old enough to be a parent is an adult. There is no in-between status. Puberty rites mark this very important passage into adulthood. Some Australian aborigines, for example, bury their young men in the belly of the earth mother. When they are released a few days later from their hole in the earth, they have been born again as adults. Puberty rites still exist in our society today, though we rarely think of them as such. For Jews it is the bar mitzvah ceremony. For Christians it is confirmation or adult baptism. By these rituals a person is asked to take on personal responsibility as a young adult member of the religious group.

Puberty rites highlight the growth of identity. Every child, adolescent, or adult has a need to grow into a specific identity, to adopt specific ways of thinking and behaving, to achieve a sense of being a specific someone who fits somewhere in particular. Puberty rites tell the young person when to leave behind the child's behavior and begin to take on an adult role. The rites can cut down on the fumbling trial and error of adolescence by assigning specific behavior patterns to anyone who has gone through the rites. The girl who played with brothers and male cousins could do so until her puberty rites. After the rites she must avoid the company of male relatives until she is married. The boy who lived at home and addressed his mother with respect becomes a man through the rites, moves into the men's lodge, and treats his mother as someone who no longer has authority over him.

It is not only through rituals that religions establish identity; the moral code also tells a person how to behave and even how to think and feel. Those who adhere faithfully to the moral rules can feel they are good persons. A sect that tells people it is immoral to dance, drink, or play cards, may be depriving them of occasional fun, but it is providing them with a clear set of standards that define a good person. The sense of worthy selfhood achieved by obedience to the code of behavior can be more important than a game of poker or a glass of beer.

Religious beliefs generally help establish basic human identity. They can tell us we are animals, or the offspring of the ancient heroes, or the children of gods, or made in the image and likeness of God, or godlike beings in disguise, or beings who can become gods. They can tell us we are part of nature's patterns, or belong instead to a spiritual realm, or that we do not really exist as individuals at all. These beliefs influence how we think of ourselves and one another.

Our Secret Identity

There are a number of religious traditions that teach that we are not who we think we are. Hindu and Buddhist beliefs, for example, tell us we are not as real as we might think. Neither the body nor even the individual self is of significance; the self we believe we are is an illusion. The only thing in us that is truly real is that which is identical with the eternal and incomprehensible Atman, that which is not individual at all.

Children have fantasies of being a royal foundling, that is, a prince or princess found by the parents in a basket on the doorstep with a note: "Take care of this baby until the time comes to reveal its true identity." The me you see, a child dreams, is not the whole me or the real me. I am like Clark Kent or Princess Diana. Under the right circumstances I will be revealed as Superman or Wonder Woman. Plato and the gnostics held that we are not as physical as we might think. We are really pure spirits merely trapped temporarily in bodily forms. The Rosicrucians promulgate the message that we have untapped mental powers within us, that we are more powerful beings than we know. New Age writers today propose that each of us may have lived many prior lives, perhaps as important individuals in history, and have a chance to be born yet again in the future, perhaps, in roles of great importance.

The system of thought known as Scientology makes even more impressive claims. According to one report, L. Ron Hubbard, founder of Scientology, declared that we are all Thetans, members of a race of superbeings who have lived for millions of years. By the power of our minds alone, we could leap small galaxies at a single bound and travel faster than a speeding photon. But it was all too easy for us, Hubbard explained, so we began to set limits on our powers in order to make our existence more challenging. The greatest limitation we chose was loss of memory that we are Thetan. All the frustrating limitations we now experience in life, therefore, are self-imposed and artificial. With the proper training we can become "clear," our memories restored and with them our superpowers.

Beliefs such as these promise many kinds of salvation. They offer power that people can use to overcome the alienating limitations of earthly physical life. Through such beliefs people can achieve a great sense of belonging. They also can provide a third form of salvation: a sense of individual worth. After all, we are truly Thetans!

Reassurance for a Threatened Identity

The importance of achieving a meaningful identity is most visible precisely where it is most difficult. Most of us grow into our identities with a vague sense that we are what people are supposed to be like, but we all have some doubts, some problems with who we are. Many people live an even more socially and psychologically marginal existence. Living on the margins of society, as it were, they may look to the numinous powers for a sense of personal significance.

A vivid instance of this is the snakehandling sects in the United States, made up mainly of people who are poor and powerless in society, who have little education, and who have the most reason to wonder about their own worth. They are Christians who have been told God loves them, but their lives mark them as outside the usual sphere of success and competence that other people experience. On certain occasions they assemble in simple churches to show concretely that they are actually people God has blessed with wondrous powers because they are strong in their faith.

After prayers and hymns and perhaps a simple sermon or testimony the leaders will open up a box of snakes, the more poisonous the better. According to the Acts of the Apostles in the Christian New Testament, the apostle Paul was bitten by a viper when he and others were temporarily stranded on Malta. The inhabitants concluded that Paul must be a murderer who was being punished for his crime in this way by a numinous power. They expected him to swell up and die, but Paul shook the snake off of his hand into the fire and remained unharmed. (The inhabitants then decided he must be a god in disguise.) Christians have taken Paul's immunity to snake bites as a sign of his great faith and divine protection. In lines at the end of Mark's gospel, Jesus promises that his followers can pick up serpents. So the modern Christian snakehandlers prove to themselves that they too are specially blessed and protected by God, by picking up poisonous snakes and passing them back and forth. Only rarely are they bitten. The risk is worth the rewards, apparently, of feeling that they are approved by God, regardless of how they appear in society's eyes.

Sects and cults in general have the power to transform social rejection into self-affirmation. Those on the margins of society are susceptible to the leader who comes along and tells them that their exclusion from social acceptance is a sign they are special. It is not because they are unworthy that society does not appreciate them; it is because society is ignorant, foolish, or sinful. By joining the sect or cult a person not only achieves a sense of belonging; the beliefs of the cult or sect also give the person a sense of individual significance, of worthy identity.

People can find significant selfhood through many forms of religious affiliation. In ecstatic visions, in priestly status, in rites of passage and rituals of power, in discovering their true and awesome identity—in any or all of these, religious believers discover a way of seeing themselves as significant. The unusual cases command our attention, but it is the everyday patterns that are most important. The set of beliefs we take for granted about our human identity have the strongest effect on us precisely because we do not think to question them. Our ordinary beliefs about childhood and adulthood, male and female, what is natural and what is unnatural, are the beliefs that make us who we are. To repeat, throughout human history, religious traditions have been the repository and support of these patterns of identity. Today that may be changing, but that is a topic for the chapter on modern religion.

Identity in the Stages of Religiousness

We live in a culture that is an accumulation of ideas from primitive, archaic, and historic times. We also have an individual accumulation of ideas collected from childhood, adolescence, and later years. Each of us individually and the society in which we live are a mixture of identity-patterns from different stages of individual and cultural development. Once more, the standard warning about neat categories: they are rough approximations, not the simple truth; there are exceptions to all of them. Nevertheless, it is worthwhile to describe the various stages for the sake of any insights these descriptions can provide.

Identity in Primitive and Archaic Religions

As with the issue of our place in the universe and our sense of belonging, the issue of identity does not become a profound one until historic times, after the axial age. Primitive people are apparently the least self-conscious about who they are; they take it for granted that it is right for them to be as they are, to do as they do, to maintain their traditions. In various matters such as relations between wife and husband, parent and child, cousin and cousin, neighbor and neighbor, the primitive person is aware of a need to learn the proper roles and rules and thereby achieve what we would call the correct identity. But the primitive person does not do this in a conscious attempt to discover his or her true inner selfhood. The correct identity ideas are learned for a practical reason: correct behavior earns a person the continuing right to share in the food, the common hut, a religious dance, and so forth. Correct identity is learned simply as the external pattern of behavior suitable for a human being, as part of tribal life.

Primitive people in general do not seem to have much language to identify their inner selves. They often attribute even their own inner emotions to a particular spirit within or to a part of their bodies: "My kidneys grieve." We still do this today when we say "My heart is sad." But we are more apt to recognize this explicitly as a figure of speech.

By the late archaic stage, perhaps an effect of literacy, people seem to be somewhat more conscious of the problem of identity. They can hear and even read about different lifestyles in other cities. Life is no longer just a one-possibility thing, so it is easier to wonder why this particular identity, out of many possible ones, is the one to take on as one's own. They are better able to wonder about who they are and how they should behave, and why the group's roles and rules should be followed.

Too much wondering about identity would cause a great deal of personal confusion and social chaos. If too many people question their roles as warrior or mother or prophet or servant, soon everyone might be doing whatever she or he feels like doing and everything would be disorderly. The religious beliefs often help to prevent such chaos. The beliefs explain that the social rules and roles, which define one's position in the sacred hierarchy, are assigned and upheld by the gods. Other rules and roles might have been possible, the believer knows, but the gods settled the issue for the group. There is no use protesting it.

Archaic civilizations exhibit greater conscious concern about identity than do primitive people. They show this through a great concern for explicit social status, for honor and even public glory. Their sense of identity is not merely a practical matter of earning enough acceptance to maintain a full share in the city's life, possessions, and food; it is also a matter of personal status. There is a highly developed sensitivity to insults in many archaic societies. Honor is an explicitly important standard. Heroism in battle is said to be admired even by the gods. This is largely, however, a matter of external status, not inner worth. The power, honor, and wealth a person commands is the measure of the person's importance.

Identity in Historic Religions

Obviously every culture including our own retains the archaic tendency to value people according to their external success. But historic culture and consciousness adds additional standards of worth that are based more on the inner qualities of the person. These higher standards provide an alternative to external status as a means of establishing a worthy identity.

When the axial age gave birth to the historic forms of religion, humankind developed a new form of self-consciousness. Some individuals may have arrived at this self-consciousness hundreds or even thousands of years before the axial age, but around 600-500 BCE the new way of thinking became common enough, in poetry, drama, philosophy, and religious writings. It was the age when people learned to stand back from the world they experienced and ask ultimate questions about it. So it was also the age when people became more skilled at standing back from themselves and asking different questions about selfhood. How can I judge myself and others by what they really are instead of by what they possess or their external successes? In fact what really is it to be a person, they asked.

The beginning of such questioning appears in the experience we have all had of an awkward or embarrassed self-consciousness over a period of time. The person who is moving toward historic consciousness can most truly feel embarrassment. It is not the embarrassment as such that is significant here; it is the ability to imagine ourselves through the eyes of others, to picture a "me" that is not the one I am inside myself, but the "me" that others see or think they see. We can wonder, "What am I really like to others? How do they really see me?"

Such self-conscious questions can lead on to the questions of historic thought. "What finally does it mean to be human; how do I live up to full human standards?" Historic thought connects these to further questions: "Where do I belong in the scheme of things, and what is my purpose?" These questions in turn contain at least implicitly the ultimate question about identity: what is the human person in the context of the whole universe? What is the purpose of any person or all people together?

These questions hold the possibility of full estrangement. Where primitive and archaic consciousness discovers individual problems and specific mysteries in life, historic consciousness discovers an awesomely large overall challenge, that we might ultimately not fit anywhere, have any ultimate purpose at all, or have any ultimately meaningful identity. Historic consciousness discovers that the mystery of human identity is potentially infinite. In order to find a secure and worthwhile identity, the historic culture has to discover ultimate answers to the problems of identity. It must find out how the human person relates to the infinite scope of reality.

Most of us do not worry about such ultimates on a daily basis. We live out a practical identity as persons who need to live, work, enjoy friends and family, and deal with our daily problems as they come. And yet we live in a culture where the ultimate mystery of life has become an explicit part of the religions, the philosophies, and the literature that tell us who we are. In response to ultimate questions historic religions offer ultimate answers about who humans are and where we fit. The Hindu says we are not who we think we are, but we are of infinite worth because the true reality within us is Atman, which is Brahman. The Taoist says we are enfolded in the eternal ways of Tao and must learn to accept our humble status in relation to the eternal. The Jew, Christian, or Muslim says we are beings in the likeness of the infinite God or destined for eternal union with God. Each of these answers connects the identity of the individual to whatever is Ultimate.

Each also says it has the universal truth about the relation of the individual to the Ultimate and how the individual should therefore live. Every individual can now judge his or her own worth by how well one lives in proper relation to the Ultimate. That individual is, at least in theory, no longer dependent on social approval to feel a sense of self-worth. This produces a certain kind of "individualism." But it is not the rather modern notion that every individual has a right to choose his or her own values and life-style. Historic thought links the individual directly to ultimate standards of selfhood to which every person ideally ought to conform. Socrates claimed to live by norms superior to those of Athenian tradition, so he placed his own values over that of his society. But he did claim he had an individual right to chose whatever he thought best for himself. He claimed that his values were the universally valid values, which everyone should recognize and accept. He condemned his own society for failing to live up to those standards.

The ideal self in historic religion may be too ideal. The religious traditions ask for sanctity or full submission to the will of God or complete detachment. Individuals may push themselves into the extreme behavior of asceticism, avoiding all earthly enjoyment, or into overly scrupulous concern to live a life of perfection. Such individuals may also try to impose their strict way of life on everyone around them. The famous Taliban of Afghanistan are not the only group in history to do this.

Yet the image of an ideal self can also lead to both humility and compassion. Historic religions usually say that everyone falls short of the ideal in some way. We could give more alms, be more sincere in our devotions, be less interested in trinkets and status, and so on. Such thoughts engender humility. Humility in turn aids in recognizing common human frailty. Each of us has blind spots, weakness, confusion. As we hope for understanding and compassion for ourselves in our own limitations, we can more readily extend it to others.

None of this is enough, though, to eliminate our human feelings of anxiety about our identities. Every person is still liable to suffer some lack of purpose, some loss of self-esteem, some self-doubt. Among the best-selling books today are those that tell us how to get ahead, make friends, get rich. Selling equally well are the books telling us how to become better persons. They tell us how to change our thinking, educate our emotions, gain self-confidence, create a new self. Many new religious movements try to offer instant salvation from insecure identity. They let us in on the truth about "the real you." They accept us lovingly into a community of people who tell us we are valuable. They perform rituals to give us special status. But life goes on. We keep thinking and dreaming and worrying. Uncertainties recur. The same weaknesses and faults remain in us; the easy answers were not enough. Something deeper and more enduring seems to be needed. We continue to look for ways to improve not only our external social and economic status, but also our inner self. There is nothing new in that; the historic religions have been doing it since their inception.

The Long Processes of Transformation

In the course of many hundreds of years, the historic religions have developed and tested some basic means to achieve a new, lasting, and basically valid selfhood. There are many traditional religious texts giving instructions on how to transform the self. One thing the historic religions agree on is that this is not easy to do. Transformation of self is a long process.

A branch of Buddhist thought now known as Zen Buddhism is essentially a method of self-enlightenment. By meditations and instruction over the years a person comes to perceive that the structures and things of reality as we see it are all caught in self-contradiction and meaninglessness. When we truly come to perceive this, these Buddhists say, we will finally be close to release into nirvana. Similarly, the Confucian sage spends years in study and practice, imitating the wisdom of Confucius and generations of scholars until finally the sage achieves an ideal balance in life in conformity with li, right order. Likewise Muslim and Jewish mystics spend years learning to contemplate God. Jewish and Muslim scholars devote lifetimes to absorbing the sacred laws imparted by God; they hope not merely to learn the law but to become one with it in their inner beings. These are long processes of inner transformation that integrate certain values, habits, or attitudes into the person's continuing identity. To give a clearer idea of how such processes can work, here are two examples, from two greatly different, yet somehow similar, historic cultures and religious traditions: Hindu yoga and Christian mysticism.

Hindu Yoga

The word "yoke," the collar joining two oxen or horses, comes from the same ancient word as yoga. A yoga is a way to achieve union with the supreme reality. (Often the word "marga," meaning "way" is used instead of yoga.) A simple classification divides yoga into three types. Bhakti yoga is union through devotion, through special worship of a god or goddess who will help a person achieve union with Brahman. Karma yoga is the path of morally good action in conformity with the cosmic law of justice. By good behavior a person earns rebirth into a higher life, one close to attaining union with Brahman. The third type of yoga is jnana yoga, the way of contemplation.

The most widely esteemed method of jnana yoga is one developed in the second century BCE by the Indian holy man Patanjali. His method is sometimes called "raja" or "royal" yoga because it is thought to be a noble way to achieve enlightenment and release into moksha, eternal salvation. The goal is to meditate on reality, self, and eternity until one truly recognizes that the real self is Atman-Brahman, that there is no individual self. Anyone who achieves this recognition has already achieved union with Brahman-Atman, a unity that will become complete when the person dies. Through discovery of true Self, therefore, a person achieves eternal release from the self.

Patanjali's way is arduous and complex. It begins with learning moral goodness. As we put aside all anger and jealousy and greed, we must also release ourselves from various attachments, all the little pleasures and irritations in life. This begins with a conscious asceticism, a deliberate denying to self of any particular pleasures or comforts. After some years of practicing moral virtues and asceticism, a person will begin to lose all attachment to needs. The yogi, the one following the path of yoga, will become utterly indifferent to all pleasure and pain, all comfort and discomfort.

Meanwhile, as the yogi learns detachment, he or she also begins the practice of meditation. Detachment from pleasure and pain makes it possible to give oneself over to meditation more fully, but there are still other obstacles. A person's body can be a major source of distraction. Bodily cramps, a lack of oxygen, gas in the bowels, can all interfere with the yogi's concentration. A person must learn techniques of posture and breathing and bodily control that will eliminate internal distractions. The senses also must not be distracting. With training the yogi will learn how to allow ears and skin to still function, perceiving sounds and pressures and heat, but in a way that does not distract the person. The yogi remains aware of the outside world, but his or her mind no longer pays any attention to it. The techniques of physical self-mastery are called hatha yoga. (This is the form of yoga that most Westerners think of when they use the word.)

There are yogis of sorts who have apparently mastered many of the techniques of controlling the body or ignoring pain, and who demonstrate their skills for the sake of attention or money. This is entirely contrary to Patanjali's advice. Anyone who still needs to receive attention, praise, or physical rewards is still obviously attached to this worldly maya that keeps us from our true eternal identity. The serious yogi will not be seen in the streets lying on a bed of sharp nails or walking on hot coals; the yogi who does such things has not yet begun to understand what true self and reality are.

The serious yogi will have learned moral goodness, detachment, and bodily control. Years of meditation will reveal the limits of self and the world. The meditation thereby leads eventually to insight, a clear recognition of the truth that the self and the world are maya. In time the insight will produce an inner experience of self as not-self but Self (Atman). The experience of Self is a moment of union with the infinite Atman, which is Brahman. This moment of union with the infinite will completely consume all the tiniest webs of desire, attachment, or illusion that might remain floating in far corners of the yogi's consciousness. When the yogi opens his eyes again when the moment of union has passed, he or she will still live on until natural death but will have no attachment of any kind. Family, home, personal name will not exist for the yogi. When death comes, the inner emptiness of the yogi and the total lack of attachment assures that he or she will merge completely into Brahman's undifferentiated oneness, never to be born again. This is moksha, salvation.

Christian Monastic Mysticism

The previous chapter presented a brief description of the mystic who achieves a sense of belonging to God through union with God. To achieve this union with what is eternal, the Christian mystic must endure a training process and an inner transformation just as the Hindu yogi does in seeking a union with the eternal Brahman.

Near the beginning of the Christian era, some people decided that in order to be a perfect Christian and achieve salvation in this wicked and useless world only a thorough asceticism would be sufficient. In the deserts of Egypt there grew up small colonies of solitary ascetics. In Greek they were called *monachoi*, loners. From this word "monks" evolved. Influenced perhaps by gnostic dislike of the material world (see Chapter Five), the desert loners decided they must give up all physical pleasures. They ate and drank and slept very little, through hot days and cold nights with little protection against the climate. Through trial and error over generations certain practical rules developed and were handed down on how to regulate one's own life in order to be morally good, undistracted by earthly concerns, and attached only to God. Eventually many of these rules were incorporated into organized bodies of regulations followed by whole communities of people. Individual people became organizers of such communities and the solitary ones of the desert became less solitary, as they banded together into homes for monachoi, known now in English as monasteries. From very early time women sought their own form of monastic life.

Like the yogi, the monk is supposed to practice morally correct behavior. The monk is to strive to avoid all sins. He is to practice kindness toward all the people he meets, but he is also to avoid too much contact with people. The main goal is holiness through an attachment only to God. The monk learns to avoid excessive food, drink, sleep, conversation; he learns to fill every idle moment with prayer rather than trifling conversation; he learns to see every event and person and thing as a form of the presence of God. Even as he learns to do all these things, the tradition warns, he will be tempted to become proud of his accomplishments, to be smug about how holy he is becoming. Such temptations are a sign that the person has only begun the long process of achieving holiness and has a long way to go.

A major goal that more and more monks, as well as their feminine counterparts, the nuns, came to cherish was mystical union with God in prayer. They practiced what is usually called a life of prayer; but it is not a prayer that asks something from God; it is not even a conversation with God. While it is traditionally called prayer, it is more accurate to think of it as meditation. In monastic circles it came to be called "contemplation." It requires years of training before a person can achieve mystical union in this way.

In one classic formulation a person must first go through purification or purgation, a process of detachment from pride and self-love, from one's own desires, perhaps even from pleasure. Then a person has begun to enter the second stage, that of illumination. In this the potential mystic begins to discover that the God whom the monk or nun seeks in meditation is awesomely great, the infinite and eternal One. This involves realizing ever more clearly that God is not imaginable, not even conceptualizable. Illumination thereby turns out to be, in one famous metaphor, darkness. John of the Cross, a sixteenth-century Spanish mystic, proclaimed that a person reaches God only through a dark night of the soul. In this a person knows that even the powers of the human spirit are too limited to grasp God. This mystic proclaimed God's brightness to be so great as to utterly blind a person's mind. Those who say they can conceive God in their minds are therefore deceived. By this time the potential mystic may be entering into the third stage, the stage of unity, in which all desires and selfhood are left behind and the soul is so filled with the Infinite God that the person is as nothing. For a moment the person has become united with God, transformed and overwhelmed.

In the mysticism of the West, unlike that of India, the individual self retains his or her own identity. Jewish and Islamic mystics share this notion with Christianity, although all three sometimes speak as though the individual is completely dissolved in God. In the West, unlike in Hindu thought, a person does not have to become a mystic in order to achieve final salvation. Paradise or heaven or the kingdom of God are open to all morally good believers. Moral goodness alone, however, is difficult. Monasticism, even for those who are not mystics, is a way of life involving self-transformation through a long developmental process of moral growth, asceticism, and meditation.

For the Christian monk and Hindu yogi the ultimate goal is to unite oneself with the infinite. In this union all forms of estrangement are eliminated because now the person is perfectly at home, united to the eternal truth, fulfilling the ultimate purpose of every person, achieving the fullness of what a human person can aspire to. But even as they work toward this ultimate goal, they are already achieving a sense of salvation. By dedicating themselves to the process of transformation, they already can feel they are giving their selfhood over to what alone is truly worth belonging to.

The Continuing Need for Long Effort

The previous two examples of asceticism in historic religions both center on a concern to achieve inner union with the Absolute. In general, any and all attempts to establish inner transformation of one's selfhood involve long processes.

In primitive and archaic societies only external behavior patterns require long conscious effort. Inner identity is taken for granted. Thus, the primitive hunter knows that only long practice with a spear creates real skill, but having an identity as a tribesperson is automatic. An artisan of an archaic culture knows it requires years of training to become an expert silversmith, but worthwhile identity is just a matter of being loyal to one's family and society.

When historic consciousness appears, there is also a greater inner self-consciousness and with it comes the notion of perfect selfhood, an ideal self without any failings or unworthiness, a happy self without any fears and frustrations. Even if a person recognizes that no one can be truly perfect, the image of perfection nonetheless remains present in the culture. All this conspires to make a person restless to develop a better selfhood. Then that experience begins to teach a person that such development requires years of effort.

This has remained true in modern times also, as we will be seeing. Modern thought is more this-worldly and does not seek mystical union with an other-worldly absolute. In the quest for ideal selfhood, however, modern thought still recognizes the need for a long process of personal development, accomplished through hard effort, through an asceticism that includes a willingness to face years of reflection and experience.

The modern person, like people in all types of cultures, will still look for the quick fix. The primitive and the childish in us will expect that reading one or two insightful books, or finding the perfect philosophy, or engaging in a series of seminars by psychology experts, or joining the new cult with the answers to everything, will finally make us all right. Then it turns out that even the leaders of the cult or the new psychological advisors expect that only years of disciplined community life or years of seminars, analyses, and training will lead us to the sense of worth and belonging we seek. It is not easy to achieve the salvation that is the sense of ideal selfhood. (In modern thought, in fact, a different idea will appear: that a person can be at peace even with one's imperfect self.)

Summary

This chapter has surveyed some aspects of identity and religion. Identity is a problem because we are born without one. The question of identity was not explicitly asked in primitive cultures. Archaic cultures defined it in terms of loyalty to the local gods and nations. Finally, historic cultures asked who we are ultimately in relation to the universal power or order behind all else, and even came to provide programs of growth towards our ultimate fulfillment.

End of Part II

There are patterns running through the quest to achieve salvation through the numinous. One pattern is the set of observable stages of development from primitive to archaic, historic, and eventually, perhaps, the modern. This is a progress of awareness from local to universal, from home-ground awareness to a cosmic consciousness.

This is also a progression toward more and more self-awareness. The primitive sees little of his or her interior self, attributing even unwanted emotions to spirits acting on a person. By historic times humans learned how to mentally stand outside of self in order to look back at self as an individual with certain needs, hopes, and fears. Consequently, the progression from primitive to historic times has also been a movement toward an ever deeper questioning of self. Where the primitive person need only look around to find the one natural (local) way to live, the historic person must connect in one universal and coherent picture all the ways of life with ultimate justifications of all.

All this means that the kind of salvation offered by religion, at each stage of religious and cultural development, must be adequate to the scope of awareness of people. A primitive person who is told that salvation consists of achieving nirvana or the beatific vision may worry whether there will be plenty of pigs and chickens there. A historic person who is assured that after death there is a pleasant valley for spirits to live in may want to ask whether there is any ultimate purpose to that.

Another pattern is the ongoing threefold dimension to the mystery we humans all face. The mystery can be delineated by three questions: 1) who are we? 2) where and how do we belong? and 3) how can the world in which we live be made right? Problems of selfhood, relation to others (and the universe), and the conditions of our universe have constantly challenged people and made them wonder whether it makes sense (is intelligible) and has a purpose (is worthwhile). A consistent part of this pattern of human behavior has been the faith that, in spite of the mysteriousness, in spite also of confusion and evil, our existence is indeed ultimately intelligible and worthwhile. This is religious faith in its most general form.

Primitive, archaic, and historic stages of culture have all included a firm religiousness, assured that the mystery is the realm of a numinous reality that provides a good world (here or to come), a proper and worthwhile place to belong, and a secure and worthy identity. Modern culture, as we will see, appears at times as though it is the first culture to lack this assurance. We live in days when it is possible to doubt the existence of not only the spirits and gods but even God or any other such Ultimate. It is as though the modern age of humankind is going to see whether it can face the mystery without religion.

Something like this has happened before, however. One of the charges on which Socrates was tried and condemned in Athens in 399 BCE was the charge of atheism. His universalizing way of thought seemed to call into question belief in the gods. Jews and Christians were sometimes called atheists by the authorities of ancient Rome, because they refused to worship the gods. The axial age had introduced the idea of a God in the West as far back as the sixth century BCE. But it took many centuries before historic religiousness became so strong that it dominated politically. It then turned out that atheism, in the sense of disbelief in the gods, was actually a step to a new form of religious belief.

The modern way of thinking may well be as Bellah describes it, not irreligious but a new stage of religiousness. Even in these somewhat skeptical times there is still endless mystery, there is still the need to discover who we are, where we belong, and how life can be made whole; and there still seems to be the underlying faith that even in the presence of mystery, somehow life does have meaning. Even the modern era, as we will see, still has some lingering inclination to treat the infinite mystery as numinous and not as emptiness.

The most obvious kinds of salvation are concrete and limited—having a helpful God, for example, who can also provide life after death. Equally obvious are the human needs for various kinds of salvations, needs that arise out of our experiences of helplessness before death and life's unfairness, of feeling lost and alone and worthless. Less obvious is the infinite depth of these needs. The mystery of where we are, how we fit in, what our purpose is, and where our happiness lies is an endless mystery. If none of the answers of historic religion is fully satisfying or fully convincing to some people in these modern times, they may nonetheless find that only a modern form of religiousness, not unreligiousness, is what they seek.

All these ideas, however, have to wait upon later chapters for a fuller and clearer explanation concerning modern religiousness. Before that, there are other aspects of the religions of humankind that have to be surveyed to provide a better description of the ways we humans live our lives in the presence of mystery.

For Further Reflection

1. Can you identity any particular patterns of human behavior that are clearly natural (inborn or conformed to nature) and not just invented? What are they?
2. Do you see it as good and valuable that people can establish a sense of worthy identity through their religion? Why? Why not?
3. What are the main social forces or groups or individuals that tell you who you are? Which of them are religious, if any?
4. Is there an ideal self you can imagine you might become through long effort? Is religion relevant to this? Explain.
5. What are your plans to develop your own selfhood in the years to come? If this strikes you as an odd question, explain why.

Suggested Readings

Leslie Stevenson and David L. Habermas, *Ten Theories of Human Nature*, 1998. Contains summaries and critical analyses of various religious, philosophical, and psychological theories.

Robert Carter and Sheldon Isenberg, eds., *The Ideal in the World's Religions: Essays on the Person, Family, Society, and Environment*, 1997. Some chapters in this book are also relevant to the two preceding chapters here.

Peter Berger, *The Sacred Canopy*, 1969. This book is difficult to read, but the first chapter contains the major ideas of the book.

Denise L. and John T. Carmody, *Ways to the Center*, 1981. See the sections of each chapter in Parts II and III entitled "Structural Analysis...self."

Victor Frankl, *Man's Search for Meaning*, 1967. Written by a survivor of a concentration camp.

Robert C. Neville, *Soldier, Sage, Saint*, 1978. Religious stages of individual identity.

Kwasi Wiredu and Kwame Gyekye, *Person and Community: Ghanaian Philosophical Studies* I, 1992. See Part I on African identity.

Part III

Guides to Life

To the extent that we are unfinished animals, as Peter Berger says, we need to learn patterns for living; we need ideas and practices to guide us. Throughout history religion has been the dominant source of guidance, at least up to recent times. Religion does this in many ways. In the next four chapters we will survey some of them: moral rules, sacred texts and leaders, rituals and symbols, and rational reflection about beliefs and practices.

Those who are committed to a specific religious tradition will normally follow its moral rules, respect the traditional texts and leaders, participate in symbolic rituals, and learn the formal religious thought. They will do these things because it is expected, because they are part of the way of life of a person's community or tradition. Jews observe the Sabbath, Christians the Lord's day, and Muslim do the same for Fridays. Hindus do not eat beef, while Jews and Muslims avoid pork. The star of David, the crucifix, and the crescent evoke special but different feelings from Jew, Christian, and Muslim.

It is less obvious that participation in all these practices has an educational function. Together the symbols and rituals and texts and leaders and moral rules and religious reflection educate a person in a certain way to be human. They constitute an interpretation of what life is in relation to the ultimate mysteries. They explain the origin and order and purpose of things. They offer an understanding of where estrangement comes from and how to overcome it. By participating in all the practices and forms of a religion, people take on its worldview as their own, often to an extent they do not realize. The world is "mediated" to them by religion; i.e., the reality of things is presented to them in a certain way through the medium of religion. Religion thereby guides them in how they understand themselves and their relations to others and to the universe. Religion integrates a person into a whole pattern of life.

Religion is not the only source of interpretations that guide life. There are nonreligious moral visions, leaders and texts, rituals and symbols, and rational analyses of things. Some are informal and unorganized. Thus we all learn pieces of how to interpret life from television programs, the common prejudices of school friends, a favorite magazine or comic book. Other interpretations are more thoroughly formulated, as in nonreligious philosophies like those of the American Humanist Association's Manifestoes. Not all worldviews are constructive ones. The crude, distorted, and angry worldview of the Klu Klux Klan is an example of a destructive one, though it presents itself as a religious perspective.

Whether reality is interpreted for us by religious or nonreligious sources, organized or informal ones, all of us must learn some interpretation of reality on which we can then build more of our own life, whether in full harmony with what we have learned or in opposition to it in some way. We cannot construct a whole universe of ideas and meanings and values by solitary effort and inventiveness. Even when we feel that we are rejecting our tradition and our upbringing we nonetheless reproduce much of it in our own lives. And we have to borrow from other traditions even to formulate our opposition to our own. The next four chapters will illustrate our ongoing dependence on the ideas and practices of prior generations to guide us or to give us alternatives in finding a coherent and workable way of life.

Chapter Eight

What Should I Do and Why

Religion and Morality

The Problem of Morality

One of the great mysteries of life is knowing what makes something good or bad. We do not usually experience this as a mystery because various human drives lead us to value some things, and we also have many societal standards to help us distinguish right from wrong. Inner drives such as hunger tell us to eat; social standards tell us to wipe our noses and to stop beating on our neighbor's head. Yet everyone experiences some confusion sooner or later about what is really good or bad.

Any discussion of morality is soon tied up in a thousand complexities of religious tradition, individual reasonings, societal prejudices, personal psychology, and so on. It is notoriously difficult to sort out not just what is good or bad, but even what "good" basically means. Each religious tradition will have its own ideas on this, and its own code of behavior, one related in some way to a numinous reality.

To help sort it out, this chapter will rely on some developmental theories concerning moralities, theories that fit fairly well with the theory of cultural and religious development proposed by Robert Bellah. The theories of moral development used here are those of the Swiss philosopher and psychologist, Jean Piaget, and the later work of two Americans, Lawrence Kohlberg and James Fowler. Aspects of all these theories are disputed and some of the ideas in this chapter are further speculation based on those disputed theories, so caution is wise here. The theories, however, do provide an illuminating framework for sorting out some complexities.

Different Types of Morality

To some extent the type of morality varies with the stages of culture and religion. Primitive society has dominant notions of what makes something good or bad that are different from the notions that predominate in historic or modern cultures. Each of us individually also goes through stages of personal development, with different standards of morality dominating in the different stages. Our notion of good and bad at the age of seven is quite different usually from what it is at the age of seventeen.

To make it all even more complex, each of us retains past standards to some extent, so that as we mature we end up with a collection of different operative moral standards. Sometimes, like any seven-year-old, we avoid lying only because we are afraid of getting caught in a lie, but other times we are truthful out of a general conviction that honesty is something that people owe to one another. Cultures are more complicated than individuals, so they also have many different moral standards operating in them at once.

There are four different types of moralities that will be described here, in the order that they seem to appear in the development of each person's life. The first is called "taboo morality," an egocentric concern for one's own pleasure and which defines as "bad" only those things for which a person gets punished in some way. The second is called "allegiance morality," based on a seemingly natural human desire to gain approval from and fit in with one's own group. A third kind is "universal laws morality," based on a supposition that there are objectively valid moral norms which all people everywhere ideally ought to follow. Finally, there is a "basic value morality," which claims that the best foundation for any moral judgment is whether in the long run it will best serve the basic value of general human well-being, whether it helps people rather than hurts them. Each of these four kinds of morality has a place in religious traditions.

TABOO MORALITY

Taboo Morality in General

The psychologist Lawrence Kohlberg characterized our earliest childhood morality as "egocentric." A morally egocentric person is one who calls things good if they feel good to that person, and labels something bad only if it causes pain or discomfort to that person. Stealing is bad, according to this attitude, only if you get punished for it when you get caught at it. If there is a way to steal that results only in profit without pain to the person doing the stealing, then stealing is good for that person. Morality consists in discovering what it is that earns punishment, and then in figuring out how to avoid that punishment but still get as much pleasure as possible.

This is a morality that is a collection of specific rules, learned one at a time, about what feels good to do and what results in pain or punishment. It is similar to the list of "taboos" that a primitive person learns, or to the list of "no-no's" that a child learns.

In taboo morality intentions do not count. If a person breaks a rule, violates the taboo, does a no-no, then punishment follows. The exception to this is that the taboo moralist sometimes learns that other people think that intentions are quite important, and uses this knowledge to try to avoid punishment. "I didn't mean to do it" is a plea that the taboo moralist can use in order to manipulate others even when in fact the taboo moralist definitely did mean to do it but just hoped to be able to get away with it.

Taboo morality provides some support for the social order by threatening lawbreakers with punishment. If a society has many people who seek personal pleasure, regardless of what the effects are on other people, the result will be a jungle of competing desires. Rules for social order enforced by threat of punishment will counterbalance individual pleasure seeking. This way of upholding social order is limited, though. If people are motivated only by personal pleasure and not by concern for others, they will seek ways to break the rules without getting caught.

Taboo Morality in Children

As young children we live by a taboo sort of mentality. Up to the age of about six, we define "bad" simply as whatever we are punished for. Even when the rules do not make any sense, they are to be obeyed. A four-year-old child knows it is wrong to lie, without understanding very well what a lie is or why it is bad. Grown-ups get upset when you say things that are not true. So do not do it.

Little children do not believe in the value of good intentions. Piaget told a story to little children about two little girls who played with their mother's scissors and some cloth. Alice wanted to help her mother but cut a large hole in the cloth by accident. Jane knew she was not supposed to play with scissors but did it anyway just for fun and cut a small hole in the cloth. When Piaget asked little children whether Alice or Jane should be punished, the children said that both of them should be punished. Alice's good intentions are irrelevant. In fact the children agreed that Alice should be punished more because she cut a bigger hole in the cloth than Jane did.

Children are short-term pleasure seekers, willing to make deals with one another at times, but not too reliably. Two of them exchange toys, but one of them tries to end up with both toys. This basically egocentric impulse is evident in the common technique parents use for dividing a piece of pie or cake. One child cuts the cake; the other gets first choice. The one cutting will do it with tongue-bending precision, sure that whoever gets first choice will of course choose the bigger piece. The one cutting does not want to give away a single crumb more than necessary.

Some children learn to think of life as full of dangerous forces that punish you. Children beaten by their parents grow up to experience the world that way. So also do children who are punished and rewarded inconsistently by parents who are moved easily by moods of anger or irritation. Like primitive people children assume that events have causes that make sense and that the world is supposed to work right if you follow the correct order. Children reason that if they feel pain it must be the result of something they did that was wrong. If something really bad happens, such as a divorce or the death of a parent, the child tends to feel that this is a punishment he or she has somehow deserved. Not yet able to tell themselves that maybe the world has gone awry or that the parents are at fault, such children begin to feel that there must be something basically wrong with them as persons.

Primitive Culture and Taboo Morality

Because all human beings begin their lives as children, taboo morality is part of all of our life-stories. Primitive people are no exception to this. Because primitive and archaic cultures do not have explicit universal laws morality or basic value morality, as we will see, primitive culture is an especially good place to look to see what taboo morality would look like if it were a dominant morality in a culture.

All of us are inclined to think that things that please us are good, and things that harm us are bad. The primitive person agrees. "Good" is what feels good, earns a reward, receives praise. "Bad" is what hurts, what you get punished for. If stealing from a neighboring tribe does not cause you any harm, then it is all right to do it. If being kind to a stranger results in sickness in your house, then it is bad to be kind to strangers.

Just as primitive cultures live by collections of folktales that describe various aspects of reality, they also live by collections of individual rules that have to be learned one at a time and obeyed one at a time. The primitive person has an overall concern to live correctly and thereby make life go smoothly. What constitutes living correctly is contained in a set of customs and stories handed down from the days of the ancestors. The story of the man who slept with his sister and was then turned into a goat is a story that instructs about the dangers of incest. The traditional saying that those who light their neighbor's cooking fire (meddle in their neighbor's affairs) will carry their neighbor's sores (will be the one treated meanly by spirits who are actually angry at the neighbor) is a saying that instructs people about good social behavior. (It is also a saying as obscure as many such sayings are, even to the tribespeople themselves at times.)

There are various motives at work to make primitive people observe the approved customs. An obvious incentive to keep the rules is threat of punishment from a person's neighbors. If you kill a man, his relatives may seek to kill you or members of your family in return, or demand some payment in recompense and will threaten to kill you if you do not pay up. The desire for vengeance is not well controlled in most primitive societies (or most archaic, for that matter), except by fear of retaliation.

Some acts carry their own punishment in an obvious everyday way. Sticking your hand in the fire hurts. Punching your neighbor in the nose is liable to get you a bloody nose in turn. But most of the harm that comes to a primitive person does not result from such obvious causes. You stumble and break a toe. A bag full of berries breaks, scattering them all over. Your skin erupts in sores; your children are crippled by disease; your tribe starves in a drought. All of these are bad because they hurt. The primitive tribesperson does not believe that they can be random accidents. There is a reason for everything that happens. If the cause is not an obviously visible one, then it must be a mysterious numinous power at work. If harm comes to a person in any form, the primitive person reasons, then some spirit has done it, or a sorcerer using magic. When the numinous is dangerous, as it often is, it is labeled "taboo."

Primitive people, like all people, also enjoy having status or prestige in the eyes of others. The skilled basketmaker or hammock weaver, the woman with many children, the successful hunter or fighter, all enjoy positive attention from others. (Primitive society is called "egalitarian" in spite of this because such status is earned and transitory, not hereditary.)

In fairness to primitive people it is important to note that another motive they have for keeping the rules is their social value. The rule that forbids killing a fellow tribesperson is useful to keep the tribe functioning well, gathering its food harmoniously, and defending its territory. Primitive people, as intelligent as people anywhere, recognize the need for social peace and harmony in the tribe rather than discord. They recognize that conformity to custom helps to preserve this social order; they will support the customs for this reason and not just out of fear of punishment by the numinous or from each other.

Life gives concrete evidence to primitive people, which suggests that intentions are not very important to the invisible powers. A person tries to save a child from drowning but is drowned in the process. A person who goes out in the rain to help another is killed by lightning. People who steal and kill but do not offend the spirits sometimes live long healthy lives anyway. There is much evidence to primitive people that the numinous powers that run things and cause things to happen do not really care about our intentions.

Many rules of taboo morality are externally imposed restrictions that the primitive person does not usually expect to be able to understand. The rules exist. If it were clear that they served some higher purpose then the intention to achieve that purpose might count even when the person failed or did something wrong by mistake. But the rules often are just there. They represent how life is, that is all. Laws, morality, and codes of behavior are one and the same thing: part of the collection of instructions on how to behave in order to avoid getting hurt, perhaps by numinous powers, to maintain their place in the group, and to keep social peace.

Archaic Culture and Taboo Morality

Archaic cultures are more complex than primitive. Archaic cultures that are also literate may have long and complicated myths that explain how the world came to be long ago through the great actions or struggles of the gods, and how the gods now rule the world, establishing the kings and laying down the rules that people must follow. But taboo fears remain as a major motivation to observe the rules. In the days of King David of Israel and Judah, for example, in about 1000 BCE, archaic times for these people then, a man named Uzzah tried to save the sacred ark, the throne of Yahweh, from injury when it was about to fall. As a result of this well-intentioned act Uzzah died. The people thought that Yahweh had struck down Uzzah for daring to touch the sacred ark. Rules are rules, not to be broken, regardless of intention or purpose.

The great literate archaic civilizations used their writing abilities to create a detailed body of laws. The laws were codified, put into formal lists that could be used by judges for deciding legal cases brought to them. To some extent this removed some of the laws from the control of religion and made them mainly secular or civil matters. Yet civil contracts were still signed in the temple of a god or sworn to in the presence of a god, with offerings made to the god to be a witness to the contract. Whoever violated the contract would thereby incur the anger of the god for having used his or her name in vain. The god would punish the offender. So the motive to be honest would still belong to taboo morality: fear of punishment, based on religious belief.

Taboo Morality in Adults Today

It is not just children and primitive and archaic people who live by taboo morality and motivation. Everyone probably follows some rule or other for no other reason than out of a fear of punishment. Many sexual rules have functioned in this way. The religious ban on masturbation was long supported by nothing more in many people's minds than threats of punishments. It will cause pimples or insanity, some said; others declared that God would send a person to hell eternally for such a deed. Some rules imposed under the threat of punishment might be good rules, but if a person obeys them for no other reason than fear of punishment, that is a taboo morality motivation.

There are also a good number of people in places as diverse as prison, the United States Congress, and neighborhood used car lots whose basic moral sense is to do whatever is rewarding as long as they can avoid getting caught and punished. "Fast-buck" operators who swindle the elderly out of their savings seem unmoved by the suffering they cause. They even seem totally unembarrassed at getting caught and publicly exposed. They often exhibit neither shame nor guilt. Avoiding prison or a fine is all that is important to them. They believe others would do the same as they did, if only the others felt they could get away with it. Everyone is looking for a self-serving angle on life, the taboo moralists figure. They do not seem to be able to recognize that other people have a moral motivation that is not so selfish. Many of these modern taboo moralists can be rather intelligent, as is true also of primitive people. But somehow their life's context has kept them confined to a perspective that is scarcely moral at all, just a desire for personal gain without regard to others as long as they can avoid punishment.

Even among religious people today, there are taboo moralists who obey God or the gods only because the divine beings have power to reward and punish. Their formal beliefs may be drawn from a historic religion, but their way of understanding those beliefs can be primitive or childlike. A punishing God who passes laws to be obeyed regardless of whether they make sense is a God who fits in well with taboo morality. Taboo moralists are likely to believe that society can be held together only by the threat of divine punishment. God, after all, knows and will punish every transgression eventually. Taboo moralists do not expect anyone to obey moral rules for any reason except fear of some punishment.

Allegiance Morality

The Need to Belong

Another type of morality is based on our human need to be accepted by others, to be approved, cherished, praised, or honored. This need for acceptance can be part of taboo morality in that it may function as just an egocentric desire to get attention or privileges or to avoid the irritation of being mocked. But the need for acceptance also leads a person to get beyond such narrow self-interest and to find some fulfillment through participation in a community of people. We give a group of people our loyalty and expect to receive their support in return. At times this can motivate a person to sacrifice individual interests for the good of the group. Allegiance morality can even produce great heroism. It can also, however, lead to bigotry and mistreatment of those who do not belong to the group, especially those who are perceived to be the enemies of the group in some way.

There are many kinds of groups. We all tend to have a strong allegiance to our families, feeling protective towards them even if they are in the wrong in disputes with others. In many cultures the clan is the basic unity of society. All those who are related to you, even if they are your uncle Abner's grandchildren or second cousin Bertha's husband, deserve some degree of special treatment. Patriotism is also a form of group loyalty. So is loyalty to the members of your street gang. In each case the need to belong and be accepted has its corresponding price of loyalty to those who accept us and make us significant by giving us a worthy group to belong to.

Where the need to find acceptance through allegiance to a group is strong, leaders and heroes will be unusually important. Stories told of heroes will exemplify the virtues of loyalty and courageous defense of the group and its ways. Certain individuals will provide a focus for the group, promoting its beliefs and values, bestowing approval on this person or that as a valued member of the group. The nation has its king or president; the street gang has its leader; a religion has its authority figures. (See the next chapter for more on religious leaders.)

Forms of the Need to Belong in Individuals

Kohlberg described a stage in the moral development of the individual in which a child seeks to be accepted by the people around him or her, primarily the parents but also adult relatives and teachers. This is the "good boy and girl" stage in Kohlberg's language. We have already talked about this need for acceptance in the chapters on belonging and on identity. Children need to know that their parents will not give them away or abandon them, that their parents love them even if the parents beat them. Children also become confused and angry when people make fun of them. Primitive people also, like all of us, have a strong desire to be accepted by others in their group, to be praised rather than mocked. Sometimes this need for acceptance will manifest itself only in the self-centered concern typical of taboo morality. But at other times it will lead to a much greater concern about the whole group of people to whom we belong.

Though a desire to belong arises very early in life, in early adolescence it becomes more consciously important. We feel a desperate need to conform to group standards in order to be one of the crowd, in order to be thought normal instead of weird. We experience the common human need to achieve a sense of self-worth through acceptance by others around us. Perhaps we are mainly self-centered in this; but perhaps we also begin to feel some sense of greater devotion to others, of loyalty to the group.

The need for acceptance and the impulse to give our loyal support to those to whom we belong remain part of a person throughout life. Allegiance morality is therefore part of every person and of every culture. But it may be outweighed by other types of moral motivation such as those that emerge in historic and modern culture, as well as in later stages of individual development. Allegiance morality is more clearly visible in archaic cultures, before other forms of morality take on the explicit importance they will achieve in later forms of culture (or in later stages of individual development).

Allegiance Morality in Archaic Cultures

While allegiance morality is by no means confined to archaic cultures, it stands out in such cultures as the dominant morality. These are cultures of loyalty and heroism and honor. Among archaic people as among adolescents, the virtues that are often considered most praiseworthy are the group virtues of loyalty to one's own people, dedication to the causes of the group, and trustworthiness and honesty in dealing with others in the same group. To be regarded as disloyal or traitorous brings shame and dishonor. To look out for only selfish interests is ignoble.

Honor even becomes sacred, to be guarded and protected against anything that might profane it. The purpose in going off to battle is to gain honor. Those who die in battle receive the greatest honor, because they have sacrificed themselves for the good of the group. On the other hand, to be dishonored is the greatest evil. No person is worse than the coward, who places personal safety above the needs of those to whom he or she has pledged loyalty. To be thus dishonored is to be shamed or to lose face. In some cultures only suicide can clear a dishonored family name or resolve the tension incurred by loss of face.

Archaic cultures (or the archaic element in any culture) will look to a heroic leader. Primitive culture has no formal leader. Tribespeople sit and talk and come to a consensus, albeit with some individuals more persuasive or stronger than others. Historic cultures, as we will see, suppose that there is a body of law that is superior to individual leaders. But the archaic style of culture knows no better way to make society cohere than to find a strong leader to whom people may give their loyalty and who will reward them with special attention when it is earned by devotion. This style of thought thinks that it is legitimate to break the law in service to one's leader, though loyalty to the leader is itself a kind of cultural rule. The section on historic culture and universal laws morality will explain more about this.

Loyalty to the Group

Unlike taboo morality, allegiance morality tends to value good intentions. A person who means well is one who is loyal and supportive, one who can be trusted. The loyal person may make mistakes or prove to be ineffective, but that person's good intentions are enough to compensate for most other failings. Taboo moralists are not too surprised by the neighbor who falsely pretends to be friendly or the trader who cheats. After all, who wouldn't do such things? Allegiance moralists are upset by such double dealing; it is a sign of untrustworthiness. The liar, the hypocrite, those whose intentions do not match their mien of honesty and innocence, are bad people. Of course it is often all right if one of the group or clan lies and cheats to outsiders, because outsiders do not count for much.

The allegiance moralist gives over much of his or her identity to the group. This person can feel worthwhile only if the group is worthwhile. In defense of his of her own belongingness and identity, therefore, the allegiance moralist does not merely praise loyalty above all virtues, but also praises his or her group over all other groups: "We are the noble, the true, the sacred band; others are inferior, mistaken, or evil."

Every group has those who promote, maliciously or thoughtlessly, a kind of bigotry that derides outsiders for the sake of bolstering their sense of the value of their own group and of their identity with it. Those in a group who feel least secure are most likely to have a bigoted attitude towards outsiders who are different. Because outsiders do not really count, it is also more permissible to attack them. Allegiance moralists are also most likely to feel threatened by any member of the group who seems to place some other value before blind loyalty. The person who criticizes some aspect of the gang or tribe or religion or nation is a threat to the person who is strongly driven by a need for clear standards of what the group wants and lives by.

Motivated by a need for acceptance, a person tends to feel that right and wrong, the very standards of good and evil, are identical with the group's identity and customs. Many rules of the group might be ones an outsider would judge as wise or practical, but that is not the motivation behind allegiance morality. Whether the rules are wise or foolish, practical or impractical, easy or hard, humane or cruel, matters little. The rules and standards are felt to be correct because they are those of the group. If an outsider challenges the group values, the group will draw together in self-defense, regardless of how reasonable the outsider's claim is. Only if there is a consensus within the group for some change, if the leaders or heroes whom the others use as their model recommend some change, will the group adopt new ways. This maintains a sense of belonging and acceptance.

Allegiance Morality and Religion

The person whose main objective is to achieve acceptance can find it very fulfilling to belong to a religious group. The group's beliefs and rules will provide clear standards for the person on how to remain worthy of acceptance. Ordinary churches will not be so attractive as sects, cults, or some select clique within a church. A sect or cult more clearly defines itself by contrast with other religious groups or with people in general. The sect or cult thereby provides a more sharply defined group to give loyalty to and to receive acceptance from.

Religious ties based on allegiance morality will tend to focus on religious leaders and heroes as symbols of the group's standards and as focal points of the group's authority. Wherever the leader takes them, they may follow with fervor, even to their deaths. The allegiance moralist will be likely to join a new religious group or to become part of a heretical or schismatic group not because of abstract beliefs but because the group has a leader upon whom a person can focus his or her loyalty.

The allegiance to a certain religious tradition may include intolerance towards other groups, such as a firm conviction that all nonbelievers are going to damnation. This fortifies a sense of belonging. To praise one's own religious group as the source of true salvation is an act of faith and loyalty to the group.

Among the various numinous powers it is the personal and attentive god or God who will be of greatest interest to the person who values mainly acceptance as a standard for knowing right and wrong. The allegiance moralist turns to a God or god who loves people in spite of their mistakes provided only that they are loyal followers of the authority of the religious leaders and defenders of the beliefs of the group as the unchangeable truth. If there is still some fear of punishment for mistakes or sins, a fear continuing on from an earlier life-stage when taboo morality dominated the person's thoughts and feelings, this fear may balanced by a loving trust in the care the god or God is bound to show toward a devoted follower.

The allegiance-minded person will expect that good intentions, sincere faith and feelings of devotion are important enough to earn acceptance, forgiveness, and love from God or the god. Pure Land Buddhists in Japan say that merely to invoke the name of Amida-Buddha in an act of trust in this divine being is enough to earn life in paradise after death. Catholic Christians trust to the loving help of the saints, especially the Blessed Virgin Mary; many Protestant Christians emphasize a trusting faith in God as the basis of salvation. The bhakti yoga of Hindu thought says that acts of devotion and praise toward the god, whether Krishna, Shiva, Kali or some other, can compensate for lack of moral exactness in behavior. One would expect to find such ideas especially strong in a person for whom loyalty and devotion are the highest moral values (though such religious ideas may also be part of a more complex belief-system).

Allegiance Morality Is both Good and Bad

Allegiance morality represents a normal human motivation. We can guess that over the last fifty thousand years of human development any innate impulse to loyalty to one's own kith and kin could be a powerful help to preserve the lives of the people of the group. Sociobiologists, who investigate how much of our behavior is guided by our genes, claim that we may have some innate inclination to help out those who are like us or those with whom we have been raised. Whether this is so or not, we certainly act with passionate loyalty at times when our family or friends are threatened.

Allegiance morality has much that is good in it. The loyalty which motivates a person to sacrifice pleasure or safety for the good of others seems praiseworthy. Dedication to a God who is loving and accepting rather than vengeful seems to be a humane way to live. But allegiance morality also has its down side. It may sustain the tendency to see outsiders as inferior or dangerous, and be a source of antagonisms that manifest themselves in ways ranging from petty bigotry all the way to war against the evil enemy. Like much in life, allegiance morality is both good and bad.

But if you agree with that statement, it raises a question: how do you know what is good and what is bad about allegiance morality or, for that matter, about taboo morality? What standards of good and bad are you using to make that judgment? One possible answer is that you have learned and grown accustomed to another basis for making moral judgments, one that does not clearly appear in history until historic cultures develop. That is the morality of universal laws.

The Morality of Universal Laws

Taboo morality is self-seeking and self-centered. Allegiance morality has a concern for self also, but it leads to personal sacrifice for others in the group. A third kind of morality achieves a sense of self-esteem by measuring self against what it sees as a set of objective and universally valid moral standards. It is a morality which is worked out explicitly for the first time in historic cultures, the cultures which begin to reflect systematically on the universal structure and order of things.

One sign that a culture has developed a strong historic element is the development of a moral vision that seeks perfection. Thus historic cultures tend to look outside of this world for salvation because they want something more perfect than earthly existence could provide. Similarly, in ethics there is a tendency for historic religions to propose a morality of absolute laws that everyone in theory should always obey, even though in practice people can never fully adhere to such laws, as we will discuss when we consider the disadvantages of universal laws morality.

The Idea of Universal Objective Norms

Truly objective and universally valid moral norms should be standards that are valid whether anyone agrees with them or not. If such moral standards exist, a person could use them to judge whether a given group, even the person's own clan, nation, or religion, is right or wrong. In theory, therefore, these standards can overrule the standards of allegiance morality.

By definition, universally valid standards should apply to everyone, everywhere, in all situations. They should show no favoritism to one group or person over another. Every person's moral rightness could be measured by such standards. We live in a time when belief in such standards has diminished. We are accustomed to hearing that every person has his or her own morality. Universal laws morality insists, however, that regardless of what people think, there is as a matter of fact just one true and universal set of moral laws, which all people ideally ought to obey.

Universal laws morality does not necessarily include any specific laws different from what taboo morality or allegiance morality might impose. Nor are the universal laws necessarily any more rigid than taboo rules or groups customs. The basic difference lies not so much in which laws are to be obeyed or how strictly, but in how universally the laws are to be applied. A law against cannibalism is not a universal law if it forbids eating only your neighbor but allows for hearty meals whenever strangers stumble by. It is common enough in history for a group of people to try to forbid killing and stealing among themselves but to allow wholesale plunder and murder of outsiders for pleasure and profit. At some point in a culture's development, however, it may extend its basic moral rules to all people.

The ancient Hebrews, for example, in their archaic days were not surprised that their god, Yahweh, insisted on a set of laws and rituals that were not the same as the ones that the gods of the Egyptians enforced. But by the time of the Babylonian exile many of the Jewish prophets interpreted some of the laws given by Yahweh in a new way. The laws against killing, stealing, and lying, the laws demanding justice and honesty in human affairs, were recognized as laws that all people everywhere should follow. What had been only the tribal laws of an archaic society became the universal laws of a historic religion. The prophet Isaiah dreamed of a wonderful social order, with justice and equal protection for all people, that would result from obeying the universally applicable laws of God. Because the Jewish people could share those laws with everyone, Isaiah promised that Judaism would become a light to all nations.

The Advantage of Universal Laws

Universal laws are intended for everyone, everywhere, under all conditions. Most people have some familiarity with this kind of morality. Many people have been told at some time that it is always wrong for anyone to steal or that no one should ever tell a lie. Most people today usually believe it is legitimate at times to make an exception to the rules, but a totally universal morality supposedly does not allow for exceptions. Once exceptions are tolerated at all, the principle has been established that the laws are not fully universal. There is then the practical problem that if any exceptions are allowed more and more exceptions may be granted until law and order breaks down. Strict adherence to universal law can be a strong defense against anarchy. The rules are supposed to be followed, though, because they are objectively right and not just because they are means to preserve law and order.

Universal laws can promote equal justice. Everyone is to be judged according to the law and not according to family ties, social status, or political influence. This is the principle that allows the poor and the rich equal rights; not even a king or president is above the law. It is not easy to enforce this principle. Money and power can bend rules. A traditional caste system can override it. But the principles of equality set the standard to live up to. Where the archaic style of thought is willing to make exceptions for the powerful or the famous, for the leaders and the heroes, historic cultures seek to establish the primacy of law over status, promoting the ideal of equal justice for all under the law.

Universal laws are expressions of some basic insights about human life. It is always a bad thing when someone is killed by another. Even a person favoring capital punishment can say that each time a criminal is executed it is genuinely bad that such an extreme solution is necessary. In each case it is a terrible part of life that one person's life is sacrificed. Likewise, it is always a bad thing when someone steals, no matter how valid the justification. Even if it is necessary to steal in some situations, it still is true that there is unjust loss to one person, that more mistrust has been created; it is regrettable that such stealing should ever be necessary. The basic insight of universal laws morality is that such things as killing and stealing are always bad in some respect. A universal laws morality takes this insight and transforms it into a set of laws. If killing a person is always bad in some way, then it should always be forbidden, the reasoning goes.

Universal laws morality functions as a challenge to a culture and its people to be always better than they have been, simply because no culture has lived up to such a morality perfectly. No matter how necessary it might seem at some time to lie or steal, universal laws morality stands as a constant reminder that all such exceptions represent failures in human existence, that such actions can never be simply accepted but must always be regretted, that there must be an unending search to find ways to avoid violation of the ideals expressed in the universal laws. Universal laws morality can be very difficult to apply, but attempts to follow it can have a good effect on a culture.

Universal Laws Morality and Religion

Universal laws morality is most likely to flourish when a religious tradition reaches its historic stage. In many cases ideas from archaic times provide the base upon which the later classical morality is built. As we saw in Chapter Three, belief in a yang/yin order in nature goes back to archaic times in China; so does belief in the right order called li. Egyptian belief in ma'at, the proper order to all things, is very ancient. Greek belief in a fate that rules everything predates the axial age. Such beliefs provided a basis eventually for a more historic formulation.

In late archaic cultures around the world, the need for some explicit basis for law and order and overall social coherence became greater as the cultures became more complex. The great kingdoms of China, India, Mesopotamia, and Egypt all had to find ways to unify diverse elements of vast populations with different traditions. Sheer force works only for a time. Human beings can grow restless unless someone makes sense out of the order of things by showing why things are the way they are and then, how they should be.

We can speculate that perhaps this practical need to articulate some basis for an overall and unifying social order gave cultures the drive to discover universals. Perhaps the need to provide justification for the laws, customs, and morality that an empire imposes on various people pushed them into the axial age and into universalizing consciousness. Perhaps. At any rate, out of archaic beliefs in the will of the gods, fate, and li, there materialized the historic moral systems of universal laws.

By the third century BCE, for example, the ancient Stoics discovered a morality built into nature. They perceived a divine pattern in nature, as we have seen, a cosmic structure that included human life. They called it the divine Logos ("word" or rational order); or sometimes "Zeus," though they did not think of it as really the anthropomorphic sky-god. To conform to the Logos of nature is to live naturally, they said, and therefore wisely.

Stoic thought is still influential in some forms of Christian morality today. Christians argued that God made nature. To behave naturally, therefore, is to act in conformity with God's will. The Catholic church still reflects a somewhat Stoic "natural law morality" in its arguments about sex. By its very nature, according to the purpose for which God made it, the reasoning goes, sex is meant to produce children. Therefore any sexual activity that deliberately excludes the possibility of pregnancy is unnatural activity. What is against nature is always intrinsically wrong. Therefore, the Catholic Church concludes, artificial contraception is contrary to the nature of sex and is always intrinsically wrong, as are masturbation and homosexual activity for the same reason.

The full force of universal laws morality, though, is not found just by looking at particular conclusions. By itself each law is just a law; but in the historic religions it is part of a universal harmony. To adhere to one law can be to put yourself in touch with what you believe to be the order of the cosmos. To build a life upon the set of universal laws could integrate your life into the vast unity of all things. When universal laws morality is integrated with a religious vision, it becomes a way to create an identity and a belonging that unites the person to the all-encompassing supreme Reality, to the infinite and numinous Source of life and nature. To conform to a universal laws morality is not merely to be good, it is to belong to God or to the Eternal.

An important aspect of this is that because each person's identity is no longer tied to the clan or the nation but to the universal scheme of things, a person's self-worth is therefore no longer just a matter of group allegiance. Instead, it is an objectively valid self-worth based on the objective and universal right order. This is the basis for the new kind of individualism, not one of egocentric concern for self alone but of self-worth defined by adherence to certain universal values. This is not, however, the radical individualism of some modern theories, as we will see, in which the individual can choose her or his own moral framework. In a system of universal moral laws, the individual is subject to the framework of universally valid norms that all people are supposed to obey. It is called "individualism" only because it provides a basis for the individual to break the claims of community custom and stand on individual conscience. In 1521 when Martin Luther concluded his defense at the conference in Worms, Germany, with the words, "Here I stand; I cannot do otherwise," he was claiming that as a person of conscience he had to obey what God wanted him to do, and not accept the authority of the Church. (Of course, the Catholic Church claimed that it and not Luther knew what God wanted.)

Difficulties with Universal Laws

In spite of the advantages cited there are problems with any universal laws morality. One is that rules and attitudes from taboo and allegiance morality tend to get mixed in with the universal laws. Every historic religion is made up of a mixture of people, some of whom operate more on the basis of taboo and allegiance motivation. Every historic religion is also the continuation of some culture's tradition and retains within it many ideas and values from archaic and even primitive times. The universalizing tendency of historic religion produces some basic insights about the harm involved in every act of killing, stealing, and so forth. That same universalizing tendency, however, often leads people to make supposedly universal laws out of what actually are no more than the local customs of the group or culture. Is it true, for example, as Islamic tradition insists, that charging interest for loans is always and everywhere wrong? Is it true, as some Christian missionaries tried often to insist, that public nudity is intrinsically immoral and therefore always wrong? A universalizing religion often interferes with its own claims about the objective and universal nature of moral laws by insisting that its whole set of culturally produced laws and customs are all universally valid.

A serious problem in all this, as you may have noticed by now, lies in knowing how to tell the difference between a universally valid law and one that merely happens to have been maintained in a given culture. Whatever is familiar may seem objectively correct. A person taught to fear God's punishment for masturbation, or to fear being rejected from the group for divorcing, may really act out of taboo or allegiance motivation in claiming that divorce and masturbation are intrinsically and objectively wrong. Our motives are often mixed. The motivation behind a genuine universal laws morality is not fear of punishment or rejection, but a sense that there are standards worth following simply because they are intrinsically valid, whether or not they are accepted by others or rewarded.

The greatest problem with universal laws morality is that each law appears to have some valid exceptions. The same religious traditions that insist that certain laws are always valid often allow exceptions. They say that a person may steal food if that is the only way to feed a starving child. A person may lie if that is the only way to prevent much greater and long-term harm. A person may even kill if that is the only way that can be found to save innocent lives. To forbid any exceptions at all would create a cold and sometimes cruel legalism, the law for the law's sake, not for people's sake. Yet to allow exceptions conflicts with the claim that such laws are truly universal.

Casuistry

Historic religions can say that universal laws could always be obeyed if there were a perfect world, but since this is not a perfect world there is a need for realistic guidelines that are more applicable than laws that may never be broken under any circumstances whatsoever. There has been a practical set of guidelines on how to apply the universal laws to fit an imperfect world. These guidelines make up what is called "casuistry," a name derived from the fact that they are guidelines about difficult cases in applying universal moral laws.

Casuistry has a bad name for those who believe firmly in absolute universal laws morality, because it consists of ways to soften the rules in their application. Casuistry is often described as hair-splitting and quibbling because it produces complicated justifications for not giving simple obedience to some universal law in a given case. Supporters of casuistry value it, however, as a way to deal realistically with the complexities of life.

Universal moral law has been understood to command, for example, that no killing is ever allowed, not even of one's own self. Therefore suicide is also wrong. But what if a person is trapped on top of a twenty-story burning building, asked one textbook, and the only way to escape a painful death by flame was to jump to what seemed to be also a certain death by landing on very hard concrete very fast? Jumping would be suicide and therefore immoral in itself, unless you jump intending not to kill yourself but only to avoid the flames. You jump; you just do not intend to land. This is called "the principle of double effect."

That sounds a little silly to our ears. But this principle of double effect is applied in other ways. Some of those opposed utterly to all abortions nonetheless allow ectopic pregnancies to be terminated, even though that kills the developing embryo, on the grounds that the main purpose is not to abort but to remove a diseased section of the fallopian tube, diseased because the embryo has implanted itself there. Many people who hate the idea of killing civilians in war nonetheless think it is moral under some circumstances to bomb an enemy knowing there will be what is euphemistically called "collateral damage." Are we being immoral because we end up violating a universal law when doing something that seems nonetheless necessary? Perhaps not, says casuistry. Life is complicated.

There is in fact a major principle of casuistry that sums up all the others fairly well. That is the principle it is always legitimate to do "the lesser of two evils" when it is inevitable that you will have to end up doing at least one of them. Telling a lie to save a life is an instance of this. It is an evil to tell a lie, but it is also a greater evil that someone should die. Real life often consists of complicated tradeoffs between different evils and goods. Casuistry acknowledges this and tries to give guidance on how to deal with real life as it is.

Casuistry was originally a set of rules attached to universal laws morality, rules used by people who wanted to maintain universal laws morality but apply it in a realistic way. These rules go by such names as "lesser of two evils" and "principle of double effect." Others have used the insights used by casuistry to construct a different kind of morality. Here we can call it "basic value morality."

Basic Value Morality

Human Well-Being as the Basic Good

When confronted with conflicts among moral laws, casuistry tried to discover the option that resulted in the most good and the least harm. In doing this it had stumbled upon a very general moral norm, much more general than the specific universal laws. The general norm is this: do good and avoid harm as much as possible.

But this begs the question: how does a person know what is good? Taboo morality identifies good as whatever satisfies a selfish concern for one's own pleasure even at the expense of others. In allegiance morality, good is whatever promotes the common weal. Universal laws morality breaks out of group loyalty in order to offer objective and universal standards of what is good or bad. But when even universal laws are not adequate for defining what is good, then what does it mean to say that a basic moral norm is to do good. What is "good," and how does a person know it?

Basic value morality cannot offer a precise answer to that. This morality proceeds on the basis of concern for the well-being of every human person as much as is possible. But there are many arguments about just what this well-being is and how best to achieve it. Is the invigorating challenge of a free capitalistic world better for people, or the humane security of a socialist state? Would we all be better off if we lived in a world run by robots who protected us from all possible physical danger and all confusing choices and all disturbing surprises? Or would that make life too boring and make us too immature? But then what is it about maturity, whatever that is, that makes it part of "human well-being"? For that matter, should we have a deep concern not just for human well-being but for all living things on the planet, as some ecologically minded people insist? The questions are endless.

In the nineteenth century some basic value moralists called Utilitarians defined "good" as individual pleasure. The goal of all moral decisions, they said, should be to increase the sum of individual human pleasure in the world as much as possible. This approach was labeled a "hedonistic calculus." Utilitarians believed that morality was similar to capitalism. If each person seeks his or her own happiness within the limit of not being allowed to directly interfere with anyone else's search for happiness, then in the long run, as though guided by an invisible hand, maximum human happiness would follow.

Other Utilitarians disagreed. Some said that pleasure is not an adequate good for human well-being. Other words like "happiness" or "fulfillment" would come closer to describing such an ultimate good. Yet others added that the original form of utilitarianism paid too much attention to individuals as such and needed to learn to appreciate love and loyalty and devotion to family and community life as part of human well-being.

Some moralists have tried to solve the problem of defining human well-being by sidestepping it and focusing instead on the intentions behind our actions. The way to achieve the basic value of human well-being, they have said, is to act always out of love in every concrete situation, to do whatever is most loving towards all people. (The name "situation ethics" is sometimes used for this approach.)

But this emphasis on intentions can actually be very harmful to human well-being. People who act out of good intentions may be ignorant, incompetent, or impulsive, and thus cause great harm. It may be personally very gratifying to be able to say that you acted out of love. But personal gratification is not the goal of basic value morality. The goal is to actually achieve what is helpful to others. For this reason some forms of basic value morality call themselves "consequentialist ethics" in order to stress that it is the consequences of our actions that count the most. This brings the question back to the nature of "good." If a person acts out of love in order to produce good consequences in the lives of others, just which consequences are good ones instead of bad ones, and how do you know? Having a loving intention alone will not solve this. What criterion does a person use to evaluate whether the consequences have in fact been good instead of bad?

Virtue Ethics

"Virtue ethics" is the name for another approach that focuses also on the person rather than directly on the outcome of decisions or actions. The word "virtue" has lost some of its power in everyday language. It now suggests a prim or even puritanical attitude. But the original meaning of virtue was "strength," in this case strength of character. We might think that a person of strong and good character is one who habitually feels compassion for others, values justice highly, has the wisdom to judge well how to achieve what compassion and justice require, and the courage and generosity to act on this judgment. Certainly, the more people can develop such virtues, the more we will have a world which achieves human well-being. So a basic value morality ought to seek to inculcate such virtues.

The question that virtue ethics sometimes fails to answer, however, is just how one knows which virtues are more important, or which habitual dispositions are really virtues at all. A taboo moralist may regard courage as a virtue but not compassion, and will interpret wisdom as skill at serving self-interests. An allegiance moralist will place loyalty very high on the list of virtues, and may think that standing up for abstract principles of justice at the expense of one's own group is disloyalty. A universal laws moralist will think it virtuous never to violate any of the objective moral laws in which that person believes. Stern obedience to the law is thus an important virtue. A basic value moralist may find such unbending obedience to be a vice to whatever extent it leads someone to sacrifice human well-being to the demands of a law.

Virtue ethics nonetheless makes an essential contribution to the goal of serving basic human well-being. Virtues empower a person to actually practice what moral theory proposes as the good. Perhaps, however, basic value morality should place "humility" rather high on the list of virtues, to guard against arrogance in judging what truly serves the well-being of others.

The list of virtues given here is not necessarily what each type of morality will come up with. These lists merely illustrate that the virtues a person chooses to develop depend on a prior moral vision or commitment—to one's self-interest, to one's community, to an objective set of laws, or to basic human well-being. So the question remains of how to know what is truly helpful and what is harmful.

Basic Value Morality and Universal Laws Morality

Basic value morality can partly say what is harmful and what is good by appealing to the insights of universal laws morality. Universal laws express the recognition that certain kinds of acts or events seem always to include some degree of harm to people. Lying and stealing and killing and torture and slavery and many other things are all found to be greatly harmful by those who are on the receiving end of these actions. Society needs order; people need justice. Basic value morality does not abandon the insight of universal laws morality that some actions always do some harm. But instead of making the laws absolute, it treats the laws as guiding norms which should never be violated except when that causes greater harm than good in the long run. The basic value of human well-being determines what is good or bad, not the laws in themselves. The laws are to serve human well-being. That is why even good and insightful laws can sometimes be broken.

In practice people also seem to agree on what is harmful in the other kinds of morality. We say that the selfishness of taboo morality seems bad because it is a willingness to harm others for personal gain. The group loyalty of allegiance morality extends its concern mainly to its own and not to outsiders. The outsiders may all be harmed. Universal laws morality seeks to treat all people equally but can harm people in some circumstances if the laws are applied too strictly.

None of this provides a fully clear answer to the question of what is "good." We are close here to the basic mystery of morality. Yet people can nonetheless usually agree on what is clearly opposed to human well-being.

Pain and suffering, fear and despair, deformity and death all seem worth avoiding whenever possible. As individuals mature and cultures develop, torture and slavery appear more and more barbaric, and rape or sexual abuse become intolerable. We can also usually agree that love and friendship, accomplishments and good health, hope and long life are all desirable, at least as long as they are not overburdened by all the things worth avoiding. While we continue to struggle to learn more about ourselves and what is good for us and each other, we know at least a great deal about how we can already help rather than hurt each other.

Other Characteristics of Basic Value Morality

Basic value morality is a universal law morality. It is a single moral law that applies to all situations everywhere and always. It says one thing: always do what best promotes human well-being. There are no valid exceptions whatsoever to this single law in basic value morality. This is the basis of all other laws and all valid moral judgments. Nothing is good or bad except to the extent that it serves this basic value.

Basic value morality is therefore very demanding. It can at first appear to be easier than universal laws morality because it allows exceptions to the rules. It softens hard legalism and subordinates it to a concern for human welfare. But it is not easier, because it makes everything a moral matter. All our thoughts and acts affect people eventually in some way. We are always responsible for all the ways we affect people, because every effect could be good or bad; it is up to us to worry about that and do our best to make it good. Even doing nothing, leaving things undone, is a choice open to us and therefore part of our moral responsibility. The burden of basic value morality is to put a person under a constant moral responsibility for all of his or her actions.

There are clearly limits to what we can reasonably be expected to do. It would be useless to haunt ourselves with thoughts of all the ways in which we might be failing others. Perhaps what we ought to expect of ourselves is just that we should develop the basic habits of thoughtfulness towards others that will alert us to ways in which we can be helpful and not harmful. Such a habit is a virtue.

It should be acknowledged, however, that basic value morality can be dangerous because it is vague. When people are given very specific rules of what to do, then good and bad are much clearer. When the rule is only the general one to help instead of hurt, it is open to misuse by all sorts of people who use this as an excuse to do whatever they want. They can argue, after all, that there are no unbreakable rules. Basic value morality and the casuistry on which it is based have established that, they say. But they ignore or fail to understand that basic value morality says that the rules can be broken only to help people and avoid harming them, not broken in whatever way a person wants for any reason. Morality is confusing enough, however, that once moral laws seem no longer unbreakable then some people will allow themselves to do as they please. Such people tend to do as they please anyway, so perhaps the danger here is no greater than what already existed.

Basic value morality can also be frightening because it hands over so much responsibility to the individual person. Sets of specific rules, whether taboo rules or group rules or universal law rules, are at least fairly clear most of the time. All that a person needs to do for the most part is to memorize them and follow them. Basic value morality says that this is only a useful beginning, that a person must also then reflect on and take personal responsibility for whether this rule or that should actually be obeyed or broken. While some people enjoy this responsibility, others flee from it. Virtues of wisdom and courage will help here.

Finally, basic value morality extends and modifies the notion of the individual. We saw that universal laws morality allows a person to define self clearly and as worthy by building a life based on universal laws. The person who does not steal, cheat, kill, lie, and so forth can feel assurance that she or he is a worthwhile person, living as a person ought to, regardless of what others may say or think. Basic value morality similarly offers a way of defining the worth of one's own selfhood, but now by a general standard instead of through many specific laws, by the general standard of whether the person is one who works effectively to help others rather than hurt them. Because the basic moral value is so general, however, there is more burden on the individual to define how best to live up to that value. This form of individualism is more radical than the one that emerges from a universal laws morality. There is thus all the more need for personal virtues.

The Motivation Behind Basic Value Morality

Basic value morality says that the well-being of each person should be the guiding purpose behind every act. But how does the basic value moralist know that this is so? It is difficult enough to decide just what human well-being really consists of; how can anyone know that it is really the most basic value? One approach is to ask about the motivation behind it. Discovering the motivation for accepting human well-being as the most basic value, in fact, can shed light on the nature of morality in general.

It is possible to affirm that human well-being is the most basic value on the grounds that God or society or neighbors will reward the person who affirms this and punish the person who denies it. In that case it is a taboo morality motivation at work. Or a person could support human well-being only because that is one of the commandments of the group to which a person belongs and is loyal. This is allegiance morality motivation. A universal laws morality is built on a kind of conformity also, but in this case to the supposedly objective and universally valid laws of the universe. A person can achieve a sense of true and valuable identity by making one's own character conform to this universal set of laws. Evidently there can be more than one motivation for upholding the basic value of human well-being.

There is one more motivation that may in fact be the strongest one at work in a true basic value morality, one that is a matter of personality or character. That is a sense of sympathetic compassion for others. There is a kind of compassion for others that exists in most people from a very early age. A child sees a puppy hurt and cries with it, imagining the puppy's hurt as its own. This compassion is not very deep. The same child may torture a bird out of curiosity. An adolescent has a compassion for some people that is sometimes intense: a friend or classmate in trouble, a person's suffering reported on the evening news or described in a work of fiction. This compassion is also often limited, though; not all people will be able to earn the adolescent's sympathy. The adolescent is equally likely to issue strident condemnations of those whose motivation seems foreign or hypocritical or inadequate. Many people fail to outgrow this indignant intolerance.

Basic value morality usually represents a fuller compassion, one grounded in a sense that we are all human together. We are all confused, limited, frustrated; have hopes and dreams, needs and aspirations; look for love and are lonely. We all search for happiness and learn to accept less than what we can imagine. The person next to us is like that too. As we become increasingly sensitive to the humanness we share, we can begin to feel a personal pain from other people's pain and a personal happiness from other people's happiness. Every person, no matter how much a criminal or a sinner, no matter how boring, obnoxious, disappointing or weird, is you and me—partly who we really are, partly who we easily might have been. We all hurt in various ways. We all need the same understanding and acceptance. This sense of our mutual human needs and worth can also become a habitual sense, a virtue.

This compassion still does not solve the problem of exactly what is good about human well-being nor what this well-being fully consists in. But it brings people much closer to being helpful to one another instead of harmful. And some of the answer to why we should be good and what goodness consists in lies in the realm of the mystery of the human person, as the last section of the chapter will discuss briefly.

Basic Value Morality and Religion

Basic value morality has been most evident in historic and in modern forms of religion and culture. The great historic religions of the world have often proposed the one basic value of human well-being as the foundation of all morality. The idea of subordinating all specific laws to the one basic value appears in the Christian New Testament when Jesus declared that "the sabbath was made for man, not man for the sabbath." The great Rabbi Hillel had already proposed that the whole law of Moses could be reduced to two precepts: love God, and love your neighbor as yourself. This sense of concern for every human person shines through in the endless variations from around the world, but it often takes a familiar form known as the golden rule: "do unto others as you would have them do unto you." Give to them the same compassion and patience and acceptance that you yourself would want to receive. They are human just as you are human.

In every religious tradition such sayings are repeated more often than they are practiced. For some people "doing unto others" only means making deals to scratch each other's back, a form of self-serving taboo morality. Some feel that the neighbor who deserves their loving concern is only the one who acts properly and earns a decent place in society or shares the "one true religion." This is a form of allegiance morality. Others are sure that there are some God-given laws to be obeyed no matter who gets hurt, a form of universal laws morality. The basic value of human worth has often been buried under specific universal laws, or the need to conform to the accepting group, or to narrow self-interest. Nonetheless, various traditions have claimed that service to one's fellow human being, especially the lowly or those suffering, is the highest morality in this world and the guide and foundation for all other moral precepts.

The strongest form of basic value morality is probably the religious insistence that every human life is sacred, that in the people around us we are seeing in concrete and limited form the best clue to the inner nature of the infinite God or Self. In the familiar Western religions, each person is said to be special to God. Each person, in fact, is special because to be a person is to convey something of what the divine Mystery is all about. In the words of Hebrew scriptures, God made people in the divine "image and likeness."

People turn to religion for moral guidance because religion is a source of clear and secure direction. The kind of morality a person desires is bound up with the kind of religion a person prefers. Sometimes religion provides clear lists of rules about many aspects of life, and appeals to people who need firm and clear guidance about life from the numinous. At other times religion offers only general inspiration and ideals and leaves it to the individual to work things out. The modern forms of religion come closest to this through their emphasis on basic value morality.

The differences here exist often within a single religious tradition. Thus Muslims disagree among themselves on how strictly they should apply some Islamic rules. Jews disagree among themselves on how literally and exactly they are to follow the law of Moses. Christians range from very strict to very liberal in their interpretation of moral rules about sex and marriage or about war.

The differences in interpretation of moral rules by religious people is also a difference of interpretation concerning the place of the human person in the universe. Some religious people presume that people are meant to listen and to learn and to obey. Morality then consists primarily in receiving moral instructions and carrying them out. Other religious people think of the human person as created to be intelligently free and responsible. Morality is then something that people are supposed to create themselves as they learn more about life and about human needs and possibilities. Most people probably do a little of both in their lives.

Virtue ethicists argue that it is not a system of ethics we need but a way of developing good character. Character can guide a person in responding to the complex and unpredictable realities of life. A person of character may be one who feels compassion for others, values justice highly, has the wisdom to see how to achieve what compassion and justice require, and has the courage and generosity to do what is needed. This fits well with basic value morality, changing it from just a theory about how to determine what is right and proper to a set of personal characteristics that will be effective in actually bringing about what is good and resisting what is bad.

It is not clear that the actual proposals for an ethic of character will fit with a basic value morality. One of the most well-known advocates of ethics of character, a Christian theologian named Stanley Hauerwas, seems in fact to expect that good character will lead a person towards a kind of universal laws morality, in which abortion and war, for example, are never to be tolerated. His ethics are community centered, even sectarian in style according to some critics, in that he thinks the Christian community should stand against the fallen or false aspects of contemporary society. He seems confident that people who belong to this community will be able to discern what is right and wrong on the basis of their religious faith, but he is somewhat vague on just how this discernment works. Nonetheless, a basic value moralist would probably welcome Hauerwas's belief in the importance of character, as well as his call to high standards of moral concern.

Morality and Mystery

To arrive at basic value morality is to arrive at the edge of mystery because this morality raises the question of why anyone should value anything at all. We live by the half-conscious faith that life makes sense and is worthwhile. But our minds still have the capacity to ask how it makes sense and why it is worthwhile. The taboo moralist knows it is worthwhile to enjoy life and avoid pain. So do we all. But we would give up enjoyment and endure pain to be accepted, appreciated, loved. Yet we admire the person who would sacrifice fame, acceptance, even love, for a greater cause and a nobler principle. We admire a person who sacrifices his or her life to obey a principle that forbids killing another. We might even do it ourselves. But why? Because God will reward us? Because people will admire us then? Because it is objectively the right thing to do? Because there is something sacred about life? But what is that sacredness and how do we know? The question is the universal and ultimate one: what finally is the purpose, the value, of anything and everything?

There are pragmatic answers to the ultimate questions: eat, drink, and be merry, for tomorrow we die; live, love, and grab all the gusto you can get. There are more inspiring answers: live a worthwhile life so that when you are about to die you can feel satisfied that you have not wasted your life. Pragmatic answers and inspiring answers can be satisfying, but the human consciousness has the capacity to seek deeper answers. Only an ultimate answer could provide a complete solution.

This means that morality is inevitably a religious question. It does not mean it is inevitably a matter of receiving divine commandments or obeying religious rules. Morality is deeper than rules and commandments. It is the question of precisely what the ultimate value or purpose is to anything and all things. The kind of answer it requires will connect moral values to whatever is the ultimate truth about God, the Tao, Brahman-Atman, nirvana, or the cosmos. It will connect the worth of the person with the Ultimate.

Religious questions, however, do not always receive a religious answer. A person who decides that there is no divine Ultimate, but only endless and prosaic mystery, will have to find some way to affirm life's values anyway. (In a later chapter we will see existential humanism strive to do exactly this.)

Summary

This chapter has described four different stages of moral perspectives and connected these with four stages of cultural and religious evolution. Primitive religion and culture seem to hold on to a taboo perspective more than other cultures do, though this perspective can be found among people in all cultures. Literate archaic religion and culture, with their heightened sense of honor or pride, give a stronger emphasis to the need for public acceptance, though this is a need common to all people. With the appearance of historic religion and culture, we encounter for the first time clearly universalist ethics, usually codified in many laws. Modern religion and culture have made more explicitly focal the older general notion that loving one's neighbor, helping others, is the basis of all morality. Certain virtues enable people better to live by this standard. People find guidance from religion, however, not just through moral tradition but in many ways. The next three chapters describe some of these ways.

For Further Reflection

1. To what extent is fear of punishment by God needed in society today to maintain good social order and morality?
2. Do people that you know find it easy to go against the opinions of their families and neighbors in order to do what seems objectively right in their own eyes?
3. How do you know what is really good or bad? Is it just a matter of individual feelings with no objective validity at all? Explain.
4. When others seriously hurt you or your friends or the weak and helpless, on what grounds can you say this is really wrong?
5. How would you feel if you had to admit to yourself that you are one of those who are careless about hurting others? Explain why you feel that way.

Suggested Readings

John R. Snarey, "Cross-Cultural Universality of Social-Moral Development: A Critical Review of Kohlbergian Research," in *Psychological Bulletin* 97:2, 1985, 202-232. Snarey does a "meta-analysis," comparing numerous different studies of Kohlberg's theories in different cultures.

James W. Fowler, *Stages of Faith*, 1981. See the end of the chapters of Part IV for comments on changes in moral perspective.

James Rest et al., *Postconventional Moral Thinking: A Neo-Kohlbergian Approach*, 1999. A revision of Kohlberg's stages based on extensive further empirical evidence.

Mary M. Wilcox, *A Developmental Journey*, 1979. A good general introduction to the ideas of Piaget and Kohlberg, including their theories on moral development.

R. Murray Thomas, *Moral Development Theories—Secular and Religious: A Comparative Study*, 1997.

Carol Gilligan, *In a Different Voice: Psychological Theory and Women's Development*, 1993 (2nd ed.).

Irene Bloom, J. Paul Martin, and Wayne Proudfoot, eds., *Religious Diversity and Human Rights*, 1996.

CHAPTER NINE

The Process of Tradition

Leaders, Texts, and Interpretations

RELIGIOUS TRADITION AND CULTURE

The introduction to Part II notes that we all must learn how to be human, and that it is our culture that teaches us this. Another word for culture could be "tradition." The English word "trade" comes from the same root. Tradition is whatever is passed on or handed over to someone. Our parents, teachers, community, and whole culture passes on to us a way of seeing life and living life. That is tradition. It teaches us a way to be human.

Religion has normally been at the heart of every cultural tradition. The basic religious beliefs, values, and practices are usually part of the cultural air each person breathes, so much so that people do not consciously take note of this any more than of their own breathing. In our modern culture we are used to the idea that every person has the right to determine privately which religious tradition to follow, if any. We think of religion as a matter of personal conscience, between the individual and God. Because of that we do not always see the influence that religion has on culture. Even in modern times culture is given certain forms and directions by the presence of religious ideas in the air and by leaders and texts that our culture presents to us as respectable, authentic, or sacred.

Religiousness in turn is socially conditioned, that is, formed by the social context people draw from as they become who they are. Every culture and society is formed over many generations. They are the products of historical processes, of the patterns of human behavior and choices in an ongoing development generation after generation. It is human inventiveness at work, over thousands of years, discovering endless possibilities of language, law, custom, value, roles, rules, all the things that go into making us who we are. All of this has a great impact on religious tradition because religion and culture are usually intimately intertwined.

People are not inclined to think that way about their own religious tradition. They tend to believe that the Law of Moses or the Bible or the Qur'an is to be accepted not because of cultural endorsement but because it is truly God's word. They believe in the authority of Moses or Jesus or Muhammad, they say, not because society tells them to, but because these people spoke for God. And yet it is also clear that much depends on where one was born, and to what family. Few Americans worship Vishnu or seek nirvana. Few Japanese pray to Allah and read the Qur'an. There is individual human choice involved, but choices are guided by society and culture, by a person's historical context. What most of us do is trust that our religious tradition, the cultural heritage of our people, authentically represents the numinous reality as it really is. We implicitly trust that the cultural process that has led us to accept certain beliefs and values and practices is a process that has been in touch with the reality of the numinous, with God or the Tao or the gods or the ancestors.

People do change religions, even against the current of their culture. That is why cults exist at all. People also adhere to minority positions within a larger culture. The presence of Jews in largely Christian and Muslim lands, of Parsees (Zoroastrians) and Christians in India, attest to this. In each case certain people maintain an allegiance to a tradition that is not strongly supported by society as a whole. Even these traditions, though, exist within a social context and are affected by the currents of ideas and values flowing about them. Religious traditions have identifiable roots in the broader cultural traditions and historic patterns.

The interplay of religion and culture can vary over time. In India the Jain tradition is attributed by Jains to a series of twenty-four holy men, especially the last, known as Mahavira ("great man" or hero) and also as Jina (victor). Jainism was at first, as long ago as the sixth century BCE, a rejection of the authority of the Vedas, of Hindu ritualism, and of the caste system, although like the other "orthodox" Hindu traditions, including Buddhism, it accepted belief in karma and the wheel of rebirth. But over subsequent centuries, Jainism gradually re-absorbed many Hindu beliefs and practices.

Much later, beginning in the sixteenth century in India, a guru (religious leader) named Nanak tried to reconcile Hindu and Muslim belief, in the direction of a strict monotheism, through his Sikh beliefs and practices. Too austere for most Hindus and not orthodox enough for most Muslims, the Sikhs were often on the defensive. Nine more significant gurus led the Sikhs, one after another, each adapting to the needs of their respective situations. Since the end of the seventeenth century CE, Sikh males have followed the custom of becoming religious warriors prepared to fight and die for their homeland in the Punjab (in Northwest India, though part of the original

Punjab is now in Pakistan). Sikh men wear their death shroud wrapped up as a turban on their heads, carry a large dagger, and let their hair and beard grow long. Sikhism, as it is sometimes called, is no longer so much a reconciliation of Hindu and Muslim traditions as a tradition of its own.

The prevalence of such long-term historical change makes it difficult to know the best way to characterize a given tradition. Protestant Christians, like the most traditional of Buddhists, hearken back to their original sources, as in the Bible or in classic early Buddhist texts. But Catholic Christians and Mahayana Buddhists are comfortable with a long history of further developments in beliefs and practices. Catholicism in particular can cite declarations of formal church councils, from at least 351 CE in Nicaea to the Second Vatican Council held in the 1960s. Orthodox Jews give primary respect to the Law of Moses encoded in the Pentateuch, the first five books of Hebrew scriptures. But they accept prophetic and historical books as commentary on the Law, as well as the Talmud as further commentary, at least up to the sixth century CE. Reform Jews in the nineteenth century made yet more adaptations to their times. So one can identify a tradition mainly with its original sources, or also with the results of long-term development.

If neither of these is adequate, one can look to current beliefs and practices. Certainly a Buddhist may feel that personal religious life as a Buddhist tells that person what true lived Buddhism is. Practicing Buddhists or Christians or Taoists may not be very well prepared to describe the true origin and history of development of their own traditions. Even while they ascribe antiquity to their own traditions, in practice it may be a rather recent form of it that a given person follows. Catholics raised in the forms set for the whole church by the sixteenth-century Council of Trent, for example, often have trouble recognizing that those forms are partly the result of a long developmental process and not simply truths set forth in the original Christian scriptures.

There are degrees of conformity and variety, change and stability, in every society and in religion. We will talk more about people's reasons for choosing to accept or reject their culture's tradition in a later chapter on knowing and believing. For now, though, we can see some of the ways tradition is formed, passed on, and interpreted.

The Leaders

People are normally very interested in finding out about mysterious powers and how to deal with them, or in discovering answers to life's ultimate mysteries. Anyone who can claim to understand, interpret correctly, or deal successfully with the mysterious and invisible powers in life is likely to be accorded special status and be respected. There have been a few people in history, people like the Buddha and Lao Tzu and Moses and Jesus and Muhammad, who have had enormous impact. There are many more people who are less noticed but still very influential. Every culture has numerous religious leaders of various kinds, who learn the tradition and pass it on, or who live it with special vigor, or who modify it and gather a following for their new version of it. People readily look to special leaders for guidance and help in their relations with the numinous. Here are a few of the kinds of important religious leaders. It may seem confusing to consider so many different kinds. The purpose here is only to illustrate the many ways in which religious leaders can have influence.

Technicians of the Sacred

In any primitive society there are two main religious tasks that are performed by part-time specialists; healing and augury. The healers (in English sometimes labeled witch doctors or medicine men and women) are usually called shamans by anthropologists, who borrow the term from natives of Siberia. Siberian shamans must wrestle with spirits who cause disease and other ills. Shamans are also herbalists, using a variety of roots and herbs to aid in cures. Shamans are often also accomplished at augury, though others might share in this skill.

Archaic cultures around the world employ another technician of the sacred, the priest who performs rituals, especially ritual sacrifice. Though primitive people may sometimes offer gifts to keep the spirits happy, archaic cultures believe that the gods expect regular sacrificial offerings, whether of grains and fruits, or animals, or even human sacrifice. Permanent places of sacrifice, whether open air altars or enclosed temples, provide a locale for full-time priests to perform their duties. At this same place augury is liable to be carried out, either by the priests or by full-time "prophets," whose job it is to check animal entrails or organs or to analyze the movements of the stars, in order to discern the will of the gods or the course of fate.

The ancient Brahmin caste in India is an example of a professional priesthood. As far back as archaic times in India the young Brahmin boy would be assigned thousands of poetic chants to be memorized exactly. Countless ritual details had to be mastered until after years of training the Brahmin could function in the village or town as a priest performing the rituals to end drought or cure the sick or consecrate a marriage. In cities the Brahmins also maintained the constant rituals that helped to preserve the universe and keep it running smoothly. It was usually thought best to hire three priests at once, who would repeat the ritual chants and practices together. If one should make a mistake, the other two would correct him so that the ritual would not lose any of its power.

Historic religions have set great store by priestly function. Christianity, Buddhism, and the Hindu tradition still include major groups whose leadership is in the hands of priests. Usually they are no longer considered just technicians and ritual practitioners but learned guides also. Even in historic religions, however, what identifies a priest is still the ancient function of the technician of the sacred: a careful and proper performance of the ritual, especially ritual sacrifices, to control or influence various numinous powers.

As a rule, the role of the augur is not part of historic religion. The usefulness of augurs lies in the fact that a clear prediction of the future allows a person to avoid bad events. If the goat's intestines reveal that tomorrow is a dangerous day for a journey, then a person can stay home and be safe. Historic religions tend to consider this ability to manipulate one's own future and fortune an affront to an ultimate supreme Being or cosmic Power. Trust or submission is the proper attitude toward God's unavoidable will or the Tao's ultimate influence. Nevertheless, people belonging to a historic tradition find it comforting at times to employ prophets or soothsayers anyway. Trust in God, they may say; but for greater safety yet read your horoscope and consult your palm reader.

Wise Ones and Enlightened Ones

Confucian tradition has high respect for the sage, the wise one whose learning and insight and well-balanced perspective produce a life worth imitating and wisdom worth learning. Kung Fu Tzu (Confucius) himself is held in highest reverence because of his wisdom. He received no revelations, was not divine, did not practice any particular austerities or devote extra time to worship of the gods. He was not a prophet nor did he perform rituals. He was simply wise enough that China built an entire social order on his thought and maintain it fairly well for over two thousand years.

In fact, Confucian tradition should probably be thought of as a philosophy and not as a religion. But the so-called philosophical Taoism, the other great native tradition of China, has a religious respect for the Ultimate Tao. Taoism is also based on wisdom. It had its beginning supposedly in the brief writings of the legendary Lao-Tzu. His name translates roughly as "the old man," implying that he probably was one whose age had taught him wisdom worthy of reverence. Lao-Tzu was stopped at the border of China, the story goes, by a guard who would allow Lao-Tzu to depart from China only on the condition that he write down his wisdom so it would not be lost. Lao-Tzu quickly composed a few pages that became known as the *Tao-Te-Ching*, the Book of the Power of the Way (Way-Power-Book). About 250 BCE Taoism was strongly influenced by Chuang-Tzu, whose great wisdom guided generations of Taoists. Neither Lao-Tzu nor Chuang-Tzu was said to be inspired by the ancestors or given a revelation by the gods. Their authority lay simply in the wisdom of their words.

Buddhism also could be said to have its origin in wisdom. In this case it is the insight or enlightenment of Siddhartha Gautama. Buddhism has its many priests and its holiness communities, but it was begun not by priests or monks but by the prince who turned to reflection and achieved enlightenment, thus earning the title of Buddha, "Enlightened One." At first, Siddhartha Gautama followed the path of Indian yogis and ascetics of his time, training himself in meditation and then fasting until his stomach met his spine. This did not provide release from sufferings. He was learning by experience. Finally, he sat one night in meditation under a tree and broke through into full enlightenment. He moved on then to teach others about what he had learned, giving his first lesson to a few others in a deer park at the city of Benares in northern India. Many came to follow his teachings. His insights into life somehow fit the experience of many who listened to him. Soon his teachings on life's suffering and on release into nirvana through detachment became the core of one of history's great religious traditions. (Not too many years later, that tradition began to describe the Buddha not merely as a wise man, but as the earthly form a divine being had taken in order to provide guidance to humankind out of compassion for our suffering.)

The Learned Interpreters

The Chinese sages and the Indian Buddha had all been influenced by ideas that were part of their culture. Lao-Tzu knew about the yang/yin of the Tao, because everyone in China knew about it. The Buddha believed we are all condemned to be reborn into suffering countless times, because that was becoming a widespread belief in India. Even the wisest and most learned have to start with some ideas and values from their cultural traditions. Sometimes the role of the wise and learned religious leader is explicitly acknowledged to be that of interpreter of the religious tradition. The Jewish rabbi is one such. So is the Islamic imam ("leader"), and the Protestant preacher.

After the return of many Jews from the exile in Babylon in the sixth century BCE, the priests in Jerusalem were the religious leaders and custodians of the tradition. Since the law of Moses often needed recopying, the writers ("scribes") who did the copying came to know the law in detail. They often helped to interpret it. The role of the priesthood ended with the destruction of the temple in Jerusalem in 70 CE by the Romans. Without a temple in which to offer ritual sacrifices there was no need for priests in Judaism, so the learned interpreters of the law took over as the leaders of Judaism. They were addressed as rabbi, meaning teacher or leader. Their authority to this day comes from their learning. They know the law and the great body of interpretations of the law that accumulated and were gathered into a collection known as the Talmud ("teaching") by the sixth century CE. Today, the major religious leadership role in Judaism is that of the learned person, the interpreter of the law.

Continuing what began with the Jews in the West, Christians and then Muslims also compiled their own sacred texts. For centuries the leaders in Christianity were the priests. Then with the Reformation in the sixteenth century in Europe, many of the Protestant Christian churches eliminated priests and gave the leadership role to those who knew the sacred texts of the Bible very well and could interpret it and preach its message. In Islam the name *ulama* stands for a body of religious teachers who are learned in the Qur'an and can help others in interpreting and applying the will of God that is written there.

Rabbis and preachers and imama, Confucian sages and Taoist philosophers and Hindu thinkers, and even the priests of many traditions, are all called on to know the religious tradition and guide others to better understanding and application of it. At times in all the religious traditions, there are also those who claim great learning without having it, without even understanding what learning really is. Others equally unlearned will listen and not know the difference. Every tradition has some movements within it, movements which claim the authority of the tradition but which actually depart from it, sometimes without even realizing it. The problem of interpretation is one we will return to later in this chapter.

The Messengers: Great Prophets

English-speaking people are accustomed to use the word "prophet" to label individuals inspired by God to be his spokesperson and, sometimes, to predict the future, even if somewhat obscurely. The function of predicting the future is one that primitive and archaic prophets had, inasmuch as these prophets were really augurs, soothsayers, readers of omens. The best-known prophets are not soothsayers, however, but messengers of God who deliver information and guidance from God. Isaiah, Jeremiah, Ezekiel, Hosea, Micah, and Amos are some of the messengers of God in the Hebrew scriptures. The primary prophet in the Jewish tradition is Moses. The instructions from God transmitted through Moses provide the foundation of Judaic thought. In the New Testament Jesus is portrayed at times also as prophet, a new Moses bringing to the people a new understanding of God's will. In Islamic belief Muhammad is God's final and supreme messenger. His teachings are written in the Qur'an, though they are not really Muhammad's teachings. They are the eternal will of God recited by God's angel Gabriel to Muhammad so that he in turn could recite them to others. According to

Islamic belief the teachings of God delivered to Muhammad are the fulfillment of the teachings God gave to Moses, Jesus, and other prophets.

The Appointed Agents of God: Messiahs

We have seen that the name messiah is from a Hebrew word meaning "anointed." The ancient Semitic practice (still observed in a few cases today as in the Catholic ritual of confirmation) was to anoint with oil a person who was appointed to a special role. The kings of ancient Judea were anointed. The future king many Judeans hoped for is thus the anointed one, messiah. Christians are familiar with the Greek translation of the word. "Anointed one" in Greek is *christos,* shortened in English to "Christ."

As far back as the seventh century BCE, the prophet Isaiah had offered hope for an ideal king to come. This was associated with the "Day of the Lord" when Yahweh would bring about a peaceable kingdom, the ideal life without war or bloodshed. Subsequent generations continued to hope that God would send a leader in times of troubles. Most hoped for a king, a royal messiah. Others thought Yahweh might anoint a priest, a prophet, or a teacher to be the agent who would usher in God's kingdom. Some Jews speculated that perhaps it was not an individual person but the whole nation of Israel that was to be anointed by God to bring peace and happiness to all the world in a glorious millennial Day of the Lord. One result of all this was the growth of the apocalyptic thought described earlier. Another result was the birth of Christianity, originally a Jewish sect adhering to Jesus of Nazareth as the agent appointed by God to inaugurate the apocalyptic coming of the Day of the Lord and the Kingdom of God.

The notion of messiah belongs also to Islam. Some forms of Islamic tradition have looked forward to the arrival of a person sent by God to order things the way God wants them. This messiah will not reveal any new truths or instructions. The Qur'an is the last word on such things. But there is still need for a leader who has the authority to propel people toward accepting God's will and living their lives properly. The majority group of Islam, the Sunnis, look forward to a mahdi, one who is divinely guided. He will appear on earth near the end of the world. Shiite Muslims expect that God will send a very special imam to restore all things in the end. In various religious traditions it is possible to find messianic ideas. Perhaps the Buddha and other figures who bring salvation in some way can all be called messianic figures. Anyone who claims to function as the agent of God and lead people to salvation can now loosely be called a messiah.

Holy Ones

Some individuals become authorities in a religious tradition because they are thought to be very holy. They are not appointed by God or the gods to this role. It does not necessarily even require insight or wisdom or learning, although this is a deficiency that can make holy people very dangerous.

Holiness is a difficult attribute to define. It usually consists of an intense devotion or dedication to the service of the divine or numinous. We often think of holiness as a moral quality. In that case, holiness is firm obedience of all moral laws and a superior measure of virtue such as patience and compassion. But holiness appears in other forms also. Some people are considered holy because they give up pleasures and practice great asceticism. In primitive and archaic societies especially, holiness is identical with sacredness; anything that reflects the presence of the numinous is sacred. This means that strange or mysterious persons are often considered holy, because it is the strange and mysterious that is the numinous. Epileptics are holy, for example. The words they say before or after a seizure are to be listened to as words from the spirits. Even the insane or mentally retarded are considered to be touched by the numinous and are to be treated as sacred. Religious leaders who have charism, a powerful personality and style of presenting themselves, are often treated with special reverence or followed blindly.

There are people who institutionalize holiness. The monks and nuns in Eastern and Western religions seek holiness in this way. On the other hand, there are holy people who devote themselves to the divine in very individual ways, living as hermits. There are many who cross back and forth across such lines. St. Francis of Assisi was an individualist who devoted himself to God through a simple life of prayer and kindness. But he also assembled others into what became the Franciscan order of friars and nuns in the Catholic Church, although Francis himself did not remain very comfortable in his own order. In India there are gurus (teachers) who have schools of disciples, but when the guru dies the disciples move on. In the lifetime of the Buddha one of his followers, a cousin named Ananda, took the Buddha's ideas and helped make them the basis of a religious community. Holiness is sought alone or with others, in different ways around the world. Those who are considered holy for whatever reason are also respected as guides to the right way to live and deal with the numinous.

Incarnations and Avataras

The word "incarnation" literally means enfleshment or embodiment. It is used to indicate those persons who are not merely human but are in some way actually a god or God living somehow as a human person on earth.

Kings have sometimes been considered to be the incarnation of a god. The king of the Shilluk people along the Nile in the Sudan is actually the god Nyikang. When the king dies the god moves on into the body of the next king. The pharaoh of ancient Egypt was Horus, divine son of the god Osiris. Upon the pharaoh's death he became Osiris and the new pharaoh became his son, the new Horus. For many centuries, until 1959, the ruler in Tibet had been the divine priest-king, the Dalai Lama, the major leader of a form of Buddhism in that country. When one Dalai Lama dies, other priests go looking for the signs that tell them which young child is the new reincarnation of this divine being, the new Dalai Lama. The divine and awesome power that controls reality and society is present physically in the person of the king, pharaoh, or ruler-priests in these cases.

In other traditions it might be the relatively powerless who embody the divine. The guru of India is a person who is both wise and holy. The guru whose yoga training is far advanced can guide others in the path of salvation because the guru has already achieved the insight or enlightenment into ultimate truth. As a person approaches the ultimate truth, he or she discovers that the only true reality is the Atman or Self; this divineness lies within a person. The guru is one who has discovered the inner divinity we all have and are, insofar as we really exist at all. In that sense we are all incarnations of the divine, but only the guru is close enough to this inner reality to truly grasp it and guide others to a realization of their own inner divineness.

Another example of what is meant by incarnation is the Hindu belief in avataras. This word implies a descent from godly status to human existence. According to one Hindu tradition the god who has most often thus descended is Vishnu, worshiped by his followers as the supreme form that divinity takes (though Vedantic tradition says this divinity exists in other forms in other gods also, and ultimately is Brahman, beyond all the gods). The first avatara or incarnation of Vishnu was as a fish. Vishnu has been incarnate nine times so far, in fact. The avatara of Vishnu that is most important to many Hindus is his incarnation as Krishna. According to Vishnu's worshiper, the Buddha was another incarnation of Vishnu. There is still a tenth one to come called Kalkin, who will appear at the end of this long cycle of the whole cosmos.

The Christian use of the word "incarnation" is the most familiar one in the West. The fourth gospel in the New Testament declared that the divine Word of God became flesh in Jesus of Nazareth. In its rather complex doctrine of God, Christianity came to assert that the one God has within itself three distinct aspects or "persons," one of which is called the Son. This divine Son is also called "the Word" (*Logos* in Greek). It is the Son who is incarnate in Jesus, but through the Son the whole divineness of God is said to be incarnate in Jesus.

Both Jews and Muslims reject this Christian belief on the grounds that it makes God into a mere god. A god like Zeus could beget a son on earth and did so a number of times. A god like Vishnu could become enfleshed as Krishna. But God is infinite and unchangeable, Jews and Muslims say. God is not anthropomorphic like Zeus, nor finite and changeable like Vishnu. So God cannot have a son, except perhaps poetically speaking, nor can God shrink down to a finite size to become human. In response Christians say that Jesus is not a god in disguise but is a fully human person who is nonetheless also the real presence of the infinite and absolute God. The traditional Christian formulation says that in Jesus full finite humanness and full infinite divinity meet and join but without any mixing between the two. If this seems hard to understand, the Christian tradition says that is to be expected because God is truly infinite and incomprehensible, just as many Jews and Muslims also insist.

The Significance of Leaders

Religious leaders are often people who have spent many years in pursuit of the divine or the sacred. Every culture has its significant few, those more deeply perceptive, more compassionate, more dedicated, or even more desperate for religious meaning. But they do not produce their ideas out of the air. They plunge deeply into traditions, especially their own, drawing from them the materials from which they form saving insights or build structures of wisdom, morality, community, and contemplation. These support others in their search for meaningful existence in the face of the mysteries of life. Occasionally, leaders shift the direction and focus of their own tradition in ways that constitute the beginning of a new religion, a new way of achieving salvation from limit and estrangement through relation to the numinous. The new comes out of the old, however, and there is continuity between them. A few intensely religious people become leaders because their sensibilities and perceptions are human enough, however divine they might also be said to be, to make contact with the needs and hopes of others. Religious leaders are sometimes people with very special gifts of insight, eloquence, or leadership. Leaders with great abilities to influence their followers are sometimes called "charismatic" leaders, after the Greek word for "gift" (*charism*).

Some leaders initiate movements distinct enough from prior traditions that the movements are treated as cults. When the people of the ancient city of Antioch called the followers of Jesus "Christians," the Greek word they used was the equivalent of "Christies," much as followers of the Reverend Sun Myung Moon, founder of the Unification Church, are often called "Moonies." The Christian belief that Jesus was raised from the dead seemed too far from traditional Jewish belief to be just a variation of Judaism. Likewise, the Reverend Moon's belief that Jesus saved only human souls and that salvation of the body is yet to be achieved strikes Christians as aberrant.

But members of the Unification Church can hope that someday their movement will become accepted and as revered as the older form of Christianity. In a century and a half the Church of Jesus Christ of Latter-day Saints has achieved something like this, even though their founder and leader, Joseph Smith, was killed in 1844 by members of a mob who saw him as the leader of a powerful cult. Similarly, the nineteenth-century Bahai faith has gained respectability in various parts of the world, even though in its native Iran it is still called an apostasy from Islam by traditionalists.

Religious leaders have different kinds of authority over their followers. Some lead by force of personality, by persuasion and eloquence, others by the example of their lives, some by the claim to have divine support. But all of them lead mainly because they were first accepted by a few, and then by many, and then became part of the cultural tradition themselves. All of them spoke out of a cultural context that made them intelligible to others in the first place, and in ways that touch the humanity of others. All of them are significant because they contribute to the flow of tradition, for better or for worse.

Sacred Writings

Like religious leaders, sacred texts are focal points in religious traditions. Many traditions are based on scriptures of one kind or another. The word "scripture" merely means writings. To those unaccustomed to writing, it can seem wondrously magical that strange little markings can convey thoughts and words over distance and through time. Writing was originally developed for the ordinary purpose of keeping commercial and governmental records. Yet few human inventions have changed human cultures as much as the alphabet. Among the many writings in the world, there are some we still call by the special name, "scriptures," to indicate that these writings are regarded as sacred.

To be classified as scripture or as sacred it is not enough, however, that the texts deal with the numinous. After all, libraries are filled with books on religion. Few of these books are considered sacred. To meet the standard for sacred scripture, a text must also somehow carry special authority. Those reading it must see it as a text that has a power, status, or authenticity that raises it above ordinary human writings. There are various ways of attaining this status.

Truth from Tradition

Some writings have a special status as sacred truth simply because they are traditional. The world's cultures have usually had great reverence for the past and for tradition. Things handed on from long ago have a luster and an authority. They have endured and have achieved respect. What is new is untested and may soon pass away.

The earliest Christian texts were considered inferior writing by the educated people in the Hellenistic world of antiquity. But now Christians find them profoundly inspiring. Though the Qur'an exhibits a more-than-human beauty and power in the eyes of Muslims, those who drove Muhammad and his followers to leave Mecca and move to Medina perceived only human and sometimes odd sayings in those same verses. As such writings become familiar tradition to new generations, heard repeatedly and even memorized, they acquire enormous respect and reverence.

Most of the world's scriptures have some additional claim to sacred status besides being traditional. Those who accept a certain text as sacred will tell you that it was revealed or inspired by the gods or God. But if you were to ask how they knew that gods or God had revealed it, the answer would often be simply that everyone knows that; it is tradition that hands on the belief that the text is sacred. As long as everyone has assimilated the belief from prior generations that a certain text is truly sacred, then people will find it normal and natural to accept the text in that light. The longer it has endured as sacred, the more obvious it will seem that it is in fact a true and powerful link to the numinous realities it describes.

Wisdom Literature

The original book of Taoism is the *Tao-Te-Ching*, the Book of the Way ascribed to Lao-Tzu. The book gained acceptance because it was viewed as unusually perceptive and wise in its statements. Chuang-Tzu was highly respected in his lifetime as a very wise person. His sayings were recorded and now form part of the traditional writings of Taoism. Confucius was a great sage; many of his sayings were written down. In time many other bits of wisdom were linked to his name and added to the collection of sayings attributed to him, forming the Analects (sayings and stories) of Confucius.

The authority of the names associated with these writings is part of the reason they gained respect. Ideas attached to famous figures and human personalities achieve a little more "authority" in people's imagination. But the Chinese wise men were famous because they were wise. It is not the fame of the authors but their wisdom that is supposed to be the basis for the authority of these Chinese texts. There are also texts in the Jewish and Christian scriptures, in Hindu writings, and in the Buddhist tradition that have authority because of the wisdom they contain.

Revelation and Inspiration

The most frequent explanation given by religious traditions for the sacred status of certain writings is that those texts were produced not by humans alone, not even by the wisest of leaders, but by a divine being or power. The humans involved were merely the channels for the divine influence. Ideas that have come from a divine source are called either revealed or inspired. These words do not always have clear definitions, but there is a common distinction that is somewhat useful.

Messages directly given by a numinous being are most often called revelations. The avatara Krishna spoke at some length to a charioteer named Arjuna. These words are now recorded in the sacred Hindu writings known as the Bhagavad Gita, written in the early centuries of the axial age and still among the most beloved of Hindu texts. Ahura Mazda, the Wise Lord, spoke to Zoroaster. His followers wrote down these revelations as Zoroaster passed them on, recording them in the Avestas ("laws"). In Jewish belief God gave his law to Moses on Mount Sinai and later. Muslim tradition says that Muhammad received the words of the Qur'an from Allah by way of the angel Gabriel. These messages were all held in respect not because they were the words of a holy and wise person, but because they were spoken to a messenger from a divine being and, therefore, possessed undoubtable validity and importance. When these words were put in written form, they endowed the written texts with a certain sacredness. Not just the ideas and the words, but the texts themselves are treated with reverence.

Sometimes the words of sacred writings are not thought of as directly revealed by the numinous being but only inspired by the god or God in a general way that left the writer or speaker free to choose the particular words and images. The most ancient parts of the Hindu sacred writings known as the Vedas, for example, begin with poems for use in rituals, poems composed by seers known as rishis, who were said to be inspired when composing. Even though the author of the Old Testament book of Proverbs who collected the many folk sayings in one book does not seem to have claimed that God revealed these sayings directly, Jews and Christians have traditionally treated the book as somehow the result of divine inspiration.

The Complexities of Sacred Writings

The fact that the authority or sacredness of given texts can derive from tradition, wisdom, revelation, inspiration, or any combination of these all at once, is one source of complexity. The Vedic tradition actually encompasses all of these categories. Similarly, most Christians think of the scriptures as a mix of direct revelation (e.g., God's words to Moses), inspiration (e.g., Paul's New Testament letters), and wisdom (e.g., the book of Ecclesiastes).

The historical nature of many texts is the main cause of this complexity. Religious people can mentally lump their own scriptures together as sacred texts produced "back then" when God spoke or inspired certain people. But "back then" can cover many centuries. The earliest words of the Vedic tradition may go back to 1500 BCE, but this tradition includes writings from the sixth century BCE, and perhaps even more recent times. The Jewish tradition began taking written form in the tenth century BCE, but received major additions, including a large body of interpretative writings, up until the sixth century CE.

Even texts put together in a relatively short time have a history. The Christian New Testament texts were produced in about sixty years' time (50-110? CE). But the first texts were based on sayings and stories already in circulation for over twenty years. For a long time Christians were not sure which of the many early writings should be counted as authoritative. There are lists of scripture used by Christians in the second century that include books like "The Shepherd of Hermas" and "The Epistle of Barnabas" but exclude the Book of Revelation (the "Apocalypse"). It was not until after 150 CE that there was significant agreement on just what books should be included as part of scripture and which excluded, though arguments continued for many years thereafter.

According to Muslim tradition, the Qur'an was delivered by the angel Gabriel to Muhammad over a period of but a few years. But then another historical process followed. Muhammad transmitted verbally to people around him the various sayings that make up the Qur'an. These others had to write them down, a process that continued (and may not have started until) after Muhammad's death. For a while there was more than one list of these sayings, in various orders. An early Caliph ("successor" to the Prophet as leader of the community) is said to have ordered a single text to be compiled and the other versions destroyed. Most of the sayings were put in order according to their length, rather than in chronological or topical order. The earliest versions seem to have lacked vowel marks. When vowel marks were later added, this determined the meaning of some words that were otherwise ambiguous. Even then the clearest words had yet to be applied to life's varied and complex situations, and so a tradition of interpretations, as well as methods of interpretation, arose to guide people.

Interpreting Texts

A Desire for Certainty

People who live by a religious tradition like to be able to feel that the basics of their tradition are well settled and clear. Religions fulfill very important human needs. They make sense of life in the face of suffering, injustice, and confusion. They provide a sense of belonging and identity. They give help, comfort, and security. All this is possible provided that the religious tradition can speak clearly and authoritatively. When people turn to religious leaders and sacred texts they usually do not want to hear conflicting voices and changing opinions. When they do hear of conflict and change, they either try to dismiss it as peripheral and insignificant, or they attack it as serious error. On the whole, religious believers manage to maintain some sense that what they believe is the unchanging and firm truth.

This sense of stability and certitude, however, must be won by continuous effort, especially by the historic religions. Primitive religion takes stability more or less for granted in its one-possibility universe (sometimes changing nonetheless without much fuss). Archaic religion is open to a variety of beliefs. With so many gods and powers about, there is always a new one to learn about. Historic religion, though, contains what it believes to be universal and all-inclusive truth. The one God or supreme Reality rules all things at once. All aspects of life must be integrated into one all-embracing religious story of reality. (We will see more about this in the chapter on reason and faith.)

The historic belief system expressed in some leader's words or in sacred scripture seeks to spell out the basic and final unity to everything. This will include a description of the ultimate numinous reality, ultimate salvation including identity and belonging, the moral requirements of life, and all other necessary means for relating to the numinous. It can be difficult, though, to maintain such a complex unity. Life goes on. Ideas change. New problems arise. Stability and unity of religious existence is maintained only by a constant effort at interpreting the tradition and applying old values to new contexts.

The Necessity of Interpretation

The actual use of the Qur'an by Muslims is an example of this. Muslims believe that the Qur'an is the set of instructions on life given by the Almighty, ordained from all eternity as the final and full truth for human beings. Muslims look to these words, therefore, to settle disputes about religious matters. But problems of interpretation quickly arose. To this day there is a dispute over who is to be the major political leader among Muslims, dividing especially Sunni from Shiite, but raising questions for Muslims in general. Other difficult questions had to be addressed. How were non-Arabic people to be joined to an originally Arabic religion? Must even the poorest and most distant Muslim make a journey to Mecca, as required by the Qur'an? Should the yearly all-day fast during the month of Ramadan be kept strictly, even by Muslims who happen to be living in countries where most people do not observe this fast?

In cases like these Muslims apply Hadith, sayings and practices attributed to Muhammad but not found in the Qur'an. There is no single collection of Hadith that is the sole authoritative collection. In addition during the early centuries of Islam a body of laws known as the Shari'a (the Way) was articulated on the basis of the Qur'an and Hadith and common practice. There are at least four major schools of Shari'a for Sunni Muslims. When Shari'a does not provide answers, then a consensus of opinions of learned imams may be followed. Individual Muslim scholars may also issue a ruling (fatwa) for a specific case. Interpreting how a good Muslim is to live in accordance with God's will can be difficult. The same is true in any religion. There must be interpretation; it is unavoidable. And once people begin to interpret the tradition or the texts, they may disagree.

Sometimes interpretations of scriptures are collected into a kind of adjunct scripture. In India, Vedic commentaries known as the Brahmanas and the Upanishads took on a sacred character of their own. As noted earlier in this chapter, Judaism treats the Law of Moses (the first five books of the Bible: the Pentateuch or Torah) as most sacred, but it also reveres the words of the prophets and other writings as holy commentary on the Law, and has added to all this the learned commentaries of early rabbis assembled into the collection known as the Talmud. Many Christians rely on the great councils of church leaders in the first five centuries of Christianity as authoritative interpretations of scripture. It was only in 325 CE that Christians found formally explicit words to express their belief that Jesus is truly and fully divine, the Logos of the Trinity incarnate, rather than only a god or a son of God. And it was not until the following century that they found the right words to express that Jesus is also completely human and that Jesus's humanity remained fully distinct from his divinity. Most Christians, though not all, have accepted these ideas as the correct way to interpret what their bible says. The complexity of these beliefs illustrates why interpretation is difficult.

There are countless more instances of the complex and historical process of interpretation. It is important to have seen at least a few of them in order to appreciate interpretation and why it is necessary, because religious traditions sometimes obscure or even hide their own dependence on interpretation and reinterpretation. The reason for this is that the problem of interpretation is not just how to do it well, but that it has to be done at all. The need for interpretation suggests that the answers to life and how to live it are still not fully clear, that there is still some uncertainty.

It is here that religious leaders can become especially important. Among the religious believers there can be those who officially or unofficially carry the burden of deciding for others what the best interpretation of the scriptures and the whole tradition might be. Gurus and charismatic leaders, messiahs and incarnate divinities, holy ones and priests, learned interpreters and wise ones, all can give their followers a sense that certainty does exist, that there is some clear and authoritative message people can confidently obey without doubt or confusion. Some religious groups claim that their leaders may even receive ongoing divine guidance in interpreting the tradition and scriptures. Catholics make this claim for the Pope under certain precise circumstances; Mormons do likewise for their chief elder.

Literal or Loose Interpretation

Leaders and ordinary believers alike often have difficulty deciding how literally to interpret their sacred writings. A strictly literal interpretation can provide a divinely authoritative set of specific and exact instructions, it would seem, on how to live and what to believe. A strict literalism might thereby eliminate confusion and insecurity. Such literalism has become known as fundamentalism.

Early in the twentieth century, a number of Protestant clergy, theologians, and believers reaffirmed traditional fundamental beliefs of Christianity. Among these was the belief in the "literal inerrancy" of scripture. This belief says that the sacred scriptures of Christian tradition are exactly as God wanted them to be. God inspired the writers to record without error all that God wished to be revealed through Moses, the prophets, Jesus, Paul, and others. Because these Christians called this a fundamental belief, the name fundamentalism has come to be applied to claims of literal inerrancy of the scriptures. Among Jews, those who are called Orthodox are rather fundamentalistic about the Torah and Talmud as words to be obeyed exactly. Traditional Islam has been fairly fundamentalistic about the Qur'an, though there are different schools of interpretation in Islam also. In India there is a Ninsana (interpretation) school that insists that the Vedas are absolutely and literally true.

In every tradition there are scriptural passages, though, that do not lend themselves to literal interpretation. Many Jews and Christians have come to believe that the biblical story about the sun stopping dead in the sky while the followers of Joshua battled with their opponents is not literally true, though once it was taken that way. It seems obvious now that the heaven above is not a hard "firmament" holding back the waters of chaos from descending upon the earth, even though that is how the first chapter of the biblical book of Genesis describes the world.

In every tradition there are also reasons given why even clear instructions in the scriptures should not always be obeyed literally. Not all Muslim nations now amputate the hand of a thief. Few nations with Christian backgrounds are now inclined to stone witches. Every tradition has found some ways of interpreting its own scriptures in new ways when that seems useful.

Careful research has often reinforced this tendency towards loose and more figurative or poetic interpretations. Buddhist texts tell of a virginal conception of the Buddha through his mother's side. A historical analysis suggests that this story was based more on an imaginative writer's desire to offer a strong image of the Buddha's significance than on historical fact. Jews and Christians share the biblical stories about Adam and Eve, the first humans. Scientific data about the age of the earth and about human ancestry suggest that the Adam and Eve stories should not be taken as literal history but as myth-stories that captured some general truths about life.

The intent behind a loose and more figurative interpretation of scriptures has usually been a respectful one. It is not an intent to destroy the reliability of the scriptures but to get at a broader and more symbolic meaning behind all the specific detail, in order to bring that general meaning into greater clarity for people. If there never was an Adam and Eve, for example, the Jew or Christian could still see in the stories a general truth that somehow humankind has ended up estranged from the ultimate wholeness we need. If there never was a Noah's ark coming to rest on the peak of Ararat, the story of the rainbow and the dove with an olive branch could still be a vivid image about having hope in new beginnings under God.

No matter how good the intent behind these loose interpretations, though, efforts of this kind are seen by more literal minded believers as misguided and dangerous. Religious people are people for whom the mysteries of life are real and important enough to make the religious ways of dealing with these mysteries also important. To some extent a general basic faith in the meaning and value of life carries people on in the face of mystery, but that faith is still threatened by confusion, doubts, and personal trials. As was noted earlier, highly literal and unquestioning adherence to religious instructions in scriptures can provide a greater feeling of security and certitude. Loose interpretations, on the other hand, can suggest that the sacred scriptures are just poetic stories or unclear and vague messages that must be interpreted by the already uncertain human mind.

Nevertheless, every reading of scripture, even the ones that are intended to be the most literal, will include a great deal of interpretation and reinterpretation. Scriptures and the words of religious leaders are not passed on to believers on a one-way, perfectly clear course. Instead there is an ongoing interaction. The sacred words are expressed in a particular language and a cultural context. That context provides religious leaders and writers with questions to be answered, and categories of thought, value, images, and words to be used in answering them. The religious message, whether it comes from wisdom, insight, or divine revelation, has to be expressed in a culture's categories. The message is then passed on to listeners and readers who receive the message as a way of interpreting their own lives and the reality they live in. Since they have their own way of perceiving reality and have their own categories of thought, they add their own interpretations to what is passed on to them, sometimes without noticing that they are doing so.

And so it goes down through the generations: leaders, scriptures, interpreters, commentaries, and readers or listeners all interacting and forming a chain of tradition. It is a living chain, a flowing back and forth of interpretations and reinterpretations that enable people to make sense of their lives through relation to the numinous in the face of the mysteries of existence. The guides of religion are not static signposts but living currents in the overall human adventure that is religion.

Each generation tends to focus most clearly on the particular leaders and interpreters of texts that their family and recent cultural history have handed to them. Each generation tends to place its faith in the rather specific instructions provided by the religious context in which it comes of age. Each generation faces the mystery and deals with it by means of the detailed beliefs and moral rules that its historical setting has made plausible. In every case there has been the temptation to overlook or deny that the texts, leaders, and interpretations are in fact part of an ongoing historical process. There is the constant tendency to deny that any real change ever takes place. But no tradition is a package of unchanging beliefs, values, and practices. Tradition is a living process. As we will see, it is modern (and postmodern) religion that will admit most fully the fact of ongoing change as part of its own story and life. Modern (and postmodern) religiousness will also turn out to be the most open to uncertainty and flexibility about its own specific beliefs.

Summary

Each religious tradition has its leaders and texts that interpret life and reality for people. The importance of interpreters and interpretations is attested to both by the many varieties of religious leaders and sacred texts that exist, and also by the trust that people put in their traditional leaders and texts. What is less noticed but is an intrinsic part of the story is that the religious activity of interpreting life is an ongoing process, with each generation guided in slightly new or different ways, so that to trust a tradition is actually also to trust a process of development.

For Further Reflection

1. List and explain all the ways you can think of that your ideas, values, and personality have been formed by tradition in some sense.

2. Give some examples of ways in which you and others show trust in your traditions.
3. Which specific leaders have you followed in some way? Moses or Jesus or Buddha? Luther, Wesley, Martin Luther King, Jr., or Mother Teresa? Why?
4. Is there any good way to tell which sacred writings are most worthy to be accepted as truly sacred? How about *The Book of Mormon* or the *Divine Principle* of the Rev. Sun Myung Moon or the *Tao-Te-Ching*?
5. Do you think it is legitimate to select or reject sacred texts on the basis of their rational plausibility? Their moral value? The emotional comfort they provide? On any basis? Explain.
6. If any sacred text is truly revealed or inspired by a numinous being like God, then is not a fundamentalist interpretation of it the best one? Explain.

Suggested Readings

Len Oakes, *Prophetic Charisma: The Psychology of Revolutionary Religious Personalities*, 1997.

Leonard J. Biallas, *Myths: Gods, Heroes, and Saviors*, 1986. An easy-to-read review of different types of religious leaders from a religious standpoint.

Kenneth Dramer, *World Scriptures: An Introduction to Comparative Religion*. 1986.

J. Benton White, *From Adam to Armageddon: A Survey of the Bible*, 1994. A quick textbook survey of major aspects of the Hebrew and Christian scriptures.

Pui-Lan Kwok and Elisabeth Schüssler Fiorenza, eds., *Women's Sacred Scriptures*, 1998. Reveals tensions in interpreting scriptures from women's points of view.

Dominic Goodall, ed. and tran., *Hindu Scriptures*, 1996. This is based on an earlier anthology by R. C. Zaehner of some significant segments of Hindu sacred writings.

Mary Pat Fisher and Lee W. Bailey, *An Anthology of Living Religions*, 2000. Presents extensive excerpts from world scriptures, past and present, to illustrate many religions, with liturgical texts relevant to the following chapter.

CHAPTER TEN

Living Images of the Traditions

Ritual and Symbol

As each religious tradition has developed through the centuries with its beliefs in numinous powers and forms of salvation, in moral codes and religious leaders and sacred texts, it has expressed all this not only in verbal form but also in the language of symbol and ritual. In drawings and carvings, statues and architecture, in music and dance, drama and everyday ceremony, the religious visions of reality and life have taken on vivid forms. Ritual and symbol can be as effective as leaders and scriptures in guiding people how to live in the presence of mystery and in inspiring them to do it well.

RITUAL

Ritual is ceremonious or formalized behavior. We think of ritual also as repetitious behavior because most rituals or ceremonies are repeated time after time, but it is possible to invent a ritual to be used only once. It is the ceremoniousness that makes a behavior a ritual. It is also usually not random or spontaneous behavior (though some rituals include these elements) but structured or preplanned behavior. In 1969 Neil Armstrong might have simply hopped from the bottom rung of the ladder of the lunar landing craft onto the moon's surface and said whatever came to mind. Instead, for that one-and-only occasion, he carefully paused, and just before his foot touched the lunar dust he recited, "One small step for [a] man; a giant leap for mankind." He made a small ritual out of that first-time event.

Ritual is a constant part of human existence. There is something in us that makes us ceremonialize every major element of life and many minor ones. From the simple formalized greetings of saying hello and asking about one another's health, to the days of ceremony attending the death of a pope, life is filled with rituals. Birth has its rituals of "showers," handing out cigars, and baptism. Death is thoroughly ceremonialized in funeral rites. And in between birth and death there are countless anniversaries, holidays, graduations, retirements, toasts and testimonials, formal invitations and thank you notes, rules of protocol, explicit and implicit dress codes that are more ritual than convenience. In military assemblies and athletic meets, in courtrooms and classrooms, in political conventions and show business award ceremonies, there is ritual. The list goes on and on. Why do we do this? There are three reasons. The first is to honor gods or God. The second is to make reality work right for us. The third is to make reality more real to us.

Ritual Honors Divine Beings

In most religious traditions, a major purpose of ritual is to honor one or more important numinous beings. The ancient Celts left behind evidence of worship of gods. So did the Chinese, the Sumerians, the Aztecs, and every archaic culture of the world. India still has thousands of rituals honoring various gods. Anglican, Catholic, Lutheran, and Orthodox Christians honor Christian saints.

In the Sufi tradition it has been common to venerate the saints in rituals dedicated to them. In what is now Saudi Arabia, however, beginning in the eighteenth century, a traditionalist reformer named Muhammad ibn Abd al-Wahhab (or Wahab; 1703-1791) viewed the veneration of saints by Sufis as superstitious worship. God alone is to be worshiped, say the Wahhabis still, whose interpretation rules in Saudi Arabia. Similarly in the Protestant Reformation in the sixteenth century in Europe, John Calvin and others accused Roman Catholics of treating saints as though they were gods deserving of rituals. Both Catholics and Sufis claim that rituals to honor their saints are acts of veneration or reverence but not worship.

Religious people commonly assume that the numinous beings are pleased by the honor paid to them in rituals. This is clearest in those cases where the purpose of ritual is to persuade the saint to intercede with God for a favor, or to persuade the gods to offer help, or to move God to be merciful. This assumption makes most sense in archaic religion. The gods are quite susceptible to flattery or gifts, and are even rather sensitive about their honor. The ancient sky god of the Aryans in South Central Asia decreed that only if there is a sacrifice of a horse once a year in the spring will the god guide his followers to victory in battles. In other cases the ritual of an archaic religion is simply well-suited to catch the god's attention. In ancient Canaan the worshiper of the fertility god Baal and his consort Astarte would celebrate annual spring rites that centered on sexual activity, especially in the temples and shrines.

Baal and Astarte had to initiate the fertility of the year by sexual intercourse. Their worshiper could catch the attention of these gods and reawaken their interest in fertility by human sexual ritual activity that reminded the gods what to do. In general just the showiness and ceremony of ritual might impress the gods and flatter them, and the sacrifice offered as part of the rituals adds an extra incentive to the gods to take care of human needs.

The theologians of historic or classical religions, however, argue that God is neither vain nor in need of attention. Nor does God need reminders of the divine responsibilities. God is thought of as all-good, all-knowing, and all-powerful, the Creator on whom absolutely everything depends. Anthropomorphic limitations such as need, vanity, or forgetfulness are simply out of place when speaking of the Divine Mystery. The main value of rituals, the theologians may argue, is to have a positive effect on the participants, as we will see shortly, not because God feels a need to be honored or is flattered by such attention.

Ritual Makes Reality Work Right

Ritual is often magical. The right words said in the proper way while doing the correct thing with the required precise objects control numinous powers. To get rid of warts you must stand in a graveyard at precisely midnight with a dead cat with a rope tied to its tail. Whirl the cat around your head exactly three times and say without stuttering: "Cat follow devil; warts follow cat." Within three days your warts will begin to dry up, provided that you have correctly followed the ritual prescription.

We have seen that it is not just ordinary magical rituals that are useful. There are great magical, mana-filled rituals of immense importance such as the Aztecs and the Brahmins enacted to keep the universe working right. There is a special Taoist ritual of cosmic renewal still performed in Taiwan about every sixty years. This is the Chiao ritual, a nine-day series of ceremonies to renew the power of life. The sun, the highest form of yang, must be born again each year with the help of appropriate ceremonies. Every long generation of sixty years all yang-power must be given rebirth also through Chiao. Then babies will continue to be born, the crops will grow, the village will be healthy, and there will be enough good luck for everyone. To achieve all this, everything must be done with exact correctness. No one is to wear either leather or wool materials taken from animals. The spirits must all be formally invited so that they do not get upset and disturb the ceremony. Each family, clan, and village must contribute its traditional elements, whether soap, swords, scissors, or scales. The Taoist priests will then follow the prescribed forms that have been handed on for generations and create a perfect sequence of ceremonies to renew the cosmic power of yang.

Belief in the magic of ritual power is alive today in many places. Every little ritual we ordinarily call superstition is an example of this. The person who spills salt tosses a pinch over the left shoulder to avoid bad luck. Even some historic religious rituals are still occasionally considered as magical. One person administers the rites of baptism with an extreme carefulness to get the words and actions exactly right, out of a fear that if it is not done with exact correctness, then somehow it will not have its effect. Another person is upset because the traditional wording of the Eucharistic ceremony or the Bar Mitzvah ceremony has been changed, as though there were a magical power inherent in using the exact words that had been handed down for generations.

There are many rituals with the power to make reality work right not because of magic in them but because they are well-suited to influence the gods or God who controls reality. In some cases the god has decreed certain rituals.

Ritual Makes Reality More Real to People

There are many nonreligious rituals. Wedding anniversaries have no magical power; retirement ceremonies do not influence the gods. These and countless other rituals are important without exerting any control over numinous realities. These nonreligious rituals provide us with a clue that the importance of ritual lies not only in their power to influence external reality, or to influence holy and divine beings. It has another power as well, that of influencing human consciousness, of interpreting and supporting a pattern of life.

As Chapter Seven explained, human life is not lived as the lives of animals are. Human life is enacted; it is drama that follows a script that culture has written. It is a way of living based on human biological nature in many ways, but is largely composed of themes, styles, patterns invented by the human mind and incorporated into our culture. It provides us with a set of values and larger perspectives that tell us who we are, where we fit, and what our purpose is. The life we live is but one of the many ways that are workable for dealing with reality. This life is our interpretation of how to live, of human existence, of what the meaning and purpose of life are. People disagree on which interpretations are more accurate, which are human inventions and which are based on divine guidance, but they are all interpretations.

As we saw earlier, our life does not seem like an interpretation. Instead, it seems natural, just the way things are and should be. That is a sign that our culture, like other cultures, has successfully performed its function of giving us roles, rules, values, mental concepts through language, and so forth, that we can incorporate as part of our way of being a human person. If the rituals are religious, centered on stories of the gods or on human relations to an Ultimate, the rituals may fill a participant with a sense of awe or reverence.

This adds an extra sense of legitimacy to the ideas, values, and practices which the ritual represents. The beliefs are more clearly true, the values correct, the practices proper because of their association with the numinous. Identity and belonging are fortified.

Primitive cultures rely heavily on ritual because there are no alternatives to it, no schools, and no written records. The rituals associated with birth, puberty, marriage, hunting, and death all contain guides to the tribesperson on how to act and think about themselves. The rituals are occasions to retell and reenact the folktales of the ancient figures and ancestors who made reality and its rules. For primitive people rituals usually contain reality. Most of the stories told in ritual are real life and not just stories. They are reality as it is now, and probably also reality as it was at the origins, repeated and commemorated.

For archaic or historic people, religious ritual can be somewhat more distinct from life in general, but it still is a representation and interpretation of life. On the island of Bali, for example, in the long chain of islands of Indonesia, the people have been Hindu since about the seventh century CE. A central feastday in the Balinese year is the celebration about Prince Rama, the seventh avatara of Vishnu. His story is told in the Ramayana, one of the great classics of Hindu literature. According to the sacred story, a demon abducted Rama's wife Sita. Rama joined forces with the king of the monkeys and pursued the demon to Sri Lanka. With the help of the monkeys Rama defeated the demon and rescued his wife. This story is acted out on Bali in a great live drama in honor of Rama. With special clothing, face masks, and lights, the Balinese bring the demon, monkeys, Rama, and Sita to life before their eyes and those of their children. Through this drama every new generation comes to know about the nature of heroism, about love between husband and wife, about the evil of demons, and about many other things. The ritual thereby tells the community what reality is like and makes it more emphatically real to them.

In the spring Jews celebrate a long-ago event of passing over from slavery in Egypt to freedom in Canaan. At an evening meal called the Seder, Jews recall this Passover in ritual form. The table is set with special tableware and some unusual food, such as unleavened bread and bitter herbs, in memory of the food the Hebrews had when escaping from Egypt. The youngest child ritually asks, "Why is this night different from all other nights?" The head of the family begins to tell the story: "When we were slaves in Egypt...." The combination of various symbols and stories re-creates in the minds of those at table the events of past centuries that made the Jews the people of Yahweh. The story is told not only about ancestors who experienced all these events; it is a story that says, "When we were slaves." It brings the children into an identification with the past. When those children grow up, they will talk to their own children about the times "when we were slaves." Through the ritual every child comes to know what the reality of being a Jew is, and that reality becomes increasingly real through repetition in ritual each year.

Islam structures each day around ritual prayers. Five times daily the Muslim pauses from ordinary activities, ritually cleanses hands and feet and lips, faces towards the holy shrine at Mecca, and prays. It is prayer to praise Allah for his mercy and compassion. Above all, it is prayer that accepts Allah's will. Through daily prayers, through the daytime fast in the month of Ramadan, and through the activities of the pilgrimage to Mecca which every Muslim hopes to make at least once in a lifetime, the beliefs and values of the Islamic tradition are reaffirmed. These rituals confirm the reality of Allah as the merciful and all-powerful God. They confirm the reality of submission to Allah that makes a person part of the Muslim community. These rituals thereby help create the social reality that is the House of Islam.

Christianity has a ritual that explicitly retells the story and purpose of the whole universe. That is the traditional Easter service that recounts the biblical story of God's creation of the world and the first man and woman. It tells of the first sin and the expulsion from the garden of Eden into a world of pain and fear and death. The generations down to the time of the Patriarch Abraham are listed, the story of the escape of the Hebrews from Egypt, and the expectation of a Messiah. The birth and life of Jesus are quickly retold, recalling his trial and sacrificial death on a cross. Then at dawn the story of Jesus' resurrection from the dead is celebrated. The promise of eternal life for all humankind and the messianic fulfillment of the entire universe are proclaimed with joy. Through rituals like this the Christian comes to perceive all of life in a certain way.

Ritual sometimes also includes a ceremony of dedication to the reality it portrays. A standard American marriage ritual is a clear example of this. It reminds people of what marriage is, a bond between two persons "until death do you part." This marriage rite also asks whether the two persons promise to maintain this bond. The marriage is formed by the act of commitment in the words, "I do."

The element of dedication or commitment can be less explicit but still real. In the New Hebrides in the southwest Pacific, a woman has two teeth torn out of her mouth to show she is married. College fraternities today exact a price from their pledges. The applicants for membership must suffer indignities and do physical labor to earn acceptance. Whether the cost is two teeth, psychological trials, or manual labor, this sort of ritual does not merely keep a person conscious of the new form of reality he or she is entering, but also requires a spirit of dedication or commitment from the person. This dedication to the reality that is re-presented in the ritual makes the reality more real, and also more important.

It sounds odd to speak of a reality becoming more "real." A thing is real or it is not, our common sense tells us. The sun rises in the east or it does not. No ritual makes that any more or less a fact, common sense insists. Yet it is not really as simple as that. A sun ritual at dawn every day can make people take note of a reality. The ritual can make people become more explicitly conscious of how reliable the rising of the sun is. Secondly, a sun ritual will include some interpretations about the sun. The ancient Aztecs and Egyptians both saw the sun as divine. The reality of the sun's divinity was plain to these ancient peoples because, in part, their rituals dramatized this truth to them. Thirdly, by the act of assembling together at dawn for the sun ceremony, people become more conscious of their unity as a people who worship the sun. The ritual helps to create the realness of their mutual belonging and identity. In these ways and others, ritual makes reality real to the participants.

The Separation of Magic from Ritual

When religious traditions become historic they try to eliminate the magical use of ritual. An absolute God or infinite Brahman is totally beyond the power of magic. Such a deity cannot be affected by any mana-like power inherent in any rituals. Moreover, in historic religions the universe is controlled by a universal and all-powerful numinous reality. The belief that there are little numinous powers that human beings can manipulate in magical rituals is a belief that might challenge the omnipotence of God, that might suggest there are some things that are not under the control of Allah, for example. For reasons like this, the historic religions tend to oppose belief in magic.

Yet belief in magic comes easily to human beings. Traditional rituals, performed with reverence and treated as sacred, evoke a sense of awe in the participants, a sense that there is real power in the ritual actions. Buddhists in Thailand are tempted to believe that a priestly blessing bestowed on medals bearing the Buddha's image endows those medals with powerful luck. Catholics in St. Louis are tempted to believe that the baptism ceremony has a magical influence on the inner soul of an infant. If the words and actions are done just right, the divine power flows into the medal or child, the believer is likely to think.

The Buddhist priests of Thailand insist that the medal-blessing ceremony does not bestow special good-luck powers on the medals. It is an educational ceremony, they say, that recalls to people's minds the understanding of life that the Buddha attained in his enlightenment. The Baptist movement in Christianity has tried to guard against a magical interpretation of baptism by making it a ritual for adults, not infants. Adults can participate in the ritual as an act of conscious acceptance of a Christian life.

There is a continuing struggle by historic (and modern) religion to avoid magical use of ritual. Islam typifies this in its insistence that external observance of the ritual cleansings and prayers does not fulfill the religious requirement. It is the inner intention to acknowledge, praise, thank, and obey Allah that makes the ritual worthwhile. The Catholic Church has been emphasizing in recent years that its sacraments (central rituals) are not automatic external routines for producing a kind of divine energy called grace, as some Catholics tend to think. The sacraments are carriers of meaning and have their effect through people's consciousness and faith. They require personal attention and dedication to be efficacious. Magic requires only that the external operations be exactly correct. This controls mana-like power. Nonmagical ritual does not control such power; its influence is on the consciousness of the people involved, so their personal involvement is necessary.

The Origin of Ritual

Ritual is clearly very useful in affirming the reality and significance of the way of life of a society. But almost no religious people give that as the reason why they ritualize. It is much more usual to claim that a religious tradition says that the rituals were established in the beginning by divine instructions or inspiration or example of a religious leader. This does not explain, however, why people also ritualize all sorts of nonreligious aspects of life, and add new rituals in the religious tradition as the centuries pass.

In earlier chapters we have seen some theories about why people have felt that ritual is useful. Water poured on the ground is similar to rain falling upon the ground. A water-pouring ceremony might easily appear to be useful for inducing rainfall. A voodoo doll made from clothing, hair, and fingernail clippings of a certain person is likely to be able to affect that person in an invisible way. This explains why certain symbols are chosen; it does not explain why the symbols have to be ritualized very precisely.

No one seems to have a sure explanation for our tendency to ritualize. Some have reasoned that we are born with an inclination to ritualize. Most animal species have some ritual behaviors, especially mating behavior. Perhaps there is a genetic tendency to ceremonialize. Others have noted that children ritualize as a way of learning. They watch adults do all sorts of things with ease: carry water in a cup, trim leaves off a plant, make toys roll across the floor. When children try to do the same, they spill, break, or overturn whatever they are handling. They learn that many things must be done exactly right and with care. Each movement of foot, hand, eye must be carefully coordinated. From controlled sequence of acts comes ability to accomplish things correctly. Perhaps such experiences leave even us adults with a lingering sense that if only a person learns the exactly correct actions in the correct sequences and does them with a ceremonious care, then almost magical results occur.

Ritual serves to make people feel they have techniques for taming the wild powers in us and the universe. Many experiences produce chaotic emotions. Grief over the death of a child is channeled in manageable forms by funeral rites. The powers of madness in certain drugs can be controlled by restricting drug use to religious ceremonial times. The ancient Aryans used the drug soma (or haoma) as part of religious ritual. A native American religious movement uses peyote in its ritual. The controlled patterns of ritual safely contain the awesome power of the numinous. The Yanomamö of Brazil and Venezuela inhale a hallucinogenic powder made from the bark of the ebene tree. It helps them see or get in touch with certain spirits, which sometimes make them behave so wildly they have to be restrained.

It is interesting that dancing and use of rhythms in speech are appealing to all of us as children and even as adults. Perhaps patterned and rhythmic behavior came first in human cultural development and eventually acquired mythic explanations to make sense out of them. This could be how rituals originated. First people danced. Then they began to tell a story in order to explain why they danced.

Legalistic Ritual

The legalistic use of ritual is closely allied to belief in magic. Legalism in morality is obedience to the letter of the law instead of its spirit. Legalism in ritual is obedience to the external forms of the ritual instead of participation in the meaning of the ritual. There are religious believers who maintain that their ritual is not magical, but who are still concerned mainly with the external correctness of the ritual rather than its inner meaning. In every religious group there seem to be those who dare not change ritual patterns, or the letter of any religious laws, for that matter, no matter how reasonable it might be to do so. It is a kind of taboo use of ritual, where ritual is done out of obedience to commands and out of a fear of punishment or chaos that would result from doing the ritual incorrectly.

But to adhere closely to traditional patterns is not necessarily legalistic. The Amish who retain old-style dress do so out of a sense of identity with their community. The Orthodox Jewish male who refuses to shave may find this a way of preserving a sense of continuity with tradition. The Catholic who does not eat meat on Friday may act out of a sense that it is good to retain some personal reminder of older ways. Yet among Amish, Jews, Catholics, and all groups of religious people, it is possible to find many who cling to traditional patterns of behavior almost compulsively with little sense of their meaning. Such behavior can be motivated by the human need for security, identity, and belonging, but ritual practices that emphasize external conformity to codes of dress and behavior can empty those rituals of their meaning. Legalism appears to support ritual by maintaining its externals, but legalism can actually kill ritual by depriving it of its inner life. Religious ritual has its strongest effect where its inner meaning is given full attention.

Rituals as Part of the Long Transformation

All of us are tempted to believe that the routine performance of some ritual procedure will give us easy access to what we desire, as though by magic. We want to lose weight without dieting and grow strong without exercise. In religious matters, too, we often want easy and automatic paths to moral rightness or life in paradise. From childhood through adolescence, though, we slowly grow in the awareness that dedication and effort are needed, that there is no easy shortcut through magic or merely external observances to get what we want. People who belong to historic religious traditions still might like to believe that prayers or rituals will slice through the obstacles to happiness. This is a normal human tendency. But what we come to learn as adults is that the path to achieving meaningful personal growth is arduous and involves a long process of transformation of ideas, values, and emotional perspectives.

This transformation is supported by rituals that function not magically or merely externally but as interpretations of life. The rituals describe the worthwhile goals, keeping them before people as incentives, and they reaffirm that there is a path to the goals. They offer encouragement, reminding people of the trials and pains that accompany all developments; they encourage people to make the religious vision the guiding center of their lives. The rituals will have these effects to some extent even on people who think of them as magical, but this belief in magic can also distract them from trying to learn from the rituals and from making a personal effort to grow into the reality the religious tradition offers as a path of salvation.

Symbols

Rituals are just one form of symbol. Many symbols and symbolic actions together make up rituals, but symbol is nonetheless a broader category than ritual. Every ritual is a symbol, though a complex one, and there are other symbols besides ritual ones.

In ordinary English, a symbol is something that stands for something else. Those who write about religion like to make distinctions between signs and symbols and other representations. We can overlook all those subtleties here. A symbol re-presents something more than itself. It is a word, picture, gesture, action, object, drama, ritual that brings to people's consciousness something additional. Like ritual forms of symbol, all symbols are meaning-carriers; they too make reality more real. They are not "merely" symbols in the place of the real thing; they are a kind of presence of the real thing, as various examples here will illustrate.

Some symbols are great art. Museums are filled with great art of religious origin. The eighth-century Great Mosque of Damascus is considered a stunning piece of architecture. Michelangelo's early sixteenth century Pieta, a sculpture of Mary holding the body of her son Jesus just after being taken down from the cross, envelops the onlooker in her massive sorrow. On the other hand, some symbols are rather crude, simple paintings or carvings done without artistry or taste. Yet they too can convey ideas or evoke feelings and help to make present some sacred reality.

Kinds of Symbols

There are all kinds of symbols, some rather ordinary. In a sense each word we read is a set of symbolic marks that represent various sounds. These marks and the sounds they stand for re-present to your mind some ideas. Some symbols evoke strong emotional responses: the national flag inspires feelings of patriotism. Some symbols are as simple as a handshake; others are as complex as the coronation of the Queen or King of England. The stop sign on the corner is the symbolic presence of the police power of the government. For that matter, the government in a democracy is the symbolic presence of the choices of the people.

Presence-through-symbol can be limited: a letter from a friend is a mode of presence of the friend. The friend is far away, yet her thoughts are there in front of you in written form. Her care and humor are present to you in her words. The presence-through-symbol can be a strong and close one: every person's body is a symbol of the invisible personality within. Each of us has an inner self that is always out of view. Yet we can say to one another, "I see you; I hear you; I understand you." That is because bodily motions, such as the sound waves made by voice and lips, all make present to others our inner self. The body is the symbol of the inner self because it really is the presence of that self. The only way any one of us is present to others is in and through bodily expressions. It is worth learning skills to express oneself well in order to make our inner self present to others, and to be a good conversationalist in order to draw out and discover the inner selves of others.

Religious traditions say that there is an invisible numinous reality that influences or controls things. Invisible realities can be perceived only by some visible re-presentation, by a symbol. The signs of numinous power are all symbols of the numinous; they are all modes of presence of the numinous.

The tree in the forest is a symbol of the wood-nymph that lives in the tree and makes it grow. All green growing things are symbols of the fertility-power of the goddess Demeter. The bright, dry, hot, and lively things of the world are all presences of yang-power and are therefore symbols of yang. All dark, moist, cool, and quiet things are symbols and presences of yin. If the whole universe is created and sustained by God, then the whole universe is the symbol and presence of God's power and creativity. If God is the absolute fullness of what we know as "personness," then every person is a symbol and presence of God.

As you perhaps suspect, everything is or can be a symbol. For a reality to function as a symbol, it must be recognized as a symbol. Human consciousness makes things symbolic by relating one thing to another. Water is just water until the human mind links it to other aspects of reality. Then it becomes a symbol and presence of life, of cleansing, of death, or of chaos, depending on how a person views it. For the people of the Nile, the river is the blessed source of life. For those who live near the North Atlantic, the waters of the ocean may be a symbol of death and chaos because ocean storms destroy and kill.

Core Symbols

Some symbols are central to their religious traditions, so much so that other symbols revolve around them as satellites. These core symbols re-present most of what is in the tradition. In some forms of Buddhism the simple sentence, "The jewel is in the lotus," is a core symbol. One Chinese Buddhist declared that this saying contained the complete essence of Buddhist truths, and wrote extensive commentaries on it as the "Lotus Sutra" (or lotus saying). Outsiders have a difficult time imagining how these words could contain the whole of any religious tradition, but one who lives by the religious tradition can find a wealth of meaning there. For a Buddhist the lotus, a water lily, is a symbol of human existence because though its roots are buried in the muck and it must slowly grow upward through the murky waters, eventually it breaks out into the air above where it blossoms. Each person is like the lily growing from muck and through murkiness until release into nirvana.

In Judaism the Torah is the core symbol. To the outsider a Jew explains that the Torah is the law or teaching given by God to Moses for the chosen people to live by. But the Jew finds in the Torah more than instructions for daily living. The Torah is a symbol of God's kindness and guidance; it is eternal wisdom made concrete in history; it is a call to a covenant with God; it is the presence of a divine promise for a future fulfillment; it is the primary symbol of God's presence, activity, and love. All rituals are based on the Torah. All value judgments, cultural forms, and family structures are related to Torah. This law is the center of the relationship of the Jew to God.

Other traditions have other core symbols. It is not possible to list them all here, but it is worth noting the power they can have. Because symbols are visible and concrete, they give some focus to religious beliefs and feelings. Images, statues, and stories help define the mysterious reality that is the numinous and make it easier to relate to it. The symbols of a religious tradition, in fact, usually control the consciousness of the people who follow that tradition. The symbols define and interpret reality, and the place of human existence in that reality.

Ritual, Symbol, and the Numinous

The numinous is the invisible and mysterious. Symbols, including ritual, give concrete form to the numinous and re-present it. Beliefs, moral codes, ritual, community forms, architecture, and theologies are ways by which religious traditions make the numinous symbolically present so that the human mind and imagination can deal with it.

The Symbol in Primitive, Archaic, and Historic Religion

In primitive religion little or no distinction is made between symbols and the numinous. The three rocks in front of the cave in Australia are not symbols of the old woman and her daughters who formed the landscape. They are the three women themselves turned into stone. When the aborigines perform the rituals that retell the stories of the beginning of things in "dream-time," these rituals are a way of actually living in the past and doing the original deeds.

Archaic religions sometimes show the same tendency. The statue of the god is the god. The Babylonians used to take the wooden statue of their god out for a walk after lunch and then tuck him in bed for a nap. In the villages of India a goddess mother is carried in procession and decorated with flowers and given fragrant incense to breathe. On the other hand, the people of archaic cultures also believe that statues and symbols are not themselves the numinous power, but rather are only representations of the power. The god may make her or his power known through the statue or temple but actually lives on the mountain top or in the sky above. The Indian villager is comfortable in throwing away an old statue of the goddess; he or she knows that the statue is a presence of the goddess but is not the actual goddess.

Historic religions are much more conscious that what is divine is not identical with what symbolizes the divine. Historic religions believe that there is one all-encompassing power throughout the whole universe, a power that is infinite, eternal, and incomprehensible. But all symbols including rituals are part of limited reality. No symbol or ritual is itself divine. No statue can be God; no ritual can capture infinite divine powers. Symbols are modes of the presence of the divine, but are not the same as the divine.

Historic religions have a strong need for symbol. A finite god can be directly present in an appearance to a person. The infinite God always is beyond the limits of any image or appearance. The person who wants to turn toward the infinite God or Brahman or Tao must rely on clues, pointers, symbols. To the Taoist the patterns of nature are the symbols of the Tao. To the Jew every person is a symbol of the supreme God. To the Buddhist silence is a symbol of infinite nirvana. Such symbols are necessary to re-present that reality which in itself is infinite and incomprehensible.

The Problem of Idolatry in Historic Religions

Symbols, however, are not just valuable; they can also be misleading or even dangerous. Symbols like statues, rituals, and doctrinal descriptions of the numinous are more appealing and comfortable to people than the infinite and eternal for which they stand in historic religion. They are concrete images the mind can more easily deal with. In this lies the danger of idolatry: treating something finite and limited as though it were infinite divinity itself, as though it were the actual ultimate and eternal reality that alone is God or Brahman or Tao.

In India there is some disparity between the religious practices of most Hindus and the belief in an absolute Brahman. The religious leaders do not worry much about that. Those who think the gods are the highest reality or who worship statues as gods, are simply less mature souls. After a few thousand more lifetimes these people will appreciate that nothing finite or temporal is of any lasting value or reality. Eventually they will begin to long for true moksha, total release into oneness with the eternal and infinite Brahman. Meanwhile, the religious leaders are indulgent toward unsophisticated god-worshipers, as wise adults are indulgent toward children who still have much to learn.

The Western tradition is somewhat stricter. The Judaic tradition explicitly forbids worship of any gods but the Lord God, Yahweh. While this may originally have been a form of monolatry, it became strict monotheism. As part of the defense of monotheism, Jewish law forbade the making of any carved images in order to prevent people from falling into worship of such images. Even today the Jewish temple or synagogue typically has no pictorial images. The symbol of God's presence there is the scroll of the Torah kept in each place of worship.

Christianity inherited at least parts of the Jewish law, including the ban on the worship of false gods. Yet early Christians lived in a Greco-Roman cultural context for the most part, one that used many pictorial images in statues, murals, and paintings. Christians used images of Jesus and his mother,

Mary, and included also pictures of various apostles and saints. Christian belief insisted that these images are symbols and have no power of their own. But not all Christians have adhered strictly to that belief.

As an aid to preserving pure monotheism, some Christians have tried to ban all pictorial images on the grounds that finite images of holy beings such as angels or saints distract people from God, or even lead people to idolatry. In the eighth and ninth centuries in Constantinople there were many iconoclasts (image-breakers), who tried to get rid of all statues and pictures. In the sixteenth century Protestant Reformation in Europe iconoclasm became popular again, as Calvinist reformers tried to eliminate the superstitious use of statues, medals, and so forth, by simply eliminating them altogether. Similarly, in 2001 a highly traditionalist paramilitary leadership in Afghanistan destroyed giant and revered statues of the Buddha carved into mountain walls many centuries ago. To the leaders of the group, called the Taliban, these were idols; to most of the rest of the world they were ancient art.

Islam is very strict in its monotheism. Arabian religion before Muhammad had been an archaic religion worshiping many gods, in awe of many spirits and mana-filled springs and rocks and amulets. Muhammad and the Qur'an outdid the neighboring Jews and Christians in discarding all these distractions from the belief that there is but one God. Like Judaism, Islam forbids all graven images. It also takes great pains to insist that nothing be given religious reverence except Allah. The sole possible exception to this is the Qur'an, treated by most Muslims as the eternal wisdom and will of God written in human language. Shi'ite Muslims even warn against excessive reverence for the Qur'an lest this distract from full reverence towards Allah.

Islamic tradition warns against any way of treating any limited and finite reality as though it were God. The Arabic word for this is shirk, sometimes translated as "idolatry." But shirk consists of any tendency to take some aspect of reality, whether it be a person's nation or fame or success or power, and to make it the guiding goal in life. Only Allah and submission to Allah is ultimately worthy of a person's full devotion.

The Islamic tradition on this is one form of an idea that occurs in all the historic religions. We humans face endless mystery in our lives. This mystery threatens us because its mysteriousness leaves us confused and unsettled. We want to blow away the mists of mystery and find concrete descriptions of all aspects of what is real. We want specific and fully understandable answers to all the disturbing questions of life.

This means that in a sense we are born to be idolaters. We are born to want to take some clear answer and make it ultimate. We want to find something definite we can use, not merely as a clue to the purpose of life but as the ultimate purpose itself. A historic religious tradition will usually offer definite answers, providing a belief system of ideas to be accepted as true and authoritative guides to truth: leaders, scriptures, and approved methods of interpretation; a moral code that gives definite answers to how to behave; symbols and rituals that are correct and valid. Because the beliefs and rituals and moral codes and community patterns and texts are not divine in themselves they too are symbols, ways in which the numinous is re-presented. But the temptation exists to identify all these symbols as somehow eternal and divinely sacred, rather than limited ways in which the eternal and infinite is re-presented and made more concrete.

Historic religion has a special temptation to do this because this is the form of religiousness that human consciousness accepts when it acquires the ability to conceive of universal and complete perfection. The religious symbols historic religion lives by are not symbols of just limited and imperfect numinous powers but of infinite and fully perfect Reality. It is possible, then, for historic religious believers to feel that since the symbols represent what is eternal and perfect, the symbols themselves must be everlasting and unable to be surpassed or corrected.

The constant, internal tension of historic religion (and of modern religion also in its own way, as we will see) is to live by symbols that represent the infinite and incomprehensible mystery and give it a face and presence in doctrines, codes, community forms, rituals, and images, without at the same time covering up the mysteriousness that still remains.

In many cases there are no serious consequences of forgetting the infinite mysteriousness of the ultimate. People may pleasantly devote themselves to their own religious symbols as though those symbols were the totally complete, final, and utterly correct ones, but still somehow do so with a comfortable tolerance towards those who do not agree. This temptation to idolatry, however, can also produce intolerance. If the symbols are absolutely correct, then perhaps all those who disagree are enemies of the truth, whether they know it or not. One person might then condescendingly try to help the ignorant opponents of truth. But as we have seen, another person might also try to oppress, imprison, or kill them. It has happened often enough.

The historic religion tempted to idolatry can overcome that temptation by reminding itself that its symbols can never be eternal and perfect; only the Ultimate can. There is practical value, then, to the Buddhist use of silence as a symbol for nirvana, or the Western use of the poetic image that describes God as a light so bright it blinds the soul. A famous koan (saying) of Zen Buddhism in Japan is apt: "What is the sound of one hand clapping?" That question gives a clue that our language and thought powers are limited in the face of mystery.

Sunni Islam faces a special challenge on this topic. Sunni traditionalists long ago agreed that the Qur'an as we have it in Arabic is uncreated, that before it was transmitted to Muhammad it had already existed everlastingly in God's mind. Within Islam itself more than one school has argued against this, saying that although the ideas in the Qur'an have always existed in God's mind, the Arabic wording is created and therefore open to at least some of the limitations to which all created texts are subject. But the Sunni traditionalist interpretation has dominated Muslim thought since the tenth or eleventh centuries.

The Death of Religious Symbols

Eventually, we will be discussing skepticism about religion, and intellectual doubts about the validity of religious traditions. There is, however, another kind of loss of religiousness that is not so intellectual. That is the death of the symbols, including the death of beliefs and rituals and moral codes, because they begin to lose their power to interpret and re-present reality to people.

Any symbol can die. It might be an image that no longer conveys meaning to an observer. Most of us living in modern industrial cities no longer experience daily contact with cows, so they do not spring to mind as symbols of wealth or motherhood. A symbol also might die because the meaning it conveys, however strongly and vividly, is no longer acceptable. The image of a king still has some meaning because of all the stories about kings we are used to, but if a tradition pictures God as a king in order to suggest that God is a dictatorial ruler, some people today would find this unacceptable and insist that God should be symbolized more as a loving and creative force. Symbols can also be killed by legalism, which adheres to the use of a symbol but ignores its inner meaning. People who are pressured into external participation in a ritual may become indifferent to its significance and cease to be affected by it.

Any given symbol can be replaced by a competing symbol. A whole set of symbols associated with one community might be replaced by symbols from another source. Most cultures in the past received their symbols from religious sources. Religious tradition was the main vehicle for passing on the culture's interpretation of who we human beings are and how we are to achieve some sort of salvation in the face of the estranging elements of life. Today, television and motion pictures provide images for interpreting life. The *Star Wars* series of movies tells the young about heroism and justice. *The Wizard of Oz* lets us know that brains, heart, and courage are available to all of us. Electronic images are replacing scriptural ones.

This discussion of symbols is bringing us closer now to a topic that is often thought of as of primary importance in religion: religious beliefs. The next chapter will deal with knowing and believing as aspects of religiousness. But this discussion of ritual and symbol comes first in order to make one point clear, that the beliefs and intellectual reflections on belief take place in the larger context of religious symbols and all the culture's symbols. The rituals, scriptures, revered leaders, community structures, and moral customs all together form a consciousness-context that people's minds rely on when they try to stop and consciously spell out to themselves their interpretations of life. We are able to think about life because our culture first has re-presented life to us in many ways, including religious ways.

Summary

This chapter has described ritual and other symbols. Rituals have been part of human activity since the beginning, used for their magical powers or to influence spirits or gods, but also because they tell the stories of reality in a way that help people understand how things are or should be. Rituals are symbolic, as are many aspects of religiousness. Symbols represent realities, numinous or not, so that people can apprehend what might otherwise be obscure or unknown. It often happens that people become more attached to the symbols than the realities they re-present, although at other times certain symbols lose their power and are replaced.

Religion is a symbol system that interprets reality for people, so that in the face of the mysterious dimension of reality and its power to cause estrangement, they can find instead the saving power of the numinous as the object of the basic human faith in the meaningfulness of life. That much is true of all religiousness. The next question that religions face is that of knowing how to determine just which symbol system works best. That is the topic of the next chapter, on faith and reason.

For Further Reflection

1. Which class of rituals and symbols best represents your particular values and interests? Religious symbols? Patriotic symbols? Family, economic-business, or party-time symbols? Explain.
2. Do any of the rituals or symbols you use have magical powers? If not, what is their value to you?
3. Can you think of yourself, your community, or your physical world as the symbol-presence of the numinous, such as God? Explain.
4. An idol is a finite reality treated as though it were divine. Do people ever literally idolize success, money, or power? Explain.
5. Identify any rituals or symbols that now educate you about life in any way. Are any of them religious or provided by a religious source? Explain.

Suggested Readings

Niels C. Nielsen, Jr., et al., *Religions of the World*, 1983. Ch. 1 and 2 on symbols in general, their cultural importance, and some concrete examples

Joseph Campbell, *Myths to Live By*, 1972. Ch. 2 especially, is an influential work on the emergence of human culture through myths and their enactment in ritual.

Barbara Ardinger, *A Woman's Book of Rituals and Celebrations*, 1992.

Paul F. Bradshaw and Lawrence A. Hoffman, eds., *Life Cycles in Jewish and Christian Worship*, 1996.

Paul Tillich, *Dynamics of Faith*, Ch. III, "Symbols of Faith," 1957. A brief liberal view of symbols and myth.

Pearl Binder, *Magic Symbols of the World*, 1972. Filled with illustrations and histories.

James C. Livingston, *Anatomy of the Sacred: An Introduction to Religion*, 1998 (3rd edition). Ch. 4 and 5, on symbol, myth, and ritual.

CHAPTER ELEVEN

Believing and Knowing

The Interrelations of Faith and Reason

The relation between faith and reason depends partly on what is meant by "faith." The religious person today is usually convinced that there is a major difference between faith and reason. People think of faith as a basis for belief precisely when reason fails. Faith is a trust, perhaps, in certain symbols, scriptures, leaders, and so forth, that goes beyond the evidence. Or it is a commitment to a religious viewpoint in spite of a lack of rational justification. Faith says, for example, that there really is a life after death even if there is no hard evidence of this. Reason, on the other hand, believes in things like gravity precisely because there is good evidence for it. At least that is how people often think about these matters.

A classic proponent of this notion of faith was the second-century Christian theologian named Tertullian (c.160-c.230). He declared that he believed that Jesus had risen physically from the dead precisely because it was not the kind of thing that was reasonable. If it were reasonable, he would not need faith to accept it. His concluding words are often quoted: "I believe because it is absurd." He dramatized his position by asking "What has Athens to do with Jerusalem?"; that is, what does all the rational argumentation of the philosophers and scientists of the intellectual city of Athens have to do with the religious faith that Jerusalem stands for?

Tertullian's position, however, is not the only one. First of all, while most people do think that faith is what a person relies on just where reason falls short, they nonetheless usually like to think that their faith is at least somewhat reasonable rather than totally disconnected from reason. Secondly, Tertullian treats faith as a mode of belief. Many centuries later, Martin Luther (1483-1546) will treat faith more as loving trust in God. Specific beliefs were still important to Luther, but now only in relation to this more basic and general trust. Where a Christian would speak of faith, a Muslim would speak precisely of "Islam," that is, of submission to the will of God, and a Jew would speak of covenant and of conformity to the Law of Moses. Some current theological writers even argue that the most basic faith, one that appears in all religions, is a fundamental trust in life, especially in the value of human life.

Many things in life are based on some sort of faith. We have faith in our parents and our spouses and our friends. We trust that the air traffic control systems of the world will guide our planes to safe landings. Some argue that even science is based on faith. There are ways in which this is true (though the word "confidence" may be more appropriate than "faith"). Chapter Twelve will describe the nature of science. This chapter deals with the place of reason in religious faith.

The question for a religious believer is whether religious faith should also be reasonable, or whether it can legitimately be unreasonable or even anti-reasonable? In this chapter we will first have to sort out some of the things that this might mean by looking at ways in which religious thinkers have tried to establish the reasonableness of religion. When we have looked at various ways this *can* be done, it will be easier to judge whether indeed you think that it *should* be done. In general any process of reflecting rationally on religious faith by those who believe in it is called theology. (When rational reflection on a religious tradition is done from a nonreligious viewpoint it is then often called philosophy of religion. But religious believers sometimes take a philosophical viewpoint about their own beliefs, so the use of labels here gets confusing.)

Theology

The Primitive and Archaic Traditions

No one knows how many thousands of years human beings have had religious symbols and rituals and stories. Graves that are twenty-five thousand years old have been found with stone implements buried next to the bones, as though to provide tools for the dead in a next life. This is a clue that for those twenty-five thousand years, perhaps, human beings have been conscious of the mysteries of life and have tried to make sense of them and deal with them.

Through most of those years people have eagerly thought about the many numinous beings and powers. They have wondered about the names and characteristics of the spirits, about techniques for controlling mana and divining the future. They have celebrated the reality of the powers and spirits in ritual; they have told the stories of the numinous in countless folktales and grand myths. Over and over again, religious beliefs have made sense of an otherwise mysterious reality.

But a new stage in religiousness came into power in human history in the axial age, when some people went beyond the beliefs they had used up to this point to make sense of reality, and tried to make sense of the beliefs themselves. Everywhere there had been people who had questioned one belief or another, who had doubted the power of a certain magic stone or the presence of a particular spirit; but these were not the systematic kind of doubts and questions and analysis about beliefs that finally appeared when historic religion began. At that point some people raised very basic questions about why anyone should believe anything at all.

Historic Religion Produces Theology

Historic culture in general is a stage in human development in which the culture begins to produce individuals who seek a logically coherent and fully unified way of understanding all aspects of reality at once. That is obviously an extremely ambitious goal. But it is also an implicit faith that reality ultimately makes sense, that in the end it really all does hang together. This faith took the human adventure of development and self-discovery in a new direction.

This faith in the ultimate intelligibility of reality manifests itself in three major ways. The first is philosophy. That is a name first given by ancient Greeks to their "love of wisdom" which expressed itself in the all-embracing theories about the whole universe proposed by people like Plato and Aristotle. The Stoics and the Epicureans added their versions. Similar schools of thought arose during comparable centuries in China and India.

The second way that faith in the ultimate intelligibility of reality manifests itself is in science. This was originally not distinct from philosophy. If you are seeking to make sense of everything at once you cannot easily divide your knowledge into separate packages called philosophy and science, because all knowledge must fit together in the end. But in recent centuries we have come to think of science as a distinct set of fields of study. It shares with philosophy the faith that we should treat reality as intelligible and keep on learning ever more how things fit together, though the scientists tend to settle for one thing at a time rather than take on the whole universe of all possible knowledge at once the way philosophy has often tried to do.

The third way that faith in the ultimate intelligibility of things has manifested itself is in the body of religious reflection called theology. This is work done by those who believe in a religious tradition, to show the intelligibility and reasonableness of that tradition. Theologians strive to provide a coherent account of their beliefs and rituals and moral codes and so on, in relation to each other and to all other things. (At least this is what theology has meant to people in historic cultures. In modern times some theologians have given up on this and like Tertullian are willing to separate religious belief from rationality, as it exists in science especially. Postmodern theology has yet another approach. We will see more about this in later chapters.)

What theology has done, as is true also for philosophy and science, is to look at all of existence and try to capture it in one master "story," as theologians now often call it, but a "story" that is really a thoroughgoing and usually abstract analysis, that includes the final and overall truth, meaning, and meaningfulness of everything. In the process of doing this the theologians measured all the partial folktales and grand myths against each other to see which could fit together and which could not. They threw out those that did not fit well with each other or with other kinds of evidence and logic. The ones that did all fit together in a single coherent story were translated into a more abstract language so that the logical unity and reasonableness of this story could be presented with precision.

From the beginning of this project one of the most troublesome, though also creative, aspects is that there have often been many conflicting master stories in the world. This has been true even within a single cultural tradition. The Taoists of China did not see the same overall unity as the Confucianists; the Hindus of India disagreed with the Buddhists; in the West Jews, Christians, and Muslims have variant master stories. The contrasts among the cultures of China, India, and the West are even greater. Even if a given religious tradition has one all-embracing interpretation of life and reality, one in which all the beliefs, rituals, symbols, etc., fit together in a coherent entity, it still may have great difficulty trying to establish that its interpretation is the right one. In the next town or just across the ocean or over the mountains there is another all-embracing interpretation that is quite different.

Today many people are used to allowing everyone to believe what she or he chooses, so people do not always worry very much about the fact that the Hindu interpretation of life conflicts with the Taoist, and that both conflict with the Christian. But historic religions have tended to take themselves rather seriously. This makes sense if ultimate salvation is at stake, especially if that salvation consists in something like getting to heaven and avoiding hell or avoiding endless rebirth into suffering. Moreover, if one of the historic universalizing traditions is true, that implies that the others are at least in some way false.

In defense of their own beliefs people will sometimes try to show that the other religions are false. In contemporary times there are those who attack all religious belief. If you have faith in some religious tradition, sooner or later someone will raise questions about your beliefs. If someone attacks your religion by saying that it is unreasonable or contrary to the evidence, you may want to have a way of responding. Theology has tried to provide help here.

Theology, in sum, is a name for rational reflection about religious beliefs and all the other religious symbols. It has two goals in mind. The first is to develop and maintain an overall inner rational consistency among the aspects of the present form of the religious tradition. This applies the criterion of "fit" to religious thought. The second is to show that belief in those basic aspects is sufficiently wise or reasonable that even outsiders should respect that religious tradition. This asks how well the beliefs "fit" with evidence from life and the world. To say it even more succinctly: theology is the attempt to establish 1) the coherence and 2) the truth of a religious tradition. When a theology accepts from the outset a certain religious tradition, revelation, or some inspired writings as a valid source of truth and seeks to show the coherence of ideas and practices, the theology is called systematic or doctrinal theology. When a theology looks to the book of nature, as it were, to evidence available even to nonbelievers, to show the reasonableness of belief, the theology is called natural theology or philosophical theology. We can look at these two types of theology one at a time.

Systematic or Doctrinal Theology

Faith Seeking Understanding

Systematic theology is the name often given to the kind of theology that first presupposes that the religious beliefs of its traditions are true, and then seeks to deepen the understanding of their truth by analyzing, comparing, and integrating them with one another. This establishes the inner coherence of the beliefs. Because systematic theology takes for granted the truth and value of the religious tradition and its doctrines, it is "faith seeking understanding," a classic Christian expression used by St. Augustine of Hippo in the early fifth century CE and echoed by St. Anselm of Canterbury in the late eleventh century.

The task of systematic theology is a very difficult one. There is always some degree of uncertainty about the message of the tradition. People interpret scriptures differently, and the doctrines are not always clear and simple. This is inevitable. Religion brushes up against the fringes of infinite mystery. It always has to struggle to deal with that mystery. It is hard to make sense out of life in a coherent way. If this can be done well, it provides an indirect argument in favor of the truth of those beliefs. Any belief system that manages to do so is bound to seem insightful and reasonable. Yet it is also very difficult to do, precisely because the project is to achieve a total coherence of ideas in relation to an infinite mystery. That is a daunting task, as some examples here can illustrate.

An Example: God and Evil, the Problem of Theodicy

A dramatic example of this search for over-all logical coherence is the Western analysis of the problem of evil discussed in Chapter Three. We have seen that originally Zoroastrian thought may have been held back from a full monotheism by its inability to account for the existence of evil in a world created by an all-powerful and all-good God. One Zoroastrian answer was to diminish the divine power of Ahura Mazda. Evil exists, they sometimes explained, because Ahura Mazda, the Wise Lord, cannot easily and quickly conquer Ahriman, Father of Lies. As Chapter Three noted, any theological explanation of the presence of evil in a world made by an omnipotent and all-good God is called a "theodicy," the word invented by Leibniz about 1710. (Leibniz was not doing "systematic theology," however, but "natural" or philosophical theology, to be described later here.)

The great Western monotheisms have had a difficult time on this topic. In the West belief in God has included the claims that God is all-powerful, all-good, and all-knowing. The basic theological problem of evil is to show how these three attributes of God are logically compatible with the existence of human suffering. Theology cannot say that suffering exists because God lacks the power to eliminate it. To say that would be contrary to traditional belief in God's omnipotence. Some have suggested that suffering is an illusion. What we call suffering is not really suffering: pain is an illusion, or we exaggerate our difficulties to ourselves. Western religious tradition has rejected this idea, though. We humans do suffer, tradition says. And most of us would insist from direct experience that at least some suffering is real.

If God is truly omnipotent, it seems that God could eliminate suffering, but does not. No theologian has seriously entertained the idea that God is callous, indifferent, or evil. God is all-good, the traditional doctrines assert. Nor could suffering exist because God overlooks it for a while until someone's prayers call attention to it, because God is all-knowing, the traditions affirm. The all-good God must allow suffering, therefore, for some good reason. An explanation of what that reason is would constitute a successful theodicy.

That reason might be found in another belief, that we humans were born with the power of free choice, able to choose good or evil. Without this conscious freedom we would not be human. Without it we could not freely choose good or choose to love. Freedom is so valuable, one common theodicy says, that God finds its sometimes evil consequences worth the price. Augustine put it more precisely, that God allows evil so that an even greater good could be achieved than would otherwise be possible. In this case, God allows suffering as the inevitable by-product of creating free beings. It is this human freedom, not God, that is the cause of hatred and murder and war and other forms of suffering.

The problem of evil is not so easily solved, though. Much suffering has been caused not by human freedom but by the forces of nature, by drought, flood, earthquake, and disease. Children are killed and crippled by events that no human choice could have prevented or avoided. There are theological responses to this also. One of them is the traditional Christian belief in original sin, based on an interpretation of the book of Genesis in the Hebrew scriptures.

At the beginning of things, God created the universe and placed humankind at its peak. Then the whole universe was orderly and good. But the original man and woman used their freedom to choose to sin, thereby disrupting the right order of things, perhaps so drastically that the earth itself became unbalanced. Later Jewish and Christian apocalyptic literature added the claim that at the end of the world, God will make all things right again. Then all evil will be destroyed and perfect justice will prevail. Anyone who suffered on earth without deserving it will be repaid with happiness and glory. Anyone who did evil without suffering for it will be repaid with punishment. The suffering of millions of people has been caused by original sin, but it will all make sense in the end. This is a fairly comprehensive theodicy.

Even this traditional answer has sometimes seemed awkward, though. An all-knowing, all-powerful, and all-good God might just have found a way to prevent the suffering of millions down through the ages for sins they did not commit. But everyone has committed personal sins also, the tradition replied to this objection. So everyone has also personally earned suffering. Yet those who say this have been hard-pressed to explain the suffering of infants, who presumably have not deserved their suffering.

Other ideas have proved helpful at this point. One is that God sends suffering at times even when it is undeserved, as a means of training and testing people, to allow them to become stronger and learn how to deserve even greater rewards. If this all seems a little harsh on little children who suffer, there is the final answer that Job arrived at, that suffering is a mystery.

The story of Job in the Hebrew scriptures is one of the great treasures of Western tradition. It is a very human story of a good man who suffered much. His initial response to the loss of his children, his wealth, and his health, is a well-known response. "The Lord gives, the Lord takes away. Blessed be the name of the Lord." But relentless questioning by his friends finally moved him to challenge the heavens. Make sense of this to me, Job cried out to God. God responded: Were you there, Job, when I laid the foundations of the earth and made the creatures of the deep? Can you possibly understand? Accept that the divine ways are a mystery, Job. In response Job accepted, even though he did not understand, and trusted in God.

That brief telling does not do justice to the complexities of the story of Job. The theology written about the problem of evil since the time of the story (perhaps 400 BCE) is even more complex. We do not have to solve the problem of evil here, fortunately. But it is a good example of how great a task historic theology has taken on in its attempt to show the reasonableness, the logical coherence, of the system of beliefs.

Polytheism has an easier time of it. It does not suppose there is any final unity of reality, so it does not have to figure out how everything relates to everything else in its portrayal of that reality. But if historic religion fails to do this, it will be attacked as inadequate or internally contradictory. It will lose plausibility for the inquiring mind. By default the religious tradition will appear internally incoherent and therefore unreasonable.

Making the Implausible into the Plausible

Some beliefs present a special problem in that they might not by themselves seem reasonably plausible at all. Yet as part of a larger coherent system they can gain plausibility. Most Westerners, for example, find it hard to see how some people in India could believe that the universe is not truly real. The Hindu who follows Shankara finds this belief plausible partly because it is part of sacred tradition, and partly because the Hindu is used to the idea as part of the cultural context. But the unreality of the world is plausible also because it is a belief that fits coherently with other ideas. The Hindu faces the problem of evil: Why do we suffer? Is there a way to overcome suffering? To believe that our worldly existence is maya, an insubstantial shadow, puts suffering in its place by portraying it as part of the passing insubstantiality of worldly existence. The belief in the unreality of the universe thereby helps to make a kind of sense, a coherent explanation of the human condition.

Among the various beliefs of Western religions, the Christian belief in the incarnation of God in Jesus of Nazareth is one that Muslims and Jews find highly implausible. How can the absolutely infinite and eternal God possibly become human, finite, and time-bound, in any way whatsoever? One classic attempt of Christian theology to explain this is that of Anselm, archbishop of Canterbury, in his late eleventh-century work, *Cur Deus Homo?* (Why God Human? or, more usually Why Did God Become Human?).

Anselm wanted to establish that it was very reasonable to believe that God had become incarnate in Jesus. In 451 CE the Council of Chalcedon summed up centuries of tradition by claiming that Jesus was fully human but that this humanness was also united to the full divinity of God. Though there is no mixture between the human and divine, according to the Council, the union nonetheless makes Jesus just one person (*prosopon* in Greek) with two natures, a human nature and a divine nature. This is summed up in the belief that Jesus is the incarnation of God, as John's gospel says.

As befits a theologian of a historic religion, Anselm sought a universal and unifying coherence among all his beliefs. So he offered a way of making some sense of this doctrine of one person with both a human and divine nature. Western beliefs shared by Christians, Jews, and Muslims alike said that humankind was sinful to some degree, and that God was all-good and all-just. Anselm decided he could show how these beliefs made the incarnation a reasonable belief. Here is how he argued.

A sin against God is an offense of infinite seriousness because God is infinitely good. When the parents of the human race freely sinned against God they incurred a debt to repay God for their offense against the divine honor. But the debt would have to be repaid by an act of infinite worth to compensate for the infinite seriousness of the sin. But humankind was both finite and now also sinful and flawed. Only God who was infinite and perfect could make repayment of infinite worth. Yet reparation would have to be made by a human being because it was a human debt. Thus, Anselm concluded, only a person who was both divine and human could make reparation for human sin. God's infinite justice demanded that reparation be made. And God's perfect goodness required that humankind be able to be reconciled to God. It made good sense, Anselm concluded, that God's justice and goodness would lead God to do the one thing that could overcome the infinite offense of sin. That was to become incarnate. This, Anselm went on, is why the suffering and death of Jesus saves humankind. By this sacrifice a repayment is made by a human being, a repayment of infinite worth because the human being is also God incarnate.

Since the eleventh century, Anselm's explanation of the value of the suffering and death of Jesus has become accepted by many Western Christians. Anselm took the belief in the suffering of a God incarnate, a belief offensive to many monotheists, and explained it in such a way as to make it seem more plausible or reasonable. In actual fact Anselm's arguments have probably appeared reasonable only to Christians who already accepted belief in an incarnation. But those who were Christians could say after Anselm that their belief in the incarnation and in the value of Jesus's suffering and death was not foolish belief but reasonable belief.

We have seen that systematic theology integrates and justifies beliefs by working within a belief context, by accepting certain basic beliefs as already true. From the earliest times of historic religion, however, another challenge to belief has existed: How do the believers know that their basic beliefs are true? How can the believer show that the symbols of the tradition are correct? Why should anyone trust that its revelation is true? Confronted by doubters, those who have believed have tried to do another kind of theologizing, one that has been called by many names including "philosophy of religion" or "philosophical theology." Here we will call it by another of its names, "natural theology."

Natural Theology

By Reason Alone

Natural theology tries to rely only on the natural human powers of reasoning and not at all on prior belief or doctrines. In practice, natural theology usually ends up confirming many traditional beliefs. Every human mind is inclined to see as reasonable what is already customary. Religion is no exception. In principle, however, natural theology defends itself against doubts or attacks by using reasoning alone. It cannot support its conclusions by quoting a sacred authority or text. It assigns itself the job of making sense to people on the basis of reasoning and experience, not on the basis of beliefs already accepted.

Natural theology has been very influential in Western civilization. Beginning with the ancient Greeks of the axial age, Western thinkers have tried to use reason to uncover the ultimate secrets of the universe, to discover the universal power, patterns, and stuff of things by reflection and logical analysis. We have seen one such attempt in the example of Aristotle's argument concluding that there is an Unmoved Mover, a perfect self-thinking thought that accounts for all the motion and activity in the whole universe. By rational analysis alone, Socrates and Plato concluded that the human soul is immortal. These are but two instances of a much larger tradition of philosophical reflection. As it happened, the thought of those ancient Greeks spread around the Mediterranean world until Jew, Christian, and Muslim began to see in such thought the possibility of proving by reason much of what they also believed by faith.

A major purpose of natural theology has always been "apologetics." This is not an apology in the modern sense of expressing regret for having done something wrong. The Greek word it is based on means to offer an account or explanation of something, often to defend or justify it. Christian apologetics consists of attempts to show the reasonableness of Christian belief and practice. Some early Christians argued that the events of Jesus' life and death were clearly predicted in the Hebrew scriptures, and that Jesus obviously had divine power because he could work miracles. Similarly, Muslims have argued that the poetic beauty of the Qur'an shows that it could not have been produced by any human person, certainly not Muhammad who for all his genius was nonetheless illiterate. But philosophically-minded skeptics have not been ready to believe in miracles. So both Christians and Muslims, for example, have appealed to the high moral quality of the lives of the earliest disciples of Jesus and Muhammad respectively. Yet skeptics have argued that being good and being right are not the same thing. A noble soul can nonetheless believe in false ideas.

As a result, there is a long tradition of apologetics that appeals to criteria that even a skeptic can respect, the criteria of evidence and rational argument, of the sort that science also uses (though not with the rules of public, long-term, and open-ended empirical testing used in science). The most common instance of this is in the proofs for the existence of God.

Proving God's Existence by Human Reason

There are three major kinds of proofs. They are called the argument from design, the ontological argument, and the cosmological argument. The names are not important. The last two have lost much of their original meaning. But philosophers still use them, so we might as well also.

The Argument from Design

The word "argument" is a little misleading; it is not a two-person verbal dispute but a methodical analysis of reasons for and against an idea, in this case the idea that there must be a supreme and universal Designer of the universe. Probably the most popular argument for the existence of God, this begins with observations about the orderliness of nature.

There is an extraordinarily complex set of interrelated patterns to nature. The ecological patterns of even a small pond in the middle of summer are complex enough to test the capability of even a major computer to keep track of and analyze. Likewise the workings of the eye and hand in coordination is a marvelously intricate and balanced interplay. The eye catches the light rays of those certain wave lengths we call visible as they reflect on the surface of a baseball in swift curving flight. Signals from the eye guide the movements of body, shoulder, hand, and fingers in incredible coordination to capture the ball in flight in a smooth motion. Life forms, planets in orbits, the evolution of the stars in accordance with basic laws of nature—all seem to show a detailed pattern that could not be accidental or random. Order such as this could only be the result of an ordering Power. Both Taoist and Western monotheists agree on this.

Western theology carries the argument a step further and says that the Power that orders the entire universe must be a conscious and intelligent Being, not a mere Force. It is the order of things that makes them intelligible. Without order there would be only irregularity and unpredictability, only chaos and nonsense. But the awesome fact is that the universe is the opposite. It is as though the universe were consciously planned and intelligently ordered. No unliving and unthinking Force or Power could account for such great intelligibility. Therefore, there must be an intelligent orderer such as Westerners call "God." Because such order seems to imply a purpose or goal, this argument is also called the "teleological argument" after the Greek word *telos*, meaning "goal."

This very popular line of reasoning is, unfortunately, greatly disputed. Astronomers, evolutionary biologists, and other scientists have theories about the universe that appear to be able to explain the ordered patterns of the universe as the result of a few mechanical laws of nature operating aimlessly over billions of years. We will hear more about these scientific thoughts in a subsequent chapter. Such scientific doubts have made other arguments in favor of God's existence more significant.

The Argument by Definition and Logic

A second argument is fascinating for its logical simplicity. It was first developed by Anselm of Canterbury and came to be known as the "ontological" argument. There is a neat modern form of it synthesized by the contemporary philosopher Charles Hartshorne. In its most condensed form it goes something like this:

A. Just by definition "God" is the label for the Most Perfect Being—-M.P.B. (that than which nothing greater can be conceived: that which cannot be second to anything in any way, the totally unsurpassable Being).

B. Concerning the existence of M.P.B., there are four and only four logical possibilities. One of them must be true because there are no other possibilities.

1. The M.P.B. is logically impossible, i.e., is a self-contradictory notion like a square circle.
2. The M.P.B. is possible but does not exist.
3. The M.P.B. does exist but could cease to exist.
4. The M.P.B. exists necessarily, could not not-exist.

C. Statement 1 must be rejected. There is nothing self-contradictory in the idea of a M.P.B. (Hartshorne has written whole books in support of this.)

D. Statements 2 and 3 must be rejected because each statement is intrinsically self-contradictory: a being that does not exist or could cease to exist is surpassable and therefore is not a M.P.B. The possibility of not existing is incompatible logically with the definition of Most Perfect as given in this argument.

E. Therefore, statement 4 must logically be true, because one and only one of the four statements must be true, and 1, 2, and 3 are all false.

This argument does not appear to have the logical simplicity promised; it looks rather complicated instead. But it does not require a great deal of information about the world. It does not depend upon evidence about evolution or cosmic order. It simply argues that a Being that is called Most Perfect must be defined as one that necessarily exists (cannot not be), otherwise it is not truly a definition of a most perfect Being.

Critics of this argument, however, claim that Anselm and Hartshorne have only shown how to define the word "God" in a self-consistent way. That is not the same thing as showing that there is a reality that fits the definition. Thus, many philosophical theologians rely on a further argument.

The Argument for an Uncaused Cause

One of those who rejected Anselm's ontological argument was the thirteenth-century theologian, Thomas Aquinas, perhaps the most influential of all the great medieval Christian theologians. He offered five basic arguments. The first three of these converge on a line of argumentation partly borrowed from Aristotle. Often called the cosmological argument, it claims that the fundamental facts of the cosmos, its activity, causal order, and even its very existence, can only be accounted for finally if there is an ultimate explanation of the kind that people know as God. Here is a paraphrase of the underlying ideas.

A. Every event that takes place has a cause or set of causes that accounts for it. This means that every event is intelligible, explainable by what caused it.
B. Every event depends on what caused it. Those causes depend on whatever caused them. These further causes are dependent on still other causes, and so on endlessly. Everything is contingent on something else. This means there is no ultimate intelligibility or explanation for events.
C. It does not make sense to suppose that the overwhelming intelligibility of things (as in A above) can come out of ultimate unintelligibility (as in B above).
D. Therefore it is reasonable to assume that the conclusion of B is not correct. It is reasonable to assume instead that there must be an ultimate reality which causes everything else and thereby explains why everything else exists.
E. For this to be the truly ultimate explanation, it cannot require any cause which explains it. It would therefore have to be the sole reality that is uncaused: the Uncaused Cause of all things. This is what all people call "God," says Aquinas.

This rather abstract and bare bones summary contains a lot of ideas. It takes a common sense approach in asserting that reality is intelligible. We find it practical to assume that events do follow from their causes, that red dye makes red cloth and not blue, that loud bangs are produced by some cause and not by nothing at all, and so on. Science operates quite successfully on the premise that reality is intelligible. But it is hard to prove that reality is truly *ultimately* intelligible. Yet it is part of the basic faith of many, especially those raised in a Western tradition, that reality is intelligible after all.

A striking aspect of the cosmological argument for the existence of God is the thorough-going contingency it attributes to the universe. Every aspect and every event of the universe, it seems, could have been other than it is. There is no "necessity" to anything; all is contingent upon other conditions or causes. So a person can even ask about the universe, "why is there something rather than nothing?" Even if the universe never had a beginning, philosophers speculate, even if there has been an infinitely endless series of events preceding current conditions, we might still have to ask how it is that the universe has been existing at all. If the universe were itself a necessary existent—something that could not not exist—we could stop questioning why it is here. But a universe in which all the events are contingent on other events does not seem to be the kind of reality that exists necessarily.

This implies that even now the universe is being kept in existence, not by its own power but by the power of the Necessary Being, the Uncaused Cause. If this universe does not have its own power of existence, then there is a need for a divine "concursus," as it used to be called, a divine ongoing empowerment of the universe to sustain it in existence. In this perspective God creates the universe constantly.

In traditional Christian thought, God creates and sustains a universe with its own order of "secondary causality." God is the primary cause of the whole universe. It runs by the natural laws with which God endowed the universe. The laws are the "secondary" causes. Tradition has usually added that because God is above nature (super-natural in the strict sense), God can also intervene miraculously in this secondary causal order. But a common interpretation in Islamic thought extends the idea of the divine "concursus" to a full "occasionalism." Each and every occasion that takes place in the universe is specially and specifically created by God, so that everything does indeed happen exactly as God wills. Every event is a miracle, in a sense, done directly by God.

The Philosophers' God

The trickiest thing about the cosmological argument is that it claims only that the ultimate explanation known as God does exist. It does not claim that people can fully understand that explanation. To put it another way, the cosmological argument concludes that there must be an ultimate Uncaused Cause of all else. It does not say that we human beings can really comprehend what an Uncaused Cause is like. Just the opposite is the case. Aquinas argued something like this:

An Uncaused Cause is a cause which, just by being defined as uncaused, does not have or need anything that explains its existence or what it is like. Nothing accounts for it in any way. If anything could even possibly account for its existing or its way of existing, it too would be contingent in some way on an outside cause. Then it would no longer be the final answer to things. So, by definition, it must be the unique exception to the rule that everything is explained by its causes. The Uncaused Cause is self-explanatory. It necessarily exists. It is self-causing, if you like.

Therefore, the argument goes, the Uncaused Cause must be absolutely infinite. Any finite reality is this and not that (red and not blue, living and not dead, and so on). Every finite reality therefore could become other than it is (could turn blue and die). So a person can demand further explanation of why it is still red and living or why it has turned blue and died. The state of finite things is contingent, dependent on causes, in need of further explanation. Inasmuch as the Uncaused Cause by definition cannot depend on anything or require anything to explain it at all, it must therefore not be finite in any way at all.

This conclusion implies further that the Uncaused Cause is changeless. To change, a thing must first not be what it is to change into. It cannot turn blue if it is already blue. It must first be not-blue. But to be not something involves a finiteness, an aspect of non-being or limitation. Furthermore, a changeless reality is outside of time, because time is just the process of change. The word "eternal" stands for timelessness. As was said, this is not a mere everlastingness through all time. It is eternity outside time without any before, during, or after.

There are other logical implications, Aquinas thought, of the fact that God is the infinite and eternal Uncaused Cause. There can only be one Uncaused Cause. There cannot be two absolutely infinite realities, because then each would not be what the other was, and would therefore be limited. The Uncaused Cause must always be totally simple (without any inner differentiations) because otherwise there would be internal limits differentiating one aspect from another.

As is apparent by now, the Uncaused Cause is incomprehensible. The attributes of infinity, immutability, eternity, unity, and simplicity are all really negative ideas: no limit, no change, no time, and so on. They are not really descriptions of the Uncaused Cause so much as they are admissions that this cause must lie beyond the limits of what human minds can comprehend.

This clearly is a philosopher's God, the absolutely infinite and incomprehensible Uncaused Cause. It is also, however, the God of many philosophical theologians, those who try to argue that belief in God can be shown to be a reasonable option for an intelligent and reflective person. The problem is that the conclusion of all this intelligent reflection is very abstract and distant. Or to use a better word, the conclusion is Mystery.

When human beings seek ultimate intelligibility, final all-encompassing answers, they have set themselves on the path to the infinite. It is no wonder they find that the ultimate is Mystery. Yet to draw back from the ultimate is to settle for the finite powers again, a god or other limited forces, in order to express or explain the realities of life. There is no easy choice here.

The God of Natural Theology as Personal

If natural theology stopped at saying that the Uncaused Cause is the eternal and infinite incomprehensible One, it might fit the Brahmanistic views of Shankara but not those of Western theology. The natural theology described here comes out of the Judaeo-Christian-Islamic traditions. In these traditions the Uncaused Cause is a God that is also in some sense a personal God. As chapter three indicated, the word "personal" can have unusual meaning when applied to God. Natural theology tries to explain why the word can be used at all and what it must mean in this case.

God is infinite, the argument goes. Existing without limit, God is therefore totally perfect, the limitless fullness of being. Out of this infinite fullness, God has somehow produced a world (without any change in God, however). In this world there are various limited perfections. A limited perfection is something good that is real, but in a limited way. Whatever is good and real is a result of God's unlimited perfection. So whatever perfections exist in the world must somehow exist first "in" God in some way (a way incomprehensible to us).

The greatest perfections we know are those of reflective consciousness and moral freedom, the theologians go on to say. Reflective consciousness is an open-ended capability of absorbing things into the mind, an openness to the infinity of being. Likewise, moral freedom is an endless capacity to perceive the potential for good, to be continuously open to ever greater good. It is also a capacity to choose a positive relation to Infinite Good—to God. As consciousness and freedom are the most open to the infinite, they must be the best clues to the infinite perfection of God. Consciousness and freedom are the core attributes of personness as we know it. We are therefore closest to speaking accurately when we say that God is somehow personal or at least that God is the fullness of what we know as personness in our limited way.

Symbols of the Divine

The Western natural theology that leads to the infinite incomprehensible Ultimate parallels the Eastern beliefs in the infinity and incomprehensibility of the Ultimate. Theologians, philosophers, and mystics all find that the human quest leads them, into endless mystery. With the exception of some branches of Buddhism, however, it is not a mystery of endless emptiness, but a mystery known to be fullness and perfection, a numinous reality whose existence brings salvation of some kind.

Natural theology leads to the double conclusion that the Ultimate is Mystery but is simultaneously somehow the fullness of being and perfection. That is why symbols for the divine are both necessary and legitimate. Symbols are necessary because the divine or ultimate exceeds human grasp. Only symbols can represent it. Symbols are legitimate because there is a divine reality there to be symbolized. Whatever a culture understands to be the most real and most perfect of all finite things is a symbol for the infinite fullness of being and perfection. Personness, the flow of nature, or ritual power are the primary symbols in the great historic religions (and for some Buddhists, silence or emptiness).

Many of the great religious traditions say that in whatever manner of existence follows our final death, we will all be mystics, contemplating the eternity of the ultimate or being dissolved into it. Until then, those who are not yet mystics will have to relate to the divine or ultimate reality via finite representations of this ultimate—by symbols.

But is this truly religious? To most people, religion is a relation to some specific personal Being or beings, to spirits or gods or to God conceived somewhat anthropomorphically. People seek a divine being they can talk to and who will respond to them, perhaps even through special interventions. They want more than just One in whose presence they are reduced (or elevated) to a speechless awareness of infinite and sustaining Mystery. The answer to this, of course, lies in what a person means by "religion." The philosopher's God provides a basis for a sense of an ever-present sustaining power of God in all things, allows a person to give reverence to others and to all creation as symbols of the divine, and affirms the ultimate meaningfulness of life. Whether this is adequately "religious" depends on the person.

FAITH AND REASON

The Danger of Reason

Religious people are often uneasy about theology. Faith and reason do not marry and live happily ever after. On the face of it, all the reasoning done by theologians seems to support faith by showing it to be quite reasonable. If the symbols of faith all fit together in a coherent unity, and if basic beliefs can be supported by rational arguments, this strengthens the religious tradition's claim to be a good and valid interpretation of life and its mysteries. By being so reasonable, though, the enterprise of theology suggests that reasonableness is a requirement religion should live up to; it accustoms people to expect that all the religious beliefs be reasonable. Many believers reject this idea.

When Anselm set out to show how reasonable it is to believe that God exists or that God became incarnate in Jesus and died for human sins, he discovered many critics. Faith is precisely faith and not reason, the critics said and accused Anselm of trying to accustom people to expect that the ideas of sacred scriptures and holy tradition should be subjected to rational analysis by mere human minds. They cautioned Anselm to spend more time in humble prayer accepting God's truths, and less time relying on weak human thought to understand the mysteries of faith.

The critics were correct in recognizing the issue: Should religious beliefs have to live up to the criterion of reasonableness? Does the believing head have to submit to the inquiring mind? As we have noted, few people will say that they will believe in something that is logically incoherent and unreasonable. Yet, once the mind begins to analyze and argue in order to show the coherence and reasonableness of a tradition, there is no easy way to halt the questioning and critical analyses at some safe point. There are various ideas about the relationship between faith and reason.

Faith without Reasoning

The most straightforward way to eliminate the problems caused by rational analysis of religious beliefs is to avoid such analysis. This may never be fully possible, but there are some close approximations.

There is first of all what we can call extrinsic or artificial faith. This may not deserve the name "faith" at all, but it needs to be included in order to cover all the possibilities. Such "faith" could be a taboo compulsion to uphold certain doctrines even though the doctrines mean little or nothing to the person. A person can be taught as a child that belief in the existence of God, for example, is something that God demands of people; God will punish anyone who fails to believe. Out of sheer fear of punishment, then, a person may grow up feeling it necessary to believe that God exists, and might feel a kind of taboo motivation to defend belief in God even if he or she does not understand or value the belief at all and may even actively doubt it. This kind of faith could also be an empty dedication to certain traditional words, whether the words mean anything to the person or not. This is a kind of legalism of belief.

The same could be true of someone who clings to certain beliefs out of a feeling that that is the only way to maintain acceptance by the community, to preserve an identification with the group. This kind of motivation is more likely to lead a person to understand the beliefs in order to talk about them with others in the community group and thus strengthen acceptance. This kind of faith is liable even to be a rather intense external support for the doctrines the group shares. In this case it is really the group-belonging and not the doctrines and other symbols that are important. A person who fails to achieve acceptance by a group may readily begin to look about for other groups and other beliefs. In all of this the reasonableness of the beliefs is irrelevant; in fact, even the intrinsic meaning of the beliefs is irrelevant.

In contrast to extrinsic or artificial faith, these beliefs and practices have intrinsic meaning to most religious people. The beliefs and practices are cherished for their own sake. An intrinsic type of faith is not necessarily a reasoned faith. Intrinsic faith can exist without theological reflection, without rational process of integration and justification of the beliefs. Two things are needed: first, that a person accepts the religious symbols as true; second, that these symbols matter to the person. This is a strong and living faith, even if it is not a reasoned faith.

The most common sort of intrinsic but unreasoned faith is the everyday unchallenged faith that most people simply inherit from their family and culture. For brevity's sake we can call it just "unchallenged faith." People receive their religious interpretation of life mainly from their social context, not from hours of theological analysis. If this faith goes unchallenged by doubters, outsiders, or theological critics, the person experiences little need to show its coherence and plausibility. The tradition that is received and held this way may be a very complex set of symbols—beliefs, moral codes, rituals, and so forth—yet the faith involvement of the religious person can be the simple one of just living out the interpretation of reality provided by those symbols, without doubts or rational analysis.

Closely related to unchallenged faith is blind faith, which also does not rely on rational justification. This is a challenged faith but a stubborn one. Though it may have once been unchallenged, sooner or later challenges arise. The skeptic, the person of another tradition, the neighbor who raises logical questions, can each intrude upon the peaceful flow of unchallenged faith. Then those who care little about their religious tradition will stir slightly, mildly piqued by minor doubts. But those who are highly involved in the life perspective that their religious tradition gives them may be provoked to a stronger stand. Some will plunge into rational analysis in defense of their tradition; others will reject reason and take a more stubborn stand, affirming blindly that their beliefs are true, without regard to reason or criticism. That is blind faith.

Skeptical onlookers can find many uncomplimentary reasons for blind faith. They will be quick to recognize the human need for security that makes us cling to the traditions that give us our sense of worthy identity, our meaningful belonging, our ability to overcome limits and the powers of estrangement. Ignorance and irrationality are prices we are ready to pay in order to remain secure in the face of threatening challenges.

There may be more reasonableness or logic in blind faith, however, than is at first apparent. There are various kinds of logic to blind faith. The first is a reasonable argument to avoid the need to reason much about faith, strange as that sounds. The human quest to understand the mysteries of existence eventually ends up in the conviction that the ultimate reality is Mystery, the infinite and incomprehensible. Therefore, a person should expect that the various beliefs and other symbols of a religious tradition go beyond what reason can handle. If the truths of faith are non-reasonable, perhaps that is a sign that they are closer to the infinite Mystery which is beyond reason. This is exactly Tertullian's position. Blind faith might therefore be truer faith than reasoned faith.

Perhaps the only valid way to know the Infinite may be by the power of the Infinite itself. It has been a common idea in Christian tradition, in fact, that faith can never come from the human mind or from human effort, but instead is a gift of God. God reveals truths beyond human reasoning and simultaneously provides the mind with the inner conviction that these are indeed true. It is not human reasoning therefore but the grace of God that empowers people to know the truth about God. Blind faith is therefore correct to trust in God, this logic says, in spite of any human reason that challenges it.

There is a second and different kind of logic at work in blind faith, a more hidden logic. This is the logic of practicality. The average religious believer lives for years by a religious interpretation of life's meaning and structure in the face of the various threatening mysteries of life, its suffering, confusion, and injustice. The religious interpretation makes sense of it all, offering a theodicy to explain the pains of life, and promising some form of salvation. Estrangement is under control; identity and values and belonging are clear and strong. Somehow the whole religious interpretation of life works well for the believer, even if that person cannot give a good theological or philosophical or scientific analysis to justify that interpretation. The believer can ask whether it is truly reasonable to abandon a faith perspective that makes such helpful practical sense out of life. The person of blind faith cannot often articulate this argument in a reasoned way, but may feel it in a hidden way nonetheless. It would be foolish to give up a faith that guides and enlightens and encourages a person just because of all the rationalistic doubts raised by others. That, at least, is the second and hidden logic of blind faith.

Faith as a Reasonable Commitment

The existence of a logical basis to blind faith is a clue that we have a hard time divorcing our lives utterly from reason. To do so, we would have to divorce ourselves, after all, from our own inner nature as the peculiar beings with reflective consciousness. Ignorance and irrationality represent a partial loss of our own humanity, which is a very high price to pay for the sake of religious faith.

We have seen two major examples of the application of the power of reason to religious reflection; these are systematic and natural theology. In the past they have often represented immensely ambitious attempts to achieve perfect logical coherence and intellectually compelling arguments in favor of certain beliefs. Historic religions reflect the ambition of historic post-axial culture to make ideal, coherent sense out of everything at once.

In modern times a more modest goal has gained prominence. Instead of seeking perfect logic and fully compelling arguments, many theologians today are happy to achieve a position of reasonableness. They maintain the basic faith that life is intelligible and worthwhile. They assume that the same ultimate God is the source of all the universe, consciously reflective human beings included, so that the intelligibility of the universe and the intelligence of our minds should fit together. The reasonableness they expect of their faith, however, is not quite the perfect logic that historic religions have usually sought.

The theologians of modern culture are highly conscious that there is no compelling rational proof that the world is real and not maya, or that the Mystery is divine and not everlasting chaos, or that life really and finally is intelligible in spite of all the uncertainties that hover about us. No interpretation of life, including the religious ones, can be shown to be absolutely reasonable and guaranteed to be true.

As a result, many people now cautiously abstain from religious interpretations and settle for an agnosticism that seeks only to make do as they go. But such pragmatic caution comes close to denying that there is any basic value or direction to life we can rely on. (We will see more about agnostic pragmatism in a later chapter.) If a person still seeks some clear and basic direction to life, but also agrees that no one can finally prove the truth of one interpretation over another, one religion or philosophy in preference to all others, there is still a way to be reasonable about it. The American philosopher William James (1842-1910) recommended a faith of this sort. He criticized a famous earlier attempt made by the French Catholic philosopher Blaise Pascal (1623-1662) to play the odds and wager that there is a God. Pascal had argued that if there is a God, the positive payoff for belief is eternal reward. In relation to so great an outcome it would be silly not to place one's bet where it counts. Pascal acknowledged that this was not true faith (we could label it extrinsic faith), but he claimed that if a person began to live as though he or she had faith, true faith would then develop.

James thought this wager was a bit too cold and calculating to count as real faith. Like Pascal he thought a person still might make a reasonable choice to believe, but he took a different tack. James recommended stepping back for a moment from any specific religious tradition such as Catholicism or Islam, and defining faith in a more general way. He calls it "the religious hypothesis," by which he meant that the best and final things in life have an eternal quality to them. Unfortunately, James is not very clear what he means by this. We have to imagine that he means that basic values like love and truthfulness have an ultimate or eternal validity.

James also claims that we will be better off even now in life if we believe that such values are of eternal worth. We have the option to believe this or not. But we do not have to make cold calculations. James argues that this is a live option, of real and intrinsic appeal to many people. It is also a momentous option because it can transform a life. It is finally a forced option, because even to decide to do nothing is to make a choice. We should not allow ourselves to be held back from making this live, momentous, and forced option in favor of the religious hypothesis out of fear of being wrong, says James. We choose our friends and our marriage partner even though we cannot be certain we are correct. Life would be poorer without friends and family. So these are choices well worth making in spite of a lack of certitude. If the religious hypothesis is a live one, intrinsically attractive to a person and clearly beneficial in life, it is well worth choosing also.

It is not necessary to use James's particular analysis to see that it is possible to make a reasonable commitment to a religious interpretation of human existence in the universe, even though that interpretation is not provable. A person can reflect on the human condition, on life's possibilities and limitations. As actually lived, life can be set side by side with a religious interpretation for conscious and explicit comparison and correlation. As in the case with the hidden logic of blind faith, there is a kind of practical test, but now done deliberately and reflectively.

The test is to ask whether the religious interpretation really makes some overall sense of who we are and what the meaning of our lives might be. Does it offer an understanding of where we come from and where we are going, an understanding that is at least reasonably possible even if not provable? Does it produce a moral vision that helps instead of hurting? Can it be lived, celebrated in ritual, symbolized effectively, all in a way that fits life's experiences and gives extra meaning to life? If it can do all this, then it can be reasonable for a person to consciously choose it as his or her religious faith.

This has been called a "theology of correlation" by the theologian Paul Tillich. We correlate our experiences of life and our understanding of the basic questions about life's meaning with the interpretation of life offered by a religious tradition. When we find that this match-up produces a coherent and intelligible vision that in practice resolves our feelings of estrangement, then it can be reasonable to accept the religious symbols expressing that vision as our own faith. The act of faith for Tillich is therefore a choice, an act of making a reasonable commitment to a religious vision. It can be difficult to go through such a process of reflection. But it offers a way to reconcile faith and reason.

The Tensions of the Human Quest

Faith and reason are part of the human quest to see life as coherent and meaningful. Sometimes they can work in harmony, but there is an underlying tension that is unavoidable in the long run.

A particular faith perspective gives security to our lives by providing a way to deal with threatening mysteries. It gives the security of identity and belonging and the hope of overcoming all estrangement. It is reasonable to seek such security, at least in the hope that it can be found and maintained.

But what is the basic choice or commitment that a person wants to make: to personal security or to reasonableness? Is it legitimate to give up being reasonable entirely in order to preserve the security which religious faith can provide? Which is a person more committed to, maintaining a reasoned honesty about reality, or maintaining a sense of security even if that involves some self-deception or illusions?

We human beings are still on the great adventure of becoming ourselves. We grow in knowledge through searching and questioning, exercising our capacity for reflective consciousness in new ways. Each time we do this, we run the risk of breaking some symbol that has been our guide to life's meaning so far. The tension exists every time we begin to doubt some traditional belief. Even to continue to be fervently religious can place us in the tension between security and questioning, if the religiousness itself seems to call us to some new interpretation of beliefs. In the presence of Mystery, the religious symbols that interpret existence are always in tension between security and adventure, between past and future.

Summary

This chapter has been about theology and faith. Theology is conscious and reasoned reflection on religious beliefs and other symbols. Faith is a name for the act of commitment to the reality represented by a given religious symbol system. Theology attempts to show the reasonableness of a set of religious symbols, both in terms of their logical coherence with one another and also in terms of the rational plausibility of the basic beliefs. A person's act of faith might or might not be a reasonable one, however. Some people care little for rationality in religious matters; others care a great deal.

End of Part III

The heritage of human cultural development and of our own individual development provides us with a mixture of beliefs and other symbols, some of them primitive in style, others archaic, and still others historic. The interplay among these styles and symbols can be very complex, but we can identify some dominant themes that each style tends to impose in the overall pattern of religiousness. Each style a guide to life, in its turn influencing the specific guides provided by moral codes, leaders, texts, rituals, reason, and faith. There is one more dominant style that guides people's religiousness: the modern style. The next part describes modern religiousness.

For Further Reflection

1. To what extent do you think it is good for people to be unreasoning about their religious beliefs and practices?
2. What would be the most important purpose for reasoning about one's own beliefs and religious practices? To support them? To understand them more deeply? To disprove the claims of others?
3. How much should religious people be consciously reflective about the overall coherence of all beliefs with each other and with other human experiences? Why?
4. We usually say that people have a right to believe whatever they want. What limits would you set to this right, if any? Not to practice human sacrifice? Not to contradict science?
5. Which in fact is closest to how you would describe your own faith: blind faith or reasoned faith? Which do you think is better and why?

Suggested Readings

Monika Hellwig, *A Case for Peace in Reason and Faith*, 1992. A Catholic's analysis.

C. Stephen Evans, *Faith Beyond Reason: A Kierkegaardian Account*, 1998. An evangelical Protestant viewpoint.

Richard Swinburne, *Is There a God?*, 1996. A relatively brief but current example of theologizing about God's existence.

José Ignacio Cabezón, ed., *Scholasticism: Cross-Cultural and Comparative Perspectives*, 1998. Identifies rational theologies in seven different major religious traditions of the world.

Paul T. Brockelman, *The Inside Story: A Narrative Approach to Religious Understanding and Truth*, 1992.

Thomas Aquinas, *Summa Theologica*, Part I, question 2, article 3. The five arguments for God's existence.

Anselm of Canterbury, *Basic Writings*, 1962. See "*Cur Deus Homo*," Why God Became Man.

Part IV

Modern Religiousness and Beyond

Different people mean different things by the word "modern." For most of us it means whatever has happened in our own lifetimes. Historians say that the modern era in Western civilization began about four hundred years ago because it was then that a number of ideas that are still influential today began to gain acceptance in Western culture. Because what is usually meant by "modernity" was originally a development in Western culture, the following chapters will focus mostly on Western developments in religious thought and practices.

During these last four hundred years, a new form of religiousness has slowly developed as part of the overall cultural transformation that makes up "modernity." Some aspects of it grew comfortably from within traditional religion. Other aspects of modern religiousness originated first in opposition to certain religious beliefs or practices. This opposition sometimes ended up changing religion, to the point where ideas that were once considered unreligious or even antireligious eventually came to be part of some peoples' religion.

It is difficult to be clear on what is "modern" in religion because many religious groups that exist in contemporary times are not themselves very modern in their type of religiousness. Even religious movements inspired by modern perspectives are not entirely modern. All religious groups are made up of us human beings, all of whom are inheritors of primitive, archaic, and historic modes of thought, both from our overall cultural history and from our individual development from infancy to childhood to adolescence to our always incomplete maturity. Even though we might hold some of the modern ideas that will be described soon, we also might believe in spirits, be influenced by some taboo morality, think of some rituals or symbols as semimagical, and so forth.

The complexity of all this will be laid out in more orderly form as we go along. Nevertheless, it can help now to provide a simple guide to identifying what is meant by the modern stage of religious development. There are four major aspects of it. (Eventually, some modern aspects will be reinforced by the "postmodern" thought to be described in Chapter Fifteen; other aspects will be challenged by it.)

A first aspect of modern religiousness is the elimination of the great gulf between earthly imperfection and divine perfection that historic religiousness often emphasized. Modernism has not wiped out the distinction entirely, but it has changed it. Most Christians, for example, were once taught to think of this earth as a fallen and corrupt place, infected by sin and death, doomed to pass away at the apocalyptic end of the world. Now the modern idea has crept into Christian thought that this world and its comforts and challenges, its loves and joys, are also divine gifts, worthy and even holy enough to rejoice in religiously.

A second aspect of modern religiousness is its appreciation of freedom, variety, and change. This is a radical idea for historic religion. Religion traditionally has offered stability and security in the face of threatening change and anxious uncertainty. Modern religiousness, however, is tolerant of variety and freedom and may actively support them. Modern religiousness tends to believe that no religious doctrine is the final word on any subject. It defines ideal human "personness" in a way that emphasizes individual choices, with all the uncertainty and instability this might risk. This second aspect of modern religiousness makes religious tolerance possible. The great historic religions are tempted, logically enough, to want to suppress other religions as erroneous and dangerous to the true faith. Modern thought preaches mutual tolerance among religions and, eventually, even for the nonreligious.

A third aspect, closely tied to the first two, is a fairly individualistic humanism. We will see again that there are different meanings to the word "individualism." In general, modern culture, building upon some classical notions, argues that every person has certain basic individual rights, as well as individual responsibility for one's choices. This individualism implies a humanism, a belief in the ability of us humans to take constructive charge of our own lives and in the basic value of human well-being. It usually implies that traditional authoritarian institutions, including religious institutions, must not seek to abrogate basic human rights and freedom.

Archaic cultures define a person through the person's group, usually characterized by a combination of religious and political authority. Historic cultures define a person through the person's relation to the universal or cosmic structure, often defined and enforced by religious leaders. Modern culture has come to define the person as a center of personal freedom and responsibility. Combined with openness to change and a greater worldliness, this often appears in the form of a humanistic belief in progress here on earth, in the hope for better earthly conditions for future generations through human efforts.

A fourth aspect is skepticism about miracles. Such skepticism is almost as old as the earliest classical thought of Greece, India, and China. But the development of science and scientific attitudes has led many more people to be skeptical of miracles. Many a modern religious person will prefer to define religion in such a way that the notion of miracles is omitted completely. This includes a general reluctance to speak of the supernatural, of revelation as miraculous, of divine healings, or of any other sort of specific divine interventions into the events of nature and history. God's activity is portrayed instead as a more general ongoing supportiveness and presence. This is a major characteristic of what has been called "liberal" theology.

In Chapter Fifteen we will deal with those who have adopted what they call "postmodern" thought. The postmodernists usually claim that there is a fifth characteristic of the European Enlightenment that is specifically modern. That is an emphasis on rationality.

It is certainly true that modern culture has included an emphasis on rationality, especially in the form of modern science. But an emphasis on rationality is not specifically modern, nor is it solely European. Rationality in the West flourished long before modern times, from the axial age in ancient Greece through twelfth- and thirteenth-century scholasticism in Europe. Rationalistic philosophies can also be found in the axial age in China and India. Rationalistic analyses had a significant impact in ninth-century India, among philosophical Muslims during the same time and later, and in the Neo-Confucian movements in China in the eleventh to thirteenth centuries. But it is good to be aware that many writers now ignore or underplay this history. They claim instead that the strongly rationalistic temper of modern science is peculiarly modern and not a characteristic aspect of much of human thought in different times and cultures. At stake here is the question of whether a rationalist approach is simply a local custom of some Europeans at a certain point in history, or whether a rationalist approach represents a common tool that humans have found valuable and valid in many cultural contexts. Chapter Fifteen will deal with this when describing the perspective known as cultural relativism.

The combination of an emphasis on rationality and skepticism about miracles may make modern religion sound irreligious. There is certainly no common agreement among Westerners about what religiousness should be like in these contemporary times. What we can do is go back to the approximate beginnings of modern thought and sort out some of the events and ideas to better understand and evaluate modern religiousness. For convenience we can start at about 1600, the time of Galileo.

Chapter Twelve

Science and Secularity

The Modern Era Begins

We have seen that adherents of historic religion tend to believe in a perfect existence that lies beyond this earthly existence. By contrast with the mind's image of perfection, concrete earthly conditions appear as dismal and fallen, unworthy of concern except as a temporary condition to endure righteously on the way to perfect happiness. Modern thought, however, begins with a new confidence that somehow or another earthly life has intrinsic importance and is worth taking very seriously, worthy of enthusiasm and dedication for its own sake.

In the West this modern turn to the world has its roots in the fifteenth-century Renaissance in Europe. For a variety of reasons, Renaissance Europe experienced a great surge of energy and optimism about life in this world. The new art, architecture, and music exhibited a fascination with worldly life and beauty. Great exploratory expeditions sailed from European ports to discover new continents and new wealth. Mechanical inventions multiplied; mathematical methods improved.

All of these were an early part of the great cultural development that led to the modern era. All of them together contributed eventually to a different perspective on human existence, on mystery, and on hopes for the future. This meant that there would also develop a new sense of what religiousness is, a new sense of the deepest mysteries of existence, and how we are to discover meaning and hope in them rather than threat and confusion.

This shift towards a new way of understanding existence did not occur overnight. In the sixteenth century many people still expected the apocalyptic end of the world to arrive soon. These same people were more often inclined to see humankind as fallen, weak, and sinful rather than wise, good, and creative. These more pessimistic souls were also likely to fear Satan's power and to persecute witches. Even as the foundations of modernity were laid, the worst persecution of witches in European history broke out. By the

Enlightenment of the eighteenth century, though, many elements of modern culture were in place. It is a shift that is still just beginning in the lives of many people around the world, including those in supposedly modern cultures. The growth of early modern science was a major aspect of this shift in culture.

Early Modern Science

From about 1600 to 1800 in Europe and America there developed a pattern of thought that soberly celebrated the complex orderliness of the universe. In this orderly universe there was no place for miracles, spirits, and omens. Believers identified themselves by various names: natural philosophers, enlightened ones, free thinkers, deists. Many of these we would now call scientists, though that word was not invented until the nineteenth century.

Galileo and the Beginnings of Modern Science

Galileo Galilei (1564-1642) died after more than fifty years of prodigious scientific work. He is popularly remembered for his support of Copernicus' argument in favor of the theory of the ancient Greek Aristarchus, who claimed that the earth went around the sun. But Galileo did more than support the Copernican theory of the solar system; he promoted much of the basic method that came to be known as science.

Up to Galileo's time and beyond, science was a part of philosophy. It tried to explain not merely what patterns existed in nature, but also their ultimate purposes. As we have seen a number of times, the human mind tends to presume that things make sense. The animist and polytheist assume that many events are caused by spirits and gods who have some humanlike motive for intervening in life. Those who believe in a personal universal power, such as God, say that all events are under God's control, so that all things that happen do so in accord with God's purpose. To understand reality thoroughly, then, it would be necessary to explain why God made them happen that way, for what purpose.

One theologian of Galileo's time, for example, is said to have contradicted Galileo's claim that the planet Jupiter had moons. Because no one on earth could see the moons without a very good telescope, he contended, there was no purpose for God to put moons around Jupiter. They could not be guides for the navigator as the stars were. They could not move people to admire God's talent as a creator since they were invisible to most people. Therefore they could not exist. One clever person responded that since Galileo's telescope showed that the moons did exist, there must be intelligent life on Jupiter, beings who used the moons for navigation on Jupiter's oceans. This person obviously agreed that it was indeed important to show the purpose for the existence of the moons.

In his many investigations of the pendulum, of motion, of centers of gravity, and so forth, Galileo had long been taking a different approach. By profession, Galileo was a mathematics professor. Forget about figuring out what purpose there is behind the events of nature, Galileo insisted. Concentrate instead on finding out with mathematical accuracy just how things act, just what the reliable patterns of physical nature really are. That is enough.

Science today no longer asks why God puts the seeds on the outside of strawberries, or why God gave Mars two moons, or why God created mosquitoes. When science asks today why something happens, it does not seek to know the ultimate purpose of each thing, but only how reality is structured so as to have caused given events to happen. Before Galileo it was hard to do science without eventually mentioning God and God's purposes. Since Galileo's time we have become accustomed to leaving God and other numinous powers out of scientific theories.

This is true of both kinds of physical events, the regular and the irregular. The unusual or irregular event is one such as lightning striking a house, a comet appearing in the sky, or a disease suddenly afflicting a healthy person. From the most primitive times to today, people have found it plausible to say that such irregular events are the work of numinous powers. Up until Galileo's times, everyone was certain that each comet was sent individually by God to warn people of a calamity to come. Every lightning bolt was God's punishment. Every sickness was caused by a demon. Many people today still speak of every flood or tornado as something God sent or permitted for some divine purpose. But under the influence of the new science that Galileo helped to establish, we are no longer so sure. We usually think irregular events in nature are actually manifestations of basic and highly regular patterns. Our scientific explanations of diseases can omit any mention of God. Also dead and gone are the spirits that once lived in the tree, the river, or the cloud.

Religious believers often combine their belief in scientific explanations with at least a vague sense that it is God also who is at work in the events of nature. A meteorologist may pray as though it were God who guides the tornado even though she also believes that tornadoes follow a course laid down by natural atmospheric conditions. When she studies what is known about tornadoes, she would be surprised to find any reference to God in her textbooks as part of the explanation of how tornadoes form, why they are so powerful, what paths they tend to take, and so on.

Scientists find they can also describe all the regular aspects of nature without any mention of numinous reality. These are the various reliable patterns of nature, ranging from the extremely regular forces such as gravity and electromagnetism to the fairly regular patterns such as the movement of the tides and the chemical reactions of an acid with a base. A famous meeting between an emperor and a mathematician illustrates how science has come to describe such patterns without reference to God.

The French mathematician Laplace (1749-1827) had developed a theory of how the universe might have slowly evolved into its present form. The Emperor Napoleon invited Laplace to describe this theory to him. Laplace elaborately explained the mathematics of gravity and mass and motion, perhaps losing Napoleon in the details. But Napoleon did notice that Laplace had not once mentioned any part God played in the whole process. As the story was told by an astronomer present at the discussion, Napoleon challenged Laplace on this: What about God? Laplace supposedly replied, "I have no need of that hypothesis." These word do not deny God's existence or power; they just state what science has come to take for granted, that the patterns of nature have a regularity of their own. There is no need to slip some mention of God into a description of nature's patterns in order to explain how they operate and what events they cause.

This was not entirely new. Even the science of Aristotle's day as well as the science of late medieval theologians proposed that nature followed regular patterns of secondary causality that operated without extra divine intervention. But after Galileo's time the sheer number of events that could be explained as part of the patterns of nature constantly increased. Therefore the number of things that seemed instead to be the product of divine intervention—miracles—constantly decreased, to the point where miracles no longer seemed plausible. In short the active presence of God in the particular events of life became less directly evident to people.

Deism

By the middle of the eighteenth century, the century that came to be known in Europe as the Enlightenment, many scientists and science-minded people had come to share a kind of natural theology known as deism. This was a new form of historic religiousness, which accompanied many other new and radical ideas such as belief in democracy and free speech.

Deism usually divided all of reality into two distinct realms: the physical and the spiritual. Galileo had earlier recommended treating the physical as matter-in-motion, as nonliving stuff that acted always in accordance with basic mathematical patterns that were built into the nature of physical reality. By the time Isaac Newton died (1642-1727), there had been a century-and-a-half of success after success in science by the use of Galileo's method of treating physical reality in this way. Deists felt entirely reasonable, then, in agreeing with this approach.

The success of science also encouraged the belief that the physical universe was entirely intelligible, and intelligible in mathematical or mechanical terms. "The force of gravity is equal to the product of the masses (and a constant), and inversely proportional to the square of the distance between those masses." That is a scientific statement. Gone from science were claims such as "God made gravity to hold the universe together." Gone also were older ideas that said, "Rocks fall because they seek a natural state of rest." Rocks do not "seek" anything, the new science said. Language that suggests any life or consciousness in raw matter is simply inaccurate, most deists believed.

The mathematical order of things awed the new scientists. Where once there had seemed to be countless unpredictable happenings caused by demons, saints, angels, or God's intervention, now there was order. Now there was dependable regularity built into physical matter. Every irregularity in nature turned out to be caused by an intersection of regular natural laws in a way that could be predicted by the mind that knew the laws of nature. This led the new scientists to support certain ideas about God's power and activity. These ideas together constitute the core of deism.

First of all, there was common agreement that the orderliness of nature, its thoroughgoing mathematical intelligibility, could not possibly be an accident. It must have been designed. The older argument for God's existence known as the argument from design took on new power. The Designer, it seemed clear, must have been a perfect intelligence capable of designing and creating a whole universe of such detailed orderliness that in spite of its enormous complexity it could run on its own by its own built-in constant laws of nature, its own natural set of secondary causes. In one famous image, God was compared to a master clockmaker who designed and created an intricate timepiece, wound it up, and then let it tick away on its own. Some deists insisted that God was also continuously sustaining the universe in existence by the divine "concursus."

The same deists who were sure that God the Designer must exist promoted a second idea: this Designer did not intervene in the orderly operation of the clockwork universe. There were no miracles, in other words (though some deists made an exception for the miracles of the Bible and the general miracle of revelation). Robert Boyle (1627-1691), the English scientist and acquaintance of Newton, said God is not a puppet master pulling strings from behind the scenes.

Deists provided a logical argument against divine interventions. To believe that God intervenes in nature is to suggest that God did a sloppy job when God first designed or created the universe. People once believed God had to work to keep the planets moving in their orbits or to make the fertile rains fall each spring, as though God had made a rickety universe that required tending. We know better now, the new scientists said. We know the almighty and perfect God did a perfect job in creating. Now it is just up to people to understand that creation

Naturalism

From the deists onward, scientists have thought that science has to be guided by "naturalism," a presumption that every event can be accounted for fully by natural (secondary) causes. Naturalism comes in three forms. Metaphysical naturalism is a claim that the natural universe of time and space, matter and energy, is truly ultimate. Nothing but this natural universe exists. There is no God or other Ultimate. So metaphysical naturalism is atheistic rather than deistic. Because it denies that there is a supernatural reality such as God, it says that no divine interventions are possible.

Cosmic naturalism is the second form. It says that the events in the entire cosmos are due to natural causes. This can be agnostic about whether God exists. Or it can be religious in a deistic manner, supposing that God planned and produced the universe to operate entirely by secondary causality.

The third form is known as methodological naturalism. This merely assumes that the method of science is restricted to explaining all events as though they had only natural causes. It is not a claim that there are not or cannot be divine interventions. Some religious scientists even speculate on how God might intervene in such subtle ways that the supernatural influence would be undetectable. Methodological naturalism is a claim that science can use only natural causes to explain things, because the object of scientific study is nature, not the supernatural. (The Epilogue will look at this issue again.)

Naturalism works well in science. To abandon naturalism at any point and say that only divine intervention (or secret manipulation of the forces of nature by spirits or demons) accounts for an event would be to give up trying to understand how the event came about, beyond the bare assertion that some sort of non-natural cause was at work. By never giving up on the naturalistic approach, by assuming that there were natural causes that could be understood by the human mind, science has produced a vast array of highly precise, reliable, and effective ideas that all fit together with each other. Over and over, things like comets and lightning that had once been thought to be miracles, interventions by God into nature and history, turned out to be the effects of the great web of natural causes.

Deism as a Religious Humanism

The new scientists had great confidence in the power of human reasoning. God made the world intelligible and made the human mind intelligent, able to understand the world's intelligibility. Science was what God made people for, they thought. By the end of the eighteenth century, many people, including both some deists and some irreligious skeptics, were assuming that there were also natural laws of human behavior in addition to the natural laws of physical nature. The new sciences of economics and sociology and psychology began to appear, seeking to understand the regular laws of human life in order to tell us how to live wisely and happily. There should be no need, therefore, to ask for God's help in life, to hope for miracles or expect divine guidance. In the beginning God made all things quite orderly. We can trust that this world is a good place to live. All we need to do is to understand it thoroughly and then set to work to make it all better for us humans.

Of course, there would still be a lingering source of trouble in this magnificently ordered universe. The human person is not merely a physical and emotional being subject to the laws of nature, the deists said. The person is also a spiritual being, with a soul that has the power of free choice. The spiritual aspect of our humanness is not controlled by the natural laws of the physical universe. It can cause disorder, confusion, and evil. But if God made people free, God nonetheless would not allow freedom to wreck the overall order of things, the deists argued. God must have provided some way of regulating the human use of freedom. In light of this, a traditional Western belief seemed quite logical, namely, that God must eventually punish those who use their freedom to cause the evil disorders of life. So God is not completely at rest but, somewhat anthropomorphically, is watching us. After our deaths God will pass judgment on us and reward or punish us in accordance with the choices we have made.

Those are the ideas that constituted deism. It was called a "natural religion," one based on natural theology rather than revelation. The God of deism was the Designer God and the Judge, the God who created the world at the beginning and who will judge all people in the end but who does not intervene in the meantime. The deists were humanists. They believed that they especially did not need God's intervention because they had now discovered the wonderful power of human rationality. Traditional religion stressed the importance of obedience to religious scriptures and authority. The deists believed that human reason was the highest authority. This and the disbelief in miracles set the deists in opposition to the traditional religious groups, although they were still explicitly religious in their own way. Even in the eighteenth century, however, some science-minded people began to abandon this untraditional but real religiousness in favor of a nonreligious position. By the nineteenth century the rise of evolutionary thought contributed to more widespread skepticism.

Religious Tolerance

English deism was rooted partly in the writings of Lord Herbert of Cherbury (1583-1648). Edward Herbert was made Baron of Cherbury for his service as ambassador to France during the Thirty Years' War, a series of religious wars fought in Europe between 1618 and 1648. Killing in the name of God disgusted Herbert, so he looked for a way to leave religious divisions behind. He believed he had found it in "rational religion," a few basic ideas that he thought all rational people everywhere in the world could accept. He formulated this religion as belief in a God who designed the universe, created humans with intelligence and moral sense, and left it to people to honor the God who made them by behaving intelligently and morally. You can see how this might grow into full deism in the years to follow.

Herbert's plan to eliminate religious conflict by creating a simple universal religion has not worked. Most people in Western nations now enjoy freedom from religious wars not because all share in a single rational religion, but because most religious groups respect the right of other religious groups to follow their own beliefs and practices. Even in those European nations where one religious group is supported by the state, all religions are normally granted freedom. Norway is officially Lutheran; the clergy are paid by the government; the churches are built by tax money. But other Christian denominations, as well as non-Christian religions, enjoy freedom of worship. Nevertheless, as Chapter Six indicated, mutual religious tolerance does not come easily.

While Lord Herbert was ambassador in France, the Huguenots (French Calvinists) enjoyed some degree of religious freedom that had been granted by the Edict of Nantes in 1598. But by 1685, when the effect of the Edict was already eroded, it was repealed and bloody conflict between dominant Catholic power and the Huguenots broke out again, with many of the latter leaving France for other nations or the New World. (The official separation of church and state did not arrive fully and lastingly in France until early in the twentieth century.) In the same century a major civil war in England was fought on religious issues. In the North American colonies, the Puritans (Calvinists also) kicked Roger Williams out of the Plymouth colony for preaching religious tolerance. Quakers sought religious freedom in William Penn's American territory.

Religious tolerance was not easy to find in Europe. Spain was one of the last nations of Europe to grant full religious freedom, at the death of its fascist leader, Generalissimo Francisco Franco, in 1975. Until then, Franco followed the old Catholic rule, overturned by Second Vatican Council in 1965, that error has no rights. This meant that erroneous religions—every religion except Catholicism—had no legal or moral rights and should not be practiced openly lest it lure others into error also.

These examples of religious intolerance from Western history can be matched, of course, by similar intolerance in many places. As earlier chapters mentioned, historic religions are universalist, claiming to have the single truth and true way for all humans everywhere. In some places like China and India, various religions often managed to live side by side in peace nonetheless. Hindus and Jains share beliefs in karma and the cycle of rebirth. Buddhism was once persecuted in China, but eventually the more philosophical Confucian and Taoist traditions interacted peacefully with Buddhist ideas. But in the twentieth century in India, tension between Hindu and Muslim, and between Hindu and Sikh, have led to bloody conflicts. Muslims everywhere are hearing the call of intolerant traditionalists to cleanse non-Islamic elements from Muslim lands. If only a few heed that call, that is enough to cause enormous trouble. Many a good Protestant fundamentalist still feels an obligation to convert people everywhere in the world, if possible, on the grounds that only the converted and baptized have a chance at heaven.

A historic and universalist religion finds it logically difficult to practice religious tolerance, as Chapter Six indicated. Those who believe that divorce and remarriage are sinful can be dismayed by civil laws which allow them. Or for the word "divorce" substitute abortion, pornography, homosexuality, and artificial contraception. Religious tolerance demands a degree of privatization of religion, as not all moral norms are shared publicly by everyone. But in practice this seems to imply that these norms are not truly universal, that each group has its own norms. Each universal religious tradition can still claim that its own norms are the only ones that are correct. But religious tolerance tends to make people think in a relativistic rather than universalistic way—that moral norms are relative to one's group, or to one's time and culture. We will return to this topic of moral relativism when we look at cultural relativism in Chapter Fifteen.

The increase of religious tolerance in the West was made possible partly by the deist search for a common rational religion. Even though this search was not successful, deism took a critical look at existing religious beliefs that led so often to war and hatred. This weakened the hold of traditional religion a bit. It would not be long before agnostic and atheistic ideas would challenge the influence of religion even further.

Evolution and Agnosticism

Evolutionary Theory

The deists lived in a universe they saw as static; no significant changes were expected in its basic structure. A few thousand years earlier God had placed the sun in the center, with the earth and other planets around it and the stars in their appointed places in the sky. But then astronomers began to think that perhaps the universe had evolved. In the mid-eighteenth century Emmanuel Kant (1724-1804) propounded a theory of cosmic evolution. By the end of the century, Laplace also said that the universe was not static but was a changing process, that the sun and planets had slowly formed over very many thousands of years out of some heavenly gases or matter.

During the eighteenth and early nineteenth century geologists had ample evidence that the earth had evolved physically also. The Bible had seemed to indicate that the earth was created around 4000 BCE. The only major geological changes in the biblical record were catastrophes caused by God's intervention, such as the great flood which only Noah and his family had survived. (That seemed to account for the strange phenomenon of seashell fossils on mountain tops.) By studying the numerous layers of different kinds of rock formations, however, and comparing them to current processes of sedimentation as well as volcanic and glacial activity, geologists became convinced that only a slow process of change taking place over many millions of years could account for the appearance of those layers.

It was not long before many people began theorizing that maybe not only heaven and earth evolved but life also. The numerous fossils recovered from mine shafts, mountain sides, and special excavations were startling. In higher layers of rock, mammals abounded, were harder to find in lower layers, and were entirely absent from yet lower layers. Great lizards (dinosaurs, they came to be called) had once dominated the land when only tiny mammals lived, but in lower layers there were no lizards of any kind at all, nor even amphibians if one dug deeper. Below that there were no land animals or insects, and so on. Especially odd were major transitions, when thousands of species seem to have been wiped out in a relatively short amount of geological time, after which there was a proliferation of new species, some of which often seemed to be variants of a few species that had survived earlier catastrophes. The fossil record indicated that there had been what we now call an evolutionary process, a very long and rather meandering process at that.

It was difficult to construct a suitable theory about how this evolutionary process could have occurred. There were many attempts, each with its own problems and limitations. Finally, Charles Darwin (1809-1882) captured the attention of the scientific community with a theory that has turned out to be amazingly fruitful. He published this theory as *The Origin of Species* in 1859. For thirty years Darwin had gathered bits and pieces of information about fossils, seashells, and mountainsides, about similarities between species, and about odd animals in strange places in the world. But evidence is not really evidence until someone sees how it fits into a theory.

Darwin provided theory borrowed from economics. Nature was like a capitalist economy, said Darwin, hearkening back to Adam Smith (1723-1790) and Thomas Malthus (1766-1834), in which a struggle for survival weeded out the inefficient and weak. In Darwin's theory there are three main factors at work. The first is superfecundity, which is the tendency of every species to give birth to more offspring than would or could survive. The second factor is that there are random variations among members of a species. The offspring are not all exactly alike. The third factor is what Darwin called natural selection. Some variant forms survive and produce others like themselves. Less successful variant forms die or fail to reproduce. The philosopher Herbert Spencer (1820-1903) summed it up as "survival of the fittest," a phrase Darwin himself eventually used also.

There was a variety of responses to this theory. Many religious authorities rejected it completely as they had rejected other theories that seemed to contradict the Bible. Some deists traded in their static deism for an evolutionary deism, proclaiming that the evolutionary pattern followed a God-given natural law, that of the survival of the fittest. How ingenious of God, they said, to have built into nature an evolutionary process. These evolutionary deists, along with traditional religious people of various beliefs, at least agreed that there still was a Creator God. Not everyone else did.

Atheists and Agnostics

As noted in the Introduction, atheism is a name for the belief that there is no God. Agnosticism is a name for the conviction that no one can know whether there is a God or not. The true atheist says that the mystery we humans face is ultimately a meaningless emptiness. The agnostic just says that the mystery is a mystery. In practice, both the atheist and the agnostic get along without God.

When the new science had begun to cast doubt on some aspects of traditional religion, many turned to the nontraditional religion of deism, but others simply turned away from religion altogether and became atheists. Belief in miracles diminished or was disparaged. Church authority had been weakened by the Protestant Reformation and by later strife among religious factions. New methods of historical research called into question attempts to interpret the Bible literally. In this context, the reasoned arguments of natural theology still favored by the deists were no longer as convincing to everyone as they had been.

Darwin's evolutionary theory gave an additional boost to atheism in a number of ways. One was Darwin's claim, published only in 1871 in *The Descent of Man*, that humans had descended from apes. This made many persons doubt there was a soul or any place for the soul such as heaven or hell.

It made God less necessary, no longer needed as a hypothesis to account for human existence, nor even as a judge for the soul in an afterlife.

Of particular importance in Darwin's theory was the notion that evolution operated by random variation. The evolutionary process, as Darwin described it, was long and aimless. Each generation begets dozens of offspring. Randomly, each offspring is a little different from its parent, and that difference, also by random chance, occasionally is of use in the offspring's struggle to survive. As a result of this double randomness, that particular offspring is more likely, though not guaranteed, to grow up, breed, and pass on that lucky variation. As long as that variation helps for survival, it will tend to become more common. Many billions of such random variations over more than the last three and a half billion years of life on earth, according to current estimates, have given rise to the present species.

All theories that stressed the factor of randomness in the evolutionary process made it seem less and less reasonable to accept the traditional belief that the universe was guided by a God who intervened to guide things, or even the deist belief that God was a master designer. This impression was fortified by observations of nature's seeming cruelty. Even before Darwin published his theory, the poet Tennyson had written of "nature red in tooth and claw" caring not for individuals but only for species, and even then wiping out many scores of species over the eons. Neither tiny brachiopods nor massive mammoths survived nature's processes. Thus those who were already inclined to be atheistic saw evolutionary theory as additional support for their atheism. The theory also helped produce the new word, agnosticism.

One of Darwin's main supporters was biologist Thomas Huxley (1825-1895). In the heat of arguments about God's existence, he was asked whether he was a theist or atheist. In order to have a label for his position, he invented the word "agnostic." It means "one who does not know" or more literally "not-knower." Huxley heard those who argued that an evolutionary process that resulted in humankind could not be purely accidental but must have been planned by God. He also heard those who said the randomness of evolution proved there was no God. As a scientific-minded person, he could see no way in which either of these claims could ever be tested scientifically. He came to what seemed to him to be the most rational conclusion, therefore: no one can know whether God does or does not exist.

Agnosticism and Social Darwinism

Agnostics usually claim they arrive at their position by reasoning. It is intellectually sound, they say, to acknowledge that the ultimate state of things is simply unknowable. But we humans do not live by intellect alone. It is easier to be an agnostic or atheist if there is also no practical and emotional need for a God. The nineteenth-century agnostics could feel comfortable in a godless universe because they believed human beings could do quite well without one. A movement known as social Darwinism is a good example of this kind of agnostic optimism. Herbert Spencer was its best-known advocate.

It is reasonable to believe, said the social Darwinists, that the pattern of evolution will continue as social evolution. Human reasoning is a product of life's evolution, they said, and is itself evolving. With reasoning as a tool for survival, those who use it best will survive best. Those ideas that would best promote survival are ideas that promote better health, international peace (or at least military victory over enemies), and economic prosperity. Therefore, these ideas would steadily increase in influence until one day humankind would enjoy health, peace, and prosperity everywhere. Thus does society evolve.

Because social evolution was doing all this by itself, there was no need to rely on God's help to improve things. People would be saved from hunger and war not by divine help, but by the natural process of evolution. The millennium was coming, but not because of ancestors, gods, or God. This time of joy and peace and love would arrive, liberating people from their limits and their estrangement, because this was the pattern of evolutionary progress.

Secular Evolutionary Humanisms

A Substitute for Religion

From nineteenth-century thought until today, there have been visions of salvation that are similar to this agnostic evolutionary optimism. They are most often called secular evolutionary humanisms, or just "secular humanism." There are various forms of them (we will look at two), but they have some characteristics in common.

First, they are secular, which means that they are thoroughly this-worldly. They do not believe in any numinous powers—not spirits, gods, or God (although they sometimes believe in a God-substitute, as we will see). They are also this-worldly in that they do not believe in any life after death. We humans are born into nature and history, live our lives and die, they say. Our meaning, value, and purpose must be found within the limits of these earthly lives and our effect on the lives of the generations to come.

Second, an evolutionary view holds that reality is in constant process of development. There is ongoing change which is not merely repetitious but is a process of improvement, at least in the long run. That includes human culture, its social conditions, morality, economics, politics, and so forth.

Third, as we have seen, humanism is a viewpoint that trusts in human abilities, and maintains that the quality of human life is the most basic value there is, to be sought above all else. A humanism is a basic-value morality that proposes that a humane, loving, free, and creative existence for all people is the most important goal there is. (Note that there can be religious humanisms as well as secular ones.)

A look at secular evolutionary humanisms can help to understand modern religiousness because these humanisms are often modern substitutes for religion. Secular evolutionary humanisms agree with modern forms of religiousness in their renewed appreciation of this-worldly existence, their emphasis on growth and freedom, and their skepticism about miracles. This can be seen in the nineteenth-century belief system of Karl Marx (1818-1883) and in the twentieth-century belief system of Julian Huxley (1887-1975; Thomas Huxley's grandson). Each is a quasi-religious vision of salvation.

Marxism

The most famous—or notorious—secular belief system in the world today is probably Marxism. People who are antagonistic to the socialist or communist ideas associated with the name Karl Marx would not call Marx's thought progressive. That implies improvement. For many Marxism is just the opposite. Yet to Marx himself and to millions of Marxists, his theory is truly progressive. We can more easily see why Marxists believe this if we look at a rather simplified version of basic Marxist theory. (In passing we might note that Lenin changed Marx's theory somewhat. Communism in the former U.S.S.R., China, and some other places is not quite what Marx predicted or wanted.)

Karl Marx felt great sympathy for the suffering of humankind. He knew well that people have endured sickness, loneliness, hatred, oppression, and hunger throughout history, but he believed that history had been following a certain developmental pattern that was now producing a series of events leading to an ideal earthly life, a secular millennium. History, to him, was a kind of pattern of events operating by its own inner laws. At times Marx treated the flow of history almost as a Taoist treats the yang-yin pattern. One major difference between Taoism and Marxism is that the Taoist does not believe that there can be strong and useful progress in culture, politics, or economics, but Marxism does. To Marx, social and political, and, above all, economic developments were precisely the chief manifestations of the progressive power of history.

Marx was highly impressed with industry. Late eighteenth-century and nineteenth century techniques for using energy from steam engines held the promise of a transformed human existence. Coal (not to mention water, oil, gas, nuclear, and solar) power changed into usable machine-driving energy could accomplish something unseen and unheard of prior to this time: it could produce enough food, clothing, and shelter for everyone. In fact, Marx claimed, industrial power could even create such incredible luxuries as leisure time for most people, education for everyone, the ability to travel and learn about others. Everyone might be able to live life more freely and comfortably than even kings once could. Marx has turned out to be at least partially correct about this. In highly industrialized countries this has become generally true. The average American citizen now lives better than Henry VIII of England or even Queen Victoria.

There is something that Marx considered more important than material goods. Adequate material possessions were only a base for supporting the higher values of freedom and equality. Marx believed that in the past ages of desperate scarcity humankind had become accustomed to valuing possessions and wealth as a means for survival. It was because of this, Marx thought, that people had learned to measure their own worth in terms of the quality of their clothes, the size of their home, their social class, instead of by what should be the true measure of worth: compassion and concern for one's neighbors. The ideal society would reverse this and give primacy to justice and compassion. (Piaget and Kohlberg would say contrary to Marx that the desire for outward status and possessions is just a normal if regrettable stage in growing up; Hindu tradition agrees.)

Marx was wrong, dangerously wrong, about how the ideal human society was to come about. He thought it would begin in industrial nations unlike Russia and China. He thought the industrial nations would experience class conflict and eventually violent revolutions. These would lead to the overthrow of capitalism and the establishment of ideal socialist states. Regardless of Marx's errors of prediction, this general vision of the perfect society is still an inspiring one, shared by many who are not Marxists. It is a vision of society of material abundance. More importantly, it would be a free and equal society in which all would work together in harmony, sharing the products of the collective effort. It would be a thoroughly democratic state with equal justice, rights, and power for everyone.

With such a vision it is not hard to see why Marxism became so popular in the world. Marxism does not offer an afterlife. Nor did Marx believe there was a God such as Jews, Christians, and Muslims believe in. Moreover, Marxism has not proved correct or even wise in its effect on many nations in the world. Nevertheless, it has been an appealing vision because it promises salvation from hunger and hatred, from oppression and futility. To the person who dedicates his or her life to the advancement of Marxism, it offers a sense of being important, of contributing to a grand and glorious humane world. Moreover it encourages hope by claiming that the flow of history is like an all-embracing pattern driving cultural developments towards a perfect earthly realm.

Marxism is often considered antireligious because of its opposition to belief in God, in divine help, or in heaven. Marx described religion as the opiate of the masses, numbing their present pain by promising happiness in the next world. Marxism sees religion as a force supporting the traditional economic and political powers that oppress people. Yet Marxism functions as a kind of quasi-religion. It offers an equivalent for God in its belief that history can be trusted to act as a kind of ultimate power influencing everything to move towards the ideal state in which many limits and forms of estrangement will be overcome. One person's atheism is sometimes another person's religion. Marx proposed his vision as one worthy of a faith commitment.

Huxley's Earthly Religion

Karl Marx is probably the most famous of the secular evolutionary humanists, but many view Marxist thought with suspicion. So it is good to give at least one other example, that of the evolutionary philosophy of Thomas Huxley's grandson (and Aldous Huxley's brother) Sir Julian Huxley (1887-1975) proposed in his book, *Religion without Revelation* (1928, revised 1956). As the title of the book suggests, Huxley does not believe in any supernatural revelations from God. In fact, he is rather thoroughly secular, rejecting belief in miracles and heaven and hell, and taking a strongly agnostic position about the existence of any other-worldly power or being.

Nonetheless this secular viewpoint is also a religious viewpoint, according to Huxley. He defines religion as a unifying perspective on reality that expresses people's deepest convictions about the ultimate nature and purpose of life. Huxley's unifying perspective treats evolution somewhat as Marx treated history, as a force or pattern within the universe moving in a predetermined direction. For Huxley, therefore, the pattern of evolution is a sort of God-equivalent, not all-powerful but nonetheless universal in its influence and transcending the limits of all smaller powers and forces. Huxley believed that salvation would come through cooperation with evolution, a this-worldly salvation of an ideal human future.

Huxley's vision includes a theory of purposeful cosmic evolution. At the beginnings of the universe, the primal energy divided into various forms including the many subatomic particles. Because the particles are different from one another they organized into complex atoms. Because there are different kinds of atoms they react to one another in complex ways, causing chemical reactions and new organized bondings. These molecules interact and become organized into amino acids, proteins, and eventually into living cells. The incredibly complex organized living cells develop in different ways and eventually interact to form multi-celled organisms. The complexity of interactions between cells increases and the multicellular organisms become complex plants, animals, and eventually humans. In particular the extraordinarily complex interactions of the various nervous system cells produce the human ability to interact consciously with the environment and with one another. Because of the complex organization of individual consciousness, people are able to interact with one another to create social structures, farming, politics, literature, and so forth.

Throughout this long process of cosmic evolution, Huxley says, there is a pattern. Whatever exists differentiates, i.e., takes different forms. The different forms can then unite in something more complex. This is a higher level of organization. The more complexly organized forms differentiate further through ongoing evolution, which allows them to then unite in even more complexly organized ways. Differentiation, complexity, and organization are constantly on the increase. The first major aspect of the pattern of cosmic evolution can be summed up, therefore, as the law of increasingly complex organization.

As complex organization increases it also produces ever higher levels of consciousness. This is the second law of cosmic evolution. The highest form of consciousness produced by this evolutionary process so far is human consciousness. And it has already differentiated into different sets of ideas, languages, tools, institutions, roles, rules, values, visions, poetry, religion. These now interact in complex ways to constitute the different cultures of the world. These cultures are more complex levels of organized consciousness. A world culture which in which all the prior cultures retain their distinct identities but interact positively with each other would be an even higher level or complex organization and consciousness. All of this is part of the same single cosmic evolutionary process.

We humans are part of cosmic evolution, not only in our biology but also in our ideas; not only physiologically but psychologically, socially, and culturally. There is but one evolutionary process and it encompasses all aspects of the universe from the birth and development of stars to the birth and development of cultures; one pattern runs through it all. There are many moments of apparent randomness, Huxley acknowledges. The potential for chaos in history and nature is evident. This makes it all the more awesome that cosmic evolution has occurred as it has, effectively making use of the possibilities of greater diversity, complex organization, consciousness, and the complex interactions of consciousness in culture.

Most striking of all is Huxley's idea that we humans are now cosmic evolution become conscious of itself. We are not merely aware of evolution; we are evolution's highest self-expression so far. Now that we are cosmic evolution's most conscious form we have great power in our hands. We might fail to make use of our power, Huxley acknowledges, but he is basically optimistic. We can increase our consciousness of evolution, of ourselves, and of our potentials.

This increase, itself a more complex consciousness, will be our path into a secular sort of salvation. As we become enthused with evolutionary potential and dedicate ourselves to it, we can create a future society of peace and prosperity, of humane and loving existence. Huxley saw this as a vision worthy of a faith commitment. It is his secular religion, a secular evolutionary humanism.

The Hidden Forms of Salvation

Secular evolutionary humanisms sometimes offer millenarian visions of a this-worldly salvation. There will be a utopian lifestyle on earth one day, they assure us. Other secular humanisms are more modest in their aspirations than Marx or Huxley. Some settle for getting by as we go along, believing that even small gradual improvement is a good deal when compared to the fearsome alternatives of nuclear war, mass hunger, or the spread of totalitarianism. In general, though, it is the future, the improvements to come, that constitute salvation, even if we do not yet recognize this.

There are other, but hidden, kinds of salvation that go with allegiance to some secular evolutionary humanism. These are the salvations, also often hidden, that go with belonging to any large movement.

A vision like Marx's or Huxley's offers a picture of the universe, an interpretation of nature and history, that can tell us the meaning of life. It can offer a high moral challenge, inviting us to rise above short-term pleasures and pursuits in order to make our life more meaningful. It challenges us to give our time and energy to the well-being of future generations. If we are dissatisfied with the achievements of life yet also doubtful about any afterlife or numinous powers, we might experience a restlessness, a longing for some deeper and lasting purpose. Marx, Huxley, and others offer us that; they tell us that children now being born need not starve, because of us; that the oppressed of the world can find freedom, with our help.

Even then our enthusiasm might waver. A solitary person can do so little. Is it really worth all the effort? Marx and Huxley offer more at this point. They tell us that our efforts are not merely small human attempts to deal with one more problem. Rather, they are contributions to the great pattern of history or evolution. These efforts we exert are like helping a God bring about the millennium; they identify us not just with the morally right, but also with the ultimately victorious inner drive of nature and history. In this we can find a lasting value for our life; in this we are saved from meaninglessness. No wonder Marxist thought has had a strong appeal to many people. It and other such visions are very much like religions in their appeal, offering a share in lasting truth and deep purpose. They offer salvation in the face of troublesome mysteries.

The End of Easy Optimism

From Galileo to Marx and Huxley there grew a confidence in the intelligibility of the universe, and in the capacity of the human mind to grasp that intelligibility and live by it. This world increasingly appeared to be a potential utopia. Human society was seen more and more as something perfectible. As a result secular humanisms began to gain wider acceptance and to replace traditional religiousness. But then came the shattering experience of the First World War.

People were too rational to kill each other for a few miles of earth or for national pride, the optimists thought. Yet for a few miles and for pride millions died. Technology would bring only health and wealth, the optimists expected. But mustard gas and improved armaments contributed to the slaughter. People had outgrown blind patriotism and military pride, optimists believed. But for the glory of the fatherland people were eager to spill the blood of their neighbors. Two hundred years of "enlightenment" were not enough to eliminate war. In some ways the development of scientific rationality made it even worse.

Thoughts such as these released other doubts and confusion. Old beliefs had been breaking down for a few centuries now. Many people were uncertain about religion, about the social and economic order, about all the new ideas and inventions, about changing morals. The twentieth century was going to prove to be a very difficult one. The next chapter will describe one of the greatest difficulties for religion, atheistic skepticism.

Summary

Traditional historic Christianity had relied on divine revelation and church authority as the source of true understanding. From Galileo on, science-minded people began to trust human investigation and reasoning more. An early result was deism which promised a religion based on reason, celebrating a watchmaker God who did not intervene in history. Evolutionary thought then moved further from traditional religion by suggesting that the process of evolution was too random to have been planned or guided by a God, but was orderly or purposeful enough to provide hope for an ever-better worldly existence, even one without any God.

When the twentieth century began, World War I subverted many people's hopes for human progress even while skepticism about religion was still widespread. That is the topic of the next chapter.

For Further Reflection

1. How do you distinguish miracles from non-miraculous events? Explain why it seems reasonable or not to you to believe that miracles do happen.
2. Describe any ways in which scientific ideas about laws of nature and evolution have an effect on your religious beliefs. Should they?
3. Which position seems most reasonable to you: atheism, agnosticism, or theism (belief in a God)? Do you decide this entirely on the basis of reasonableness? Explain.
4. Does the description of Marxist thought make it sound appealing? Is Marxism an adequate substitute for religion? Why or why not?
5. Julian Huxley perceived a great cosmic pattern behind the cosmic events of the universe. Could this be evidence that there must be a Designer-God? Explain.
6. Are you optimistic about how we human beings will handle issues of war and peace, of economic justice, of the environment through our growing knowledge and our moral commitment?

Suggested Readings

Peter Gay, *Deism: An Anthology*, 1968. Includes significant excerpts from major deist writings.

Richard A. Fortey, *Life: A Natural History of the First Four Billion Years of Life on Earth*, 1998. Nicely summarizes geological and other evidence that supports evolutionary theory.

Karl Marx, *The Communist Manifesto*, 1964 (1848).

Julian Huxley, *Religion without Revelation*, 1956.

Noel G. Coley and Hall Vance, eds., *Darwin to Einstein: Primary Sources on Science and Belief*, 1980.

Phillip E. Johnson, *The Wedge of Truth: Splitting the Foundations of Naturalism*, 2000. Sustains his attack on evolution and naturalism begun with his 1991 book, *Darwin on Trial*.

Daniel C. Dennett, *Darwin's Dangerous Idea: Evolution and the Meanings of Life*, 1995. A leading philosopher explores the multiple implications of the theory of natural selection.

CHAPTER THIRTEEN

Life without Religion

Twentieth-Century Skeptical Humanisms

Throughout history, people have perceived mysteries in life and have had faith nonetheless that life is coherent, intelligible, and meaningful on the deepest level that they could imagine for their time. The primitive person took it for granted that various stories could explain the pieces of life. Archaic people, who believed in larger powers at work in reality, were less sure that life could be fully happy, but they usually lived with some confidence that their myths explained the structure and events of life. Historic religions believe that notwithstanding all the chaos and evil in the world there is an underlying ultimate intelligibility and value in life.

In this twenty-first century, however, skepticism about life's intelligibility and value has increased. A variety of factors, including the end of nineteenth-century optimism, have led to increased doubts that there is any ultimate intelligibility and value to human existence.

Skepticism has a long history. In the axial age when the gods were demoted to lesser status, philosophies arose in which religion had no place. In ancient India, for example, even as classical Hindu and Buddhist and Jain thought were taking historic form, a few such unorthodox philosophies appeared. They rejected the newly orthodox belief shared by the religious traditions of India that we are caught in an endless cycle of rebirth controlled by the cosmic law of karma. The sixth-century BCE Carvaka school of thought, for example, rejected belief in the gods and in any life after death, on the grounds that there was no good empirical evidence for either of these beliefs.

One could also count Confucius (Kung Fu Tzu) as unreligious. Confucian thought more or less ignored the gods, focusing instead on social relations and on cultivating good character. (Neo-Confucian thought of the eleventh century CE and later was more metaphysical—concerned with the ultimate principles of reality—but still not really religious.)

In ancient Greece, Epicurus (341-270 BCE) declared that the gods were uninterested in human affairs. It was useless to worship them, though one might strive to imitate their divine serenity. Gods and people alike were beings caught in the endless flow of events. The universe is composed of atoms streaming through space ("the void"), moving partly by natural forces (necessity) and partly at random (chance). So chance and necessity rule all things, not the divine Logos as the Stoics said, not the Unmoved Mover of Aristotle, not the One of the Platonists, and not the God of the Jews. There is no ultimate meaning or purpose in the universe.

And yet in all these civilizations, religious thought prevailed over skepticism. In China popular Taoism retained a rather archaic religiousness. Buddhism spread into China, eventually dominating religious thought among intellectuals there. In India Hindu (and Jain) traditions won out. And in the Mediterranean world religious philosophies spread among the educated, until they were overwhelmed by the growth of Christian theism.

Early Attacks on Traditional Religion

Modern skeptics have more than intellectual doubt about the truth of religious belief. They are often also convinced that religion is a harmful element in human life. Religion, the skeptics often say, is not merely mistaken but dangerous.

The history of religion and science in the West is a story of frequent tensions. Traditional religious authority sought to maintain the power of the theological system, while the new science promoted ideas that threatened both the system and the authority behind it. Although many histories exaggerate the conflict between religion and science, there has been conflict. Century after century, there were religious leaders who opposed parts of the new science and even oppressed those who favored it. The story of Galileo's forced recantation is a well-known instance. The Copernican astronomy that Galileo favored cast doubt on the literal truth of the Bible and undermined traditional religious authority. So religious people fought Galileo. In many lesser instances individual religious voices spoke out against scientific innovations. The lightning rod is an affront to God, some said, for God sends each bolt of lightning to warn people or to punish them. How dare human technology intervene! Likewise, disease is a punishment from God. Some even claimed that the new medical technique known as vaccination against smallpox was ungodly.

Allied with the new science was a new political philosophy that promoted equality and the free exchange of ideas. Religious leaders repeatedly opposed these innovations as threats to traditional authority and therefore to social order. Freemasons and other freethinkers (called "libertines") had to flee countries such as Germany or France to find refuge, often in the

Netherlands, from a political oppression that church authorities supported.

Those who experienced oppression also became more sensitive to the amount of intolerance that religious life could foster. In Christ's name, Christians had persecuted Jews, Muslims, and one another for centuries. From 1618 to 1648 the Thirty Years' War had devastated the German-speaking states, as Catholic fought Protestant for political power. The Inquisitions burned heretics at the stake, often after first torturing them.

Concomitant with the rise of the new science in the midst of the Enlightenment, as though to stamp religiousness for good with the seal of superstition, were the great witch hunts of the late sixteenth and seventeenth centuries (The Salem witch hunts in Massachusetts in 1692 produced one of the last major hanging of witches.) The times were troubled by changes in politics, science, religion, economics. For the new scientists this was a time of glorious learning; for the new political philosophers, a time of promise. But for many religious people it was merely a time of insecurity and doubt, so they looked for a cause of all the troubles, or at least for something on which they could focus their fears. They found it in the witches. Thousands of women, along with some men and even children, died accused of being agents of the devil.

In the nineteenth century conservative Christians attacked theories of evolution, especially Darwinism. These Christians respected the word of the Bible more than the rational arguments of evolutionists. Some Christian critics of Darwin were themselves respectful of rationality, but not all. The evidence was clear that the earth must be at least several millions of years old. The Christians who trusted the Bible more than the geological evidence helped to give faith a bad name in the eyes of the skeptics.

Throughout all this, a major point of contention was the significance of earthly existence. Even if Marx and Spencer and other nineteenth-century secular humanists had been too optimistic about earthly progress, at least they cared about the quality of earthly life and tried to promote a more humane existence for people. Many religious leaders, threatened by so much that was new, classified it all as too worldly or materialistic. They recommended instead keeping our gaze fixed on heaven, where rust and moth do not consume. One effect of this other-worldliness, as Marx pointed out, was to distract people from useful efforts to make this world a better place for future generations.

By the twentieth century, then, there was already a long list of complaints against religion. According to the harshest skeptics religion is an opponent of potentially beneficial progress in human ideas and techniques. It is authoritarian and repressive, even vengeful against its enemies. It is intolerant and even bigoted against those who disagree with it. It promotes irrationality by supporting beliefs that go against reason, thereby making it seem legitimate to be irrational. It is other-worldly, calling people away from the kind of efforts that might feed the hungry, clothe the naked, and free the oppressed. In brief, although religion promises people heaven, it makes their lives more hellish.

Not all skeptics were this harsh in their critique of religion. In the early nineteenth century, the social reformer Auguste Comte (1798-1857) portrayed the religious mentality merely as intellectual immaturity. The human race was religious in its cultural childhood, Comte said. It reached intellectual adolescence in classical philosophy. But now, finally humankind has arrived at mental maturity by turning to empirical science for concrete or "positive" evidence. Comte called these three stages the theological (religious), the metaphysical (philosophical), and the positive (scientific). His position was known as "positivism."

Others, like Freud, classified religion as a mildly debilitating illusion, as we have seen. Still others, such as the sociologists who simply noted its social function of supporting cultural forms, spoke of it more neutrally. In general, though, the various skeptics, atheists, or agnostics had decided that religion was not only wrong but on balance harmful.

In the twentieth century some forms of skepticism about religion amount to no more than casual doubt; but there are at least two kinds of movements that are fully skeptical. Both are secular humanisms: American pragmatism and French atheistic existentialism. To understand them, it helps to begin with two other sets of ideas. One concerns a new way of understanding reality; the other is about a new way of understanding what it is to be a human person.

A New Way of Understanding Reality

From the time of Galileo a number of philosophers had stressed that the way to know the truth was by checking out theories empirically, which means to test them against sensory evidence. As far back as the thirteenth century, Robert Grosseteste (1175-1253) and his student Roger Bacon (1214-1294?), a Franciscan philosopher-scientist, had urged philosophers to use this method. Do not simply believe what has been handed on to you. Do not believe even whatever seems to make more logical sense. Test ideas out. Test truth-claims by finding physical evidence of some sort. If necessary devise special instruments to detect what is going on. If there is no evidence that the eye can see or the ear hear or the hand touch, then you cannot claim to know what the truth of the matter is.

As we have seen, this method of empirical testing produced wonderfully reliable results, especially when coupled with Galileo's approach to measuring matter in motion. What is measurable can stand as evidence for or against a theory; what is not measurable, such as God's purposes, can only be a matter of speculation. Using this as the basic method of approach to knowledge, the centuries following were lighted by the results of geniuses and of ordinary but persistent researchers.

The Scientific Method

Science is a method of learning about reality. Part of the method is active doubt. No matter how many learned people have accepted an idea as true, doubt it. It might be wrong. Test it. Then when you have doubted and devised tests and have come up with a new answer fully verified, let others doubt. Let people know what your theory is, how you tested it, and what results you achieved, so that the others can doubt you and doubt your theory, your tests, your results. If your theory survives new doubts and new tests, it is more probably true in some way. By this open-ended and public testing of data, science advances. We are accustomed to thinking of science's conclusions as certain and reliable. Those that have survived many decades of testing by constant application seem to be very reliable. But every claim of science remains open to further questioning and further testing.

As the previous chapter noted, this was not fully apparent in the early days of modern science. Scientists who became angry at the dogmatic stubbornness of religious authority developed their own dogmatic attitudes. Sometimes they were modest in their claims. Copernicus' theory was first published with an introduction that said it was only an interesting, different way of describing how the sun, planets, and stars *might* move. But the early success of the new scientific method led many people to forget about doubts and become convinced that science was going to provide people with the complete, final, fully accurate truth about everything.

Another dogmatic aspect of some early science was the conviction that all human problems could be solved by the application of scientific reasoning. The confidence that science could provide the final, fully accurate truth fit nicely with the evolutionary hopes for a steady progress into a glorious future. Dogmatism, naturalism, and optimism were a potent combination in some early science.

By the late nineteenth century scientific dogmatism was sometimes allied with a radical reductionism. We can understand this reductionism by comparing it to its opposite in Julian Huxley's theory of cosmic evolution. Huxley celebrated the development of matter-energy into atoms and then compounds and then life-forms and cells and multi-celled organisms and eventually conscious processes in us and our cultures. Reductionism stands this on its head by emphasizing that culture and consciousness are, after all, only the product of brain activity, that brains are only organized cells, that cells are only chemical processes, and that chemicals are just atoms. The reductionist attitude warns us not to get too impressed with consciousness and life because they are just variant forms of matter-energy.

This thorough-going reductionism done in the name of science had the effect of excluding religion and philosophical speculation from the scientific effort to understand reality. In the nineteenth century some philosophers had argued that science would have to admit to the existence of souls or some cosmic Spirit in order to explain life and consciousness. Many scientists treated these spirit-centered ideas as threats to their methodological naturalism, and therefore as impediments to the progress of science. So they responded by reducing life and consciousness to nonliving and nonconscious atomic and chemical activity. This left no room for souls or a cosmic Spirit, with the unfortunate result that the human spirit manifested in noble thoughts, great moral concerns, and grand works of art, is reduced to nothing more than chemical processes. The radical reductionists may be said to have thrown out the baby with the bathwater.

It is possible, though, to adhere to naturalism without also being reductionistic. Julian Huxley's thought was fully naturalistic. But Huxley admired the higher and higher levels of complexity that have arisen through cosmic and biological evolution. He respected each new level as a special achievement of nature. He was especially impressed with the qualities of human thought. He was not a reductionist of the sort who says thought is just biology in general. He said that the power of thought is instead an extremely special form of biology. He was not a reductionist of the sort who says that biological life is just chemistry. He thought life was a very special form of chemistry.

Even religiously minded scientists are methodological naturalists. They say that science can attain to real understanding only of what is natural. That is because only natural causes and effects are part of a reliable and regular pattern that can be discovered through scientific study and testing. If there are indeed supernatural causes (God or other non-natural beings) at work, they are causes that cannot be studied and tested. There is no way to predict what God will do. So there is no use in trying to have a science about divine activity. Certainly theologians would agree that it is not the job of science to study God.

The End of Dogmatism in Science

The twentieh century administered shock treatments to shake science into a different frame of mind. Even as World War I spead doubt about human reasonableness and the beneficence of science, new ideas jolted scientists out of dogmatic attitudes. Newton had drawn a basic picture of the universe as stable and predictable. Evolutionary theory removed a little of the stability, but many physicists at the turn of the century thought the universe's laws were now settled, once and for all.

Then came the new physics, like that of Albert Einstein (1879-1955). Suddenly the whole universe had been taken apart and put back together in a new kind of unity. Newton had been accurate enough about certain events in the universe, but in order to include such extreme phenomena as light or energy particles at one end, and the interrelation of time, space, and energy at the other, a new set of theories was needed. Einstein said strange things. If you travel in space, for example, at extremely high speeds relative to your friends back home, when you return they will have aged more than you. The physicist Werner Heisenberg (1901-1976) declared that though the universe had once seemed fully predictable and therefore fully intelligible, it turned out that aspects of the subatomic level are unpredictable, except statistically.

In subsequent years there were enough new, odd ways of looking at the universe to get scientists accustomed to treating their own theories more critically. As far back as 1790 the philosopher Immanuel Kant (1724-1804) had carefully pointed out that the ways in which we see the world, even in our most reasonable and well-tested interpretations, are still interpretations to some extent. This tentative approach to knowledge was actually recommended by ancient Greek philosophers called "skeptics" some two thousand years ago. But it is only in modern times that have accepted this approach and found a very positive use for it in science.

It was especially in the twentieth century that science found out for itself that Kant and the ancient skeptics were on to something. The theoretical scientists of today are accustomed to the idea that when they describe electrons and gravity and the furthermost edges of the universe and black holes in space, they are not stating the whole truth. Instead they are providing good working models of how things might well be, based on the available evidence. Science provides models, tentative maps, of reality.

Imagine a map of the Amazonian jungles of Brazil that is based on reports from a few explorers, sightings from a dozen hot air balloons, and some examination of debris taken from the river at its mouth. Many highly reliable claims could be made about the jungle on the basis of this evidence, but the overall map might have to undergo serious changes as new evidence came in. Scientific theories are like such a changeable map.

Scientific theories are sometimes like practical instructions telling a person how to get certain results. Treat light as though it were collections of tiny particles, say the instructions, each particle having a certain minimum size. If that is true, then you should be able to get certain results. And you do. The problem is that if you treat light not as particles but as waves of energy, you could get a different sort of result. And you do. What is light, then: particles or waves? Scientists are accustomed to saying that the particle-model is a useful one to predict some results, and that the wave-model is useful for predicting others; but it is not possible to say which is more "true."

The method of science seems rather arcane at times, but it is just a refinement of the everyday method of verifying the reliability of a truth-claim. This checking can be done by comparing the claim with the relevant evidence available, especially evidence that would really put the truth-claim to the test (that could "falsify" it, as the philosophers of science say). The checking can also be done by comparing the truth-claim with all other relevant truth-claims that fit well with the evidence relevant to them. The method of science takes this ordinary method further in two ways. One is to devise extremely precise and ingenious ways of determining how well the truth-claims fit with the evidence. The means of measuring and testing have grown exceedingly careful and complex. The second is to make the process of testing the truth-claim a matter of public record so that anyone, even those with opposing viewpoints, can try things out for themselves and look for any flaws in the fit among evidence, logic, and conclusions.

This method might sound like a recipe for chaos. Everyone can challenge everyone else, and the potential challenges are endless. It sounds like a rather unpromising method for obtaining reliable results. That may explain why it took two thousand years from the early search for rational knowledge in the axial age, before a particular culture—Europe of the sixteenth and seventeenth centuries, as it happened—stumbled upon a recognition of the extraordinary effectiveness of this seemingly unpromising method for the particular task of evaluating hypotheses and models to see whether they function so reliably that they can be regarded as true.

The twentieth-century experience of scientific work has reinforced the idea that a person should only accept truth-claims that are well tested, but with a heightened awareness that even a well-tested theory is still a working model that must always be left open to challenge. This is not an expectation that science will always be changing its conclusions, but rather the conviction that scientists must always be prepared to accept changes in their conclusions if someone devises a better interpretation of the evidence.

The public nature of the scientific method imposes a critical honesty on the part of scientists. Every once in a while deliberate dishonesty shows up in a scientific work nonetheless. A cancer researcher fakes certain results in the skin condition of laboratory mice because he is certain he is on the right track and needs impressive results to get the grant money to continue. A noted psychologist falsifies data about identical twins raised in different environments in order to support his firm belief that intelligence is inherited. In addition to deliberate dishonesty, unconscious bias also leads scientists to overlook or misread data that would lead to an uncomfortable conclusion.

Yet the public and open-ended nature of modern scientific inquiry counterbalances fairly well the dangers of dishonesty and unconscious bias. Every truth-claim must be published publicly with the evidence. Any person, friend or foe of a theory, has a right to challenge it and test it again. All theories must stand up to ongoing testing, review, and critical analysis, regardless of who likes the theory or who does not, regardless of the impact of changes in theory on social, economic, political, and even religious beliefs. The scientific method works well because it forces scientists to be more honest than people are usually inclined to be. Scientific questioning has broken traditional beliefs that supported harmful superstitions such as belief in witches. The methodical honesty of science has broken many prejudiced claims about religions, races, cultures, and the sexes. The honesty of science, however unsettling in its unending willingness to doubt, seems to be morally constructive.

The result has been a new way of understanding what the world is like. Traditional societies, primitive and archaic, rely on the authority of the past, whether recorded in folktales and customs or in sacred texts. Traditional authority remains a powerful force everywhere today. Early philosophy and theology, however, produced a competitor to tradition in the form of rational analysis. Philosophers especially relied on systems of thought that appeared to make overall coherent sense of many aspects of life and reality, even when these systems were in conflict with tradition. Early modern science added increased attention to precise measurements of empirical evidence. But it eventually became clear that it was the public and open-ended testing of ideas against the evidence that made science successful. So this scientific method now challenges not only tradition but also philosophical or rational analysis done without adequate checking. It is not enough for an idea to be old and revered, nor to be rationally systematized into a coherent theory. It must also fit with the evidence through public and open-ended testing.

Is Science Based on Faith?

Some have argued, however, that even science is based on faith. As noted at the beginning of Chapter Eleven, there is some truth to this claim, though it can be misleading. There are several ways in which a kind of faith appears in science.

First, the everyday scientist certainly has some faith that the scientists who have gone before have actually done the experiments they claim to have done and have collected the evidence they claim to have collected. But the scientist also knows that this faith can be put to the test by further scientific work. Even if no one sets up a formal test of a theory, every time someone applies the theory in practice, results that conflict with what the theory predicts provide evidence there may be something wrong with the theory.

Second, and more basically, scientists in general have a faith that the world they study really exists. This is contrary to what some Hindus seem to say, following Shankara. Similarly the Chinese wise man, Chuang Tzu, dreamed that he was a butterfly; and when he awoke he asked how he could be sure that he was not a butterfly dreaming he was a man. We cannot prove that we are human and not butterflies. But the everyday evidence makes it very reasonable to believe that we are, and rather unreasonable to believe that we are really butterflies instead. Similarly, the belief science has in the reality of the world seems also to be reasonable. It is a belief that works consistently in practice as though it were the simple truth. When science tests its theories against what seems to be the real world, this testing process works as though the world is indeed real.

Third, scientists also operate by a faith that they can understand the intelligibility of reality. This is a faith in themselves and their methods and their powers of observation and analysis and criticism. But this faith also seems quite reasonable in that it has proved to be an exceedingly effective faith. Science seems to have achieved a great deal of highly reliable knowledge about how reality operates.

Fourth, science also has a kind of faith in certain criteria of reasonableness. "Reasonable" is a word with many meanings, of course. We use the word most loosely (and perhaps inappropriately) when it stands for whatever we want to think is correct, without applying any further tests to determine whether we are right. We use the word a little more precisely when we claim that we find an idea reasonable because it fits with our ongoing experiences. Experience, after all, is a kind of evidence. Yet we also know that we have made what we later acknowledge to be incorrect judgments on the basis of our own prior experience. A scientific conclusion is said to be reasonable only if it has the double "fit" described earlier. First, it must fit with the available relevant evidence; second, it must fit with other conclusions that fit well with their relevant evidence. This double fit must also have been exposed to public challenge over time to make it more fully reasonable to accept the conclusion.

So there is some truth in the claim that science rests on a kind of faith also, in fact on various acts of faith. But science demands that its own various types of faith be tested, publicly, rationally, and empirically. A scientist can claim that it is more accurate to describe these acts of faith as confidence rather than faith. It is a confidence based on the evidence of the effectiveness of science in the important work of devising and testing truth-claims about the world to see which best explain the data.

Nevertheless, scientific theories are still interpretations of reality that are produced by human beings. Scientific theories are models of reality, even symbols of reality, not reality itself. It is also important to note that it is a human person who has the ongoing job of interpreting reality and testing the interpretation, and who must be honest and open to change in understanding things. This has provided a basis for a new understanding of what a person, a self, is.

A New Way of Understanding the Self

From the late eighteenth-century writings of Kant to the experience of modern science, we have become increasingly aware that we are responsible for our interpretation of reality. How we think of the world and ourselves, how we think of what it all ultimately means, and how we actually live and believe because of this, are all very much in our own human hands.

One way of illustrating this is to imagine that you suddenly had an overwhelming spiritual vision and saw an image of God or heard God's voice, so to speak, telling you the truth about life and how to live. What would your response be? One possible response would be to accept gratefully this revelation and follow it. But there is an alternative response.

The human person has some capacity to step back from such a religious experience and, as with all experiences, treat the instructions from God and the experience of God both as something to be questioned, as a scientist might question certain test results and their meaning. A person might not want to do this or be in the habit of doing it, but a person is capable of doing it. Was that really God? How do I know? How honest am I being in examining this?

Even if I conclude it was the voice of God, should I just agree? Or should I make my own analysis of how wise or good or useful these ideas are? These questions represent the human ability to take personal responsibility for the ideas and values we live by.

A word often used to represent this human potential is "autonomy," the power of conscious self-ruling. There are many ways we are not consciously self-ruled. Our biological characteristics determine some of our behavior. Our social conditioning has a very strong influence on us. In moral behavior we normally tend to be heteronomous, i.e., ruled-by-another, rather than autonomous. The taboo moralist obeys others who can reward or punish. The allegiance moralist follows group standards. A universal laws moralist looks for the ultimate objective set of standards to follow. These are all instances of heteronomous morality.

It is not enough, however, that a person obey his or her own inner rules rather than external rules or standards in order to be called fully autonomous. The inner standards must also be those the person has consciously chosen on the basis of his or her own consciously evaluated morality. A person who just follows inner habits or conditioning is not autonomous but is under the control of habits or psychological and sociological conditioning. True autonomy is inner freedom.

We often call ourselves free when in fact we are acting out of habit or unreflectively responding to an impulse or desire. We may well be free from external restrictions, free to act on our desires or habits. But this is not the same as inner freedom. Philosophers argue strenuously about whether there can be true inner freedom. We can dispense with long arguments by saying that we are inwardly free to the degree that we are able to make consciously reflective choices. We have some real ability to be aware of various influences acting on us. We can develop in ourselves the useful habit of reflecting on our possible choices in order to foresee their probable consequences, and let this awareness of consequences influence us also. We can consciously compare these potential consequences to values we have carefully chosen. The more we make our choices in this consciously reflective manner, the more we are behaving autonomously.

This means that a fully autonomous person accepts full responsibility for his or her own moral standards and decisions. This is a person who believes it is not enough to obey orders or be loyal to the group or live up to supposedly objective external standards for their own sake. The autonomous person may well obey social rules, be very loyal, and honor high standards, but only because these fit with his or her best moral vision. This person might sit in judgment even on God's instructions, therefore, and ask whether those instructions lived up to the person's own best moral standard.

There is a dangerous kind of free-wheeling behavior that sometimes goes by the name of " autonomy" also, that of the taboo moralist who has found how to avoid punishment and simply chooses to grab all the pleasures available no matter who gets hurt. Most people who recommend autonomy actually have in mind not this taboo autonomy, but an autonomy built on a basic value morality. This kind of autonomy would lead a person to listen to God's voice and then ask whether agreeing with God would promote human well-being. This type of autonomous person would be responsible for accepting or rejecting God's instructions, a religious tradition, various civil laws, a group's standards, or any other guides to life, on the basis of compassion and concern for others.

Existentialist philosophers (whom we will discuss soon) call this sort of responsible autonomy "authentic existence," a shorthand expression for "authentically mature human existence." Children cannot take autonomous responsibility for their own lives. They are dominated by emotional drives, societal conditioning, and short-term practical judgments on how to get along. Only adults have a chance at coming into the kind of reflective self-possession that enables them to choose the very foundation of their moral orientation through careful conscious reflection. As we mature, the distinctively human capacity for conscious reflection on our lives becomes stronger.

We develop an increasing ability to take personal responsibility for our ideas, biases, values, and behavior. The more we do this, the more we are doing the thing that sets us apart from other animals. Those who favor such autonomy can therefore claim that it is an exercise of real humanness, that autonomous freedom constitutes authentic human existence.

This idea of authentic existence presents a challenge because we humans often try to escape from our own peculiarly human capacity to be responsible for our own values and decisions. The psychologist Erich Fromm (1900-1980) summed it up nicely in the title of his book, *Escape from Freedom*. We all tend to say we want to have freedom, yet real inner freedom can make us nervous. Do we really want to carry individual personal responsibility for every one of our decisions? It would often be more comfortable to be able to let someone else make the decisions and be responsible for the consequences. There is security in obedience and conformity. Even if that should include bigotry, intolerance, persecutions, and war, at least someone else is to blame. (There is evidently danger in a lack of autonomy as well as in autonomy.)

The emphasis on authentic existence, on personally responsible autonomy, can be dangerous, then, when misinterpreted by a taboo moralist, whose only concern is to do what feels good. This emphasis is also meaningless to the allegiance moralist, who needs to have group rules to follow. A strong emphasis on autonomy will make only limited sense to a universal laws moralist, who is convinced there are objectively and universally valid rules that no one has the right to disobey.

Those who most stress responsible autonomy, though, are usually convinced that all our interpretations of reality, including even our ideas about morality, are interpretations, models, symbols. Alternative interpretations and models and symbols are available. Because we have the capacity to reflect on these interpretations and evaluate them in an ongoing way, we have the capacity to be responsible for them. To refuse to reflect and choose is to be responsible for avoiding personal responsibility. Dangerous and difficult as it is, therefore, authentic human responsibility is an ideal that has gained a great deal of support among humanists.

That, in turn, means that there is a new emphasis in the way modern culture understands what it is to be a self. The "authentic human existence" of the modern person would not sound authentically human to other cultures: primitive cultures seek to do what the ancestors established; archaic cultures obey the gods of their people; historic cultures know that ideal human life is one of submission to the single, universally correct way of things. Modern culture is not sure of the final truth or the single truth or the universal truth, so it defines the ideal person as one who accepts individual responsibility for the interpretation of reality that person lives by, including responsibility for how that affects others.

Modern culture has thereby become even more explicitly conscious that human life is lived in the presence of mystery, that all our beliefs, values, traditions, and lifestyles are encompassed by a larger field of mystery, by an infinitely receding horizon of mystery. There are religious interpretations of life based on this awareness. Chapter Fourteen will describe some of them; but there are also nonreligious interpretations. Here are two of them.

Two Skeptical Philosophies

Contemporary skepticism, which grew out of earlier attacks on religion, includes the new scientific understanding of how to know reality, and the understanding of the human person as autonomous. It also accepts the basic view of the universe suggested by the astronomers' big bang theory and the evolutionary theory of life as random variations. We can see all this in two philosophies about life, American pragmatism and French atheistic existentialism.

American Pragmatism

American pragmatism is the approach found in the writings of John Dewey (1859-1952) among others. (A more recent form of pragmatism, as exposed in the thought of Richard Rorty [1931-] is really postmodern, a topic for Chapter Fifteen.) It is a school of thought that is generally agnostic, cautious about making unsubstantiated claims. The universe is a vast and somewhat confusing place, the pragmatists say. We have learned a lot about it. We have a lot to learn. We will never know all there is to know. The most honest and reasonable thing to do is to learn what we can when we can, and to make the best use of it we can.

Pragmatists have usually been suspicious of religious belief. The history of humankind is a history of unsubstantiated beliefs, they say, many of them religious. Adherence to these beliefs has usually prevented the growth of genuine well-tested knowledge and has bred intolerance and hatred. It is good to be wary of such beliefs. Even the belief systems of a Marx or Julian Huxley claim more than can be verified rationally. There is no adequate evidence for the existence of any ultimate Power, neither God nor history or evolution turned into minor God-equivalents. The pragmatists conclude that there is little profit in trying to argue out all the ultimate questions about the origin, pattern, or purpose to everything. There is no need to take such questions too seriously. It is reasonable to act as though there is no God, to live as practical atheists without being dogmatic in our denial of God's existence.

There is nonetheless a faith we can all live by, says Dewey, a common dedication to meeting our human needs for material sustenance and ethical ideals, a dedication to honesty and cooperation in order to achieve what we can for our fellow human beings. We live in a changing universe, open to progress; we are free beings, open to development. Let us learn to cherish the openness of things and selves in order to improve life.

This faith is a form of secular evolutionary humanism, but its emphasis is much more practical-minded than the quasi-religions of Marx and Huxley. Dewey was willing to live with a great deal of uncertainty about the basic thrust of history or the ultimate answers to life's direction. Make do as you go along, Dewey said; much can be achieved this way if we just try to be honest, reasonable, and deeply concerned with the well-being of human life on this planet.

This has been the major contemporary atheism or agnosticism in America. Groups such as the American Humanist Association or the Ethical Culture Society reflect many of the same views. There is another and more radical contemporary atheism, however, that takes ultimate questions with great seriousness. That is the perspective associated with the French existentialist, Jean-Paul Sartre (1905-1984).

Atheistic Existentialism

The pragmatist turns away from the ultimate mystery in order to pay attention to practical possibilities for improving the human condition. The atheistic existentialist, on the contrary, keeps an eye fixed resolutely on the unendingness of mystery as an awesome but important reality. The fact of infinite mystery reveals to the existentialist the strange situation of the human person.

Central to existentialism is the concern to define who we humans are, both immediately and ultimately. Even on the everyday level, says Jean-Paul Sartre, we humans are terribly odd. We are the beings with self-consciousness, able to take our lives into our own hands to some extent through our conscious decisions. This is the power of free self-determination. It is inner human autonomy. That means that in contrast to all other living beings, we "ex-ist," meaning that we stand out. We stand apart from the unfree and unthinking patterns of inanimate nature. We stand out from all the animals, who have a kind of conscious awareness but not the self-consciousness that would allow them to make decisions about themselves and their lives.

Our identity is in our own hands, Sartre says. We can look ourselves over and see how we act and think. We can measure our acts and thoughts by various rules, standards, values, or goals. We are responsible for how well we measure up to our standards, and even for choosing the standards. All this is a terrible burden because we are the beings with the capacity for the infinite. Our capacity to question and reflect and then question again makes it impossible for us to arrive at the final and complete truth. That is true also in moral matters. And yet we must do our best to choose standards of morality and truth, to live and treat each other with honesty and love. The great blessing of our freedom is therefore also a difficult burden.

There are no preset limits on how far our minds can range in our quest for the answers to life. When we begin to seek the purpose of our existence, that which makes it truly worthwhile and will tell us how to live, we are on an exploration without apparent end, because we can raise the ultimate questions. Perhaps ultimately all is mindless randomness, as some scientific theories suggest.

The historic religious traditions have answers for those who worry about such things. Our ultimate purpose is to belong to the infinite, the Tao, or Brahman, or God. By learning the tao of nature or the path of contemplation or the mystical way we conform to the eternal fullness, these traditions say. But Sartre sees a great threat to our humanness in these traditions. Our human selfhood lies in our self-possession as consciously free ex-istents. To hand ourselves over to some ultimate path, or Being, or Power, he claims, is to give up responsibility for ourselves; it is to lay down the burden of having to choose for ourselves the identity, belonging, thoughts, and actions that together make up our life stories.

Perhaps Sartre might have been able to accept the idea of handing over one's life to the infinite Mystery only by a basic trust that it is fullness and not emptiness. This trust might be sufficiently general that it could give confidence that life is ultimately worthwhile, without taking away individual responsibility for each decision made in a lifetime. But Sartre feared that the religious impulse is always to sacrifice responsible autonomy on the altar of security. Faced with endless options about who to be, how to live, where to find a sense of certainty, we are all too eager to submit to the specific beliefs, roles, rules, rituals of a religious tradition. So Sartre believed.

What Sartre proposed as a philosophy of life for the being that ex-ists is a life of courageous affirmation of selfhood in a universe where selfhood is ultimately meaningless. To Sartre, it was clear that the processes of this enormous universe are indeed mindless and purposeless. He was surprised that anyone could find a purposeful direction buried within the evolutionary process, which has been a long and messy one, built on the bones of countless species that failed and died. History has scattered countless bodies killed by starvation, flood, disease. For the last fifty thousand years of human existence, war and torture and suffering have been the rule, so much so that it all seems natural. If there is some God behind this process, Sartre concludes, it must be a grossly evil or incompetent one to set in motion all that misery and chaos.

To Sartre, sheer reasonableness requires that we must all accept the possibility that in the end nothing really means anything. Life may seem meaningful in the short run, but ultimately it is absurd. Since we need not merely meaning but ultimate meaning to satisfy the endless reach of our consciousness, the ultimate meaninglessness of the universe stands over against us as a crushing emptiness. In a sense, it becomes irrational ultimately to live for anything.

Sartre, like other atheists (most less extreme in their atheism) did find something to live for: his own existence as an authentic self, a self-conscious self, willing to be responsible for his own life. To Sartre this emphatically includes responsibility to value authentic existence wherever it is or might be. So Sartre tried to live by a deep moral concern for the selfhood and freedom of every person. He proposed a basic value morality of unrestricted concern for authentic human existence. For this reason, he called his own existentialism a humanism.

This is atheistic existentialism's challenge to religion. It is a very fundamental challenge. Any religion that focuses its attention on asserting that miracles do happen, that there is a divine guide and helper, or that there is life after death, may be a very satisfying religion, but it does not yet meet the full challenge of atheistic existentialism.

The Deepest Challenge to Basic Faith

Imagine that you live in a universe where there is a high god, filled with loving concern for all people (a sort of all-good super-Zeus). This would be a god who can work miracles, reveal the right path of life, bring people to a paradise after death. As comforting as this sounds, the atheistic existentialist has the same sort of questions about it as a Hindu or Buddhist might about a paradise: What is the ultimate meaning? Perhaps the high god and all people are trapped together in an ultimately meaningless reality. Whether a person's life ends in death after seventy years or endures everlastingly in some sort of paradise with a high god, what is the value of it? The question of ultimacy is present again.

And further modern concerns arise. First of all, there are the scientific theories which suggest that the best evidence points to a model of the universe as an aimless series of events without meaning. Secondly, there is still the modern awareness of our need for ultimate meaning because of our ex-istence as the self-conscious and therefore free being. To respond to this adequately, religion must somehow be able to see the possibility of truly ultimate intelligibility and value to human existence. The basic faith that humankind has lived by from the earliest times, at least implicitly, has finally been challenged in modern times: Does it all ultimately make sense? Is it all ultimately worthwhile?

These are questions we can individually choose to ignore. If there is a God who works miracles and offers life after death, perhaps we can worry about the ultimate meaning of everything after some few billion years in heaven or paradise. But modern religion, whatever else it does or does not say about such things as miracles, divine guidance, and life after death, has been challenged to look at the universe and human existence and show how a reasonable and honest person, willing to take responsibility for his or her own life, can find good reason to affirm that the mysteries we all face are signs not of ultimate meaningless but of a divinely numinous Ultimate, which somehow is the meaning of everything.

Language becomes abstract and difficult when we talk about these things because it is talk about the Ultimate. It is talk about what the civilizations of the world have found to be the infinite and incomprehensible God or Tao or Brahman. For the atheistic existentialist it is not merely difficult to talk about any such Ultimate; it is difficult to show that a reasonable person could believe in it. That is a challenge modern religion faces. The next chapter will describe the responses of modern religion.

Summary

In recent centuries religion has been severely criticized. At the same time agnostic or atheistic alternatives to religion have gained currency. The developments of science have convinced many that modern scientific honesty, self-criticism, and openness to change constitute the only legitimate kind of knowledge. This has brought about an emphasis on the responsibility of the individual person not to follow traditional authority unthinkingly, but to be freely self-determining. Scientific honesty and responsible autonomy are two ideas that inspire modern unreligious humanisms, such as American pragmatism and atheistic existentialism.

The ultimate mysteries of life still exist, however, and the attitudes of agnosticism or atheism towards them can be much less than satisfying. Modern religion has tried to provide a religious humanism as an alternative. That is the topic of the next chapter.

For Further Reflection

1. Do the criticisms of religion made early in this chapter seem accurate and fair to you? Why? Why not?
2. Give any reasons you can think of why a religious person could be fully dedicated to human progress in this world.

3. Find examples in your own life of beliefs you hold that seem very reliable to you but which, like scientific knowledge, are open to change if the evidence demands it. Which of them, if any, are religious beliefs?
4. Do you share the belief that ideal adult authentic existence is a willingness to take full personal responsibility for one's own values and choices? Explain.
5. If Sartre is wrong about the absurdity of life, explain what you think is the ultimate purpose of human existence.

Suggested Readings

Franklin L. Baumer, *Religion and the Rise of Skepticism*, 1960. A vivid history of anti-religious thought.

Bertrand Russell, *Why I Am Not a Christian, and Other Essays on Religion and Related Subjects*. 1957

Thomas Henry Huxley, *Science and Christian Tradition*, 1896. Includes Huxley's comments on agnosticism and his response to critics of the idea.

Anthony Flew, *Atheistic Humanism*, 1993. A set of lectures defending atheism.

Douglas E. Krueger, *What Is Atheism?: A Short Introduction*, 1998. A typical modern defense of atheism.

Jean-Paul Sartre, "Existentialism Is a Humanism," in Walter Kaufman, *Existentialism from Dostoevsky to Sartre*, 1956, 287-311.

Catriona Mackenzie and Natalie Stoljar, eds., *Relational Autonomy: Feminist Perspectives on Autonomy, Agency, and the Social Self*, 2000.

CHAPTER FOURTEEN

In the Presence of Mystery

Modern Religion

We have seen that long ago the development of agriculture produced a cultural revolution in many societies, bringing about a new complexity of social organization and thought patterns. Primitive religion gave way to archaic religion, which absorbed the primitive beliefs into its own more complicated and hierarchical worldviews. Then came the axial age and all the primitive and archaic beliefs had to meet a new test imposed by a strikingly ambitious mode of human consciousness. These beliefs now had to fit within the all-encompassing integrated interpretations of reality proposed by historic thought, as humankind sought a perfect and eternal unity, a mysterious wholeness behind all the complexities of existence. After more than twenty centuries of historic thought, another mode of interpreting reality has emerged in Western culture. This style of thought includes but redefines the various symbols from past historic, archaic, and primitive stages of thought. That is modern culture and its religiousness.

As the Preface to Part IV warned, the word "modern" is ambiguous. Early modern thought is to a large extent a variation on classical historic thought. This systematically logical and universalizing approach was almost lost in the early middle ages in Europe (c. 500-1000 CE). But with the aid of Muslim sources it revived in the twelfth and later centuries, got an extra impetus with the translation of new Greek texts in the fourteenth and fifteenth centuries, and eventually took off in a new direction in the seventeenth and eighteenth centuries. Recently, "postmodernism" has challenged the universalizing rationality of modernity. We will see more about that in Chapter Fifteen.

THE MODERN CHALLENGES TO RELIGION

Religiousness in modern times does not constitute all of modern religion. There are still classical and archaic and even primitive forms of religion in modern cultures. And modern religiousness itself, like all historical developments, is far more complex than any simple description can suggest. For simplicity's sake, however, we can identify what is modern in religiousness by looking at how religion has responded to four serious challenges posed by modern thought: 1) the new scientific worldviews, 2) an appreciation of the secular or worldly, 3) an emphasis on autonomous selfhood, and 4) the idea that all knowledge is imperfect or incomplete.

The Challenge of Modern Scientific Worldviews

The universe is a vast and strange reality. It is billions of years old with a hundred billion galaxies of hundreds of billions of stars each, exploding outward to either an eventual cosmic death or a collapse into another great explosion. The wondrous process of life on this single little planet may have been a random process, mindless and meaningless. The overall story of human life has included many instances of great evil, pain, and despair. In all this, there can seem to be little hard evidence of a divine Being guiding the universe in a coherent way toward some ultimately meaningful end. The atheistic existentialists claim that the evidence even points in the opposite direction, to an ultimate meaninglessness to all things. There also seems to be very little reliable evidence, such as we would ordinarily demand for scientific conclusions, that there is a God who intervenes in nature or in human lives to work miracles, to provide a kind of supernatural help or guidance beyond what the ordinary processes of nature already accomplish. In fact, the scientific approach to reality works well precisely because it does not accept this kind of explanation for any event.

The challenge of the modern scientific worldview to religion is this: Can a reasonable person maintain belief in a divine or numinous dimension to our existence in the face of scientific theories, evidence, and method? Modern religion says yes, but it has had to do more than just say yes; it has to work out a justification for this bold affirmation.

The Challenge of Modern Secularity

The atheistic and agnostic secular humanists have abandoned reliance on divine help. They have also turned their hopes away from heaven or any other life beyond this limited earthly one. These sixty to ninety years are ours and nothing more, say the secular humanists. It is up to us to choose how to use them well. We are on our own.

Because of that, the secular humanist claims, we ought to devote all our energies towards the needs and potentials of our fellow human beings. We ought to work to eliminate oppression, poverty, hatred, and war. We ought to learn to love one another as well as we can in ever more effective ways.

The traditional religions have usually meant well, the secular humanist continues. These religions have usually preached love of neighbor and performed great works of charity, but they have also distracted themselves from full attention to these ends by devoting many resources to churches and monasteries, resources that might otherwise have helped to develop agriculture to feed people, or helped to promote psychological research that could free people to be more humane toward one another. These religions have undercut secular efforts for human growth by relying on divine help that is at best extremely unreliable, if it exists at all. They have led people to accept unjust conditions, oppressive governments, bigotry, and war, all on the grounds that such temporal matters ultimately do not count because heaven or nirvana or such is our true home.

Altogether, then, the challenge of secularity to religion is this: can a morally concerned person devote time and energy to religion when there is so much to be done out of concern for our fellow human beings? Modern religion says yes to this also, but it has had to show how religiousness does not have to diminish the importance of human welfare but can actually sustain and promote it.

The Challenge of Modern Notions of Autonomous Selfhood

Modern culture fought its way into learning the value of individual freedom. The early scientists, then the deists and Freemasons, and eventually many others came to appreciate the value of free thought and the free speech to express it. They came to believe that it was not merely true, as Western religions had long said, that every single person was of infinite value; it was also true that every single person ought to be able to live in accordance with his or her identity as a free and equal person. Out of all of this came the ideal of responsible autonomy as authentic human existence.

The model of behavior celebrated by modern thought is that of the self-determining responsible individual. The model of behavior prized by the more traditional religious thought is that of the person who humbly submits to God's truth as found in scriptures or in religious teaching. The religious ideal has been that of the person who uses individual freedom to submit obediently to the one truth of God.

All along the way, religious leaders and believers alike were in the forefront of those who opposed freedom. Traditional religious wisdom did sometimes acknowledge that every person had to follow his or her conscience in making decisions, but it also insisted that the only correct decisions were those in accord with the Bible, with religious tradition, and with the established authorities of both state and church. Those who freely went against what was correct had to be silenced or punished, or both.

The challenge the modern notion of person poses to religion is this: can religion truly promote the growth of each person toward authentic selfhood, a selfhood that exercises responsible choices in a free society? Modern religion also says yes to this, but it has had to show how promoting this autonomous selfhood is religious rather than somehow foreign to true religiousness.

The Challenge of Modern Belief in the Tentativeness of Knowledge

The fourth and final way modern thought has struck at traditional religion has been by shattering the idea that we can possess the final and correct understanding of reality. The experience of modern science fortified what many philosophers had been pointing out, that all human understanding is a way of interpreting reality, as hypothesis, theory, map, and model. It is often very reasonable and very useful knowledge, but there is always the possibility that some other different map or model might be a better tool for understanding how things probably are.

The incompleteness of knowledge makes the ideal of autonomous selfhood more important. If the truth about reality is obscure, uncertain, or changeable, then no person can rest content with tradition. Everyone must be prepared to look over new ideas, evaluate them, and accept those that seem to be both more reasonable and valuable, even if this means discarding or changing older ideas.

This means, in turn, that there will be a plurality of positions on any topic, whether in science, history, or economics—or religion. Pluralism is now a fact in contemporary cultures; there is no longer a single accepted system of thought, moral code, or religious tradition. To the modern mind, pluralism is not merely a fact but a positive value. A plurality of interpretations is necessary in order to allow for the emergence of ever better ones through free interplay and competition among them. This will also best serve the secular desire to improve the human condition through the growth of knowledge. Pluralism is a strong form of tolerance. It is not a tolerance that merely puts up with what is different. It is a tolerance that values the fact of differences, even among religious viewpoints.

Religion, however, has not often been the friend of tentativeness, pluralism, and tolerance. As we have seen more than once, religion serves to provide security in the face of life's threats; it is a haven from insecurity and confusion. Religious people have frequently insisted that their beliefs offer security precisely because they are not tentative models of reality, but instead are the clear and firm God-given unchanging truth. Religion trusts its doctrines to be true. Classical religion trusts its doctrines to be the only fully accurate truths.

Here the challenge to religion is whether there can be a religiousness that accepts the idea that its symbols and beliefs are tentative interpretations, symbols of ultimate truth, rather than rock-like unchangeable doctrines. Can there be a religiousness that sustains people in their needs but is still open to changes in belief, and to a free competition of religious symbols in a tolerantly pluralistic context of autonomous people? Modern religion says yes to this also, but it has to explain how.

Before looking at modern religion in some detail, it is good to remember that most religion today is not very modern. That is not necessarily a criticism. There is great value in tradition, and "modern" is not a synonym for "good." But in those areas of the world where modern ideas and values have flourished, religious beliefs have been affected. There are modern forms of Hindu thought, such as that of the Indian philosopher Sarvepali Radhakrishnan (b. 1888). Reform Judaism, originating in nineteenth-century Germany, is quite modern. Most of the examples to follow here will be taken, however, from contemporary Christianity. But first, to put modern religiousness in context, consider some contemporary nonmodern alternatives.

Non-Modern Religious Beliefs Today

Traditional Faith with Accommodations to Modernity

In cultures around the world today, traditional religious faith predominates over both modern forms of religion and skepticism. (Chapter Fifteen, however, will outlline the rather high degree of skepticism that prevails in Europe.) But in the West some of those who think of themselves as following tradition may have made more accommodation with modern thought than they notice. Though they still firmly believe in God, they expect fewer miraculous interventions than past generations once did. Though they still hope for life after death, they are willing to invest more energy in worldly social concerns about poverty and injustice. Though they believe that each person is a child of God, they also believe that we are the products of an evolutionary process. Though they believe in the importance of God's work for all humankind, they are willing to make this a matter of personal belief and individual free choice rather than accept the mandate that everyone should belong to the one true religion.

This traditional faith is often not conscious of how much accommodation to modern ideas it has made. This-worldly emphasis on justice, acceptance of evolution, and the rights of individuals to publicly disagree on religious matters were once radical ideas, considered to be misleading or dangerous. There are conservative religious groups today that are not so ready to accommodate such ideas.

Fundamentalism

The most intransigent religious style is the one that has come to be known as fundamentalism. As Chapter Nine indicated, the name came from a conservative movement among American Protestants in the early twentieth century. Against the growing force of modern thought in religion, known then as liberalism, a set of twelve volumes, entitled *The Fundamentals*, was published, which set forth and defended traditional Christian faith. The viewpoint was thoroughly unmodern and even antimodern, rejecting all four of the main points of the modern challenge.

Fundamentalism rejects the idea that the basic religious beliefs might be only tentative formulations, useful but never fully adequate symbols. The doctrines of the Bible are God's literal and unchangeable truths, given once and for all, says fundamentalism. Modern religion is especially wrong to call into question the reality of the many miracles described in the Bible, wrong to try to interpret these miracles as just educational stories or symbols of deeper truths. (Such scriptural literalism is a key mark of other fundamentalisms in the world.)

There is no purpose to human autonomy, according to fundamentalism, except to make the one valid choice of obedience to God's will and adherence to God's truth. We humans are too sinful to rely on our reason, or to be self-determining. In fact, it is a sinful pride that inclines us ever to do so.

Involvement in this world is dangerous and misguided, insists fundamentalism. The secular world of history is a contest between good and evil. Those who follow God should help others in all kindness and charity, it is true, but they should not expect that justice and love can ever reign on this planet through human involvement in social causes. Only God's power, to come in full force some day, will finally defeat the powers of evil and establish a righteous kingdom.

Fundamentalism also rejects modern science's conclusions whenever they conflict with the fundamentalist's interpretation of God's truth. This is not a vast, twelve-billion-year-old evolving universe lacking any clear plan or goal, says fundamentalism. Instead, it is a more recent product of God's creative activity; it is under the ongoing general guidance of God and is directed specifically by God through many miraculous interventions. Fundamentalists tend to be creationists, believing that God made the earth and every living thing, including the first parents of all humans, about six thousand years ago. Some creationists have tried to claim that their interpretation of this is scientifically respectable, but scientists see overwhelming evidence for an evolutionary process of several billion years' duration.

Sects and Cults

Modern thought creates insecurity and confusion. The modern emphasis on tentative truth, on a need to be autonomously self-directing, on dedicated involvement in even the frustrating confusions of this world, and on the scientific method with its demand for honesty and self-criticism as well as its often pessimistic worldviews, has led many religious believers to cling more tightly to the security of traditional beliefs of fundamentalism. These same threatening aspects of modern thought may also have a lot to do with the intensification of sectarian and cultic religion.

Christian sects, by and large, are fundamentalist in their attitudes. Strict in defining beliefs, strict in providing moral rules, strict in expecting people to follow the single truth, they provide clarity and security. Variant or quasi-Christian sects do the same. The Mormons follow *The Book of Mormon* and not the Bible as such. The Unification Church reads *The Divine Principle* of the Reverend Sun Myung Moon, loosely based on Judaeo-Christian tradition. But by strictness of belief and morality they provide a refuge from the ambiguities of modern thought.

Cultic groups, some of them Hindu-inspired, as in the case of the Krishna Consciousness movement, accomplish the same thing. Behind saffron robes, shaved heads, bells and incense, are the same human needs and hopes and fears all people share, and the same desire to find clear answers to life in the midst of its mysteries. These cults generally reject the modern challenges to religion, finding no value in secular, scientific, autonomous life according to tentative symbols.

Not all members of sects or cults feel a conscious need to escape the uncertainties of modern thought and life. Many will find their religious group attractive simply because they feel at home there, because they have connections there to family or friends and because the group offers a way of life that the members can understand. This is especially true in the second and later generations of members, who have grown up in this way of life and find it so normal they would not think of departing from it. The hidden logic of blind faith is probably at work here.

Traditional faith, together with fundamentalism and even sects and cults, are all alternatives to modern religion. The next chapter will discuss various New Age movements as well as New Religious Movements, as they are called. Many forms of nonmodern religiousness are strong today. But, finally, it is modern religion that remains to be described, as it addresses the four modern challenges.

Modern Religion

Religion and Scientific Worldviews

This world as seen through the best available theories of science has little or no room for miracles, unlike the worldviews of prescientific cultures. This world also can easily appear in scientific theories as a random and aimless series of processes, rather than as one filled with divine guidance or directed towards some ultimate goal or value. There are three major categories of responses by modern Christian theology to these ideas of science: segregation, integration, and patience. You will find many different names and positions described here; they are mentioned only to illustrate that religious thinkers have found modern science rather challenging, and have proposed a variety of responses.

Segregation of Religion from Science

The first position has been to segregate religion from science, to quarantine religion in order to prevent its contamination by skepticism.

Schleiermacher's Liberal Theology

A German theologian named Friedrich Schleiermacher (1768-1834) led the way as long ago as 1799 when he published *On Religion: Speeches to Its Cultured Despisers*. True religion, he said, is not the kind that is based on miracles. In fact, it is not dependent in any way on evidence from the world, evidence such as science depends on. This theology without miracles has been called "liberal" theology. Modern religion is very much a liberal form of religion. Modern liberal theology, in fact, is precisely what provoked a return to the fundamentals on the part of those we now call fundamentalists. Above all else, fundamentalism defends belief in miraculous revelation along with the miracle stories contained in that revelation.

True religion, claimed Schleiermacher, is not based on miraculous revelations. It is based on an inner intuition or feeling, a sensitivity to the utterly awesome mystery of the universe. Every item in the world is dependent on something else, and all things together proclaim: we do not account for ourselves. The perceptive soul will sense deeply and thoroughly that there is a God, the Other who is the Independent upon whom every person and all reality depend utterly. This is an insight or feeling, not a scientific conclusion, said Schleiermacher

More than a century later, Rudolph Otto, the German theologian who popularized the word "numinous," echoed Schleiermacher. Otto's book, *The Idea of the Holy* (1910), proposed that a person may experience a *mysterium tremendum et fascinans*—a mystery both awesome and fascinating. Both Schleiermacher and Otto defined God as Aquinas might have, as the infinite and incomprehensible Ultimate on which all things depend. But both arrived at this, they claimed, through profound inner experience rather than through philosophical argument. Otto even claimed that it is enough to have the experience in order to know that it is valid. A person who has not had this experience, on the other hand, is counseled by Otto to read no further in his book, for that person will not be able to understand truly what Otto is talking about.

Between Schleiermacher and Otto, however, the philosopher Ludwig Feuerbach (1804-1872) also analyzed our inner insights and feelings, but did so in order to show how our inner feelings about God or religion can deceive us. In *The Essence of Christianity* (1841) Feuerbach claimed that the intuition of God's reality of which Schleiermacher spoke is really only an intuition of our own inner capacity for the infinite, out of which we invent the idea of God.

Feuerbach described the ability of our minds to form ideas of infinite perfection, to create images of perfect love and total power and unrestricted knowledge. But we see ourselves as finite. In order to find the embodiment of infinite perfection, said Feuerbach, we invent it and call it "God," and then demean ourselves before this fiction through obedience and humility. Feuerbach wanted people to recognize "God" as nothing more than a product of their own wonderful infinite capacity and thereby take pride in themselves. He wanted people to stop being obedient to their own invention called "God," and put control of their lives back into their own hands.

Feuerbach could not prove that his theory was true. But he did sow the suspicion that maybe we had invented God as a projection onto the heavens of our own inner potential for the infinite. About seventy years later Freud would give these suspicions new energy, as Chapter Two described. All this made it more difficult to appeal, as Schleiermacher had, to one's own inner intuition or feeling or conviction that God exists. After all, inner intuition might just be self-delusion. Yet the popularity of Otto's book many years later suggests that Schleiermacher's approach makes sense to more people than Feuerbach's analysis.

Barth's Neo-Orthodoxy

A semi-modern response to all this appeared in Switzerland just after the First World War. A Calvinist theologian named Karl Barth (1886-1968) was modernist enough to abandon belief in miracles, but traditionally orthodox enough to claim that faith in God is a gift of God, not dependent on science or inner intuition or any other merely human source. This mixed response was called "Neo-orthodoxy."

Barth was modern in that he translated all miracles into non-miracles. He treated the Bible, for example, not as a set of writings miraculously revealed or inspired by God, but as a recording made by people of their human responses to Jesus. He spoke even of the Christian doctrine of life after death not so much as literal truth but as a symbol of a more general trust that somehow human life has ultimate meaning in spite of the fact that we all die.

Barth was not very modern, though, in his insistence on the very traditional Christian doctrine that faith in God is an inner state created in us by the action of God's grace working in us. No human power, not human reason as in science, nor human intuition and feeling as in Schleiermacher's theology, can possibly bring us to faith in God. Only God can produce faith in God, said Barth. A person who shares in this Christian faith knows that the faith is a gift from God. This was the main emphasis of neo-orthodoxy.

Unfortunately Barth was never very clear on explaining how God can do this if God does not literally work miracles, because the action of God's grace on people seems to be a kind of miracle. Moreover, Barth's claim was open to the criticism that it is a circular argument. Barth said he believed in God because God gave him the grace to believe. But how did Barth know there even was a God to be the cause of belief in God? The followers of Feuerbach (and later Freud) were still suspicious. Maybe the belief in God's grace is just part of the overall fictional idea that God exists at all.

Bultmann's Existential Theology

In response to all this a German scripture scholar named Rudolph Bultmann (1884-1976) proposed another way of segregating religious belief from threatening scientific worldviews. He was called a Christian existentialist because he too thought that we humans "ex-ist." The best scientific evidence, Bultmann believed, makes the universe look like an aimless process with no ultimate meaning to it. Yet we humans are the kind of being that the existentialists say we are, in need of meaning, even ultimate meaning, in order to have some direction and purpose to our lives. So we stand out as the beings whose conscious awareness makes them seek ultimate values as a ground for a meaningful life in a universe where there is no ultimate value. On the surface, therefore, life does appear to be absurd.

In spite of this existentialist interpretation of the human situation, Bultmann was a Christian because of the way he responded to the situation. What was needed, said Bultmann, was a free human decision to face down the awful implications of science and cry out, "Nevertheless." Because we are limited and sinful we cannot grasp God, who is indeed the Wholly Other. Nevertheless, Bultmann said, I will choose to believe that there is Ultimate meaning and value. Regardless of external scientific evidence I will rely on my internal courage and freedom and stand up to emptiness, stand up to death, and believe. As a Christian Bultmann took his inspiration from the example of Jesus of Nazareth. In Bultmann's interpretation Jesus leads the way for this great and courageous "nevertheless" by his willingness to take on even a horrible death on the cross because of his dedication to God as the ultimate meaning of life.

Bultmann was not entirely original in recommending this existential choice. The Danish philosopher Søren Kierkegaard (1813-1855) had argued that the true Christian had to be ready to accept absurdity, as Abraham had done when ordered by God to sacrifice the very son that God had given to him and Sarah in their old age. Kierkegaard claimed that the "knight of faith" will choose to leap off a cliff, if necessary, rather than be restrained by ethical rationality. Long ignored, Kierkegaard's writings were promoted by Barth, who proclaimed in his own way that his faith was not based on rational analysis.

Eliade's Phenomenological Approach

Kierkegaard's and Bultmann's responses have not appealed to everyone. Much more popular in recent decades is Mircea Eliade's phenomenological approach (shared most famously by Gerardus van der Leeuw, 1890-1950). This approach is part of the package of ideas described in Chapter Two that says religion is based on experiences of the sacred. Eliade got this idea from Schleiermacher and Otto. But Eliade had a very positive view of primitive religion. He claimed that primitive and archaic religious experiences of sacred places, things, and rituals were just as important as the experiences that Schleiermacher and Otto described.

Eliade also claimed that the sacred is unique—*sui generis*. It is not the sort of profane or everyday phenomenon studied by the sciences. Only religious involvement can lead a person to truly understand the sacred. Otto was correct, in fact, when he said that religious experience is self-validating. If you have had it, you will know it is true; therefore, religion can be legitimately segregated from rational inquiry. We will return to this topic in the Epilogue.

Integration of Science and Religion

The deists had united science and religion by replacing traditional sacred sources such as the Bible and church teachings with human reason, and by using that reason to produce a religious view of God as Great Watchmaker-Creator. When evolutionary thought filled the intellectual air, a German philosopher named G. W. F. Hegel (1770-1831) set out a massively complex theory in 1807 that the universe of science was not aimless and dead but an evolution of God, of a divine Spirit evolving into greater and greater spiritual self-awareness.

By the twentieth century some French philosophers were exploring similar ideas. An Englishman, Alfred North Whitehead (1861-1947), came to Harvard to propose a philosophy of nature that had a clear religious element, based on scientific descriptions of nature. (Charles Hartshorne, mentioned in Chapter Eleven, is one of the major proponents and developers of Whitehead's position.)

Teilhard de Chardin's Cosmic Vision

A French paleontologist and Jesuit priest, Pierre Teilhard de Chardin (1881-1955), integrated science with religion by an interpretation of the universe that is easier to explain here because it is close to the views of Julian Huxley, which we have already seen.

Teilhard (to use the usual brief way of referring to him) looked at the whole cosmic process of change and did not see aimlessness there. Like Huxley, he saw a process of complexification going on, as each stage of cosmic evolution produced variant forms, which then combined in more complexly organized unities—from particles to atoms to compounds to basic genetic material to life forms to cells to organisms to humans and their stages of social development. Like Huxley, Teilhard also saw this as a process with a direction toward higher and higher consciousness. This in turn was producing higher and higher levels of interpersonalness, as human consciousness led to family life, social connectedness, global communications, and so forth. The evolutionary goal of the cosmos was apparently an ever greater "personalization" of reality.

Teilhard thought that it was scientifically legitimate to claim that there must be a force at work throughout the entire cosmos, driving it along the path toward ever more complex organization, and hence also towards ever greater consciousness, humaneness, and interpersonalness. Just as a scientist argues for the existence of the invisible force called gravity to account for the observed actions of physical bodies, so Teilhard argued for the existence of an invisible cosmic force behind the directionality of evolution toward personalization. Teilhard felt it was therefore scientifically sound to claim that there must be a supreme Personness or Person that was the primary driving force of evolution. This is actually a variation of the "argument from design" for the existence of God.

In fact Teilhard felt it was legitimate to claim that the tendency of all things to unite in ever more complex and conscious ways was a sign that love, a tendency towards union, is the ultimate force behind everything. God is love, Teilhard claimed. The goal of all cosmic evolution is a final and complete union with God, a goal that is already beginning to be realized in the growth of conscious love in the human element of the cosmos.

Teilhard tried to prove too much, perhaps. He was offering an apologetic for Christianity in a scientific era. He managed to find all sorts of ways in which scientific theories could support his own Christian faith, even on many specifics concerning God and Christ and the eventual end of the world, though he had to reinterpret some traditional doctrines to make it all work.

Scientific Mysticism

Religion and science continue to intersect. The process theology based on Whitehead's thought remains highly favored among many theologians and scientists who seek to integrate their religious faith with a scientific perspective. It is a complex theology, worked out in different ways by different thinkers. It would be difficult to summarize here adequately. There are other ways in which religion and science meet today, however, that can be briefly described.

One of these is closer to a New Age mysticism than to regular science. Various writers find religious inspiration in a holistic interconnection among matter, energy, and spirit. They speak not of quantum mechanics but of quantum mysticism. The physicists David Bohm and Paul Davies are two names associated with such thought. Mysticized science does not have an apologetic intent, does not attempt to make a rational case. It has an allure to those who have religious sensibilities of the sort that Schleiermacher and Otto described. But unlike Schleiermacher and Otto, they connect their religious experience to a broad view of the cosmos that borrows from modern scientific cosmology. They call people to a kind of intuition of a religious dimension to the universe. Many science-minded people disdain this approach. These critics claim that it is not legitimate to mingle testable scientific theories with what they see as mystical mumbo-jumbo. Those who favor mysticized science, however, feel that the critics have simply not had the religious experience needed. The other recent major form of integration between religion and science appears in two contemporary arguments from design.

The Anthropic Principle

The first current argument from design has been called "the anthropic principle," though it may be more informative to refer to it as the argument from fine tuning. The argument states that the universe appears to be quite finely tuned so that it would evolve from raw energy to more complex forms of matter and then to life, to conscious life, and finally to intelligent life.

The fine tuning is not easy to see at first. Given billions of years of existence and billions of galaxies in which things can happen, even the most highly improbable things will eventually occur. This seems particularly likely when one applies Darwin's theory of evolution in a broad sense to the history of the whole universe.

In the overall history of the universe, variant forms of energy, matter, compounds, and life have existed, all occurring partially through randomness. The four forces of gravity, electromagnetism, and the subatomic weak and strong forces limit the random variations of forms of matter. These forces affect the nature of quarks and other sub-atomic particles and how they interact in forming atoms. The nature of the atoms limits the random variants of chemical connections that are possible. The nature of chemical connections limits the ways in which life forms may appear. And so on. The second half of Darwin's theory, natural selection, is also a partially random factor. Reality blindly "selects" for destruction any variations that do not fit the limits of reality, whether those are limits imposed by the basic forces, by atomic structure, by chemical possibilities, or by the whole environment. According to Darwin's theory, this long process of variation and selection has produced the great variety of life on this planet, including us human beings, without any plan or guidance. The elements of randomness in this whole process seem to exclude any fine-tuning.

But the fine-tuning argument says to look again at those limits. The four basic forces do indeed impose limits. The limits are in fact precisely what is needed to form a universe that lasts long enough to produce the complex atoms like oxygen and carbon needed for life, and then long enough to produce even heavier elements like nickel and iron to make a planet like ours possible. For this to occur the universe must first exist for eight billion years or more, because it takes that long for stars to form, go through a few life cycles, and generate heavier elements in each cycle. But for the universe to last this long, the strength of gravity must be tuned with extreme precision. If gravity were a tiny fraction stronger, the universe would have collapsed back in upon itself a billion or so years after the Big Bang, and life would never have had a chance to evolve. If gravity were a tiny fraction weaker, the stuff of the universe would have spread out so fast it would never have formed stars, in which nuclear fusion eventually forms elements like oxygen and carbon and nickel and iron.

Arguments in favor of fine-tuning continue into excruciating detail to show that any variation in the other three basic forces would also have made impossible the evolution of the universe into an environment that could support the evolution of life. The conclusion drawn from this is that the random aspects of the universe are far overshadowed by the very precise conditions or limits which make this a universe in which intelligent beings could eventually appear. It is as though the basic forces of the universe were all fine-tuned from the beginning for the purpose of allowing *human-like* intelligence to evolve. Hence the name "anthropic" principle.

Many religious scientists are quite comfortable with a faith that there is a supernatural God (or equivalent) who created and sustains the entire universe, for some divine purpose that may not be known to us. As scientists, they are nonetheless methodological naturalists, using their science to look only for natural causes, not supernatural. Many are also evolutionary theists, whose religious thought does not lead them to expect to find any divine interventions in this universe. This fits well with belief in an initial fine tuning designed to lead eventually and inevitably to intelligent life somewhere in the universe. This is a kind of evolutionary deism, a belief in a designer God that does not intervene.

Intelligent Design

The other major current form of an argument from design is called "Intelligent Design" or ID theory. Most ID proponents strive precisely to identify instances of interventions by a Designer. ID proponents claim to be able to find in nature not just evidence of an initial cosmic fine tuning, but very specific instances of things that are "irreducibly complex" or have a highly "specified complexity." The biochemist Michael Behe, for example, points to what he calls an irreducibly complex aspect of biology in the highly complicated sequence or "cascade" of chemical interactions that must occur for blood to clot. If any of the multiple aspects of this cascade were to fail, an organism would bleed to death. Therefore, argues Behe, this clotting cascade could not have been gradually produced by an aimless step-by-step evolutionary process. It would have had to be assembled all at once by an intelligent designer. To assemble this complex clotting sequence, the intelligent designer would have to intervene at a certain point in evolutionary history, after evolution had produced creatures with blood.

The ID proponents therefore conclude that scientific naturalism is mistakenly restrictive, because it deliberately excludes significant specific instances of intelligent causality intervening in natural processes. To ignore genuine causes of any sort is a mistake, a path to ignorance about those causes. Perhaps we cannot know the purposes and methods of a non-natural intelligent intervener, because these interventions are not reliable and regular like the laws of nature. Tough luck, say ID proponents; it may be true that such an intervener has been at work anyway.

The specific arguments of ID proponents such as Phillip Johnson, William Dembski, and Michael Behe are too intricate to describe here, as are counterarguments in books by Robert T. Pennock and Kenneth R. Miller. The main point here is to illustrate ways in which a rational or scientific approach can still be part of religious apologetics today. Scientific evidence and rational analysis can provide standards for judging religious truth claims, even though not all religious people would accept these standards.

Patient Moderation Concerning Science and Religion

Some have severely divided religion from science; others have made them fit together very intimately. A third approach has been one of patience and hope. This middle ground is taken by those who do not claim to have the answers about the eventual interplay between religious beliefs and scientific theories, but who will nevertheless trust that in the long run good science and reasonable religious faith will prove compatible.

Such a position is sometimes a generally nonmodern or traditional faith that has adapted slowly to a few aspects of modern thought. Modern religiousness easily takes a position of cautious hope because it accepts science, secularity, human autonomy, and the tentativeness of knowledge. It is willing to insist that faith should be a reasonable choice of a free person concerned with the temporal welfare of all people.

On the whole, this position accepts science rather than rejects it. It accepts the scientific notion that claims about what is true or not true should not be merely a matter of individual inner experience, obedience, or commitment, but also, at the very least, a publicly defensible position. Science corrects its own tendencies toward prejudice, bias, or premature conviction by insisting that all people who are willing to try should be given a chance to test the evidence and study the reasoning behind any conclusions. This process of public debate is one that many of the patient moderates are willing to engage in concerning their own religious beliefs as well.

In general, it is safe to say that modern religion tries to be honestly reasonable. It shares humanism's trust in human reason; it trusts also that religious claims about life's meaning have not been invalidated by the methods or conclusions of science. A later section will say more about all of this.

Religion and Secularity

Modern religion also trusts the world. Schleiermacher, Teilhard, Barth, Bultmann, and moderates in between are all modern in their willingness to live without expectation of miracles, without specific interventions by God to control individual events or give directions on how to act. That means that this religiousness is not primarily a means to get help and guidance from God. It has a more secular purpose. The secularity that arose in recent centuries often advocated a total secularism, a denial that there is anything at all to existence except the ongoing problems of life, a denial of any numinous or divine dimension. But in the nineteenth and twentieth centuries, modern religion has begun to see secular interest in this world as part of its own purposes.

As the Infinite, God is a symbol of all that has yet to be done, of the more that is always possible. Meditation on God is reflection on goodness to be achieved. God is the one who calls and empowers people to do everything of value that can be done. In the modern style of thought this is a symbolic way of speaking to represent a human trust that the divine reality is somehow there behind our efforts to live life for one another, even if we cannot know just how that divine presence works. This trust is a basis for taking charge of human life in this world in order to make it as good as can be.

Bishop Robinson's Secular Theology

Traditional historic religion in the West views this world as fallen, a source of sin, unable to be improved (unless it is first destroyed). The "secular" theologians of the 1960s disagree. The Anglican bishop John A. T. Robinson (1919-1983), sums up a rather modern religious appreciation of this world in his small book, *Honest to God*. The world is not ungodly, but a sign of God's presence, says Robinson. God is not "up there" or "out there," Robinson declares, not a figure in the sky as though divine realities were removed from worldly ones. Instead the infinite divine Mystery is the ground and source of all creation, especially the ground and source of personness. So to find the presence of the mystery of God, look to what exists around us, to creation and especially to other persons.

To Robinson, these are not just traditional pious thoughts about the presence of God in all things. They have implications for how to be religious. Robinson recommends a secular religiousness, a "worldly holiness" as he calls it. This means a deep and consistent involvement in all that touches us in the world. Concretely it means that concern for political freedom, social equality, psychological well-being, physical health, and other desirable aspects of human life are ways of involvement in the presence of God.

This is especially secular because Robinson and others like him do not say much about a life after death as salvation. The salvation they are mainly concerned about is a worldly one. It is a continuous healing of the world's wounds, a constant attention to the needs of personness, which he regards as being of ultimate value here and now.

Though the label "secular"was popular in the 1960s and 1970s among theologians, few of them today would use the word. Many, in fact, are trying hard to recapture a stronger sense of the sacred. Yet many of these same theologians still have great concern to attend to the problems of this world.

Liberation Theologies: Black, Feminist, Latin American

Striking examples of this secular religiousness can be found in the various Christian liberation theologies, as they are called. Black liberation theology is a theology that interprets human existence in terms of the experience of oppression. To understand and feel what it is to be oppressed is the foundation of an approach to life that works for a transformation of earthly conditions—material, political, economic, social, and psychological. Black liberation theology sees this work as the basic meaning of the idea of building God's "kingdom" on earth. It is not enough to pray for liberation, says the theologian James Cone (1938-); it must be brought about through the thoughts and actions of the oppressed.

Likewise, women's liberation theology brings to the fore the reality of domination through power, of a division of people into the higher and lower, then rejects these as a model for human existence. Equality, cooperation, and mutual supportiveness are the ideals of feminist theology, not just as useful virtues but as the key images for interpreting where life's ultimate values and meaning lie.

Similarly, the Catholic social-political movements of Latin America all claim that the most immediately imperative religious project is not getting to heaven at some future time but of transforming earthly conditions as much as possible now in an ongoing way. Trusting that God will take care of the ultimate destiny of peoples' lives, these liberation theologians respond to God as the God of the poor and oppressed, the God of those who live under stifling oppression. The oppression itself and all the social, economic, and political structures that support it are the "sin" that these religious liberationists attack.

Religious Environmentalism

A final secular interest of modern religion is ecology. Traditional Christianity had a number of ideas that went contrary to a concern to preserve the earth. Apocalyptic-minded Christians even today have said that God will destroy the earth before long, so that attempts to preserve the earth are foolish.

Christians who look to heaven as the only true home may also lose interest in caring for the planet. And the scriptures tell its readers to subdue the earth; they do not explicitly say to protect and preserve it. But some modern Christians claim that the first concern should be for this universe, which is God's creation, and which deserves to be cherished and respected. These Christians take it as their God-given responsibility to care for the earth as stewards rather than masters, preparing it to be a better place for the generations still to come. "Deep ecology" is the name sometimes used for ecological concern based on a religious respect for the earth.

Religion and Autonomous Selfhood

Modern thought values individual freedom very highly, emphasizing that the capacity for self-determination means that each person is personally responsible for all of his or her values and for his or her choices. Traditional religion in the West has also held each person responsible for her or his choices. But there is nonetheless a difference between modern and traditional views. That difference lies in the amount of confidence placed in human ability to do what is good.

The most conservative form of traditional Christianity describes us humans as fallen, weak-willed and confused. We are fallen people in a fallen world, unable to reason clearly, whose autonomy leads to sin, whose secular involvement is a mistake, and whose science is not to be trusted when it conflicts with revealed truth. The modern humanistic evaluation of the person, on the other hand, maintains that our capacity for autonomy is to be trusted and encouraged for the sake of making constructive and creative decisions for improving temporal existence, sometimes with confidence in science as the best way available to judge what is probably the truth.

In response to this conflict modern religion has become more humanistic. A number of theologians even perceive a religiousness within secular humanism, a religiousness that is also intrinsic to science, secularity, and a concern for autonomy. Various persons have recently supported this idea in similar ways, including Bernard Lonergan (1904-1984), Karl Rahner (also 1904-1984), and Schubert Ogden (1928-). The names are not important here; a general presentation of the basic idea will do. To have a handy label we can call it the implicit-faith position.

The main theme is that there is a genuine religiousness that is part of any trust in human responsible autonomy, although it may be a hidden or implicit religiousness. When human persons take the burden of using their own human efforts in science, for example, to determine what is true, or the burden of making their own decisions about love and loyalty to others as the most basic value of their lives, they are making implicit acts of faith that there is ultimate meaning and value in human life.

We have seen that whenever a scientific inquirer pursues knowledge through the human method of investigating and theorizing and testing, that inquirer is showing faith that reality is intelligible. This has turned out to be a highly reasonable faith; it works exceedingly well in practice. The inquirer is also making an act of faith in her or his own intelligence and responsibility. This also is a reasonable faith. The human scientific enterprise has worked. We have some reason to trust our powers of understanding and commitment to truth, in spite of our many failures.

Most important, there is a fundamental faith at work in science that it is really worthwhile being a knower, being a person in pursuit of understanding. Atheistic existentialism challenges religion to show that ultimately anything makes sense. Without answering that challenge directly, even seemingly nonreligious people pursue knowledge through science as though it really were ultimately worthwhile. They thereby act as though they had an implicit faith that it really does make sense to be a human person, using one's intelligence to learn and to develop new knowledge.

The same implicit faith appears when we love one another or give deep loyalty to others or bring children into this world. We thereby act as though we trust that life makes sense. This manifests an implicit faith that our selfhood, our consciousness, our ability to learn and choose and love are ultimately meaningful. All this can be seen as faith in the value of autonomous selfhood because it is precisely our ability to learn and choose, to think for ourselves, and to make responsible choices that constitutes autonomy.

The implicit faith position argues that in principle this faith in ourselves is not ultimately valid if in fact the ultimate truth about life is that it is a meaningless accident in an aimless universe. Our selfhood is ultimately valid only if it somehow rests upon a source or ground of ultimate meaning and value. Belief in God as Personal is a belief that personhood is grounded in Personhood. The Hebrew scriptures expressed this by saying that every person is made "in the image and likeness of God." In this belief every person is therefore a symbol, a re-presentation, of the Ultimate.

Notice that in this implicit faith a person does not believe in God on the basis of an outside authority instructing the person to do so. Belief in a personal God is instead based on a prior act of self-affirmation. Theism thus becomes a reasonable way to spell out and affirm a person's basic faith in the ultimate worth of being a person. This implicit-faith position supports the idea of faith as a reasonable commitment.

The Christian theologians who argue this way go a step further. They claim that belief that Jesus of Nazareth is the presence of the mystery of God in history helps to express and maintain this faith in personness. Similarly for the Jewish religious philosopher Martin Buber, every time we encounter someone else on a personal level, as a "thou," to use Buber's language, we encounter the presence of God. In these theologies the modern emphasis on individual and free personness is not found to be unreligious but intrinsically religious.

In the next chapter we will see a new challenge to this emphasis on autonomy. The challenge is from those who say that their religious tradition helps to highlight an excessive individualism inherent in the modern idea of the autonomous self. Modern thought may well be right in seeking to develop fully the capacity of the person to reflect and choose. But modern thought often overlooks what is most worth choosing, which is positive relations with other people, in family and community. Such relations require giving up at least some of each person's autonomy from moment to moment. Love of family and friends and strong social bonds in a larger and meaningful community are highly important aspects of life. Many religious traditions remind people of the importance of community for individual fulfillment.

Religion and Tentative Knowledge

Fundamentalists strive to maintain a strict adherence to what they see as the single truth delivered by God. Even those of a more accommodating but traditional faith attach a high degree of certitude and permanence to their religious beliefs. In contrast, a result of modern reflection on science and history has been an understanding that all our ideas have changed and will change again, even our religious beliefs.

There are religious thinkers who have found that their faith could get along quite well with the idea that all knowledge, even religious belief, is tentative. They have found that they can be modern in their religiousness by emphasizing an idea that is actually rather traditional. This is the notion that God is a name for the Ultimate Reality that lies beyond human comprehension. The infinite Mystery of God can never be captured by any name, category, or belief that the human mind can comprehend. Many religious beliefs may be valid, but every valid belief is also inadequate. Every legitimate idea about God is a clue to the full reality of God but is not the simple truth. Therefore, all ways of speaking of God are open to improvement. Alternative ways may also be legitimate as different paths toward the same God.

Religious traditions usually ignore the limitations of their beliefs and practices. It is more comfortable to feel secure with firm and clear doctrines than to stand before Mystery. But the actual history of the traditions is a story of many changes. Rituals, moral codes, leadership roles, interpretations of sacred sources, ideas of salvation: these have all undergone changes. The changes might be infrequent in some cases, but if even one unexpected change is legitimate, then many more may eventually turn out to be legitimate also.

Religious tradition has made use of some core symbols. It may be that some of these in particular remain basically unchanged, generation after generation. A thousand years from now people will likely be still praying "I believe in God..." or "There is no God but God..." or "Hear, O Israel, the Lord your God is one." Yet the ways in which these words will be understood by future generations are never fully predictable.

Historic religion has usually been committed to many specific doctrines and rules as the universally valid truths for all people, everywhere, at all times. The elaborate systems of theology such as those constructed by an Anselm or an Aquinas are testimonies to this. Modern liberal religion, on the other hand, tends to commit itself not so much to the many specific beliefs and practices as to an underlying, more general faith in the ultimate meaning and value of being a person in the universe. Or it focuses on a general religious experience which may be expressed in a great variety of different ways.

To sum up: modern religious faith is focused on the ultimate meaning and value of being a person, a real, concrete, temporally developing person, free and capable of responsibility, conscious and able to grow in understanding. It is a faith that scientific honesty is not ungodly, that secular concern is not a distraction from God, that self-affirmation is not a sin of pride, and that openness to change in religious forms is not an abandonment of religion.

Modern Religion and Other Stages

Religion will continue to take many forms. This is true partly because there are many traditions, each with its own symbols. It is also true because even if there were but one religious tradition in the world with one set of symbols, different people would still interpret them in different ways.

Each of us has some primitive-style memories and feelings and thoughts, a sense of meeting and sharing in something mysterious and even numinous. Each of us has some archaic inclinations to see reality as an arena of conflicting finite powers, some of them numinous perhaps. Each of us has some exposure to the historic style, the universalizing impulse to believe in an overall unity, a single truth, the one right way to be and to act, perhaps expressed in a belief in one God. And each of us has been touched by modernness in some ways.

Historic religion did not eliminate primitive or archaic ideas. Instead, it transformed them by taking them under its universalizing umbrella. Modern religion will certainly not eliminate or replace primitive, archaic, or historic thought. What it will probably do is exert a continuing influence on the great historic syntheses by relativizing them.

The absolute doctrines of historic thought will be tempered by the modern sense of tentativeness. The historic passion for perfection beyond this world will be diluted by an involvement in the less than perfect ambiguities of this world. A patience with science and an enthusiasm for its method of honesty will counterbalance the historic desire to affirm final answers once and for all. A modern appreciation of autonomy will guard against the historic temptation to make all people follow the one true path.

A constant temptation modern religiousness faces is to become impatient with other styles of religiousness and to abandon them. This would be foolish. The other styles, primitive, archaic, and historic, are part of the life of each of us. It is unwise to try to ignore part of one's own life story. The other styles are also an endless source of riches. Without all the symbols, moral codes, and belief structures of the past, modern religiousness would be an attitude without specific expression, an orientation without concrete form.

Modern religion faces its own special danger, however, the danger of increasing vagueness of belief and values and direction in life. Where historic religion offers clear and precise beliefs, where archaic style religion provides inspiring myths to symbolize the meaning of life, modern religion is open to so many stories and to so many interpretations of beliefs and so forth that it can lose all focus. That will be one of the issues of the next chapter.

Summary

This chapter has reviewed the main challenges of modern thought to religion, and the responses of modern religion. Most religion today is not all that modern. Fundamentalism rejects the modern orientation entirely. Much of traditional faith has accommodated itself to modernity in some way. There is, however, a religiousness that is rather thoroughly modern in that it has come to terms with scientific world-views, has a secular orientation, promotes responsible autonomy, and lives by an openness to new ideas and changes. Modern thought in religion will never replace earlier forms, but it will continue to influence them as well as draw upon their heritage.

For Further Reflection

1. Which of the challenges of modern thought to religion are the most serious: the challenges of science, secularity, autonomy, or tentativeness of belief? Explain why.
2. Is it legitimate and possible to maintain traditional faith in these modern times? Why? Why not?
3. To what extent does your religious faith rest mainly on inner experience or choice rather than on external evidence?
4. Why should the three liberation theology movements cited in this chapter—black, feminist, and Latin-American—be taken seriously?
5. Are other people worth loving because God says so, or because they are of intrinsic value? Explain.
6. How useful is a religion that cannot guarantee the stable permanence of its beliefs and moral rules and so forth?
7. How much more must a religion do for people beyond affirming its basic faith that there is ultimate value in being a person in the world? Explain.

Suggested Resources

Rudolph Otto, *The Idea of the Holy*, 1958.

Rudolph Bultmann, *Jesus Christ and Mythology*, 1958.

John A. T. Robinson, *Honest to God*, 1963.

Diana L. Hayes, *And Still We Rise: An Introduction to Black Liberation Theology*, 1996.

Gustavo Gutierrez, *Liberation Theology*, 1973 and 1995.

Ann Loades, ed., *Feminist Theology: A Reader*, 1990. Includes excerpts from Elizabeth Cady Stanton, Mary Daly, Sally McFague, Letty Russell, and Ursula King.

Karl Rahner, *Everyday Faith*, 1968, 101-18; *Do You Believe in God?* 1969.

CHAPTER FIFTEEN

The Future of Religion

Religion in the Twenty-First Century

THE VITALITY OF RELIGION

The Secularization Thesis

Chapter Thirteen described the growth of various forms of nonreligious secular evolutionary humanisms (Recall that there is also a religious humanism.) In the twentieth century many became convinced that religion would continue to diminish, especially among the educated. Secular ("worldly") forces would replace religion. One of the more famous books on the topic of secularization was mentioned in Chapter Seven, *The Sacred Canopy*, by sociologist Peter Berger. As a sociologist, Berger interprets religion as the product of human social processes. We humans, unfinished animals, need some social norms and practices in order to have stable identities and patterns of life. These norms and practices are developed over hundreds and even thousands of years of cultural evolution. This is "the social construction of reality."

But we have now become consciously aware that we produce society, Berger continues, including perhaps even the religious beliefs which support society. This means that we think that religion comes at least partly, perhaps even entirely, from us rather than from God or the supernatural. This undermines religion's legitimacy. We are in a position to evaluate social and religious patterns, and perhaps choose to modify them or even replace them entirely. So whether we like it or not, says Berger, we can expect the process of secularization to continue. Another sociologist, David Martin, has called this "the secularization thesis."

It was not just sociological theory that led Berger and others to predict the continuing diminishment of religion. Earlier attacks on belief in miracles by deists, and on religion in general by critical skeptics such as Comte, Feuerbach, Marx, Freud, and Dewey undercut the plausibility of religion, at least for those educated in such skeptical ideas. As a result, in some

European nations only about half of the populace says it believes in God. Perhaps it is just a matter of time before the U.S. catches up with this European trend. As the previous chapter noted, modern religion in general is more accepting of this world. Perhaps modern religion is just a stage on the way to a thorough secularity.

Yet Martin thinks the secularization thesis has proved to be wrong—and now so does Berger, for that matter. There are various reasons for this conclusion.

Increased Church Attendance in the U.S.

In the United States, a popular but mistaken idea seemed to support the secularization thesis. This was the idea that the colonists who founded the United States were all deeply religious and that religion has been on the wane ever since, except for an occasional burst of fervor now and then. Some colonists were indeed seeking religious freedom. Puritans in New England, Quakers in Pennsylvania, and Catholics in Maryland fit this mold. But they were exceptions. Most colonists were simply looking for a new start in life, a place to get land of their own and have an opportunity to rise above the station in life they held in Europe. Regular churchgoers in the years before the American Revolution were in the minority. Recall also that many of the leaders of the American Revolution were deists, who rejected any traditional religious beliefs they considered irrational.

Sociologists who have tracked religious behaviors from colonial times up through the twentieth century, however, claim that there has been an overall, if not steady, increase in church attendance. A "great awakening" of religious fervor here and there in the mid-eighteenth century and another in the early nineteenth century produced intermittent swells of religiousness which were not sustained. Nevertheless, the long-term picture of religion in the U.S. shows a gradual increase in church attendance. Religious faith certainly involves more than just going to church. But an increase in church attendance is hard to reconcile with the claim that people are getting less religious. The secularization thesis is not working well in the U.S., nor in Canada for that matter.

Liberal Religiousness and Supernaturalism

Another reason why the secularization thesis looks less plausible is that even as there has been a relative loss of attendance at the more liberal churches, there has been a revival in the churches that offer direct experience of supernatural interventions by God. When history books speak of religion in the U.S., they often focus on what are sometimes called the "mainline" Protestant churches. This includes Lutherans, Presbyterians, Anglicans, Methodists, and Baptists. But with the exception of the Baptists, these are no longer the most significant centers of religious population in the U.S. Membership in these mainline churches has increased over the last two centuries, but not nearly as fast as the population as a whole has grown. They have lost "market share."

There is reason to suspect it is the liberal theology favored in "mainline" seminaries that makes these churches less appealing to many. Ever since Schleiermacher at the end of the eighteenth century, liberal theology has interpreted the Bible rather symbolically, often concluding that the miracles described in scripture are not to be taken too literally. Religious groups which reject liberal theology and promote belief in the power of God to intervene in human life have experienced the greatest increase in membership.

These interventions take many forms. Baptist meetings often lead a person to feel moved by the Spirit to make a commitment to Christ, and thereby be born again in the Spirit. Pentecostal churches feature miracles of healing, gifts of prophecy or of tongues, and being raptured by the Spirit. Assemblies of God and other Pentecostal churches have grown the most in membership in the U.S. Catholicism, which has also retained beliefs in miraculous interventions by God, has maintained its market share.

The Growth of Expressive Individualism in Religion

In Western nations a significant shift in the form of religiousness has been taking place, from adherence to traditional doctrines and morals and practices to more individualistic forms of religion which allow a person to choose particular doctrines and morals and practices. Previous chapters noted that "modern" religion treats beliefs and morals more flexibly than historical religion. This seems to have legitimized a greater degree of freedom for people to form their own religious ethos. People who move in this direction often themselves refer to it as a shift from "religion" (meaning institutionalized religion) to "spirituality."

It is wise to be wary of exaggerating the extent of this shift. The majority of religious people still belong to traditional religious groups which teach that there are certain basic doctrines and moral rules that are correct and to which everyone ought to adhere. Baptists are taught they must accept Jesus as their savior through a personal act of faith, and that the Bible is the inspired word of God. Roman Catholics are taught that the Pope, in communion with the rest of the church, has the official duty and authority to define true Catholic doctrine and moral teachings. Orthodox and Conservative Jews adhere closely to the Torah. Muslims consider the Qur'an to be the final and definitive revelation from God.

Yet current cultural patterns have loosened the hold of tradition for many, allowing them to formulate and express their own beliefs, in accord with their own individual sense of what is true and good. This new style of religiousness is described variously as "expressive individualism," "privatization," or "pluralization," because this new freedom of individual expression in religion often leads to more private and varied spiritualities. Thus many of the people who no longer attend church have not become more secular or unreligious; they have simply adopted a more individualistic spirituality.

New Age Beliefs and Practices

One of the more striking forms of expressive individualism can be found in New Age beliefs and practices. There is no simple definition of what belongs to the New Age set of ideas and what does not. But it is possible to identify several characteristic elements, and these elements can be divided into two sets. One set is more "classical" or historic; the other is more archaic or even primitive. The classical elements include belief in an all-embracing unity to things; the primitive or archaic elements focus more on spirits and mana-power. The same person, of course, may find both the archaic and classical elements attractive.

Among the classical elements is the one that has given its name to New Age religion: the belief that a new age of universal peace among people and between people and nature can be achieved if people will learn certain deeper truths and adhere to certain wise practices. This has been called a "soft apocalypticism." Like apocalypticism in general it proposes that the old order of pain and alienation and sin will be overcome. Unlike traditional apocalypticism, however, it expects the new ideal order will arrive through a constructive transformation of attitudes and actions rather than through a terrible period of destruction.

The expectation of an age of peace is related to a second classical element in New Age thought, which is belief in an overall cosmic unity or harmony. New Age ideas are usually "holistic" (occasionally spelled "wholistic"), which means that they seek integration of various parts rather than opposition among them. Male and female, body and spirit, nature and persons, cosmos and history—New Age proponents claim that all of these are part of a deep harmony that has been obscured by dualistic notions, which falsely divide the body from the soul, the person from nature, the heavenly from the earthly. This holistic approach is a major point in many of the spiritual guidance books that fill bookstore shelves.

Third among the more classical elements of New Age beliefs is a sense that each person is either a part of the divine or can directly experience the divine. Belief that the self is part of a great and ultimate divine unity is similar to Hindu belief that each person's atman is part of the Infinite Atman. In fact the transcendentalists in early nineteenth-century New England and Great

Britain, and then the Theosophical Society, with Madame Blavatsky as its driving force, looked to India for many of their ideas. Belief that each person can have a direct experience of the divine is a continuation of ancient Neo-Platonist ideas, which had a great influence on mysticism among Christians and Jews, and of various forms of the Sufi movement in Islam. This is reminiscent of the emphasis by Schleiermacher and Otto on an experience of the Whole or the Holy, though their thought is usually not called New Age.

New Age is also the label, however, for a set of beliefs and practices that are much closer to primitive or archaic beliefs. Those who "channel" the spirits of ancient people are usually put in the New Age category. A person channeling speaks with the voice and ideas of someone who has already died, perhaps even many centuries ago, as though the person's body has been taken over by the spirit of a dead person. Those who communicate with angels may also be called New Age. Like archaic or primitive beliefs, these concern specific spirit beings, not the Ultimate nor the universal unity of things. Those who believe crystals have the power to create certain moods, or who believe that the proper magical spell can really be efficacious, manifest the perennial human tendency to believe in mana-power. This also is usually called New Age, though it is as old as the most primitive magical beliefs. New Age ideas of this sort are thus not so much an abandonment of religion as a return to some of the earliest elements of religion in human history.

New Religious Movements and Cults

The proliferation of New Religious Movements (NRMs) is another reason to be suspicious of the secularization thesis. In recent decades it has been hard to keep track of the many NRMs, though all of them have a rather limited number of members. The Unification Church founded by the Korean leader, the Reverend Sun Myung Moon, is strongly Christian, yet places an emphasis on family that may reflect Confucian influence. Scientology, originally a pseudo-scientific movement which then got itself classified legally in the U.S. as a religion, offers ways to unblock the power of the inner spirit-being each person supposedly truly is. The International Krishna Consciousness Movement (ISKCON), derived from ancient Hinduism, trains people, many of them at its university in Iowa, in methods for tapping into the universal cosmic force.

All the many NRMs, including dozens not mentioned here, are part of a long history of new religious movements. From the nineteenth century in the United States alone, for example, we now have the Mormons (Church of Jesus Christ of Latter-day Saints), Christian Science (First Church of Christ Scientist), Seventh Day Adventists, and Jehovah's Witnesses (of the Watchtower and Bible Society), as well as the continuing New Age tradition of Theosophy.

Non-western NRMs attest further to the continuing attractiveness of religion. Notwithstanding fifty years of official atheism in China, the Falun Gong has apparently found more than ten million adherents. That is less than one percent of the population of China, but it is still a great number for such a young group. It is a kind of New Age movement, even though one of its major elements is a long-standing Chinese belief in chi as a vital power in the universe, which proper meditation can tap into.

Especially striking are those rare instances of self-destructive behavior associated with religious or quasi-religious groups. In March, 1997, in a suburb near San Diego, California, thirty-nine members of Heaven's Gate quietly committed suicide together to move to a higher mode of existence, with the aid of beings arriving in a spacecraft (a UFO). In October, 1994, members of the Order of the Solar Temple committed mass suicide and/or homicide in both Quebec and Switzerland.

A year earlier in Waco, Texas, David Koresh (original name: Vernon Howell), under attack by federal agents, led almost eighty of his followers, including children, to a fiery death. Koresh promoted an offshoot version of Seventh Day Adventist belief, and preached that a catastrophic apocalypse would come soon. In 1978 over nine hundred people joined in a mass suicide (with some homicides) in Jonestown, Guyana, following the orders of their leader, the Reverend Jim Jones. Far less lethal but still disturbing are reports about The Family, originally called The Children of God by its founder, Moses David Berg. The beliefs and practices of this group once included "flirty fishing," young women offering themselves for sexual relations in order to make connections with potential converts. The leader recommended educating young children into at least some sexual contact with adults.

Such self-destructive or disturbing forms of new religious movements should not be taken as at all typical. In spite of many charges made by anti-cult groups, most NRMs are not much different from traditional religions in the effect they have on their adherents. On the other hand, the extremes to which people can be brought by religion illustrates that for many people any religion, no matter how odd, has more appeal than a secularized life.

The Vitality of Non-Western Traditions

Islam remains energetically alive around the world. From the largest Muslim nation, Indonesia, westward around the world even to the Americas, Islam is growing. Westerners hear of "Muslim fundamentalism." Those who write on Islam more often refer to this as the Islamist movement. It includes both a traditionalist religious dimension and a political goal.

Many Muslims have experienced colonization by European powers, find themselves still politically weak on the world stage, and see secular humanist and exploitative capitalist elements intruding where Qur'anic morality ought to rule. In reaction, Islamists look to their own traditions to find an alternative social and political format, true to the Qur'an, and more likely, they believe, to provide a Godly rightness and strength to their lives.

Islamic tradition holds that the civil government ideally should not be divorced from religious influence. The government's actions should always be approved by the uluma—the scholars well educated in the Qur'an and hadith (tradition), able therefore to give valid interpretations. Where Shi'ite (partisan) Islam predominates there may be an official clergy who can perform this role. Laws, election processes, and candidates for election in the Islamic Republic of Iran must be approved by the Council of Guardians, composed of some of the highest clergy in Iran.

As Chapter Ten mentioned briefly, a strict Sunni (traditional) version arose in Arabia in the eighteenth century, called the Wahhabi movement, named after its founder Muhammad ibn Abd al-Wahhab (1703-1791). It was intent on cleansing Islam of Sufi accretions such as fervid dancing, which the Wahhabi called "magical rituals," and the veneration of certain Sufi leaders as saints, which the Wahhabi thought of as idolatry. The Wahhabi leaders succeeded in imposing their views on most of Arabia through an alliance with the Saud tribe, whose eighteenth-century sheik was an excellent military leader. After more than a century of successes and failures, King Ibn Saud regained authority for his family over Arabia in the early twentieth century, and re-established the strict and traditionalist Wahhabi approach to Islam.

The Saudi family has considered it its duty to promote Islamist movements, and has done so in various countries. Members of this family, along with other citizens of the oil-rich gulf states, have the money to fund many Islamist groups. Sufism has long predominated in Sudan, for example, but a Sunni Islamist movement took over the government not long ago, under the name of the National Islamic Front and with roots in the Muslim Brotherhood that is also active in Egypt. Gulf oil money flows to charitable institutions to help the poor and weak, as well as to terrorist groups. It is usually difficult to keep track of where the money goes.

Finally, amidst all this, in various nations at least some modernizing Muslim voices recommend that more attention be paid to the rationalistic Muslim philosophers of the ninth and later centuries, CE (second century A.H. —*Anno Hegira*). These are called the Mu'tazili, some of whom strongly influenced late medieval Christians like Aquinas. These modernizing voices invoke the Mu'tazili as an authentically Muslim precedent for entering more fully into the scientific rationality that pervades the world today. The ferment among these and other variants of Islam shows the continuing vitality of this complex tradition.

Islam is not the only tradition to manifest continuing vitality. In India, many of the better educated leaders had their own version of a secularization thesis, though they were willing to link it to the more philosophically sophisticated aspects of Hindu thought, as in the theology of Shankara. But throughout India the traditional caste system is still extremely strong, the thousands of gods still receive their care and worship, the stories of Krishna and Rama are still cherished, and religion strongly influences politics.

Buddhism is still powerful across southeast Asia and the Far East. A Japanese variant called "Zen Buddhism," which stresses meditative practices, has proved popular in the Western world. Soka Gakkai International is expanding into various Western nations. It too has ancient roots, as a lay offshoot of a form of Buddhism developed by a thirteenth-century Japanese Buddhist monk, Nichiren. He taught that devotion to the mystic teaching of spiritual cause and effect, symbolized by the lotus which both blossoms (effect) and seeds (cause) at the same time, will create a deep compassion for all suffering and lead to world peace. An interesting Buddhist-derived NRM is developing currently in Kenya. A Englishman named Benjamin Creme proclaims that a Kenyan of Indian origins is the Maitreya Buddha, the fifth appearance of the Buddha in cosmic history, one whom people have been waiting for also in the form of the Christ or Messiah, Krishna, and the Mahdi (the one guided by Allah).

In the light of these and other ways that people show continuing interest in a religious approach to life, the secularization thesis might seem untenable. On the other hand, the example of Europe shows that secularization can reduce religions collectively to a minority position. It is probably too soon to predict the long-term fate of religion in Russia, for example, where Orthodox Christianity now has more freedom than in the past, but where it has to compete with eager Christian fundamentalist missionaries from the West. Predicting the future of religion in general is an even more difficult task.

It may be more useful first to take note again of differences in basic styles of religiousness, from primitive to modern. They exist together today as different styles of religiousness even among people in the same synagogue, temple, church or masjid (mosque). Different styles of religiousness lead people to respond differently to skepticism and secularization.

Stages and Styles of Religion Today

James Fowler's Stages of Faith

There are numerous analyses of stages of individual development. Piagetian and Neo-Piagetian and post-Piagetian scholars argue over many aspects of cognitive development. Kohlbergians and post-Kohlbergians do the same about moral development. James Fowler has used the ideas of Piaget and

Kohlberg and others in his own study of what he calls "stages of faith" in a 1981 book by that name. Because he both integrates the ideas of a number of sources and is concerned with faith development, his analysis forms a useful guide for the following summaries.

Much of this book has been devoted to showing differences among primitive, archaic, historic or classical, and modern modes of religion. As the Preface indicated, individual development proceeds along a path similar to cultural development. To explain this there need be no hidden power pushing history along a certain path, as some nineteenth-century philosophers believed. There need be no law of history that individual development "recapitulates" cultural development. Both cultures and individuals may simply require time to develop more complex modes of thought. History shows that cultures need centuries or even thousands of years to develop complex cognitive tools such as literacy or formalized logic. Similarly, in an individual's life, a person first learns simpler cognitive methods and slowly becomes educated in the more difficult modes of thought that took the culture many centuries to develop. This occurs also in religion.

In the case of both cultures and individuals, the process of development is not one in which earlier modes of thought are simply rejected and replaced by later ones. Rather, it is usually a cumulative process, where earlier and simpler thought styles are enriched or reinterpreted through the addition of new and more complex thought styles. We have seen, for example, that preliterate cultures use simple folk tales to express their origins and how things came to be in the world, and that only after literacy appears do cultures develop complex epic myths with a unified plot. Yet often the folktales are not left behind but are incorporated into the larger myth. Similarly in individual development, the tale of The Three Little Pigs or of Little Red Riding Hood are beyond the full comprehension of a two-year-old, but are easily understood by the five-year-old. Not until the age of ten or so will a child be able to grasp that the many chapters of a bigger book contain not many separate stories about the same cast of characters but a single long complex story. Yet the ten-year-old will still enjoy telling the story of The Three Little Pigs or Little Red Riding Hood and explain aspects of them to a younger sibling.

Those who readily accept the power of crystals to change moods, or hear the words of ancient souls channeled by certain people today, seem to rely on the imaginative powers that we all first enjoy from as early as the age of two or so. The fast growing minds of young children latch on to countless ideas without much ability to distinguish between what is fact and what is fantasy. Whatever ideas lodge in the child's mind seem true just by their vivid presence. Thus a four-year-old believes readily in Santa Claus, has an invisible friend, and fears monsters under the bed. For the four-year-old, adults and older children constitute the major authoritative source of beliefs. This susceptibility to believe whatever is truly vivid and interesting can remain with people throughout their lives. So the earliest standards of belief—the authority of people in the know, and the vividness of ideas—are always with us in any society.

Around the age of seven or so, however, as Fowler and others describe it, most children enter a new stage of thought. They become aware of a clear distinction between fact and fantasy. They become capable of using firsthand experience and simple logic to test some ideas. They realize, for example, that not even a Santa Claus could possibly bring toys to all the millions of children of the world in a single night. If they are told that they used to have an invisible friend, they are likely to insist that they were never so silly as that. The monsters under the bed disappear (most of them, at least). Yet if authoritative adults assure them that angels really do exist, even if Santa Claus does not, the child will accept this. Imagination is now under the control of a serious intent to distinguish between fact and fantasy, but the standard of listening to authority remains. The seven-year-old child also begins to have a clearer sense of the reality of a larger society. As the child matures, society takes on an authoritative role as a source of knowing what is true or false, good or bad, proper or improper to do. Obviously, this also remains true for people throughout their lives.

In early adolescence, yet another stage usually appears. The adolescent's awareness expands to include the larger world, in a kind of late archaic perspective. The adolescent needs a large narrative which encompasses major aspects of life all at once and, most importantly, tells the adolescent where she or he may fit in this story. It might be the story of the cosmos told in the Mahabharata, particularly in the Bhagavad Gita's story of Krishna, the charioteer, explaining all of life to the warrior Arjuna, on the verge of a great battle among clans. Or it may be the epic of the universe in Hebrew, from the six days of creation, through a long history of interaction with God, to the messianic age. Christians find their main focus in the story of Jesus, whose teachings and sacrificial death and resurrection into new life make sense of things for Christians.

The stories have greatest effect if there is a heroic figure or two with whom the listener might identify. These grand narratives are "personal" in the sense that they are not abstract analyses; instead they are vivid tales of personal beings to whom the adolescent can feel some relationship. The religious narratives themselves are accepted as the proper standards for evaluating all beliefs and morals and practices, though the consensus of the larger religious community and the tradition behind the narrative provides authority to authenticate it.

Fowler calls this early adolescent style of thought and faith the "synthetic-conventional." This basic style may remain dominant for the person's whole life, even though continuing life experiences will enrich it greatly. Most of us synthesize or sum up the meaning of life through some grand narratives, whether about Moses or the Buddha or Krishna or Jesus or Muhammad. Most of us are conventional in the sense that we accept certain narratives as part of the conventional truths we learn from others. Most people continue to learn from pastors, priests, and rabbis, from gurus and imams. Most find these instructions reinforced by their religious community. The synthetic-conventional style supports social cohesion and cooperation, and provides a secure identity and set of values for the individual. On the other hand, it also supports conformity, even to ideas and values and practices that might otherwise be rejected.

By late adolescence, however, a fourth stage may emerge. People in cultures with elaborate systems of formal education receive training in the more abstract and systematic methods of analysis that historic culture first developed. Mathematical training in school prepares the way, through the logical structures of geometry and algebra. Techniques of debating issues pro and con challenge students to carefully line up evidence both for and against certain positions, to search out logical inconsistencies in the arguments used to support those positions. Essay writing, social science classes, the sciences, philosophy and theology, all include lessons in how to think logically and analytically. People in any culture have the innate intelligence to use these methods, but not all cultures provide training in them.

Not all people who are trained this way will find these methods appealing. Some may learn to use them in certain restricted areas of life but exclude them from other areas. It takes long years of formal training to become comfortable with highly abstract and systematic thought. It may also seem simply wrong to be too logical about one's interpersonal relations. The religious relation a person has with God or Krishna or Amida Buddha may be exempted from any sort of rational analysis or criticism. That is why "faith" is more often the norm for religious belief than "reason." It may also be why the synthetic-conventional approach has continuing appeal.

We have seen many people, however, who think it quite appropriate to apply strict standards of abstract reasoning to their religious beliefs. This practice sometimes turns excessively self-confident as in the case of both religious dogmatism and early modern science. But it can also be a positive tool for identifying inconsistencies and increasing internal coherence in a religious tradition. Or it may serve an "apologetic" role, to show the reasonableness of the beliefs. The theology discussed in Chapter Eleven relies on tools of rationality. Enlightenment deism is another example.

A recent school of thought called postmodernism claims to have surpassed the universalizing rationality of the Enlightenment, by showing that we cannot know whether any truths or values are universally valid, because all truths and values are "socially constructed." This has implications for religious thought.

POSTMODERISM AND RELIGION

So far in this book, the word "modern" has been used as Talcott Parsons and Robert Bellah used it, to identify in a general way how religion has been influenced by the style of modern science, which is now more tentative than it originally was, and by other prevailing ideas in European-based culture, such as greater religious tolerance and an acceptance of this world. But as the first part of Chapter Fourteen indicated, the meaning of "modern" has shifted in the last two decades. Unfortunately, the shift of meaning has not been towards clear and well-defined usage. So it would not help much to try to change each use of the word "modern" in this book. But here are some guidelines on how to understand the word when it is used today.

People tend to think of their own times as "modern," and previous centuries as pre-modern. We have already seen, however, that this common usage is not what historians and philosophers have in mind when they use the term. For them, "modern" may apply all the way back to the early seventeenth century. In fact the core era of the European Enlightenment, the eighteenth century, is the epitome of what the word "modern" has recently come to mean. Philosophers and historians (and literary critics and theologians and others) now identify the "modern" precisely with the great confidence in rational inquiry and analysis that characterized the Enlightenment. (Ironically, as the Introduction to Part IV indicated, this means that the label "modern" has come to be used for the devotion to rationality one can also find in ancient classical or historic thought, as in Greek philosophy and in some Chinese and Indian philosophies.) According to this use of the word "modern," some claim that we no longer live in modern times but in postmodern times, though the modern lingers with us, as do the archaic and primitive also. Yet there are others who think of postmodernism as just a recent competitor to an equally vital late modern approach.

To sort all this into clearer categories, we can divide the modern into early and late forms, and then compare both of them with the postmodern. Early modern thought consists of the classical self-confident rationality of early modern science in the Enlightenment. (Note again that many people still maintain this approach to knowledge.) Late modern thought consists of the more cautious approach that slowly developed in science, as scientists and philosophers began to recognize that science advances precisely by maintaining a degree of self-critical doubt or skepticism about its own conclusions (as described in Chapter Thirteen). This gets us closer to the notion of "postmodern."

Postmodern is the label for various theories which argue that the rationality of both the modern Enlightenment and also of late modern self-critical science share an important limitation. Both of them, like all human ideas, are socially constructed. (Some philosophers speak more of a "linguistic" construction of reality, to highlight the role that language plays in transmitting social reality to us.) Just as Berger argued that social norms, identities, and religious viewpoints are constructed by people over time, postmodernists argue that all human ideas are products also of their time and place. According to postmodernists this includes not only religion, morality, and the social order, but even science.

A religion may appear to its adherents to be the single universally valid religion. The postmodernist, however, says this is a socially constructed belief, reflecting the bias and interests and values of the social history behind it. A postmodernist could perhaps say that this or that religion might actually be universally valid, but that there is no outside objective place to stand in order to figure out which religion that is. So in practice believers can go on believing in the single universal validity of their own religious tradition. But they should not expect an outsider to agree (especially if that outsider is a postmodernist).

A postmodernist will likewise say that every moral code is a social product. "Modern" Enlightenment thought argued that there are universal human rights. "All men are created equal and endowed by their Creator with inalienable rights to life, liberty, and the pursuit of happiness" says the 1776 U.S. Declaration of Independence. Postmodernism points out that the Declaration of Independence was the product of Enlightenment theories, formulated in the West, by peoples with a common religious heritage. Therefore this declaration of rights is valid in those societies which support it, but not necessarily in other societies.

Postmodernism usually treats science the same as it treats religion and morality. Both early modern science and later modern science are produced by people with certain ideological biases and certain local interests and certain presuppositions that are shared by people of their time and place. Therefore a scientific picture of reality may just reflect the social context that produced it and have no lasting or universal validity. In general, then, postmodernists claim that no framework for understanding things is universally valid.

Postmodernism and Cultural Relativism

To an extent postmodernism is just cultural relativism given a philosophical justification. Cultural relativists argue that every culture has its own beliefs and practices that constitute a well-functioning social reality ("functionalism" is another name for this viewpoint). This means that the beliefs and practices of a society can be judged only in terms of how well they function in that society, not in terms of whether they are compatible with the beliefs and practices of other societies. This leads to the further conclusion that European and North American imperialists and colonialists should not impose their values on other cultures. Every culture should be respected as it is.

That includes a culture's religious beliefs. If a group that is called "primitive" from a European-American perspective happens to believe that the spirits of the ancestors offer guidance through dreams, then the European-American visitors to that group should respect those beliefs and not call them superstitious or primitive. The same would be true about belief that all illness and death is caused by sorcery, or that certain animals are sacred and must not be killed. Missionaries should not try to replace one society's traditions with outside traditions. So says cultural relativism.

There are at least two problems with cultural relativism. One is that not all the beliefs and practices of a culture are truly well-functioning. The belief that illness and death are caused by sorcery leads to constant suspicion and fights. Innocent people are accused of sorcery, just as in the witch hunts of early modern Europe. Feuds between families break out, to avenge the death of the supposed victim. When given a chance to use modern medicine to cure a child, many primitive people have decided that modern medicine is more effective in promoting the child's health than the traditional shamanistic rituals for driving out harmful spirits.

A second problem with cultural relativism is that it is very hard for even the cultural relativists to maintain when the relativists are faced with certain practices. Should we treat infanticide and forced female "circumcision" and slavery simply as the customs of others which we cannot legitimately judge? Should abuse of the poor by a small, well-armed dictatorial class be deemed acceptable as long as it is part of the religious tradition of the culture? Cultural relativism seems to imply that a society which does not respect human rights, has a long tradition of not respecting human rights, and lacks a religion which argues for human rights, can therefore legitimately ignore human rights.

The type of answer usually given by a postmodernist is that those of us who believe in human rights should try to get other societies to change their social customs until they do accept and support human rights. Our belief that every human being everywhere deserves to be treated with at least a certain minimum human dignity is a belief worth propagating. But this puts the postmodernist in the position of trying to make certain values universal. The postmodernist is stepping beyond a given social context to try to get all societies to share some ideas. The goal then is to make some values universal and not just relative to certain cultures. This will not be entirely difficult.

It is not European-American culture alone that provides a basis for human rights. Many historic religious traditions of the world tend to preach universal compassion, or that people everywhere should not do to others what they do not like done to themselves.

Postmodernism also steps beyond relativism in at least one of its conclusions. Postmodern thought arrives at what it claims to be a universal truth, that every society is constructed by people's subjective ideas, and that people's ideas are first formed by a prior social context. To be consistent, they should say that their own social context thought led them to think this way.

Postmodernists also step beyond relativism by the way they arrive at this conclusion. They use rational arguments based on evidence. Postmodern thought appeals to the evidence about how we learn and think, about the variations among cultures, and about the dependence of every person upon a social context for the person's language, early beliefs, sense of identity, and values. Postmodern thought then makes a rational case of what the evidence implies. By using evidence and logic to make their case, postmodernists are participating in a human practice that is far older than postmodernism, and which is spread across historic or classical as well as modern cultures. They may in fact be using a universally effective method of thought when they rely on evidence and logic, as Chapter Eleven indicated.

Postmodernists, then, have some problems with inner consistency. They say there are no universally valid truths, yet in practice they promote universal values, use a universal rational method, and promote their own theory as universally valid.

Nevertheless, postmodernism has many adherents because it offers methods other than scientific rationality for evaluating truth-claims. Postmodernism says there can be many methods for deciding what is true, depending on one's community. Many postmodernists also insist that there is more than one kind of truth—literary truth, moral truth, religious truth, for example. Others like postmodern relativism because it helps to establish respect for different cultures, including hunting-gathering cultures. Among those it especially appeals to are religious thinkers who find postmodernism useful as a defense against both secularism and challenges by science.

A Postmodernist Form of Anti-Secularism

Modern theologies have tended first to accept the modern secular world and then to see how religious tradition can be interpreted in response to that world. There are many in religion who think the opposite should be the case, that theology should either reject the secular world or challenge that world to change and conform to the ideals promoted by religion. Christian Fundamentalists do this. Islamists do also. But they are not alone.

Among religious people there are two camps that might be called accommodationists and anti-accommodationists. The accommodationists engage in a form of what Tillich called "correlational theology" (see Chapter Eleven), a phrase that eventually came to mean a reciprocal interaction between the religious tradition and the modern secular world. The accommodationist perspective maintains that both the religious tradition and the world can not only challenge each other but that they can learn from each other as well. Each side will sometimes end up making accommodations to the needs and vision of the other. Accommodationists are usually "modern" in their willingness to appreciate secularity and the value of religious tolerance.

Anti-accommodationists, as you might expect from the name, think that the job of religion is not to accommodate itself to the world but to confront and guide the world. Theologians should spend less time re-interpreting their own tradition and more time being true to it. Secular rationality is the problem, not the answer. On issues of war and poverty and abortion the churches ought to take a stand like the prophets of the Hebrew scriptures, standing up against the common wisdom of secular culture in order to pass judgment on that culture where it fails morally.

Postmodernism provides a way to justify anti-accommodationism. In an influential book, *The Nature of Doctrine* (1984), George Lindbeck (1923-) argues against the claim by Schleiermacher and other liberal theologians, that the basis of religion is an individual experience of the Whole, an experience that any person anywhere can have. Instead, Lindbeck argues, we should recognize that every person becomes religious through some particular social context. Every religious group is a social reality, what he calls a "cultural-linguistic" form of life for a community. Each community has its basic narratives which deal with the most important dimensions of life. There is no need to give in to or accommodate the standards of other groups, including secular standards. Each community of faith can legitimately focus on its own way of life, strengthen that way of life, and speak from it to the rest of the world. Lindbeck calls this application of postmodern thought to religion a "postliberal" theology.

This means that postmodernism gives at least implicit support to the hidden logic of blind faith described in Chapter Eleven. By default, there is no place to go to find the truth and basic values about life except to some community, to some society and its tradition. What counts in the end is simply whether the community and its tradition provide a coherent and meaningful form of life. Postmodernism tends to emphasize the role "master narratives" play in teaching people people in the community who they are and what is important and how to live. If the narratives of a religious tradition enable people to deal well with all the confusion and challenges of life, one could then argue that is enough. If the secular world fails to provide a compelling enough story for a fully meaningful life, that makes religious faith all the more reasonable.

Postmodernism Limits Science

Science can challenge religious traditions both by the conclusions that it reaches and by its method. Fundamentalists are bothered by any conclusions of science that run contrary to a literal reading of scripture. That is a major reason fundamentalists oppose the theory of evolution. The book of Genesis says that God made the first man and woman, probably about six thousand years ago. To attribute human origins to evolution taking place over billions of years must therefore be wrong. But fundamentalists often try themselves to use scientific methods to attack evolution. They gather evidence to show evolution is incorrect. (It is incompetent science, short on relevant data, misleading in its arguments, and has often been irresponsible in its use of citations from other sources, but it nonetheless tries to appeal to empirical evidence and rational analysis.)

As we saw in earlier chapters, both the method of science and some of its conclusions challenge even those religious believers who are not fundamentalists. As was said, science operates by methodological naturalism, treating every event as though it were due to natural causes alone. That means that science cannot allow the hypothesis that some supernatural cause was at work. So the method of science at least implicitly challenges belief in miracles. Recall also that as science has progressed it has been able to show that many things that once looked miraculous have natural explanations. Hence the expression "God of the gaps," to indicate that divine intervention is appearing only in fewer and fewer apparent gaps in the natural order. The implication is that perhaps all the gaps can someday be closed up. Similarly even non-fundamentalists can also be bothered by the implications of the theory of evolution, as we have seen, because it makes the world look unplanned and human life just an accident of a partly random process.

Postmodernism provides a shield against science by arguing that even science, that supposedly objective and universally valid enterprise, is actually the product of a certain social context. Historians of science have written influential histories of this or that scientific discovery, starting with Copernicus, Galileo, and Boyle, to show social influences at work in the formulation and spread of various methods and conclusions. (Thomas Kuhn is the most famous of these historians. He is the one who popularized the word "paradigm" to stand for a big theory or a basic worldview.) The implication is that science is not objective, and that when society changes science may change also. If a religious person, then, has a religious community that provides a vivifying guide to all of life, but disagrees with scientific thought on some point (such as the reality of miracles), postmodernism says it is legitimate to ignore science and be true to the way of life of the religious tradition.

The Late Modern, Postmodernism, and Fowler's Stages

Four of Fowler's stages have been described already. The last of them mentioned so far is the tendency among many in late adolescence to have such great certainty in the power of rationality that their religiousness becomes rather dogmatic. Early modern science shared this characteristic. Later modern science recognized the tentativeness of ideas, even though there was great confidence in those that had withstood a long process of testing and application. Similarly, in their adult years many people become less dogmatic about their beliefs and values, even while holding on to them. It is a stage of increased self-awareness, of self-transcendence in the vocabulary of Chapters Four and Fourteen here. This is the ability to step outside oneself, as it were, to be aware of one's own ideas and values as an observer of those thoughts and values and ask questions about them. The late modern self-reflective person is called upon to take individual responsibility for one's own theories, beliefs, values, and commitments. This is the new way of understanding the self discussed in Chapter Thirteen.

This is quite similar to what Fowler describes as a fifth stage of faith development. He calls it "conjunctive" faith, in which a person faces various deep issues in life and brings them together (conjoins them) coherently by making some fundamental commitments to an overall vision of life. The morality of this fifth stage is much like basic value morality. This faith is a decision to trust in life's meaningfulness, in spite of an inability to prove that any clear set of beliefs about life is the ultimate truth.

Fowler says that a danger of this stage is a temptation to passivity, despair, or cynicism. If no one really knows for sure what is valuable or not, why is anything worth choosing? If all of our beliefs and values are just fictions produced by this or that social context, why take any of it seriously? A person might just as well drift along on the surface of life, grabbing a little enjoyment as opportunities arise.

Postmodernism can respond to this danger not by the late modern appeal to individual commitment but by an appeal to trust in the community which formed the ideas and values by which the person lives. Postmodernism argues that we can never be fully responsible as individuals, because our beliefs and values are all the product of some community or another—even our belief in individual responsibility, if we have such a belief. When we commit ourselves to a certain way of life, then, we are really trusting in the community that formed us.

But we have just seen that even the postmodernists are not quite as post-modern as they claim. They want to make universally valid statements about the human condition, in particular about the effects of social contexts on all people, on all ideas and values. They also act as though using evidence and logic is an effective way to arrive at such universally valid statements. They act as though it were worth being a knower in the world (Chapter Fourteen). They usually promote concern and compassion for all people, including those who are different in any way. Their belief that different social contexts may all be valid makes them extend concern towards every one who is "other." Regardless of race, ethnicity, religion, gender, or sexual orientation, say the postmodernists, we should respect everyone.

So both late modern people and postmodernists often end up doing the same thing—make commitments. Without dogmatic certitudes, they can nonetheless commit themselves to a view that there is ultimate value in personness and in the world. The commitments of both late modern and postmodern people may be guided by ideas from tradition and authority figures passed on in a community context. But some communities teach people they must finally make their own individual commitments—who to be, how to live, what values to live by and for, how best to learn what is probably true, and whether or not to choose a given religious perspective. This is the "conjunctive" stage which Fowler describes as a fifth and final stage of religious development.

It would take another book to address these issues adequately. But it is important to at least look at a problem raised by postmodernism and cultural relativism, the problem of whether it is legitimate to evaluate religion except from within. The Epilogue will take up this task. It shifts the focus of attention from an attempt to describe religion, which has been the main goal of this book, to attempts to evaluate religion.

Summary

Predictions that religion would fade away have not come true. Some forms of traditional religion have weakened, but new religious movements, New Age thought, revivals such as those among Pentecostals and Muslims and Hindus, all exhibit ongoing religious vitality. Modern religion's appreciation of greater individual freedom has made religion more private and personal in many cases. Postmodernism has supported the notion that every religious group has a way of life that need not justify itself by any standards except its own. Religious people have to choose between more or less accommodation to secular and scientific rationality.

For Further Reflection

1. Do you think you have enough evidence to judge whether the secularization theory is simply wrong? Explain.
2. Give reasons why either accommodationism or anti-accommodationism is a better approach.
3. Some have said that when they read James Fowler's theory of stages of faith development, that it reminds them of their own life so far. To what extent is this true of you?
4. To what extent are you persuaded by postmodernist arguments that science is not universally or objectively valid?

Suggested Readings

Harvey Cox, "The Rise and Fall of 'Secularization,'" 135-43 in Gregory Baum, ed., *The Twentieth Century: A Theological Overview*, 1999.

Peter L. Berger, ed., *The Desecularization of the World: Resurgent Religion and World Politics*, 1999. Includes material on Islam today.

Bryan Wilson and James Cresswell, eds. *New Religious Movements: Challenge and Response*, 1999, especially the first chapter by Eileen Barker.

Helen A. Berger, *A Community of Witches: Contemporary Neo-paganism and Witchcraft in the United States*, 1999.

James R. Lewis, ed., *The Gods Have Landed: New Religions from Other Worlds*, 1995.

Ted Peters, *The Cosmic Self: A Penetrating Look at Today's New Age Movements*, 1991.

J. Gordon Melton, "European Receptivity to the New Religions," 18-30 in Helle Meldgaard and Johannes Aagaard, eds., *New Religious Movements in Europe*, 1997.

EPILOGUE

Evaluating Religion(s)

TO EVALUATE OR NOT

Evaluation is part of any academic study, including the study of religion. In a literature course students apply criteria for evaluating the literary merits of a work. In a political science course students review arguments for and against different forms of government. Why not also make evaluation part of the study of religion? The validity of the truth claims and the moral norms of various religions can be subjected to some interesting questions. So can the overall impact of this or that religion on peoples' lives.

On the other hand, religion is touchier than politics or literature. In many modern nations it is considered a rather personal matter. Because we each have the right to believe as we choose, perhaps it is better not to try to evaluate different forms of religion at all. Postmodernism and cultural relativism support this by their claim that there are no objectively valid standards to use in making an evaluation of religion.

In one sense, however, it is too late to avoid evaluation. Atheists and agnostics have already offered their evaluations. If this were a textbook on the philosophy of religion, many segments would be devoted to the criticism of religion advanced by philosophers like David Hume and Karl Marx, or sociologists like Max Weber and Emile Durkheim. Various skeptical groups today continue to challenge religious beliefs. Nonetheless, there are many who argue that it is better just to appreciate the development and diversity of religion, without engaging in critical evaluation of the truth claims and moral norms of various religions, or evaluating of the impact of religion on people's lives.

Many religions have agreed for a very traditional reason. They say that the only truth a person needs to know is the revelation from God, or a sacred text, or the prophetic vision that is the source of that religion. No human evaluation is legitimate if the evaluation challenges what comes from the divine or sacred source. Fallible human minds have neither the ability nor the right to question the divine. Orthodox Hindus know that the basic truths about karma and dharma contained in the Vedic tradition are the unquestionable truth. Traditionalist Muslims accept God's message contained in the

Qur'an as eternal truth. Fundamentalist Christians believe that God inspired the very words of the scriptures. In these and other cases, human evaluation can be an affront to the tradition itself. The only question allowed is whether a person is faithful to the tradition.

But avoiding evaluations has its costs. To avoid evaluating the plausibility of truth claims, even religious truth claims, is to act as though it were legitimate to ignore standards of truth in some areas of life. To avoid evaluating the validity of moral norms, including religious norms, is to act as though those moral rules were exempt from challenge. To avoid evaluating the impact of a religious tradition on people's lives is to act as though it made no difference whether religion is helpful or harmful. In all these cases, to avoid evaluating tradition may allow harmful human interpretations or accretions to creep in. Many religious traditions, for example, have seen nothing wrong with slavery.

Furthermore, religious traditions tend to engage in their own internal evaluation, particularly as apologetics to defend that tradition. Such evaluations are normally quite positive, of course. We have seen that a good Muslim will argue that the poetic beauty of the Qur'an shows that it was not composed by the illiterate Messenger but comes directly from God. Here literary criteria are used to evaluate the sacred text. Early Christians used prophetic messages in the Hebrew scriptures to show that Jesus fulfilled certain prophecies. These Christians were arguing that the evidence of the Hebrew scriptures pointed to Jesus. This evidence was used to verify his mission and identity. There are studies today claiming to have evidence that those who are prayed for get well more quickly, even when they do not know about the prayers. This is offered as evidence of the power of prayer.

Most religious believers would probably prefer to offer an evaluation of their own religious tradition as a whole, linking together the beliefs, moral norms, sacred texts, symbols and rituals, and form of community, with a concern to show the connection of the present forms of the religion with its roots and tradition. A Sunni Muslim, for example, appeals to the consensus of the Muslim community about traditions which can be traced back to the noble disciples of Muhammad, who wrote down the words of the Qur'an as Muhammad recited them, and who interpreted these words in light of the life of Muhammad. It is this whole tradition, not just a particular doctrine or moral rule, that deserves evaluation, says the Muslim, and a very positive evaluation at that.

Yet even the good Muslim may sometimes evaluate selectively. One who cherishes the Qur'an and the tradition might nonetheless urge fellow Muslims to recapture the more rationalist and scientific spirit of many ninth- to eleventh-century Muslim philosophers (the Mu'tazili). This spirit was suppressed by faithful Muslims concerned that rationalist inquiry could undercut pious beliefs with overly critical questions. In the scientific era of the twenty-first century, a good Muslim might argue, it may be time to recover this philosophical spirit. In almost any religious tradition, there are those who praise highly one aspect of their faith but seek some changes in other aspects. Not all aspects are considered equally worthy of belief.

This is perhaps inevitable because religions are so complex. They include truth-claims, moral standards, ritual practices, sacred texts, and forms of social relations. The methods a person uses to evaluate a truth-claim will not necessarily be the same as the methods for evaluating a moral standard. A religious tradition may even use different standards for different parts of one of these categories. The Catholic Church offers strong support for the kind of social morality that the rather unreligious American Humanist Association also supports. Both oppose the death penalty; both promote liberal social programs by the government. Yet that same Church is at odds with the AHA on abortion and homosexual activity.

Academic Evaluation

In addition to the evaluations offered by atheists and agnostics on the one hand, and by religions themselves on the other, there is a third type of evaluation that can at least be attempted. We can call it an academic evaluation. This would be an attempt to correlate religious truth claims, moral norms, and the impact of religion on people's lives with relevant criteria of truth, morality, and standards of what is or is not good for people. The ideal relevant criteria would have to be validated, as though they were objectively correct and not just criteria reflecting some social interests or bias or tradition. And these ideally objective criteria would also need to be applied with a high degree of objectivity.

Identifying objectively valid norms and applying them with objective impartiality may be impossible goals, however. We have seen Berger and the postmodernists argue that all criteria are relative to the social context in which they arose, and that every person carries some hidden presuppositions and values that will distort any criteria that are applied. Everyone is raised somewhere, by some caretakers, in some social setting. Every location and family and society educates a person into a certain way of thinking. As was mentioned in a previous chapter, that is why the people of India tend mostly to be Hindus or Muslims, and the people of Brazil to be Christians.

An academic evaluation tries to compensate for individual bias and interest in applying standards of evaluation by using rules similar to those that science follows:

1) The evaluation must be conducted through public argumentation, so that others have a chance to identify any hidden presuppositions or values at work in the evaluation;

2) Anyone should have the opportunity to challenge the presuppositions and values and ask that they be justified in terms that people in general would find reasonable;

3) The evaluation is open-ended, always subject to further challenge; and

4) In the case of truth-claims made about the religion or by the religion, the criteria of "fit" with the evidence are to be used.

The intent of these standards is to move closer to the equivalent of objectivity. In theory a fully objective viewpoint is one that any truly intelligent, adequately informed, and open-minded person should agree with. Because it can be difficult to find many such persons, the alternative is to look for conclusions and arguments that even we moderately intelligent, partially informed, and somewhat biased people find reasonable. Conclusions and arguments that survive attack from all sides can be "warranted," as the philosophers say, if they have sufficient evidence and logic to be persuasive even to people with different interests and raised in different societies.

But if some degree of objectivity can be attained in applying standards of evaluation, there remains the problem of deciding which standards are appropriate in the first place. When it is time to evaluate a religious tradition, or even evaluate religion in general (if there is such a thing), what kind of criteria should be applied? Why should religious truth-claims have to meet the criteria of evidence and logic, for example? If we cannot know for certain which standards should ideally count, can we fall back on some general agreement, among people with differing biases and interests and education and social location, as to which criteria are appropriate for evaluating religion, and how to apply them?

The descriptions in Chapter Eight of different types of moral reasoning, and in Chapter Fifteen of different stages of faith with different styles of thought, warn us that the prospects for any such general agreement are not likely. Knowledge that there are different stages of development makes us aware that each of us tends to rely on different standards of truth and value. Any given group of people will disagree among themselves on the relative importance of conforming to the group or finding specific universal moral laws. The same group of people will disagree among themselves about how much traditional authority is to be respected, or how much trust should be given to rationality and evidence.

On the other hand, the descriptions of types of moral reasoning and religious thought can narrow down the field of what we need to think about. We can compare the different kinds of evaluations that each of those stages would make. The various developmental theories suggest there are four major criteria that people use in evaluating whether beliefs are true. At each stage a different criterion tends to dominate. One criterion is how vividly the beliefs appeal to the imagination (though this is not what imaginative people would normally consider a primary criterion). A second is the authority of a community and its tradition. The third is the power of a narrative to give shape and meaning to a person's life. And the fourth criterion is to test beliefs by an appeal to reason and evidence. The point at which a person learns the limits of reason and evidence, thereby becoming less dogmatic and more tentative, may deserve to be called a fifth stage. A review of these stages and their criteria will clarify what options are available. Some of those options will probably be more attractive than others.

Stage Styles and Criteria for Belief

A description of the typical thought style of young children reminds us that adults sometimes also believe ideas just because those ideas are vivid or dramatically interesting. On the face of it, one would hardly find it probable that an image that looks a bit like Jesus or Mary appearing in a tortilla or on the side of an oil storage tank is really a divine miracle. Yet many adults have believed such imaginative claims. The gods and demons of Buddhist tradition are similarly fascinating. The great flood in Noah's time is a wonderful story. The fact that they appeal to the imagination, however, does not make them credible.

We can also learn from the behavior of older children, who are interested in discriminating clearly between truth and fancy. Like them, many adults will trust their own first-hand experiences and simple logic to identify false or highly improbable truth-claims. Like them, most adults will also trust the authority of their society. What everyone believes to be true or good, particularly that which is supported by religious leaders, is easy to hold as the truth. But there are many religions, with major differences in beliefs and values. Each of them is part of a social tradition which assures individuals that these beliefs and values are correct. And each also includes some rather vivid and dramatic ideas, for that matter.

Because some religious beliefs and values flatly contradict the beliefs and values of other religious traditions, at least one of these traditions is in some error. Muslims in India are highly conscious of this, because their tradition emphasizes the error of worshiping gods, but the worship of gods is the common religion of India. Protestants in Northern Ireland are conscious of this, because they fear that assimilation into a united Ireland will place them under laws that fit with Catholic morality. How does a person know which tradition, which set of socially approved ideas, is correct? Some criterion is needed beyond just the authority of the tradition or society.

The experience of early adolescence reminds us of the power of a grand narrative. Such narratives might be persuasive because they appeal to the imagination as vivid and dramatic tales, or because social authority stands behind them. But a grand narrative may also implicitly appeal to the hidden logic of blind faith described in Chapter Eleven. A narrative which can make sense of life, in the face of confusion and challenges, which can provide moral and practical guidance as well as courage and inspiration, is not to be lightly dismissed. It is not surprising that such a narrative itself becomes the standard that people then use to judge the validity of other ideas.

But once again, the existence of more than one grand narrative presents a problem. In the West, the Christian narrative competes with only partially parallel Judaic or Mormon traditions or modern evolutionary theisms. In the East the Hindu narrative competes with the only partially parallel Buddhist narratives. The unique narratives of the Japanese Shinto tradition, or of the modern atheistic existential narrative of life are even more distinct. Each of these narratives forms a different religious (or nonreligious) community and tradition.

If Lindbeck's postmodern analysis is correct, that is the final word. No one can really expect more than to possess some grand narrative in some social context and find therein the means to live a coherent and meaningful life. No one can expect to be able to show that one of those narratives and the life form associated with it is more correct or better than any other.

We often ask, however, whether a way of life is internally consistent, constructive in its effects on people, deeply meaningful, and so on. If we think these questions apply to every narrative, we are using them as universal standards. Such a universalist style of thought may be implicit in any interest in an all-encompassing story. But universalist thought blossomed in the more arduous axial-age style of thought that employs formal logic and seeks overall rational coherence among ideas of all kinds, as in formal theology, philosophy, and science. Late modern thought still relies on logic, but also carefully tests all truth-claims against the relevant evidence.

The four major criteria religious people may use, then, some of them unconsciously, include the vividness of images or ideas, the authority of a community, the power of a grand narrative, and the force of reason and evidence. The first three could each be called a kind of "faith." There is a faith in the power of imagination, or faith in one's community, or a faith supported by the hidden logic that justifies accepting a grand narrative that shapes and guides life meaningfully. The fourth approach is to trust mainly in reason, whether dogmatically or more tentatively.

Chapter Twelve noted that some have claimed that trust in reason is also a kind of faith, a faith that rationality will work better than reliance on a community's time-tested beliefs and grand narratives. This claim, though, will make most sense precisely to those who already rely on a community's narrative rather than on critical rationality. Others will say they have had the experience that relying on logic and evidence to evaluate truth-claims has been wonderfully effective, especially in science. To those who have had such an experience, the fourth method of trusting reason has given good evidence of its validity and need not be taken on faith.

Trust in narrative and trust in rationality are not necessarily opposed to each other, at least not entirely. A mid-twentieth century French philosopher, Paul Ricoeur, pointed out that there are three ways of treating narratives. The first is to naively accept some narrative as the truth. The second is to critically analyze one or more narratives with the tools of rationality, asking for adequate evidence of its truth-claims before accepting it.

In the case of religious narratives this in fact has often ended in skepticism. Sometimes it is skepticism about only this or that part of a narrative. The deists became skeptical about the miracle stories in Christianity, but not about the existence of God. At other times it is a thorough skepticism about a whole religious tradition or about religion in general.

There is a third way to treat grand narratives, however, which Ricoeur calls a "second naiveté." This is a post-critical re-appropriation of a narrative. "Post-critical" means that a person has first subjected the grand narrative to a critical examination, asking whether the relevant evidence and logic support the narrative, and perhaps becoming skeptical about the literal truth of the story. "Re-appropriation" stands for recognizing great and valuable power in the narrative, nonetheless. As we have seen, grand narratives can make sense of life, provide a meaningful identity, help form and sustain a community, provide values and incentives to live by those values. There can be very good reasons to hold on to some narratives, even if a person is somewhat critical of specific truth-claims inherent in that narrative.

Narratives have great power to guide and inspire us, even when we have seen behind the curtain and recognize that the narratives are products of people like us. Many a motion picture has had a great impact, even though everyone knows the parts are played by actors and the names of the director and screenwriter are there to remind everyone of the human origins of the film. A great narrative can pull people into a kind of temporary naive state where they forget for a moment to keep a critical distance and allow themselves to be swallowed up in the meaning of the story. At other times a person can be deeply moved even while recognizing the film-maker's art and the actors' skills. This is a kind of post-critical appropriation of the meanings in the film (though the word naiveté may no longer be the best to describe this state). Life lived by scientific or philosophical rationality alone would be rather cold. To contribute meaningfully to life, the conclusions of rationality must eventually be located within a humanly significant narrative.

The re-appropriation of a religious narrative in a second naiveté respects the value and power of the narrative. But if it really follows upon a prior critical analysis, it also recognizes that the narrative is the product of social history, of human thought. It recognizes that religious narratives, like scientific theories also, are open to further evaluation and development.

From the viewpoint of modern religion as described in Chapter Fourteen, this need not lead to religious skepticism. Modern religion in the West, for example, still trusts that the Ultimate Mystery is best re-represented by personness, that this world and its history are ultimately the work and presence of the divine. If it is persons, in their concrete history and communities, who produce the grand narratives, modern religion can see this as an ongoing response to the divine Mystery. Not all religious people will be comfortable with this view of their narratives, however; much depends on their basic religious style as described by Fowler.

Evaluating Three Kinds of Religious Truth-Claims

The skeptical challenge to specific religious beliefs is still part of these late modern (or postmodern) times. For some religious people part of their response to the challenge of science lies in distinguishing among different kinds of truth-claims. First, there are claims that God (or Bodhisattvas or Vishnu, etc.) intervenes in the world to make something happen that otherwise would not have occurred as it did. This is the category of miracles. The second kind of truth-claim is not about specific interventions but about the general order of the entire universe. This is the category of the cosmic. The argument that the whole cosmos seems finely tuned to produce intelligent life, for example, does not require belief in divine interventions. Proponents claim that God planned, created, sustains, and drives the entire universe forward. But God can do this by a single divine ongoing creative act. The third kind of truth-claim is the metaphysical. To assert that there is a single Ultimate behind everything, whether it is God or Atman or the Tao, is a metaphysical assertion. The first two of these kinds of religious truth-claims can be tested against relevant evidence. The metaphysical claim cannot be so tested, as we will see.

Miracles can fall into two categories, the public and the hidden. Public miracles are empirically testable truth-claims. Evidence has accumulated that a wide range of events that once were explained as the effects of invisible beings, whether spirits, gods, or God, turned out to have natural explanations. Many odd and wondrous things that were once attributed to God, Aurora, or Ares—remission of disease, Northern lights, victory of the underdog in battle—can be attributed to natural causes. Insanity is not the result of demonic possession. Lightning is a natural phenomenon, and church bells will not drive away a storm. Comets are not sent by God to warn of the downfall of a royal ruler.

In any case, miracles are specific finite events. Any event can be examined to see what might have caused it. A person can claim that an event is a miracle only if the person has examined all the evidence very carefully and compared it to all the possible natural explanations, and has then concluded that natural causality cannot account for the event. So to determine that something is a miracle, it is first necessary to examine it as a scientist would. Subjecting miracles to empirical investigation is obviously valuable in the case of fraudulent miracles. There have been religious figures who used gimmickry to create the impression that a statue or painting is crying, for example. Empirical investigation can root out such fraud precisely because any supposed miracle is a specific concrete event taking place in this physical world.

After an empirical investigation of a possible miracle, those who conclude that science cannot explain how the event occurred are using an "argument from ignorance." They are saying that because we cannot figure out how the event could have occurred naturally, it must have had a supernatural or non-natural cause. If we do not know, for example, of any reason that would account for the sudden remission of a serious case of cancer, we may be tempted to say this may be a miracle. Yet the key words are "we do not know." If we do not know of anything natural that could possibly cure this cancer, we are confessing our ignorance of how the cure came about. We may choose to believe it was a miracle. But we cannot prove it.

The argument from ignorance sometimes takes a more positive form when it claims that we do know enough to be able to say that natural causes could not possibly account for this event. But there is a lot we do not know; our knowledge has limits. It is always possible that it is the limits of what we now know about how nature operates—our current relative ignorance—that makes us certain nature could not have produced the event. Up until Darwin offered his theory of natural selection taking place over millions of years, it seemed clearly impossible that unguided natural causes could have produced something so marvelous as a spider, with its equipment and instincts for weaving intricate webs. But Darwin's theory, along with the billions of years of natural history, shows how it is at least possible that natural causes alone could produce life on this planet as we know it. It is difficult to prove that any event could not possibly be explained by natural causes.

The second type of miracle we can refer to as the hidden miracle. Some Christian theologians have suggested that God may be directing events in the universe in ways that are so subtle that they could never be identified. Perhaps God works on the subatomic level nudging otherwise indeterminate possibilities one way rather than another. Or perhaps God operates more as some Muslim theology proposes, directly producing each and every event in the universe but doing so in such a way that it all looks entirely natural. There is clearly no way to disprove such hidden activities. On the other hand, if God works only in such hidden ways, this would make it appear that God wants the process to look like cosmic naturalism, and as though God wants to leave no clues to divine intervention in the world.

Empirical evidence can also count for or against belief in a cosmic Designer, even one who does not intervene in the process of the universe. That is why there still are arguments from design, such as over the fine tuning of the universe described in Chapter Fourteen, which appeals to the evidence. For some the evidence suggests only randomness; for others the evidence clearly implies an Intelligent Designer. But in either case, evidence counts.

Metaphysical truth-claims are another matter. The word "metaphysical" has appeared a few times here already. Like many words it has too many meanings. Some New Age thought calls itself metaphysical. In the New Age vocabulary this refers to the spiritual dimension, sometimes literally a different dimension, the "astral plane,"where spirit beings dwell and where the soul may go to rest and recover between its many reincarnations. The question of whether the existence of such a dimension is open to empirical testing is interesting.

Certainly many claims about visitors or messages from this dimension have been tested and proved false. In 1848 the Fox sisters, Margaret (1836-1893) and Catherine (1841-1892), heard strange rappings, which they claimed came from the spirit world. Thousands of people took up spiritualism because of the sisters. The sisters later confessed that they had made the rapping sounds by cracking the knuckle in their big toes. The great magician Harry Houdini spent years exposing fraud after spiritualist fraud at seances; another stage magician, James ("The Amazing") Randi has been doing the same for some decades now. Strictly speaking, consistent failure to find evidence of such a dimension is not the same as proof that there is no such dimension. But the real reason for the popularity of such belief would seem to lie in its hold on the imagination, and in its ability to satisfy emotional needs for contact with a departed loved one, or for assurance of life after death.

In some philosophies, the metaphysical is whatever is universal. Thus the law of cause and effect can be called metaphysical because every event requires some cause to account for it. But then even natural aspects of the universal are "metaphysical," and the word does not really seem necessary. One could call such universals "cosmic" instead.

The most rigorous use of the word metaphysical restricts its application to one reality—whatever it is that is the single truly Ultimate that accounts for everything else. The ultimate questions described in Chapter Four are metaphysical questions because they are about the ultimate origins, conditions, or goal of all things. Thus either God, or Brahman, or the Tao is the sole metaphysical reality. It alone is the source of the universe or the Ultimate goal of the universe. It is this third meaning that the word "metaphysical" carries here. It is the kind of reality that is probably beyond what evidence can establish.

On the other hand, if you were convinced by theological arguments in Chapter Eleven for the existence of God, then you may think that rational argument based on evidence of the universe can establish at least the existence of an Ultimate, even though that theology ends up describing the Ultimate as infinite and incomprehensible. Others, less convinced by theology, conclude that we should therefore be agnostic about the Ultimate, about the metaphysical.

Still others conclude, with William James or Karl Rahner, that we have a free choice about how to interpret life, whether to choose to accept it trustingly as ultimately meaningful, or to think of it as ultimately meaningless. Those who choose an ultimate trust find allies in those who stress a positive experience of an ultimate wholeness or depth to life. Rational argument for belief, rational grounds for agnosticism (or the weak atheism described in the Introduction), a deliberate choice to trust, or a personal religious experience—all remain options concerning the metaphysical. Unlike the case with supernatural interventions, and perhaps with cosmic questions, an appeal to empirical evidence cannot resolve questions about the Ultimate. As these pages have said often, questions about the Ultimate bring us to the presence of mystery—or Mystery.

Four Types of Defenses Against Rationalistic Skepticism

The distinction among three types of religious beliefs is relevant to certain defenses of religion against rational skepticism. Each of these defenses seeks to exempt religion from outside evaluation, including the test of whether they fit with empirical evidence. We can call them "exemptive" defenses. To each of them certain responses have been offered. You may find one or more of them appealing. Many religious people do.

The first is the postliberal approach of Lindbeck, discussed in the previous chapter. This claims that no community's form of life or basic narrative can be legitimately evaluated by an outsider. Every outsider operates out of some community and its narrative, so there is no objective or neutral place from which a person in one community can sit in judgment on other communities. Each community is exempt from outside criticism. A common response to this exemptive argument has often been to note (see Chapter Fifteen) that postmodern or postliberal thought tends to believe in some universals about morality and so on. To whatever extent postmodern thinkers have such universalist norms, they can use them to evaluate other communities, including religious communities and their traditions.

A second exemptive defense, mentioned briefly in previous chapters, claims that the object of religion is *sui generis*. This is a claim that religion is concerned with the sacred (or holy or transcendent), and that the sacred is not the kind of empirical reality that science can study. The ordinary evidence of the senses, as well as evidence from various technological testing devices, is simply irrelevant in judging the reality of the sacred. A common response to this claim is to point out that those offering this defense are not always clear on just what they mean by the "sacred" (or the holy or transcendent). If they mean the infinite and incomprehensible metaphysical Ultimate, then the defense probably works well. As we have just seen, the metaphysical Ultimate is probably beyond evidence. If the defenders mean a cosmic Designer, then the defense seems misplaced, because the order of the universe can be examined to see whether it constitutes evidence for or against such a Designer. If the defenders are protecting belief in miracles by arguing that they are not subject to empirical testing, that does not seem to work either for reasons given here.

A third type of exemptive defense, often connected to the *sui generis* approach, also points to the special character of sacredness which believers attribute to certain place, objects, or beings like the gods or God. Then, as we saw Eliade do in Chapter Fourteen, this defense proposes to treat all these sacred realities "phenomenologically." It treats religions as "phenomena" in the original meaning of that Greek word—"to appear." The phenomenological approach strives earnestly to understand a religion just as it appears, and as it is understood by its adherents. Taking believers' faith very seriously, this approach refuses to apply any external criteria to determine whether that faith is correct. It "brackets" the religious phenomena. This means that it reaches the same postliberal conclusion at which George Lindbeck arrived: namely, that a religion cannot be judged by the criteria of any other religion or philosophy or science. Religious people need concern themselves only with their own religion and its beliefs and values and traditions.

The difference between the postmodern position and a phenomenological position lies mainly in how each is justified. Postmodern thought claims that every set of ideas and criteria is socially constructed and therefore has no universal validity. The phenomenological approach justifies its own restraint simply as a way of maintaining sympathetic respect for religious traditions in order to report accurately on how those traditions are experienced by their participants. But both end up saying the same thing: no outside criteria should be applied to judge whether a religion is true, good, and constructive. Only insiders can judge, by the criteria they draw from within the tradition.

One response to this defense of religion is to make a distinction between describing a religion and explaining it. The phenomenologists are correct in saying that an outsider studying a religion must understand it well enough to describe it as it appears to the participants in the religious tradition. A description of a religion is inaccurate if it fails to portray vividly and completely the religious form of life as it appears to the believers. A description of a religion should be strong and detailed enough that active and earnest participants in the religion would recognize themselves in it and be able to say, "Yes, that is what I do, think, feel, perceive, value, and pursue in my religion."

But understanding a religion from the inside in this way is distinct from the task of explaining the cause or source of the religion. Believers may say that the beliefs come from divine revelation or inspiration, and that participation in the religion depends on sacred power or divine grace. An outsider may still ask skeptically whether this is so. While believers may be opposed to such skepticism, believers themselves tend to be skeptical about religions that are quite different from their own. The alternative is to refuse to be skeptical about any religious beliefs. This does not seem prudent. At least some religious beliefs in history have been quite harmful, by most standards, from the practice of ancient Canaanites offering children in sacrifice, to the practice of the Taliban in Afghanistan forbidding women to hold professional positions.

A fourth type of exemptive defense of religion against skeptics divides all human thought into two major types: the natural sciences (*naturwissenschaft* in German) and the human or spiritual "sciences" (*geisteswissenschaft*). This division was promoted by Wilhelm Dilthey (1833-1911). The word "science" is used in the second case because the word in Europe tends to mean any organized body of study. In English the word is used only for what Europeans would normally call the natural sciences. In Europe philosophy, theology, and history, as well as the social sciences, are all called "science" (*wissenschaft*).

The natural sciences seek knowledge of the natural world, said Dilthey. But the human sciences seek to understand the realm of meaning. By this he meant that human life, individually and culturally, is a collection of interpretations of reality that expose what is meaningful in life. It is not the bare natural facts that really count; it is the value and beauty and significance and purpose of things to the human person. Religion is one of the major aspects of the realm of meaning. It is concerned not with the natural world of facts but with the meaningfulness of life expressed in various rituals, symbols, texts, and community life. So the criteria of truth used by the natural sciences are simply inapplicable to religion.

The usual response to this analysis is to agree, but only in part. Religions are indeed important because they provide a meaningful direction to life and possess powerful narratives, rituals, and symbols in support of that direction. If religions refrain from making any truth-claims about how things are in the world, then the religions are indeed exempt from critique according to the method of natural science. Or if the only truth-claim that religions made were about the metaphysical Ultimate, then the scientific method would also be irrelevant.

But religions do make truth claims, about whether the order of the world implies a Designer, or whether certain events were miraculous interventions by God, or whether certain texts with instructions on how to live are divinely revealed. Many religious believers themselves offer what they take to be empirical evidence in favor of such religious truth-claims. It should not be surprising if skeptics also appeal to natural evidence to make their contrary case. The tension between religious truth-claims and scientific method and theories will continue.

Current Options

This Epilogue has noted the appeal of imagination, the authority of a community and its tradition, the general human tendency to live by a grand narrative, and the use of reason and evidence, as different criteria for evaluating a religion. The appeal of imagination, as well as the hidden logic of living by a grand narrative, are usually only implicit in a people's consciousness rather than explicitly recognized standards. Other possible sources of religiousness mentioned in Chapter Two also usually go unrecognized. Few will say that they are religious because they have a Freudian need for a parent figure who will save them from death, or because they have a genetic tendency to anthropomorphize, as Stewart Guthrie argued.

Whether any given religion is based on divine revelation and inspiration or not, these implicit reasons for belief will remain part of human life. They will provide ongoing motives to seek explicit justification for faith, such as arguments for the existence of God or for the reasonableness of making a choice to believe. That probably means that religion is not going to fade away as the secularization thesis claimed, though it does not seem that atheism and agnosticism will disappear either.

On the supposition that religion will remain influential, there are different responses possible. Religious people will continue to differ among themselves on which aspects of religion they emphasize. For some religious people, it will be enough to enjoy the company of other participants in the practices of their faith. For many religious people, it will be a matter of some urgency to convert others to what the believers consider the true faith. For still others the goal will be to draw respectfully upon a religious tradition for its rich resources for future social developments, as the religion and the secular culture interact. For yet others, it will be very important to apply standards of rationality in religion, perhaps to place limits on what otherwise would be directionless wild imagination or to counterbalance tendencies to a mindless conformity to tradition. For others still, the main goal of their religiousness will be to exert a positive moral effect.

Those outside any religious tradition, particularly those who are atheists or agnostics, will similarly have choices. One is simply to attack all religion, overlooking differences in styles, stages, emphases, and moralities. Another is to try to create alternative forms of morality based on nonreligious science or philosophy, such as the Skeptics Society or the American Humanist Association. Yet another choice is to support those aspects of religion that seem constructive, moral, and reasonable, but to criticize those aspects that seem harmful. With such complicated issues and such a variety of choices, knowing what is best is not easy. Life continues in the ongoing presence of mystery—or Mystery.

Again the Tension of the Human Quest

This Epilogue has been rather abstract, categorizing and analyzing various approaches to evaluating religion. It has also raised questions that can seriously challenge some or all religious beliefs. It might seem better just to leave religion alone, without all the critical reflections on it. You may find yourself agreeing with Friedrich Nietzsche (1844-1900) at this point, that too much consciousness is a curse. We might be better off not to think too deeply and too critically. Or you may agree with Fromm that we sometimes want to escape from the burden of making our own critical evaluations. And yet the distinctive ability that makes us different from other beings on this planet is precisely the ability to reflect critically, to engage in this sort of "self-transcendence," and make choices based on such reflection. The last section of Chapter Eleven identified what it calls "the tension of the human quest." This is the tension between our ability to think critically and endlessly about everything, including our religious beliefs, and our need to have a clear identity and set of values in life, whether from some master narrative or from a formal theology or philosophy.

We can deal with this tension somewhat abstractly, by talking in theoretical terms about what it means to be human. Sartre did this by speaking of what he says it is to be authentically human. Authenticity for Sartre is achieved by accepting what we are, the beings who have the capacity to be free, and are thus responsible for who we are.

Sartre thus thinks that of course we should think critically about our religious beliefs. But a religious tradition may insist that we humans are children of God, born to know and obey God. When critical thought and free choice lead us from a life of obedience to God, they have gone too far. Or a different religious tradition may argue that no matter what we think and choose, the law of karma will prevail. We will be better off if we accept that as the starting point of our thoughts and choices. But Sartre, and before him Feuerbach and Freud, then ask us to engage in critical reflection on the religious beliefs about God or karma. The theoretical arguments can go on endlessly.

We can also deal with this tension more practically. At several places in this book you may have thought it would be better to cease reading and get back to real life. It is an interesting choice to consider, partly because it raises the question of how critically we should think about this choice. We can all ask ourselves the question of whether in the long run we think it is wise to get in the habit of reflecting critically on all our choices. Will we benefit more from open-ended critical thought, or will it produce more problems than benefits? There is no simple answer to this question. At some point, often long before we can be sure we have all the information we need, we must choose. As William James pointed out, if we wait for total certitude we might never make decisions.

We can also ask ourselves the sort of question that a basic value moralist asks—am I the sort of person I would admire? The answer depends on what you find admirable. Do you think highly of someone who strives to reflect honestly and objectively about her or his beliefs and practices? Do you think highly of someone who takes personal responsibility for his or her own basic values? What we find admirable depends on the particular kind of moral stage or cognitive style that predominates in our own lives at this point. So these questions might just keep us within the same circle of values and beliefs we already possess. On the other hand, by asking such questions we may open ourselves up to further developments in our own thinking. Because we all live in the presence of the ever-receding horizon of mystery, further development is always possible.

Summary

Although religious people often seek to exempt their own tradition from evaluation by outsiders, they themselves evaluate their own and other religions. Academic evaluations of religion strive for objectivity. But many factors influence the outcome. This includes the development of the person, and whether it is the miraculous, the cosmic, or the metaphysical that is under review. Various ways to exempt religion from outside evaluation do not entirely succeed. Yet religion remains a complex and powerful aspect of human history. We have our own difficult choices to make about it.

For Further Reflection

1. Explain which of the arguments for or against evaluating religion from the outside make most sense to you and why. Indicate whether you reject any of those arguments and why.
2. Do you think that a fairly objective academic analysis of religion is really possible? Explain why or why not.
3. Identify and describe in your own life or someone else's the operation of more than one of the criteria for belief: imagination, traditional authority, the appeal of a grand narrative, rational analysis.
4. Does the so-called second naiveté seem to you to be a valid and constructive mode of religiousness? Explain.
5. Of the options offered in the paragraph immediately preceding the summary, which attitude do you think that agnostics and atheists should take toward religion?

Suggested Readings

Russell T. McCutcheon, ed., *The Insider/Outsider Problem in the Study of Religion: A Reader*, 1999. An excellent collection of twenty-seven articles representing a wide range of positions on the problem of evaluating religion. The earliest article is from Kant. Articles by Otto, Eliade, and Wach, who seek to exempt religion from outside analysis, are also included, but so are a good number of those who recommend such analysis. The six major parts represent every approach, except perhaps that of the traditional theologian. The chapters consist, for the most part, of articles from academic journals, and are sometimes difficult to read.

Ninian Smart, *Worldviews: Crosscultural Explorations of Human Beliefs*, 1995 (2nd ed.). A simpler explanation of a phenomenological approach than those of his writings that are excerpted in McCutcheon's book.

Robert A. Hinde, *Why Gods Persist: A Scientific Approach to Religion*, 1999. This proposes that science-minded people who think religious beliefs are false should not attack religion but take a more balanced approach. See especially the first chapter and the concluding chapter.

Gary R. Habermas and R. Douglas Geivett, eds., *In Defense of Miracles: A Comprehensive Case for God's Action in History*, 1997. The authors represented in this collection disagree with the position on miracles presented in this chapter.

Paul J. Griffiths, *An Apology for Apologetics: A Study in the Logic of Interreligious Dialogue*, 1991. An exposition of how religions seek to evaluate themselves in relation to one another.

Index

Of Related Interest...

Vatican II
40 Personal Stories
Michael Daley and William Madges

William Madges and Michael Daley have gathered together forty personal stories of women and men who took part in the council, were there at the time, or saw the course of their lives change dramatically because of it. These storytellers include: Joan Chittister, M. Basil Pennington, Mary Luke Tobin, Martin Marty, Richard Rohr, Richard P. McBrien, Thomas Groome, Eugene Fisher, and Mary Jo Weaver.

1-58595-238-9, 240 pp, $19.95 (X-81)

An Introduction to the Old Testament
Journey into the Mystery of God
Laurin Wenig

Brings to life the people and literature of biblical times in a clear, engaging style based on solid scholarship and relevant to present day.

1-58595-167-6, 304 pp, $24.95 (X-06)

Faith, Religion, & Theology
A Contemporary Introduction
Brennan R. Hill, Paul Knitter, and William Madges

This thoroughly updated text offers students and adults an overarching perspective. The "Faith" section of the book focuses on the nature of human faith as well as Christian faith. The "Religion" section examines the personal and social value of religion, religious belief and behavior, and offers an overview of major world religions. The "Theology" section includes an analysis of the theology/faith relationship. Suggested readings and study questions included.

0-89622-751-1, 480 pp, $24.95 (C-18)

The World of Jesus
Culture, History, Religion, Politics, Geography
Joanne Turpin

Joanne Turpin takes us on a detailed tour of Jesus' world. She arranges the story of his ministry around three themes: Jesus as Healer, as Teacher, and as the Way, and looks at his religious heritage, the social and cultural environment, history, geography, politics, economics—all the elements that help shape society and individual lives.

1-58595-167-6, 304 pp, $24.95 (X-06)